Defining Their Identity

The Changing Roles of Women in the Post-War Era
as Documented by the *Valley Times* Newspaper

Edited by Christina Rice

Introduction by Joy Picus

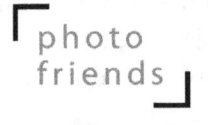

photo
friends

LOS ANGELES PUBLIC LIBRARY

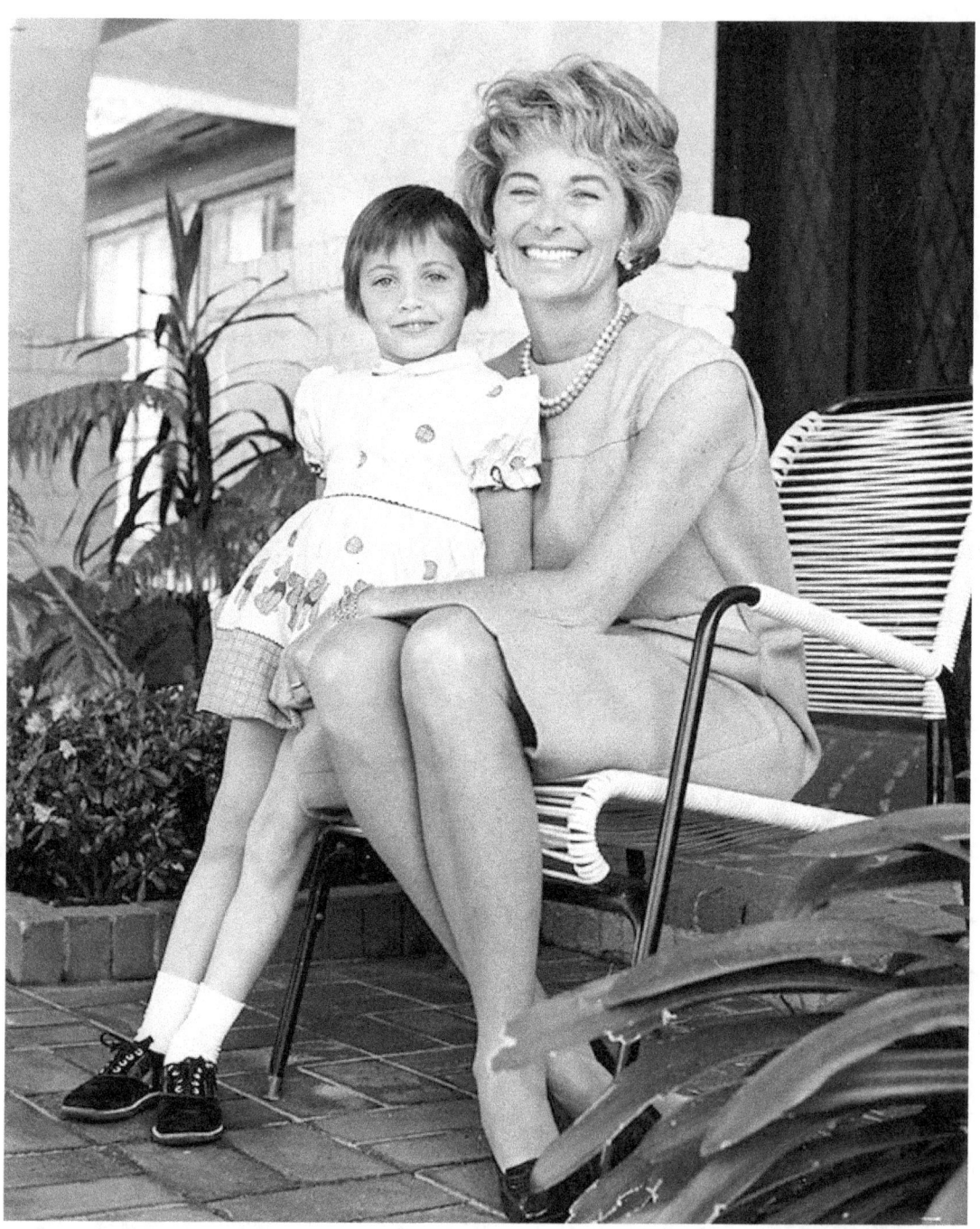

"Mrs. James Stewart, wife of actor Jimmy Stewart, is campaign chairman for annual Cystic Fibrosis Foundation Los Angeles Drive June 19 through July 19. Pictured with Mrs. Stewart is poster girl, Lisa Behr. Goal for the drive is $100,000."
May 27, 1964. (Order #00110952)

Contents

Introduction

This catalog covers an exceptional period in the history of the San Fernando Valley, as it makes the transition from a sleepy suburban community with its agricultural base still visible, to a thriving, growing, bustling city/suburb still striving to find its identify as part of the larger Los Angeles metropolis. In the foreground was the postwar homebuilding frenzy, as the area welcomed WWII veterans, their sweethearts and soon the arrival of their baby boom children.

The period this catalog reflects preceded the publication of Betty Friedan's 1963 paradigm-changing book, *The Feminine Mystique,* which altered everything for the mid-century woman. What an eye opener this catalog is! Who knew that women were landscape architects, pharmacists, heart specialists, and real estate brokers in the 1950's and '60's in our San Fernando Valley? Who knew the stunning role women were playing in rocket and missile design as scientists and engineers at our local aerospace facility, Rocketdyne? The dominant images of the times, and even our memories, are flawed.

Women were, as they are now, mothers, wives, and members of social clubs, and they wore aprons, hats and gloves. They raised money for vital charities and important causes. They were also popular celebrities, talented actors and performers, who lived in the Valley, which could be considered "Hollywood adjacent." They were educators, principals, and superintendents, and some ran for, and were elected to, local city councils and school boards. They were activists, demonstrating for peace, and against apartment development in their neighborhoods. They piloted airplanes, having learned those skills during the war, and organized the Powderpuff Derbies in the 1950's.

In contrast to the explosive diversity of today's Valley, the catalog portrays a singularly white Valley, but that's the way it looked The minority of African Americans in the North Valley were disregarded to the point of seeming to be non-existent.

Women were overlooked by our history books, if not our local newspapers. This exhibit is witness to that. Women's History Month wasn't observed until the early 1980's. Women have been making huge contributions to their communities for generations, and if the historians didn't notice it, the local newspapers did!

We have not acknowledged these beautiful, talented, exciting, challenged women for too long. Now that we have rediscovered them, let us celebrate them, our history and our limitless future!

Joy Picus
June, 2014

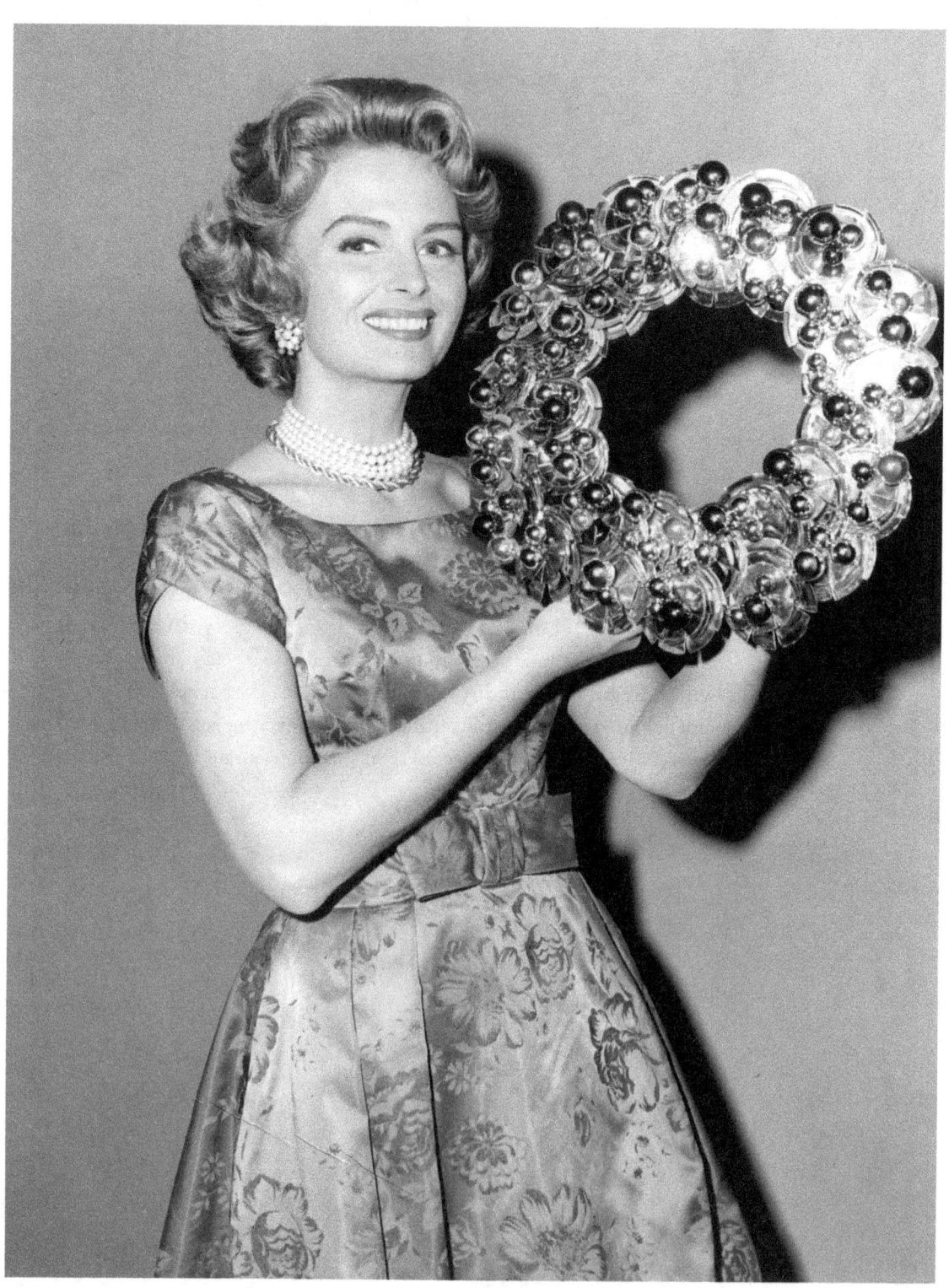

Actress Donna Reed holds a holiday wreath made of soup cans.
November 17, 1960. (Order #00109757)

Defining Their Identity

The Changing Roles of Women in the Post-War Era as Documented by the *Valley Times* Newspaper

For many, the predominant image of the post-War woman is the suburban mom and consummate homemaker as immortalized in television characters of the period such as Donna Stone (*The Donna Reed Show*), Harriet Nelson (*The Adventures of Ozzie and Harriet*), and June Cleaver (*Leave it to Beaver*). This figure did indeed exist in suburban homes throughout the county and was a vital part of the social fabric, but she wasn't the sole feminine representative in the post-War era.

LIFE Magazine ran an extensive article in 1947 discussing the "American Woman's Dilemma." Should she seek a family? A career? Is it possible to have both? Once her children are raised, will she have anything interesting to discuss with her husband? In the 1930s & early 1940s, many women had entered the workforce because of financial necessity spurred by the Great Depression or the home-front manpower shortages of World War II. For many (though certainly not all) women in the post-War era, pursuing a career did indeed become a decision more than a necessity. The American woman's dilemma could present itself, and the various paths chosen during this time were heavily documented by the *Valley Times* newspaper.

Published out of North Hollywood as a daily newspaper from 1946-1970, the *Valley Times* documented the entire San Fernando Valley, a region that was emblematic of the tremendous suburban development boom that was taking place outside of urban centers around the country. Groundbreakings, ribbon cuttings, school openings, and various civic activities became common themes of the newspaper and could at times reflect the picture perfect green-lawned life of the Cleavers. The editors of the *Valley Times* themselves seemed to have viewed its female readership as very Donna Reedesque when advertising a Women's section in 1961 which catered to the "number

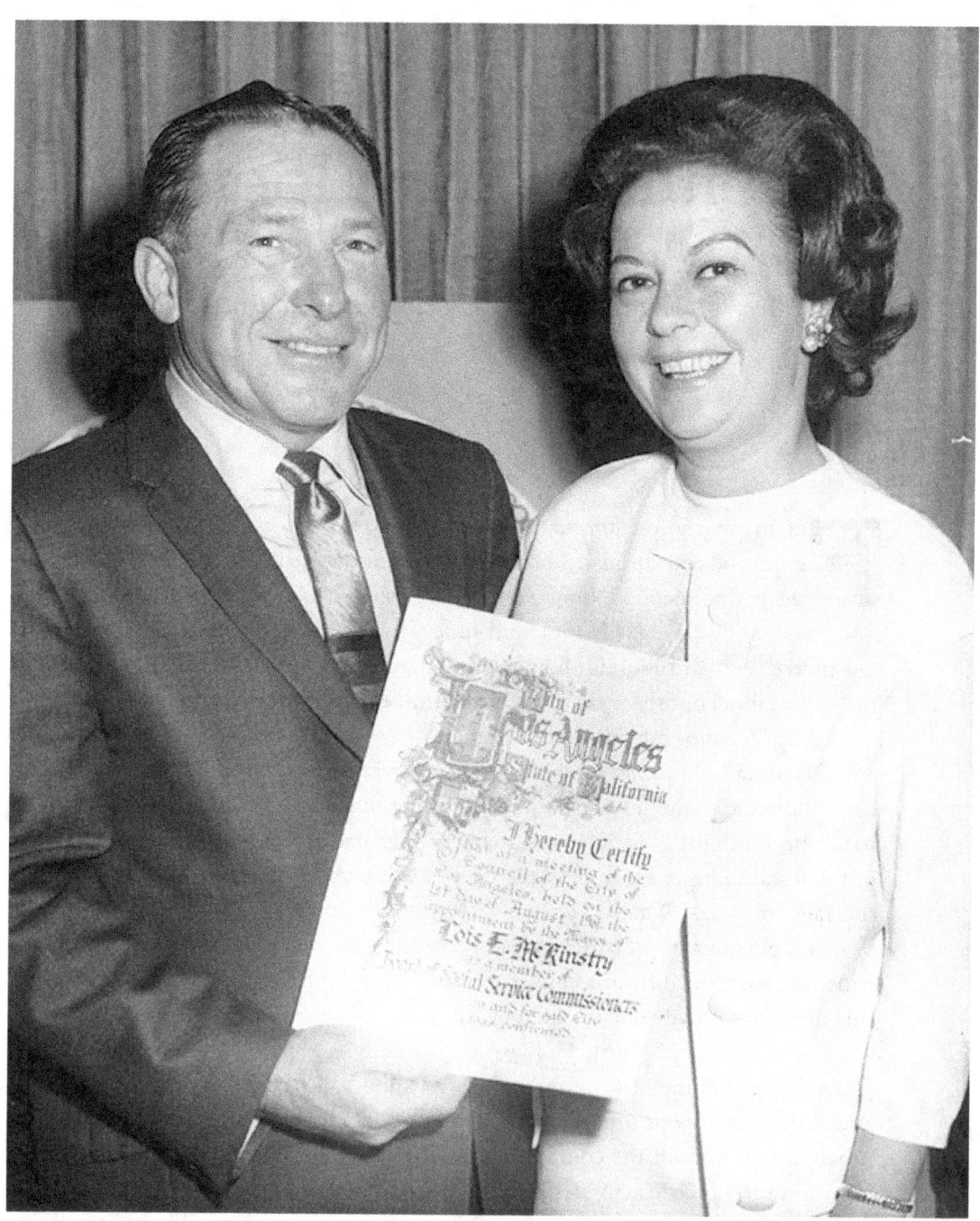

"Mayor Samuel W. Yorty presents a newly-designed certificate indicating membership on Los Angeles City Commission to Mrs. Lois E. McKinstry of Sherman Oaks. Mrs. McKinstry was appointed to the Social Service Commission at a recent meeting of the Los Angeles City Council."
August 7, 1962. (Order #00111242)

of things that almost every woman would like to be—gay and frivolous, sound and practical, fashionable, attractive, a charming companion, a clever conversationalist and a gracious homemaker."

However, in covering the various goings on in the San Fernando Valley during this time, the newspaper also unwittingly documented a population of diverse and dynamic women trying to establish their own unique identities in a seemingly homogenized suburban culture. Yes, the homemakers and beauty queens found representation in the pages of the *Valley Times*, but there also existed women of various ethnic backgrounds who were politically active, valued the advancement of education for the youth population, and formed clubs which championed charitable causes, not to mention that wide swath of those who developed professional careers; musicians, artists, librarians, flight attendants, police sergeants, nurses, doctors, pharmacists, engineers, business owners, architects, stock brokers, and physicists are just some of the positions held by women of the Valley and no doubt could be found amongst the female population across the country.

The newspaper also documented those who were uniquely "Valley Girls." By the 1950s, the San Fernando Valley had long been home to a numbers of folks from the entertainment industry and the *Valley Times* did not shy away from covering these people. Unlike today, where celebrities are predominately documented in pure social settings, the celebs of the post-War Valley were civically engaged in their communities, contributed their time to charitable causes, and took titles such a "honorary mayor" seriously. Along with these women of entertainment were the pioneers who took great pride in their long Valley lineage and sought to preserve local history for future generations. Let's not forget the Valley's own "Rockettes" of Rocketdyne, the rocket engine design and production company in Canoga Park who employed over 2,200 women in posts ranging from secretary to rocket scientists and everything in between.

The Los Angeles Public Library has been the custodian of the vast photographic collection of the *Valley Times* for over 30 years. Advances in technology have not only allowed us to gradually make the images of the newspaper readily accessible online but have also made it possible for us to discover the not so obvious themes permeating throughout the collection such as the diverse women of the San Fernando Valley who strove to define their identities.

Christina Rice
Los Angeles Public Library Photo Collection
May 2014

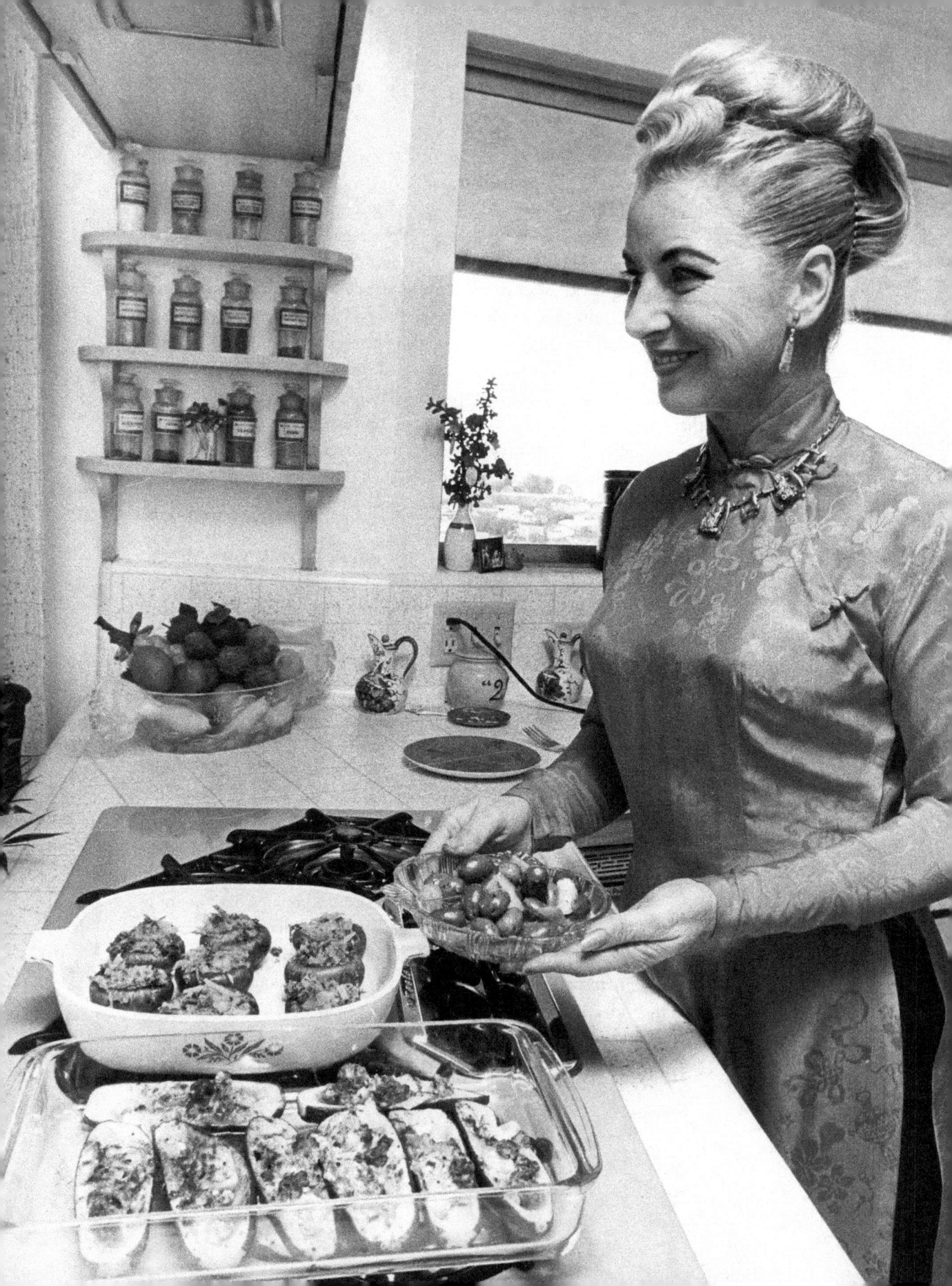

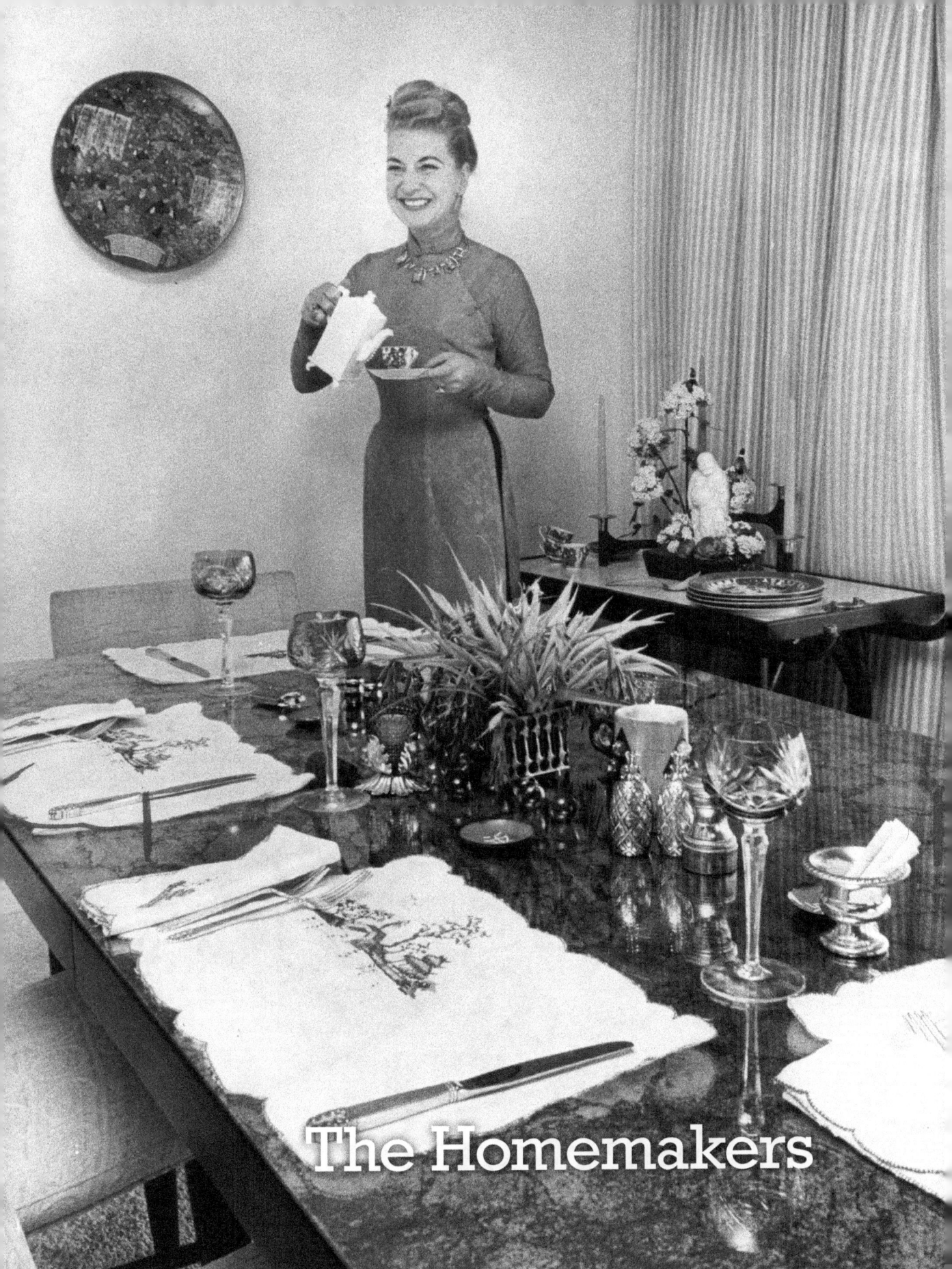

The Homemakers

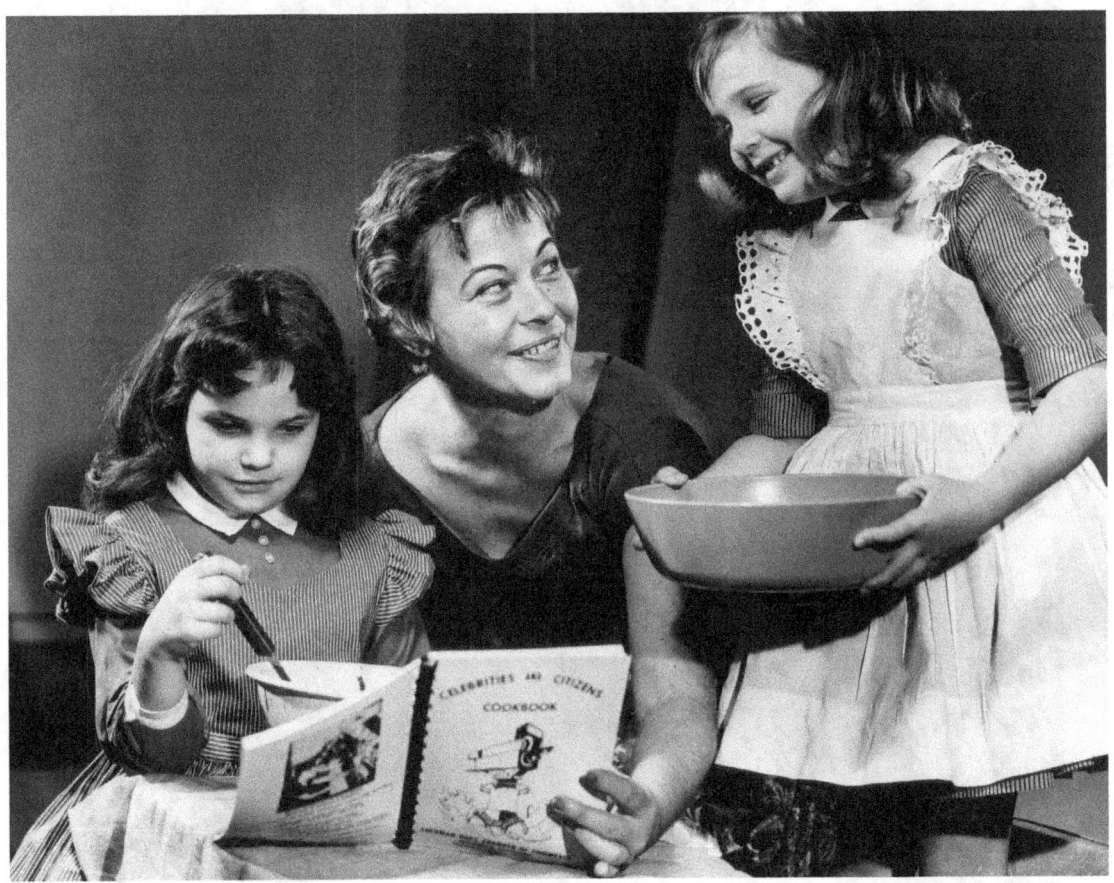

"Mrs. L.M. Stark, ways and means chairman of Women's Division of Sherman Oaks
Chamber of Commerce, starts home-making lessons with 7-year old Dana Haskins and
her 5-year old sister, Honey Anne, by showing them some delectable recipes
in *Celebrities Cookbook.*"
December 18, 1959. (George Brich)
(Order #00031139)

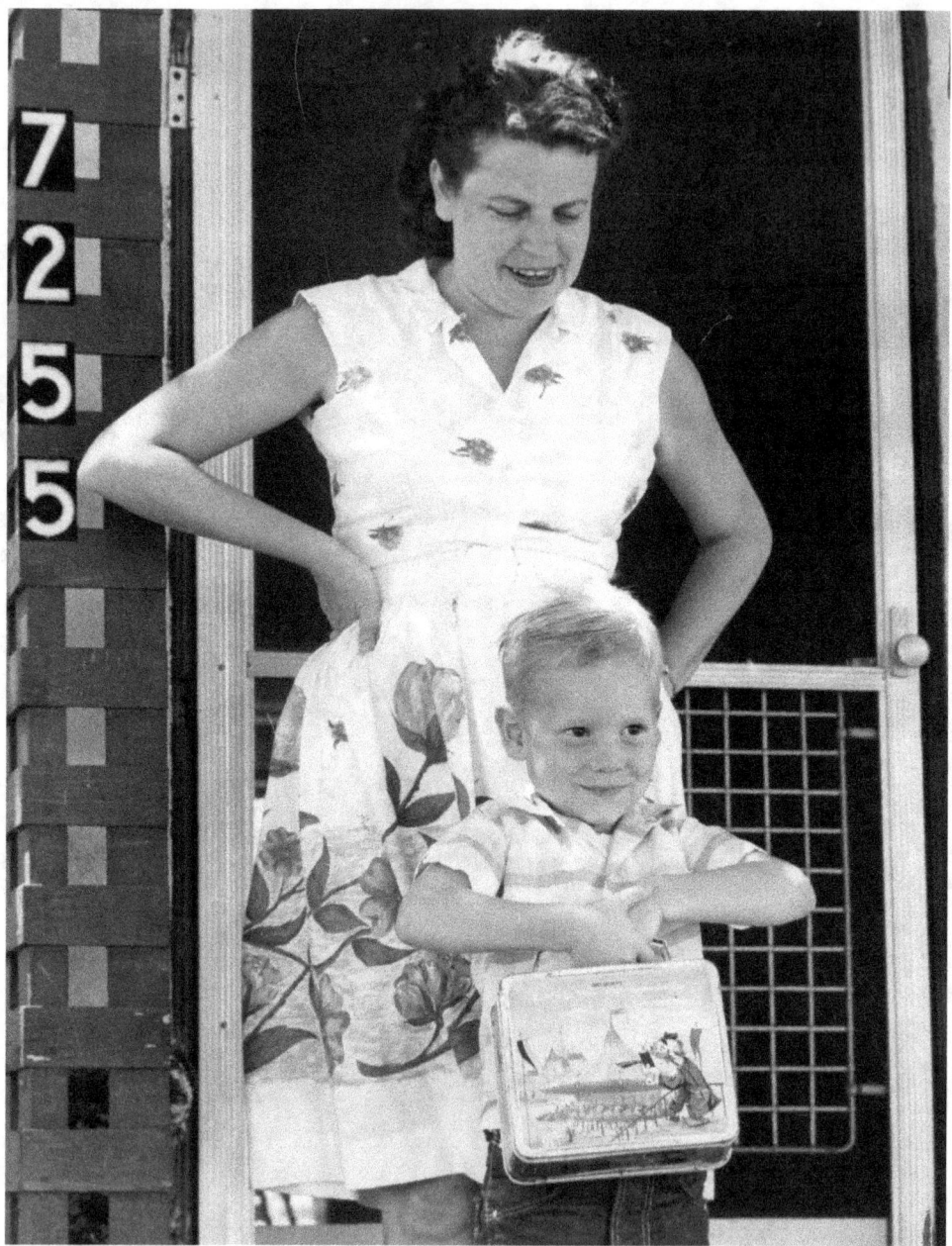

Mrs. Lawrence Garske of Reseda prepares to send 5-year-old Russell to the Anatola
Street School in Van Nuys for his first day of kindergarten.
August 22, 1963. (Gordon Dean)
(Order #00082776)

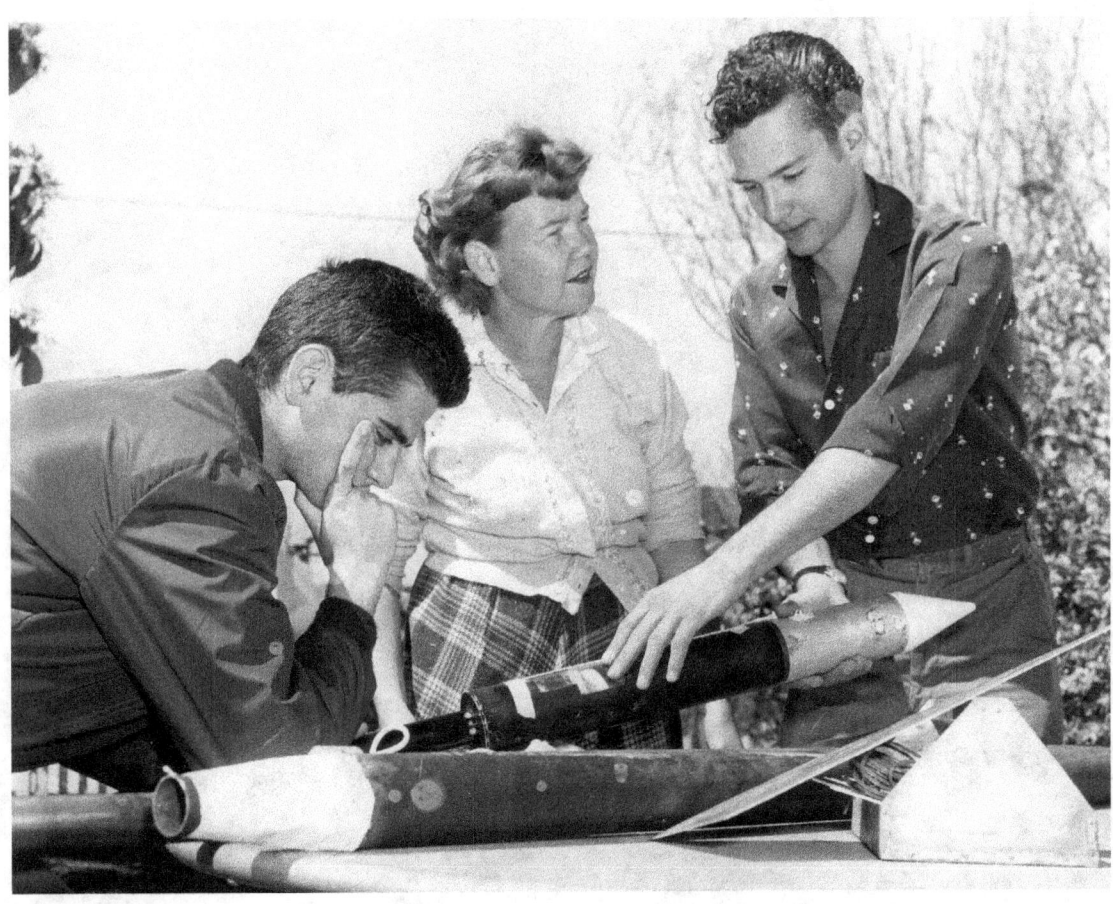

"Les Newbill points out important nose cone features to his mother, Mrs. Lena Newbill, as his partner Myron Lieberman, left, looks on."
March 26, 1959. (Order #00082700)

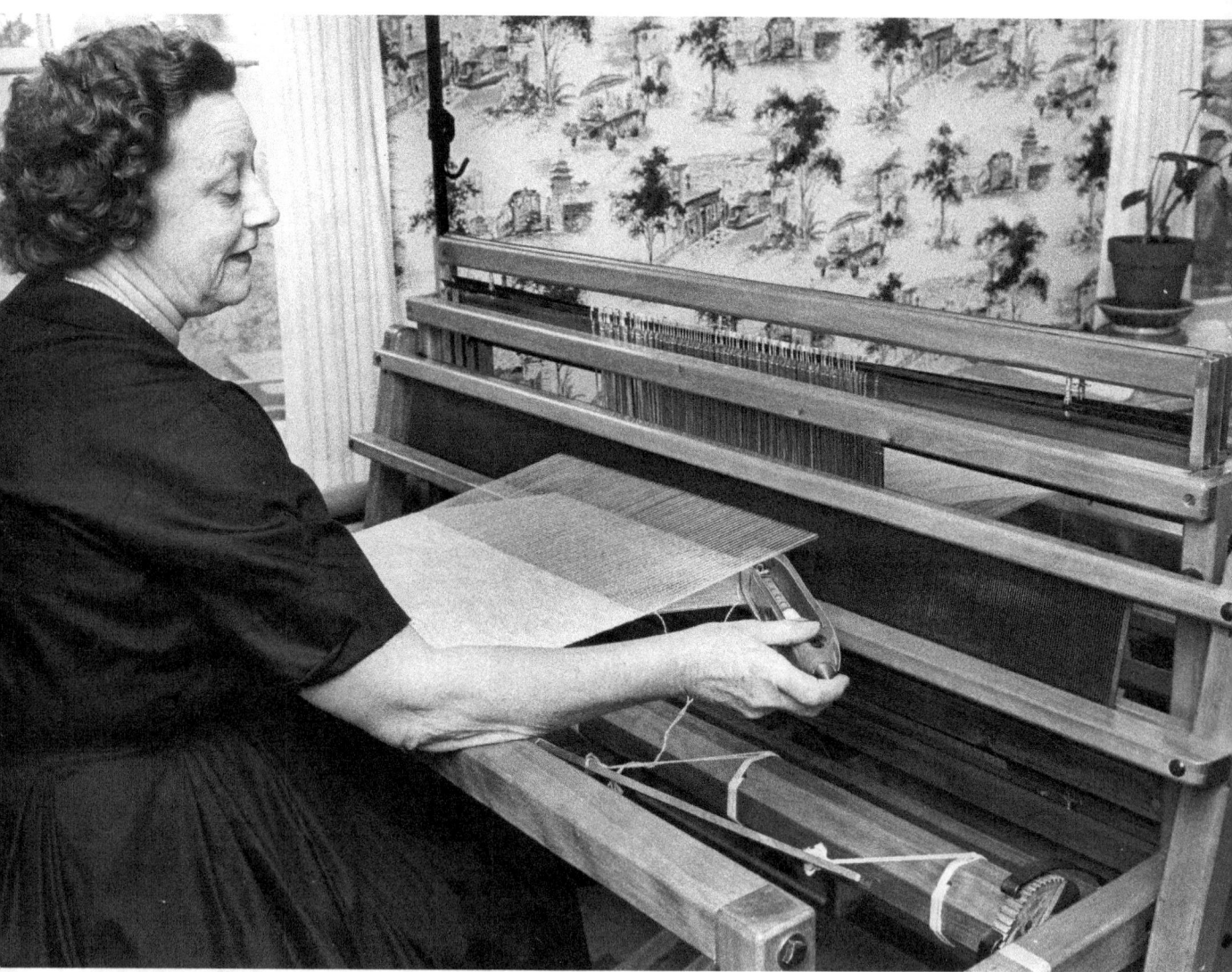

Sherman Oaks housewife Mrs. Joseph Perry weaves her troubles away by making gifts for others. Here she starts weaving a place mat set on her loom, calling her hobby fun and 'good therapy.' January 4, 1962. (Jeff Goldwater)

(Order #00082969)

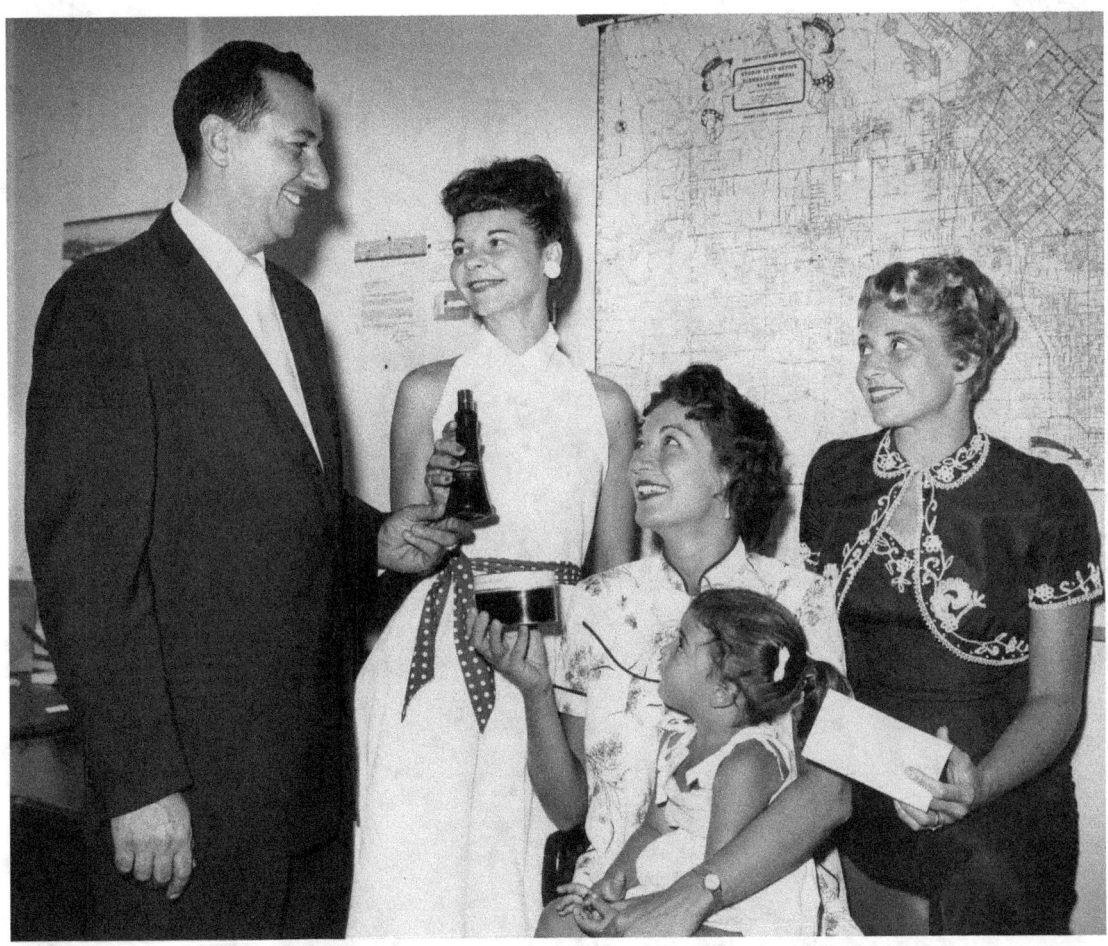

New members of the California Home Owners Service Club receive free gifts from President Paul Freeman. Left to right: Freeman, Mrs. Conrad McEdwards; Mrs. Norman Schechter, Miss Gail Schechter and Miss June Taylor.

The California Homeowners Service Club was organized to "simplify the woman's problems in home maintenance by making available to her skilled artisans in all fields...that she might need in running her household. A carefully screened list of services sources...has been compiled." A woman would apply to the organization and for a $5 annual membership fee be able to call the organization who would take care of service she requested.

September 2, 1959. (Order #00083903)

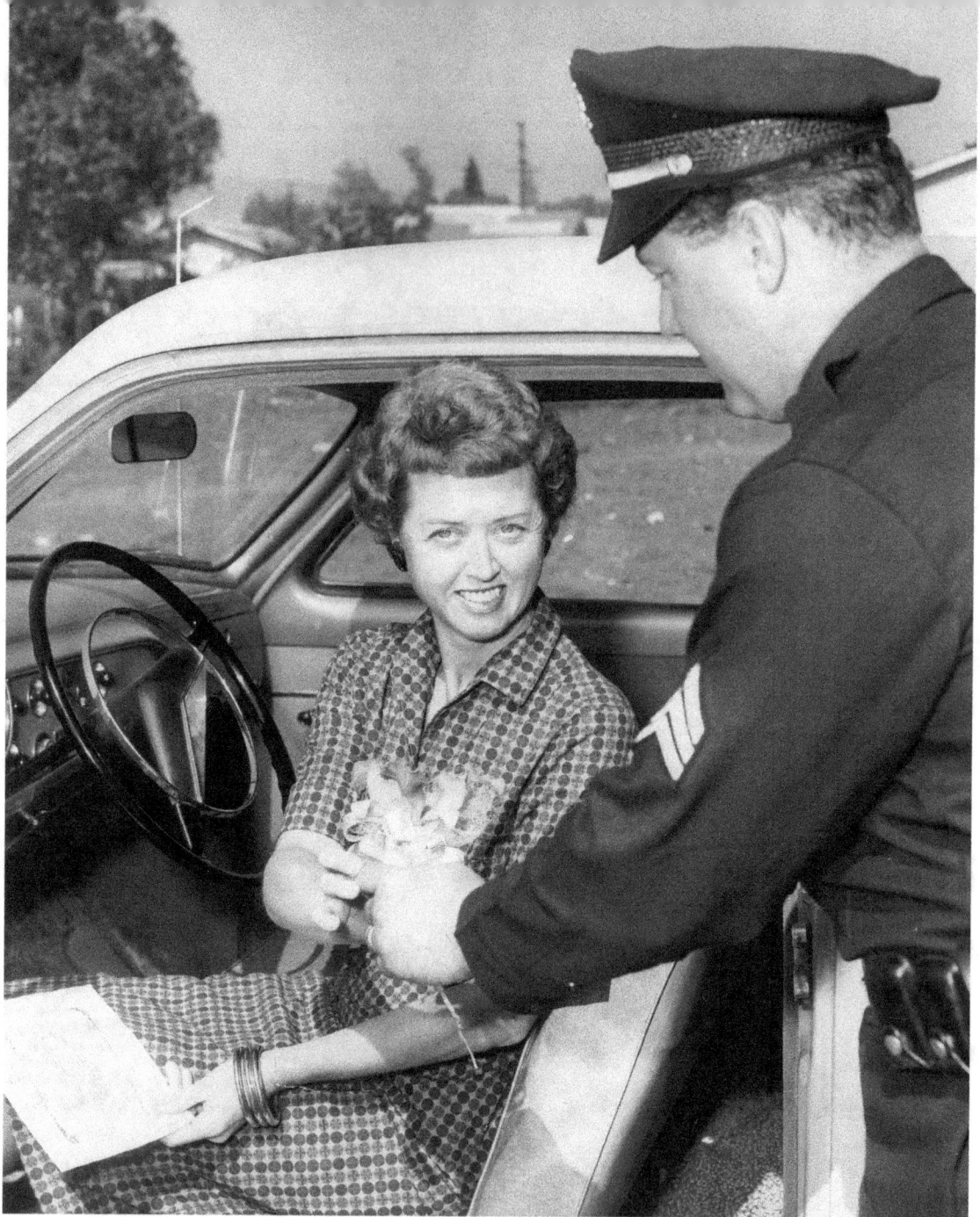

"Mrs. Harold Allen, a housewife, of 13355 Dronfield Ave., Sylmar, was grateful when presented an orchid by Sgt. Charles "Chuck" Sherwood for her safe driving practices. Sherwood made the presentation after directing Mrs. Allen over to the curb. Police Chief Winford Slaughter's men handed cigarette lighters to the men for their safe driving and orchids to women during weekend observance of safe driving practices." September 30, 1959. (Order #00084497)

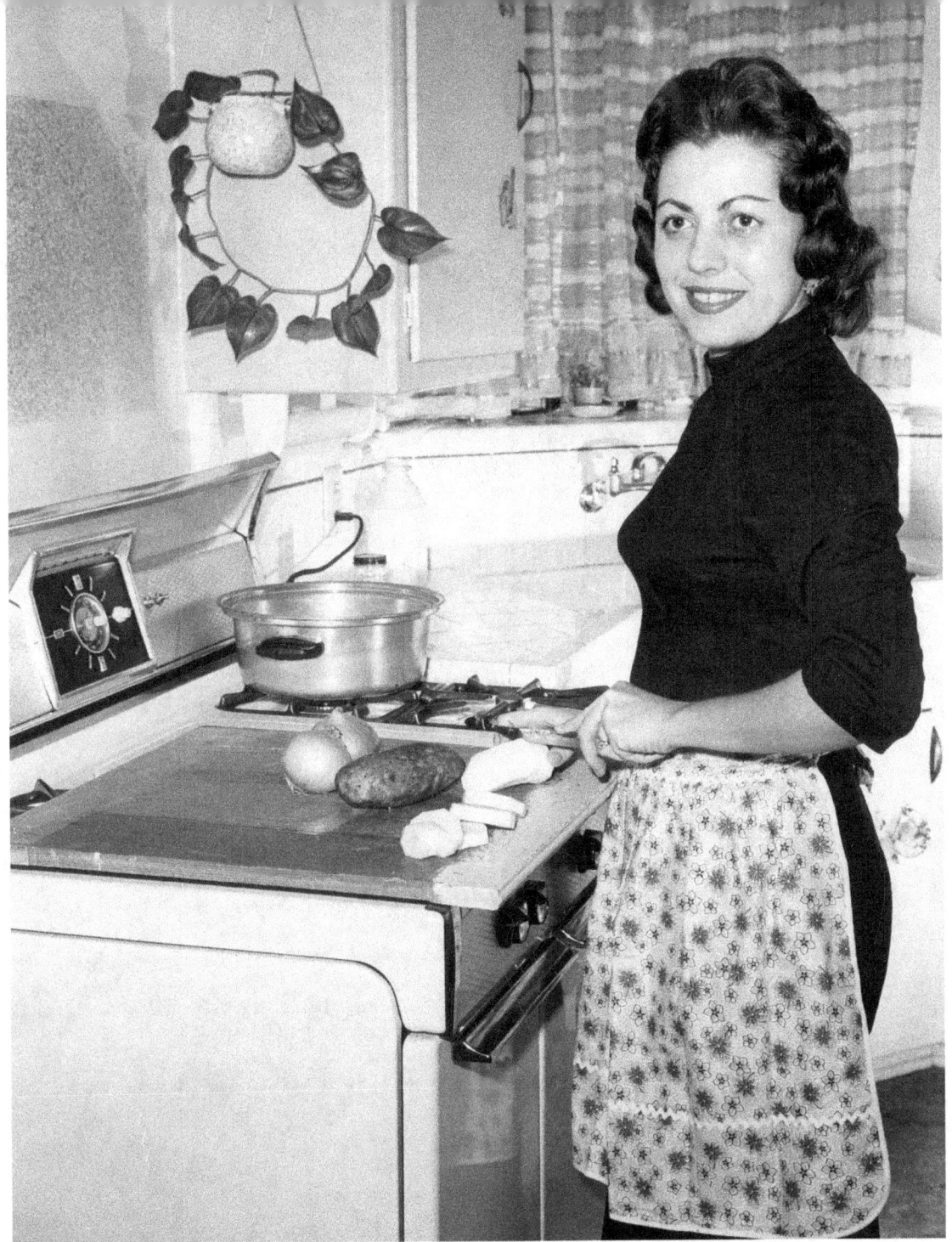

"Mrs. Bob McKay cuts potatoes and onions in preparation for the big pot of New England Clam Chowder she will serve for dinner. Being New Englanders, she and Bob say "no tomatoes" in the chowder."
January 17, 1960. (Order #00086417)

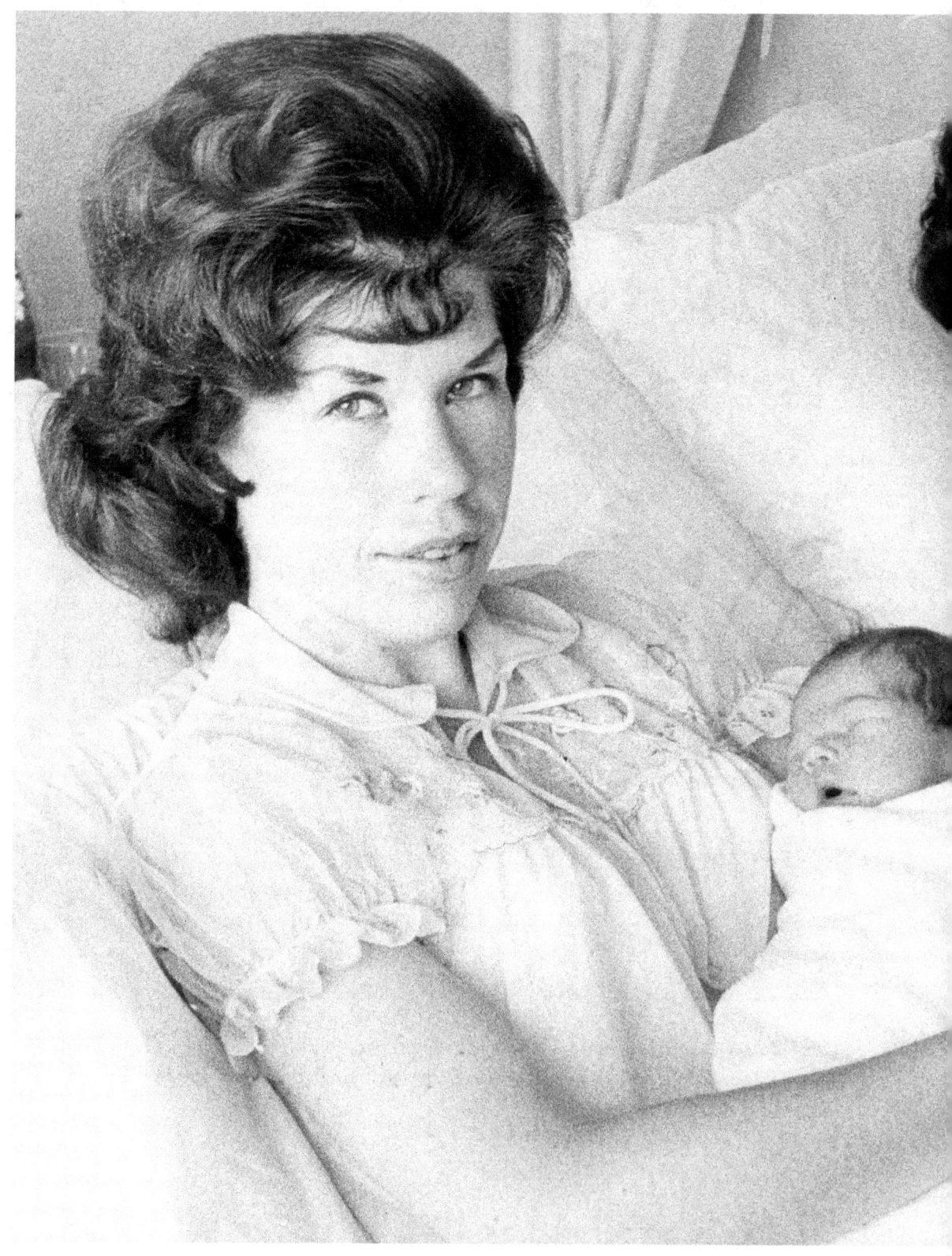

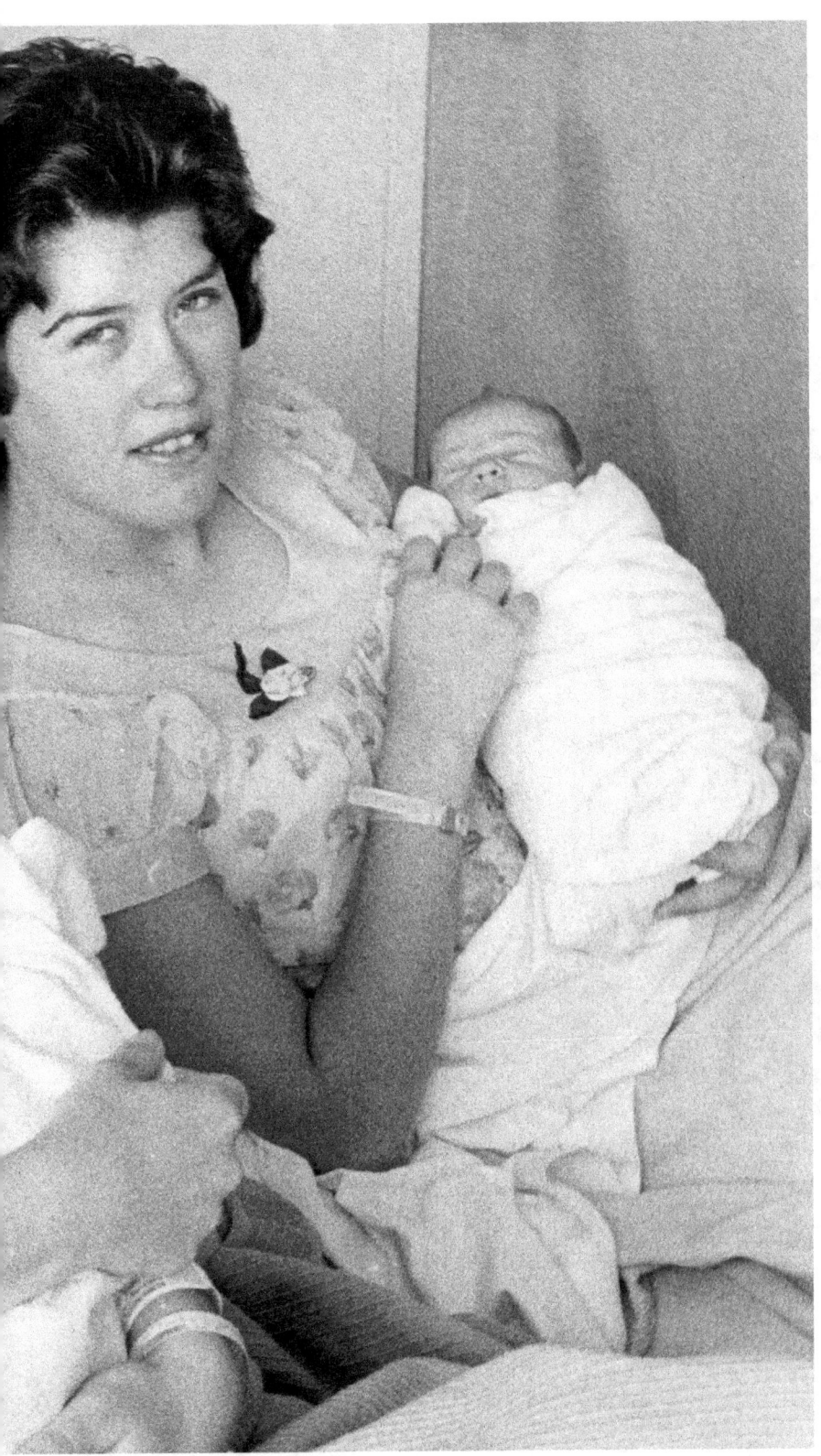

"Two Pacoima sisters, Mrs. William Klarkowski, 22, 13864 Daventry St., left, with 7-lb. 9-oz. Angela, and Mrs. Michael Thoene, 17, with 7-lb. 2-oz. Susan, gave birth to their daughters about five hours apart Monday evening at Holy Cross Hospital. The babies were delivered by Dr. Hans Engel."
August 2, 1963.
(Larry Leach)
(Order #00108820)

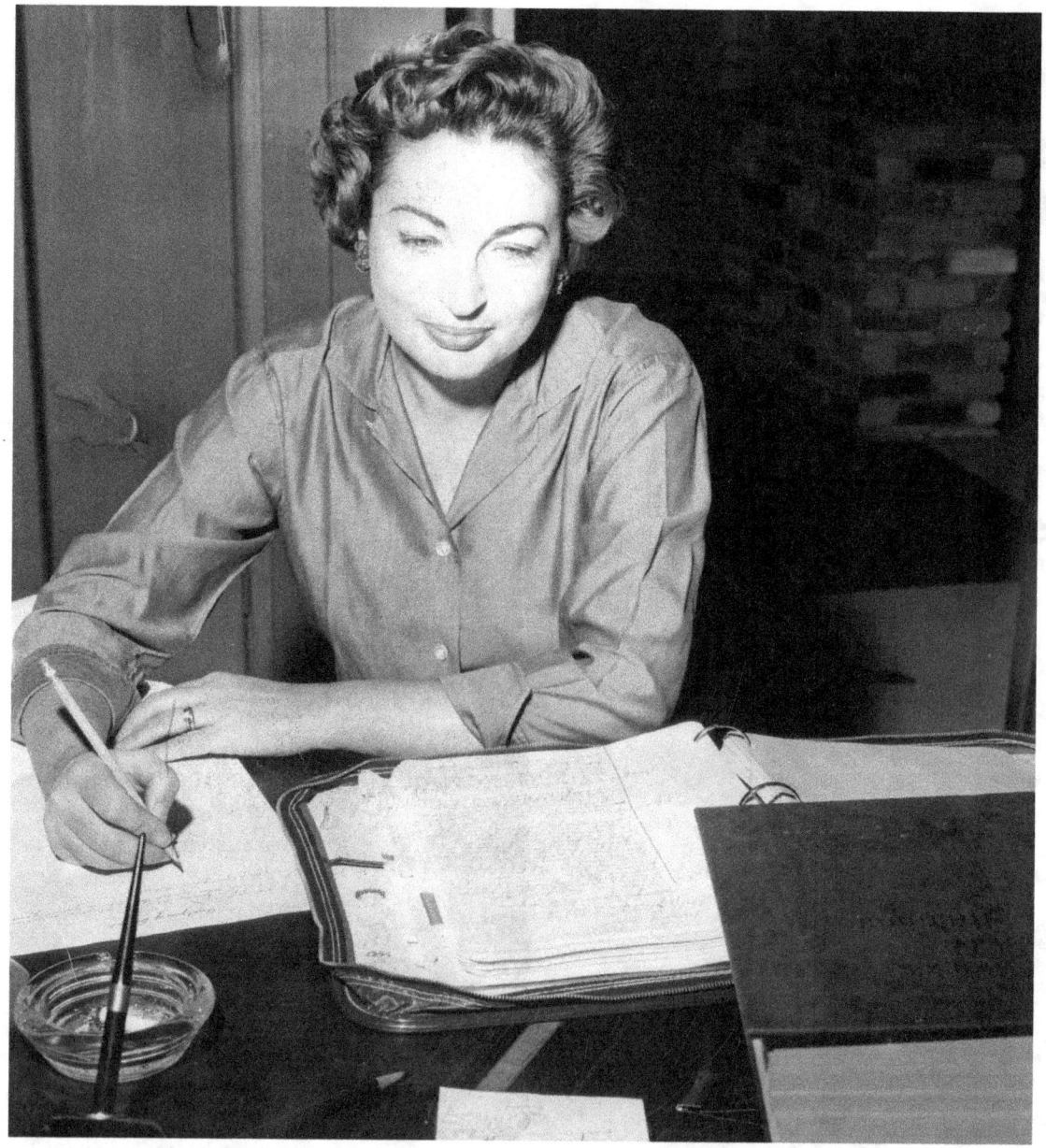

"Mrs. Iylene Weiss of Encino, mother of five children, has added law to her many household duties." Weiss would later make an unsuccessful run for the state Assembly before founding the Ballona Lagoon Marine Preserve in order to restore the 16-acre area in Venice. April 26, 1960. (Jon Woods)

(Order #00093482)

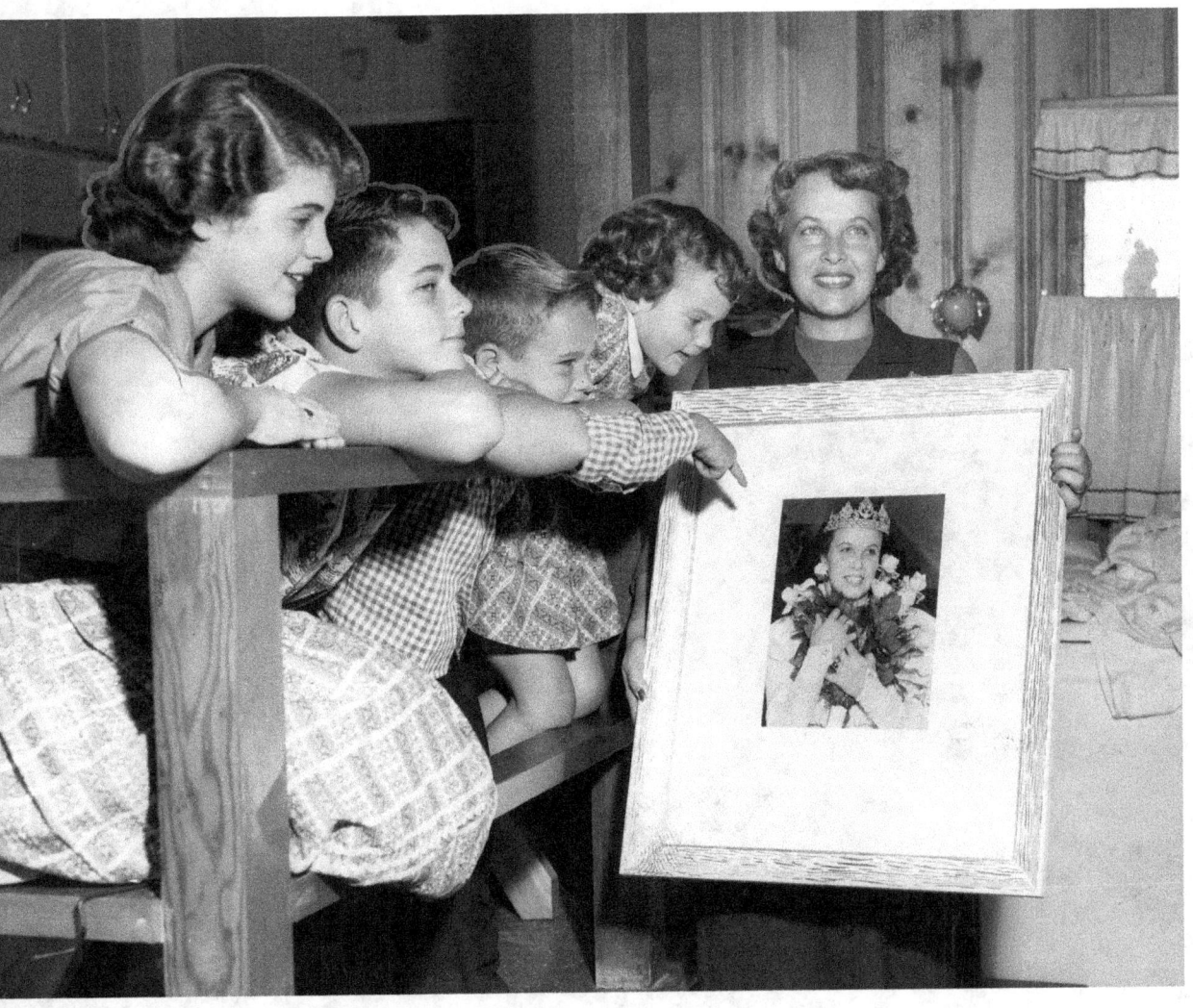

"Appreciative audience comments and compares Margaret Huntley, 1940 Rose Queen, on framed picture, and their mother, Mrs. Margaret Huntley Main, 1955 Sunland housewife and Sunday school teacher, standing. From left are Linda, 14, Johnny, 12, Marty, 6, and Sandra, 5."
December 26, 1955. (Order #00109900)

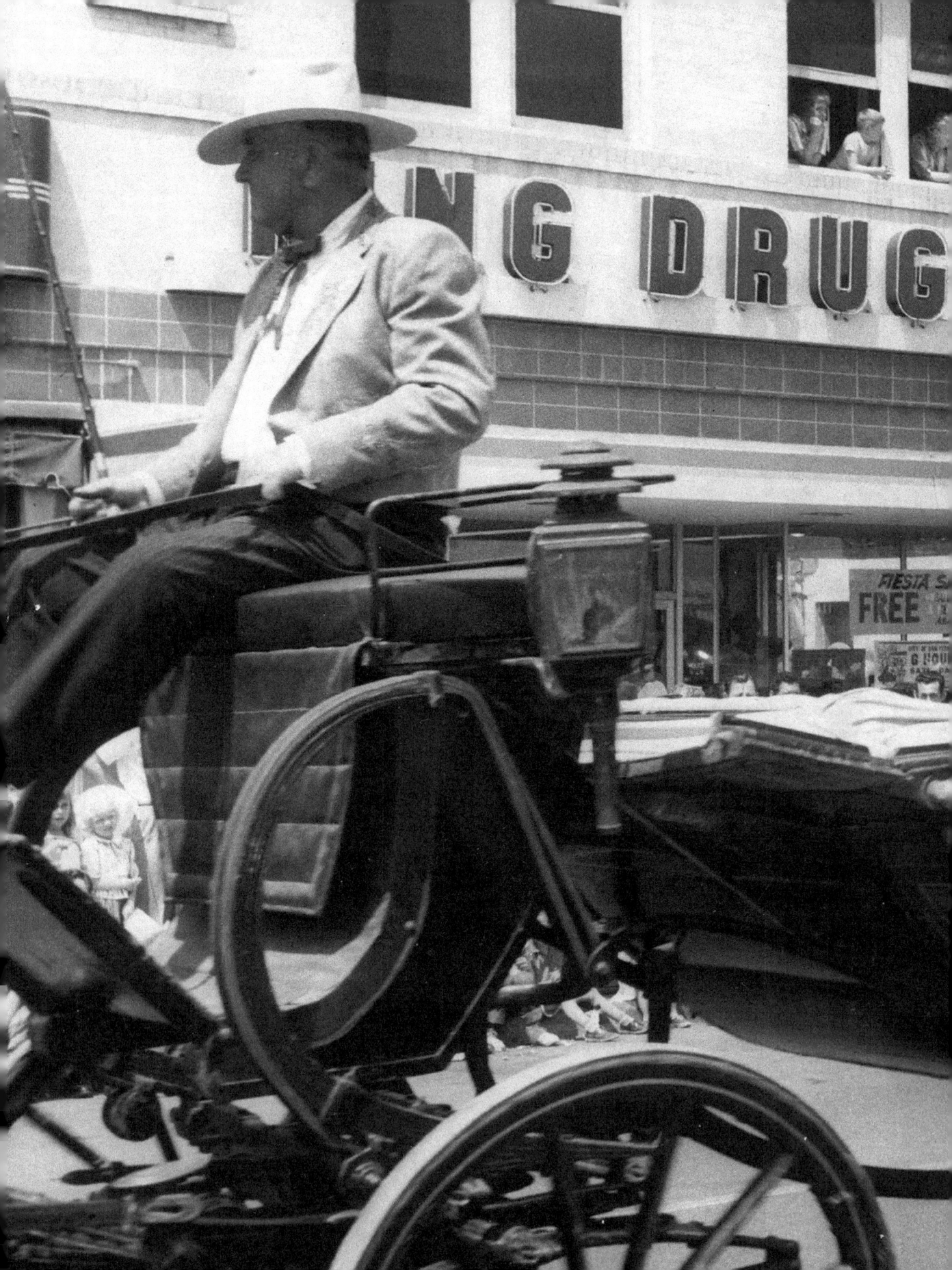

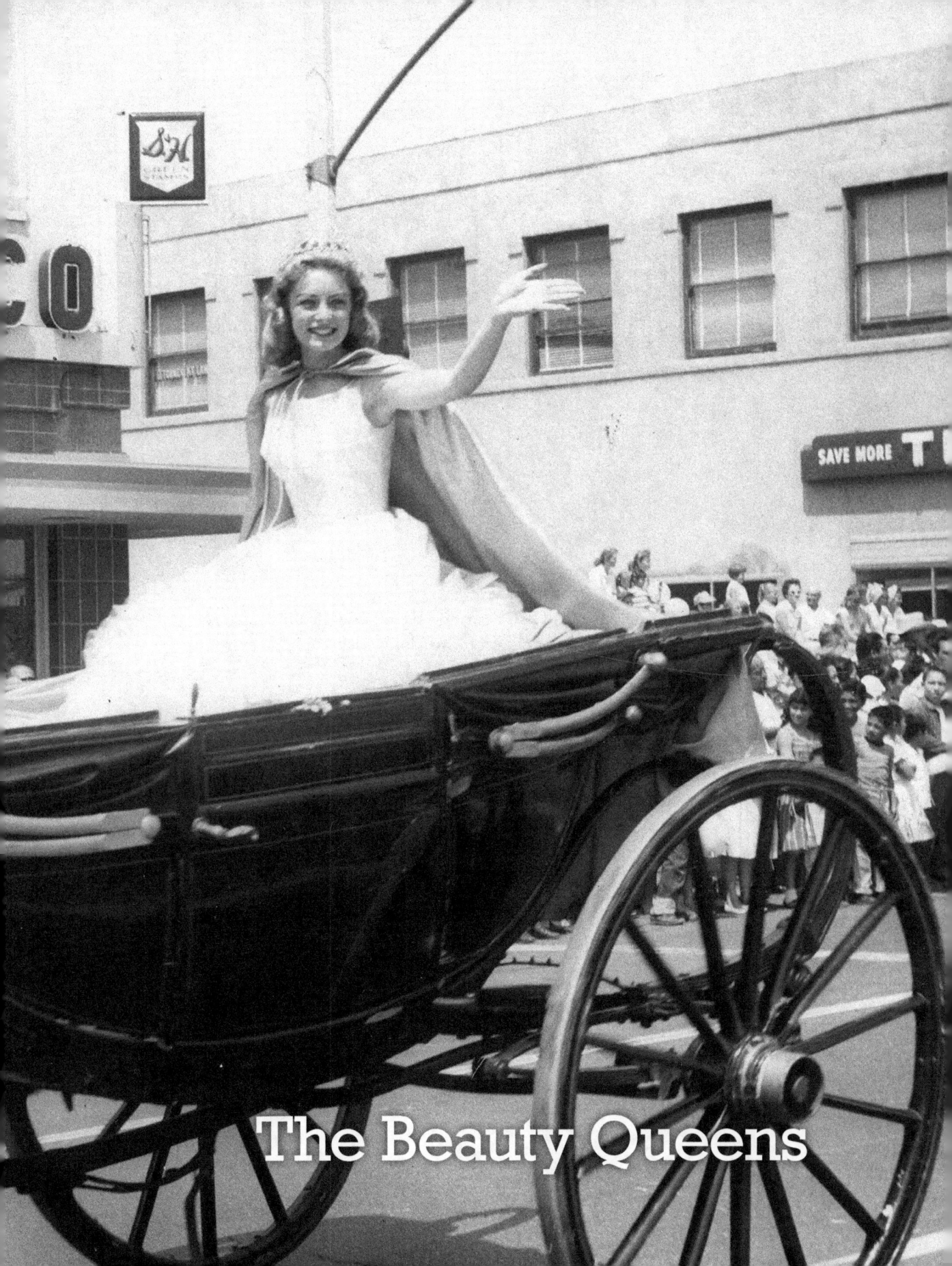

The Beauty Queens

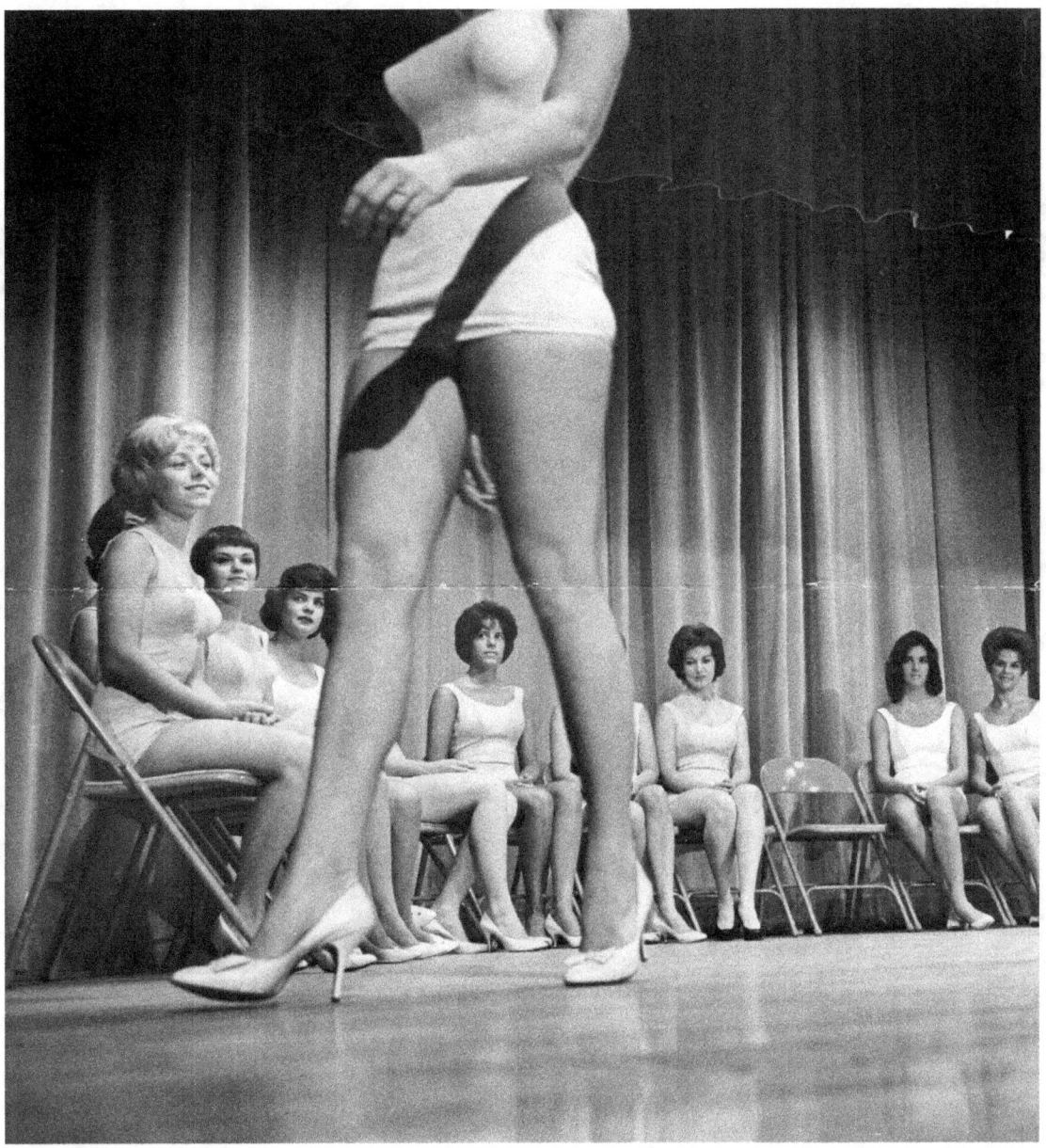

"Judges aren't the only ones who cast discerning glances at beauty pageant contestants
as the above photograph from the Miss Sherman Oaks contest demonstrates.
As one girl goes through her paces, other title hopefuls eye their competition."
July 10, 1962. (George Brich)
(Order #00082872)

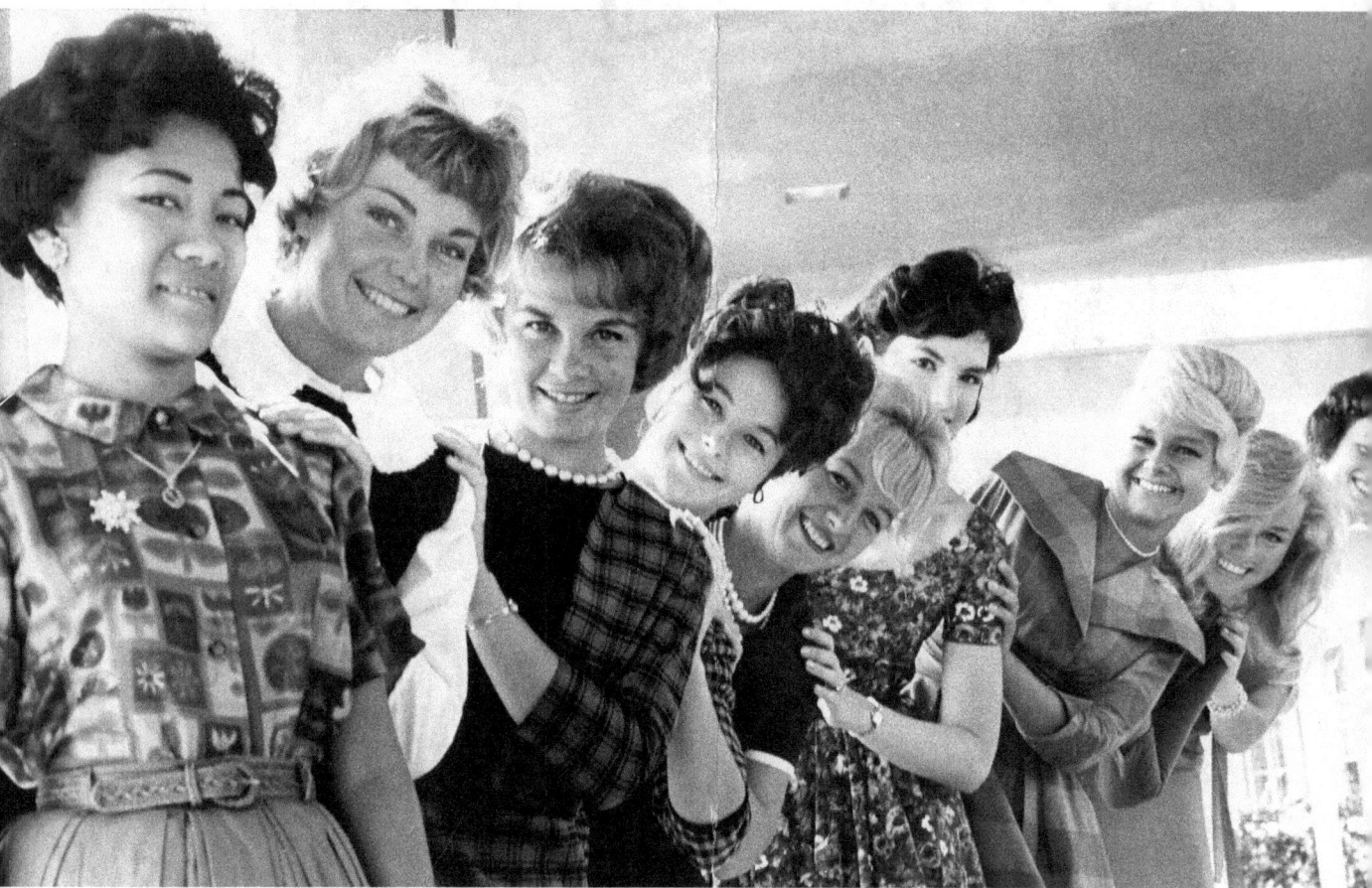

"Valley College students are a little worried. They are faced with a difficult problem.
Next week, they have to select a new queen. And just look at all the candidates. The final
decision will be made Oct. 17 and 18 through a student vote held on campus. Results of the
election will be announced at a homecoming dance Oct. 19. Candidates are, from left,
Carmen Hoo, 19; Judy Anderson, 19; Bobbi Wagner, 19; Madeline Blackburn, 18;
Marty Oeland, 19; Diana Dale Pleasonton, 16; Gail Weichlein, 17; Rae McCardie, 19, and
Robin Saunders, 18."
October 10, 1962. (George Brich)
(Order #00109405)

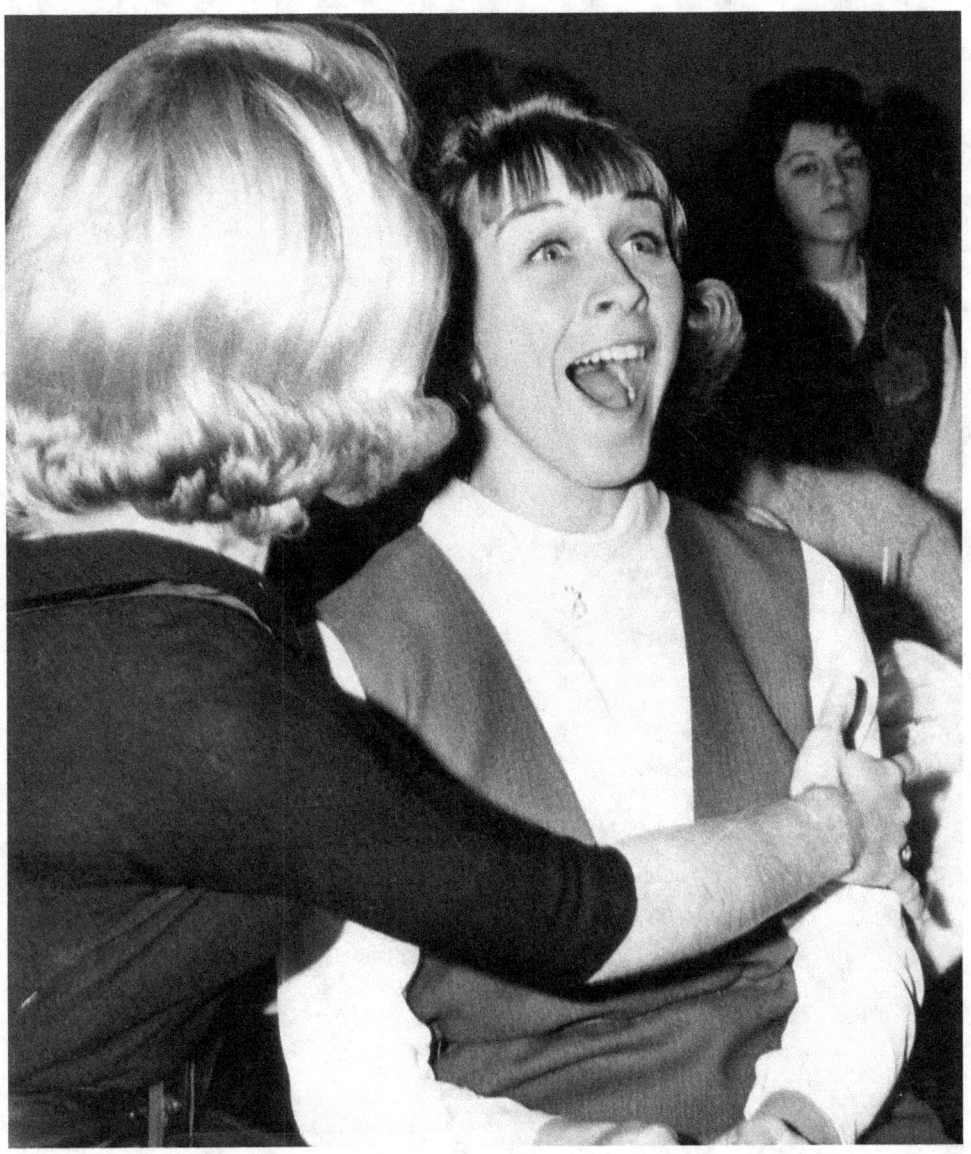

"Surprised? Pierce freshman queen speechless! Vickie Bartmus, 17, reacts with open-mouthed surprise as she is announced the winner of the Pierce College freshman queen contest Wednesday. Vickie, a psychology major, lives in North Hollywood with her parents. Congratulating her at left is runner-up Loreen Onichak, 18, of Encino. The new queen and her court will preside over the Freshman Christmas Dance on Friday."
December 12, 1963. (Jeff Robbins)

(Order #00083848)

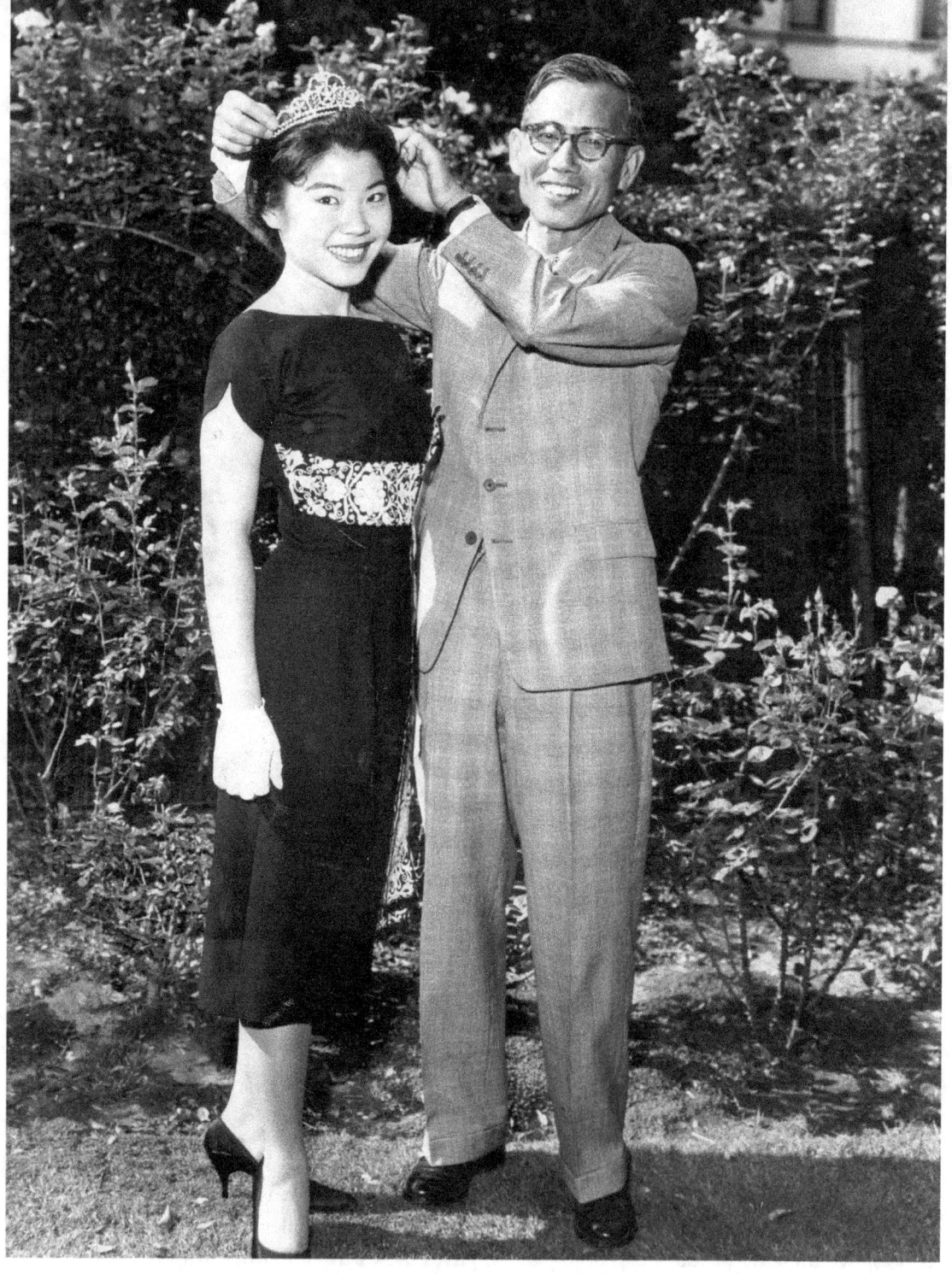

"Ayleen Ito, 18, is crowned as queen of 27th annual American Legion Fourth of July fireworks show at Coliseum by Yukio Hasumi, consul-general of Japan in Los Angeles." June 24, 1959. (Order #0083342)

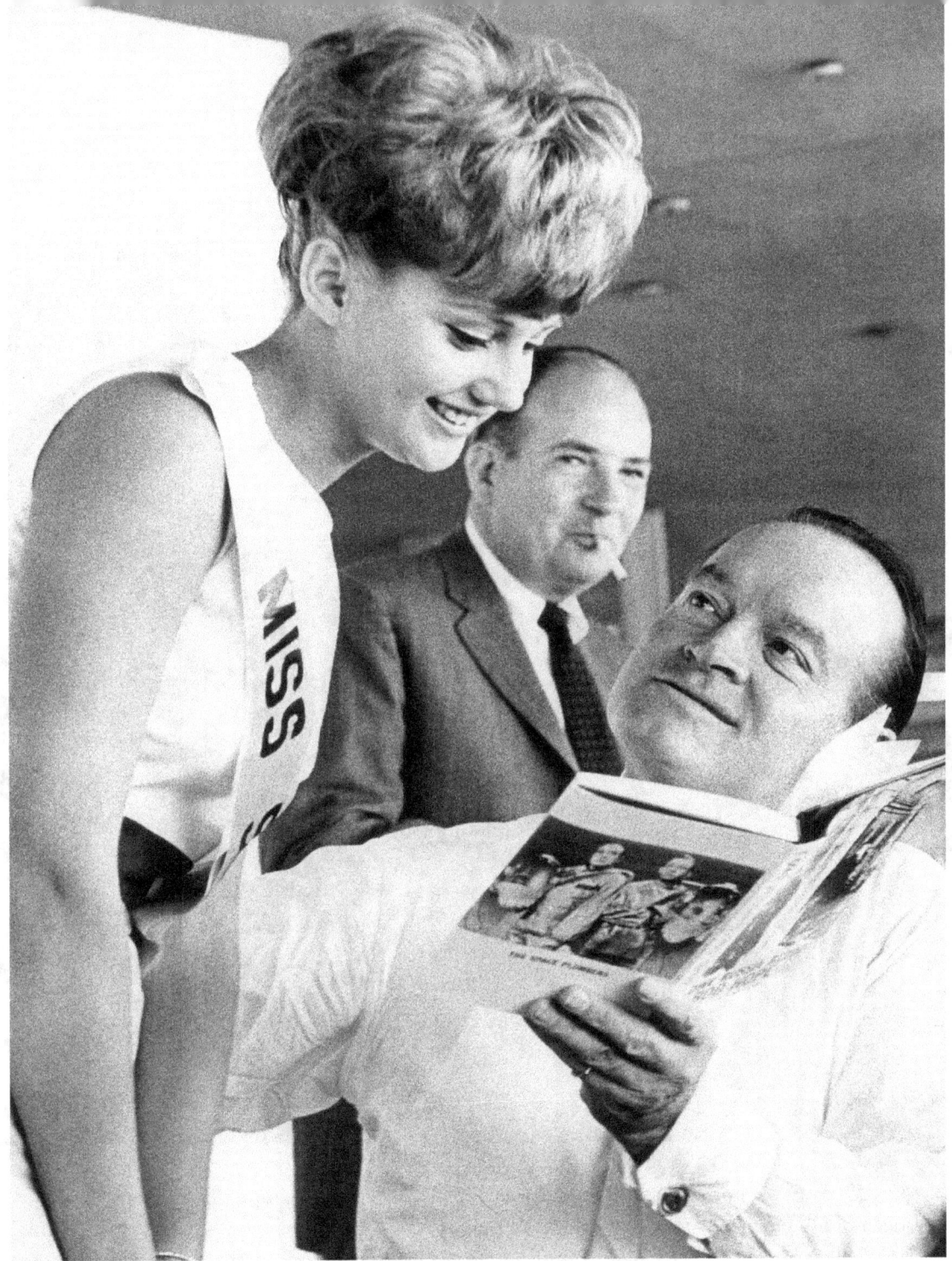

Miss Sunland, Barbara Schneider, 18, gets Bob Hope to autograph a copy of his book *I Owe Russia $1,200* during a book signing at the Broadway Department Store in Panorama City. August 3, 1963. (Bob Martin)

(Order #00084144)

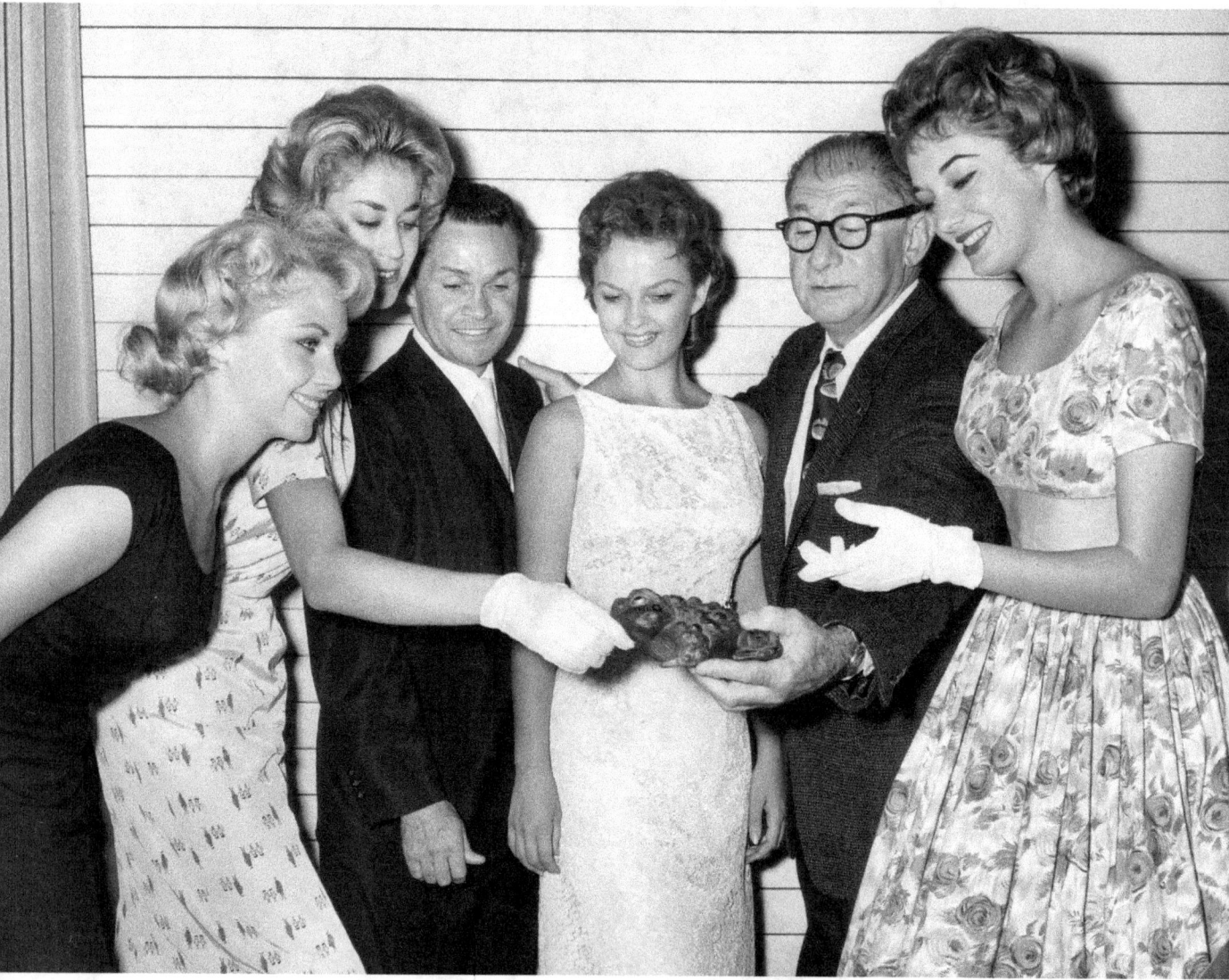

"Beauty Queens Vie For New Crown—Looking at "Lucky Toad" in hopes for success as
"Queen of Hi-Finance" sponsored by Trust Deed and Mortgage Exchange as feature of opening
of new Valley office at 5241 Lankershim Blvd. tomorrow. From left, Darlene Tompkins
(Miss Pacoima); Catherine Maguire (Miss Granada Hills); Tom Farrell, manager of new Valley
Office; Trust Deed and Mortgage Exchange; Joyce Phillips (Valley's Most Charming Girl);
Harry Gourfain, one of beauty pageant judges, and Jan Richards (Miss Van Nuys)."
September 22, 1959. (Order #00084239)

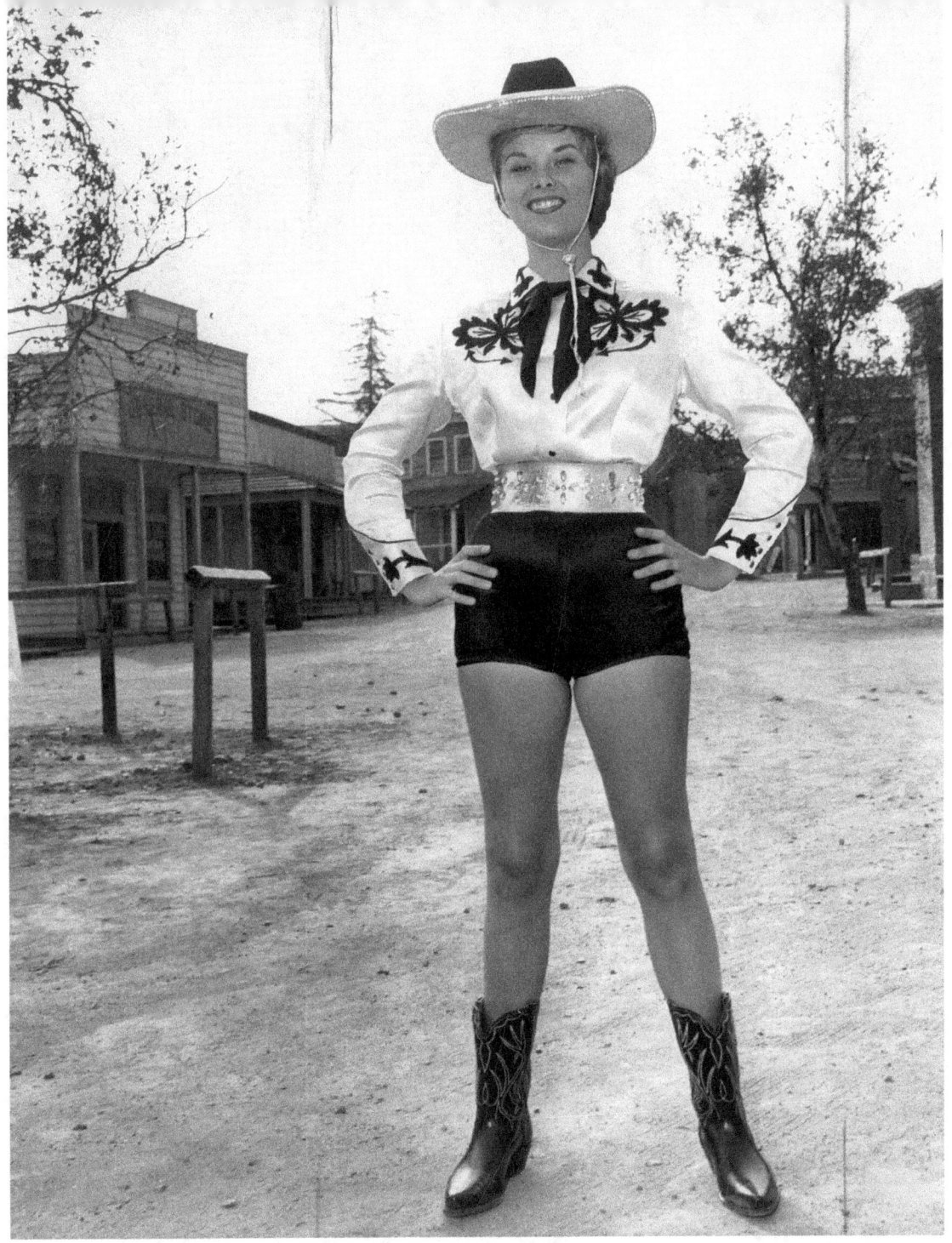

"Curvaceous Carolyn Komant, Warner Bros. actress and former Miss Maine in the Miss Universe contests, adds new dimensions to rodeo as she prepares for her role as Rodeo Queen for annual Saugus-Newhall competition slated for April 30 and May 1."
April 21, 1960. (Order #00093383)

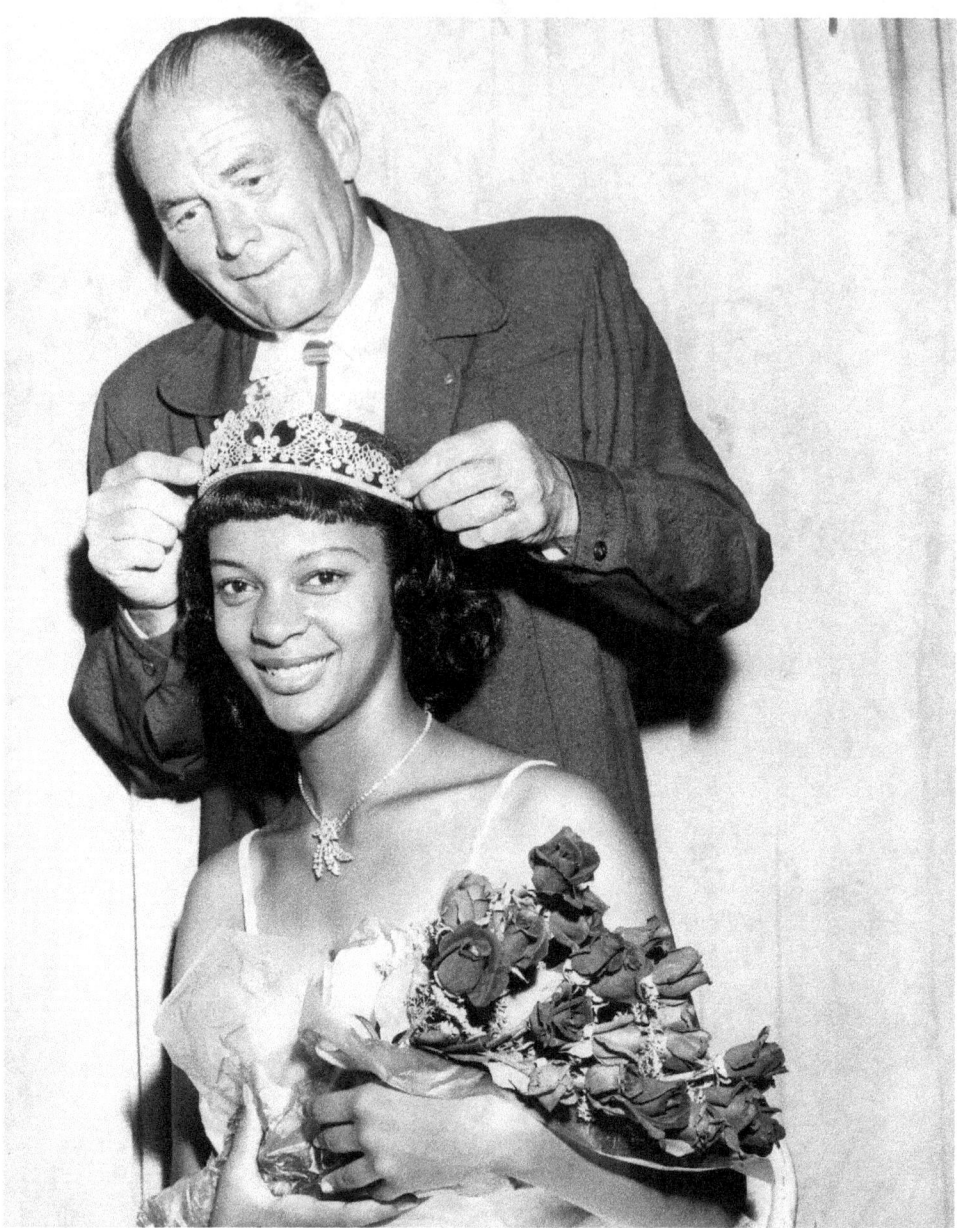

"Glenda Fields, 17, dance student and senior at San Fernando High School, is crowned queen of Pacoima's Community Fair by Earle Erne, president of Pacoima Chamber of Commerce. Miss Fields accepted prize check for $300, and plans to be career dancer."
August 3, 1959. (Order #00083674)

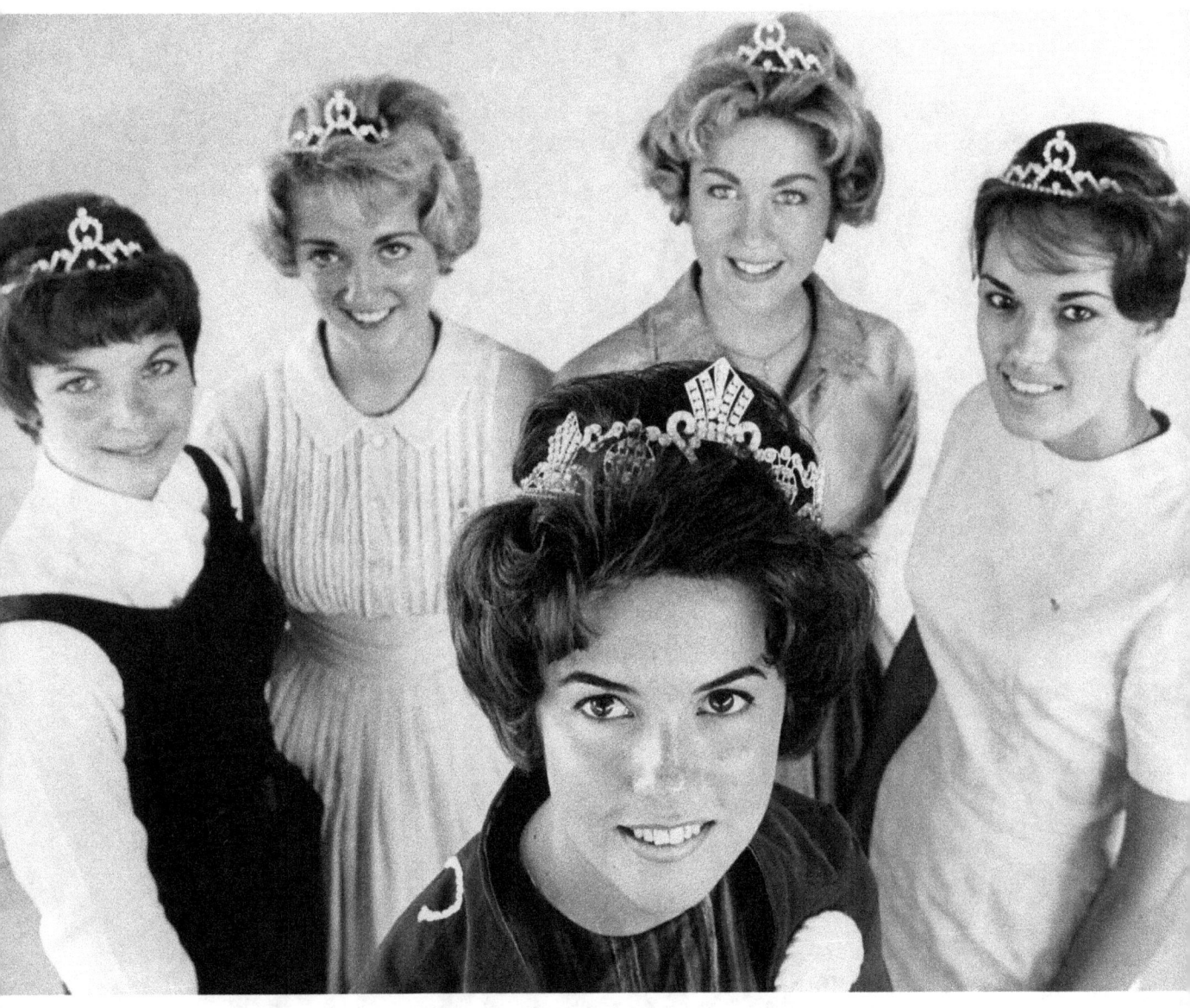

"Jan Jensen, 18, foreground, 21620 San Jose Dr., Chatsworth, has been named Homecoming Queen of Pierce College. She will be crowned officially at a dance next Friday night and will reign during the college's football season. Her court is, from left, Sharon Brodie, 18, 6500 Corbin Ave., Woodland Hills; Dianne Jackson, 18, 11502 Burbank Blvd., North Hollywood; Dianne Cain, 19, 6650 Quakertown Ave., Canoga Park; and Donna Schalyo, 18, 17557 Enadia Way, Van Nuys."
October 14, 1961. (Order #00107129)

"Three young beauties who are entered in the 1965 California Beauty Pageant are, from left, Joan Conrath, 18, of Sherman Oaks; Laurie Hogue, 19, of Burbank, and Carolyn Berg, 18, of Panorama City. The winner will be picked July 2." March 23, 1965. (Herb Carlton)
(Order #00109423)

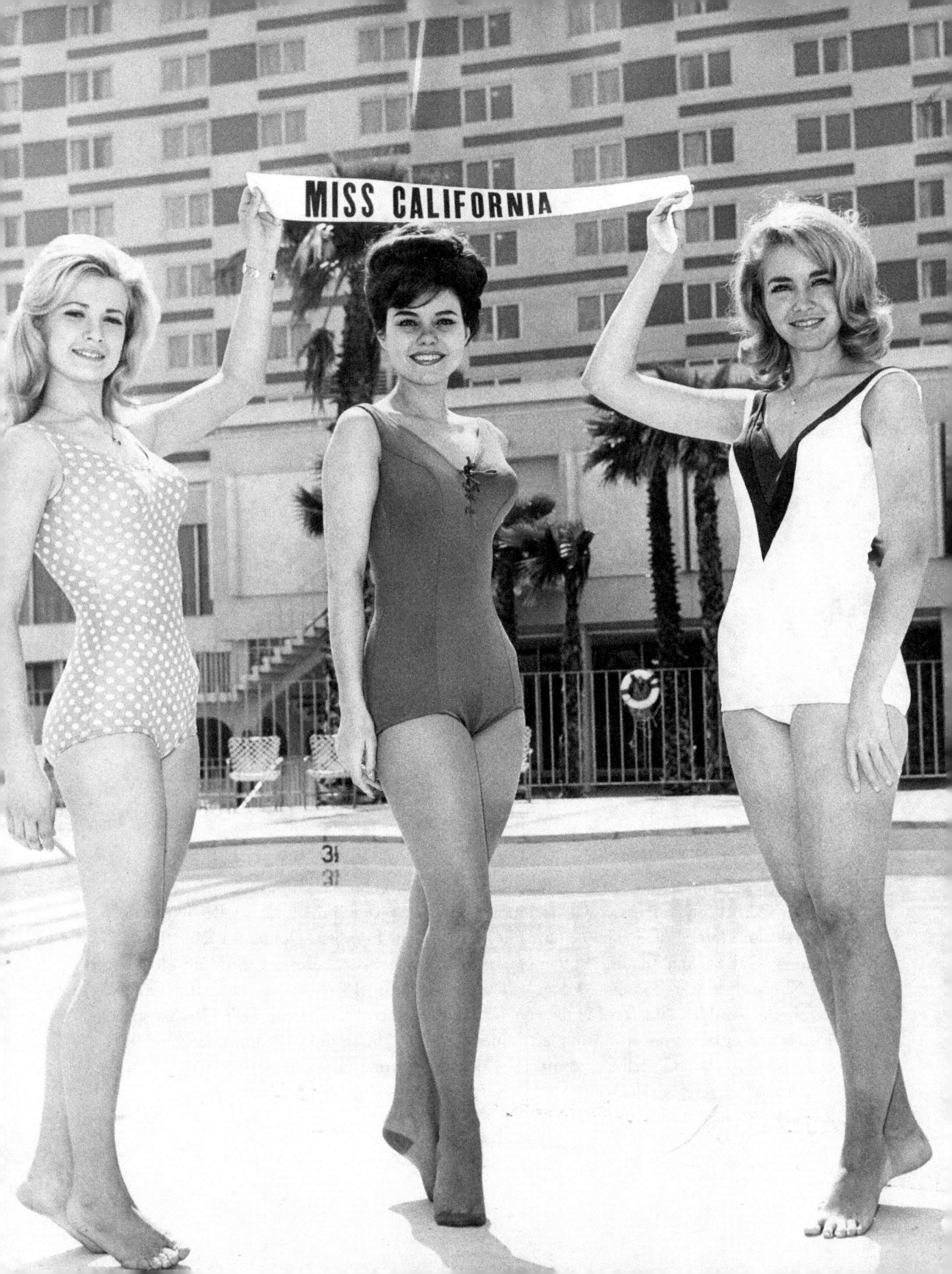

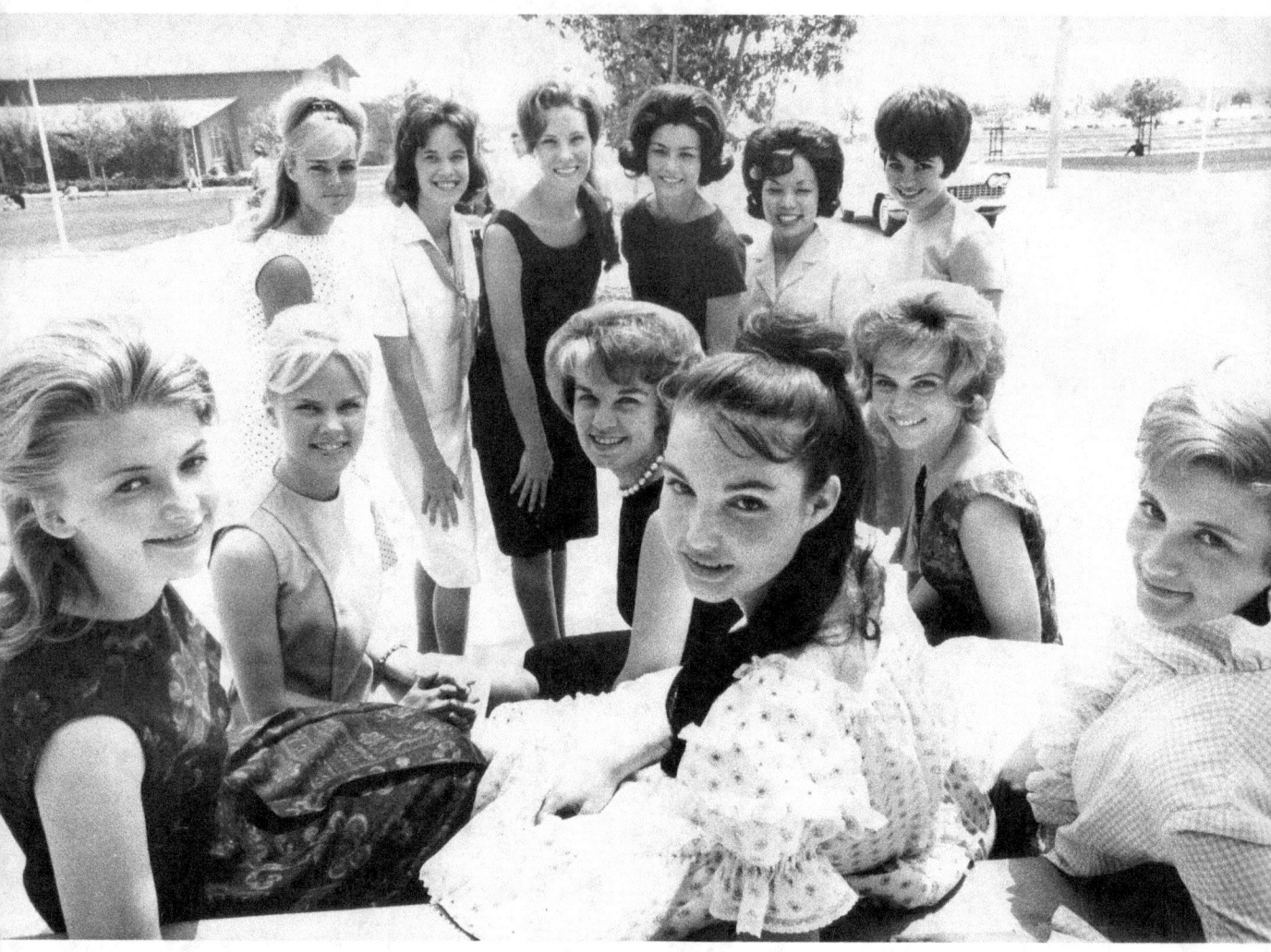

"One of these Valley College coeds will be the college's 1963 Spring Prom Queen. The winner and her four princesses will be announced at the prom in the Embassy Room of the Ambassador Hotel, Friday. The 12 hopefuls are, back row from left, Donna Russell, 19, Sherman Oaks; Dona Adams, 19, Van Nuys; Joyce Knigge, 18, Sherman Oaks; Carol Johnson, 19, Northridge; Anna Tawara, 19, Sun Valley; Sandi Herbst, 18, Burbank; center row: from left, Kathy Luedtke, 19, North Hollywood; Bobbie Wagner, 19, Sherman Oaks; Jan Yacobellis, 18, Sherman Oaks; front row: from left, Vineta Ozolins, 18, Studio City; Linda Bower, 19, Sherman Oaks, and Gladell Davidson, 18, North Hollywood."
May 18, 1963. (George Brich)

(Order #00109406)

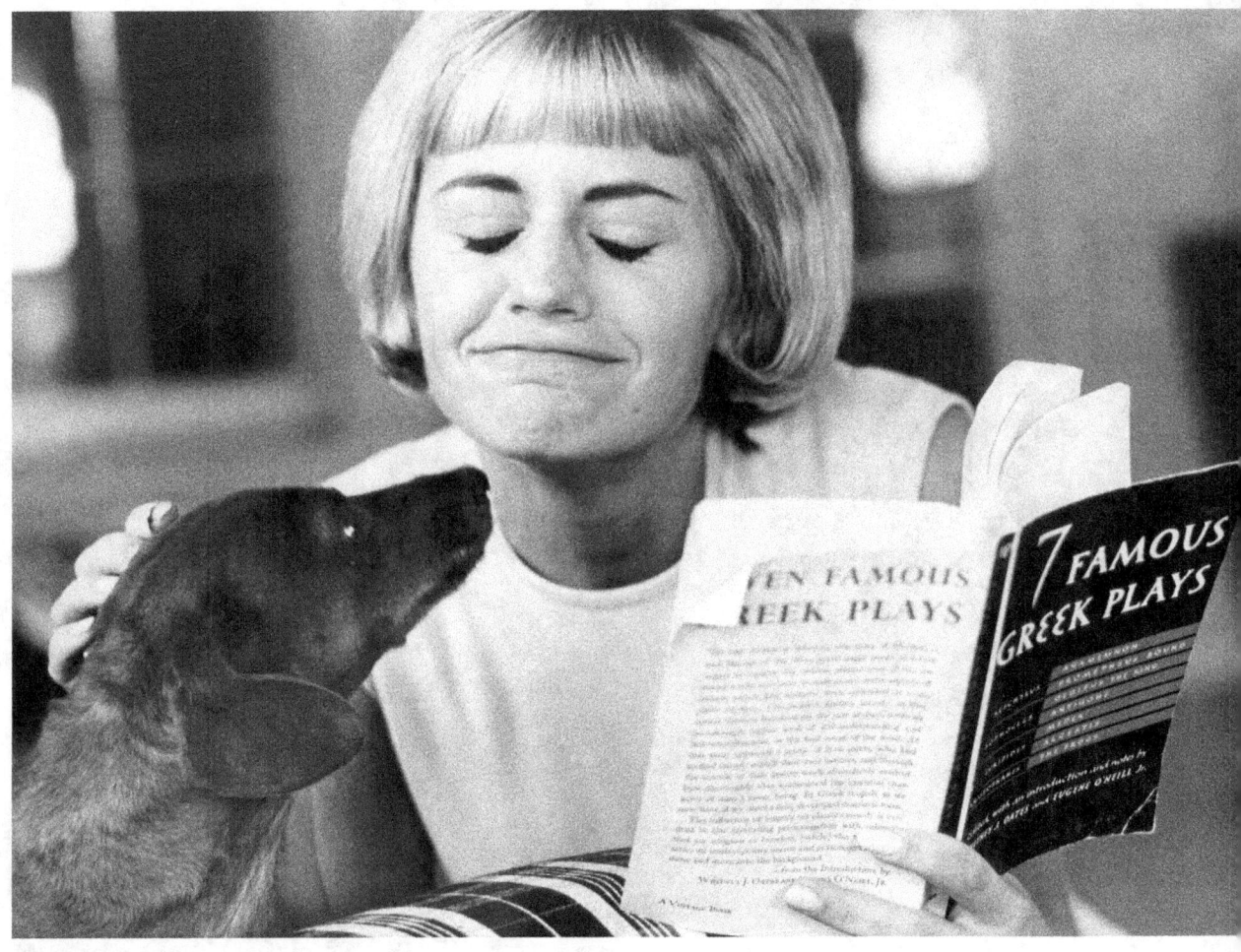

"It's Greek to me says 'Hugo,' mini-dachshund, to Diane Shaw, 19, Miss Granada Hills, as she reads her favorite Greek comedies and tragedies. Diane resides in Granada Hills with her parents, Mr. and Mrs. Robert Shaw, and attends Valley State College."
March 16, 1956. (George Brich)
(Order #00109641)

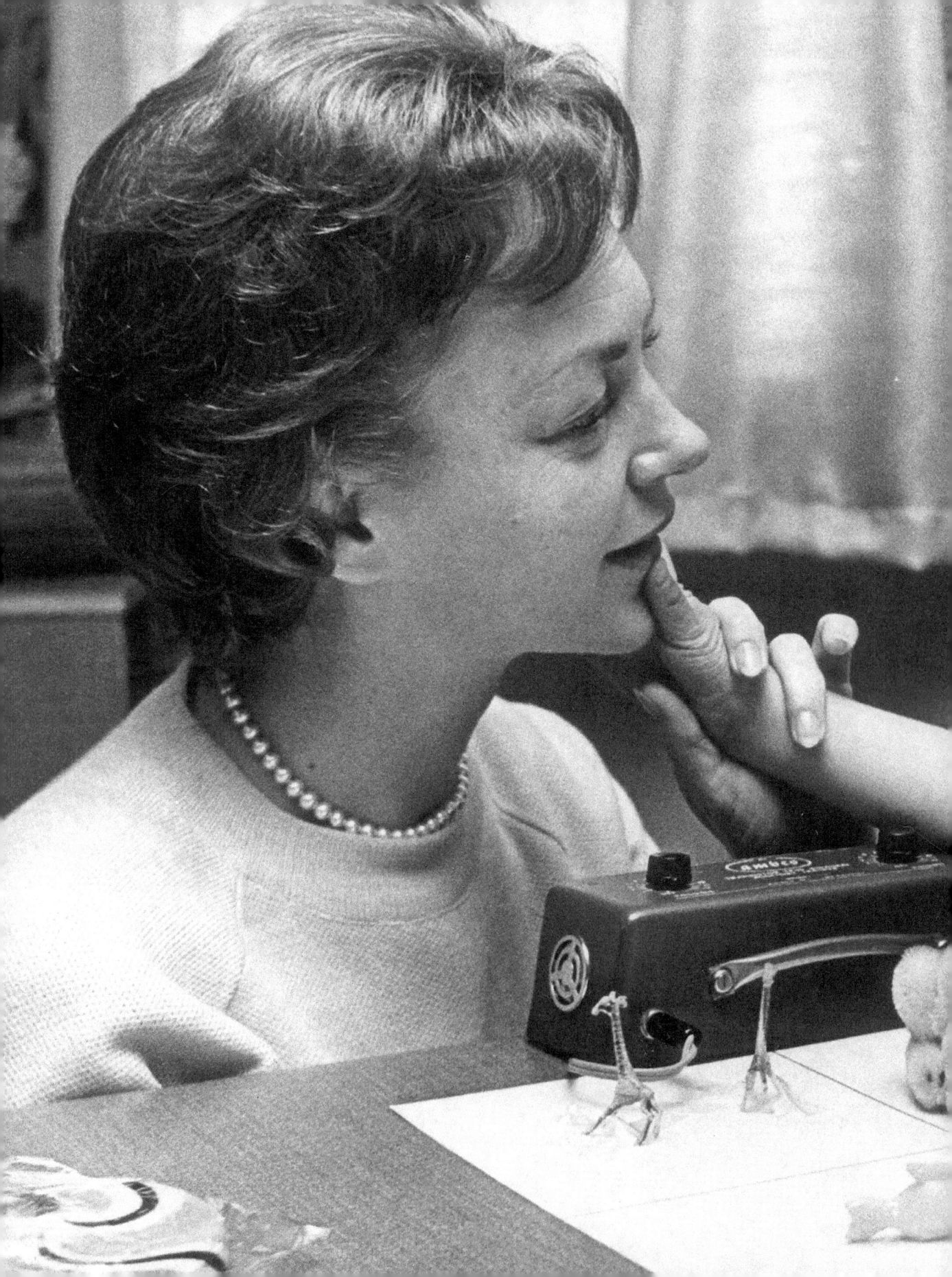

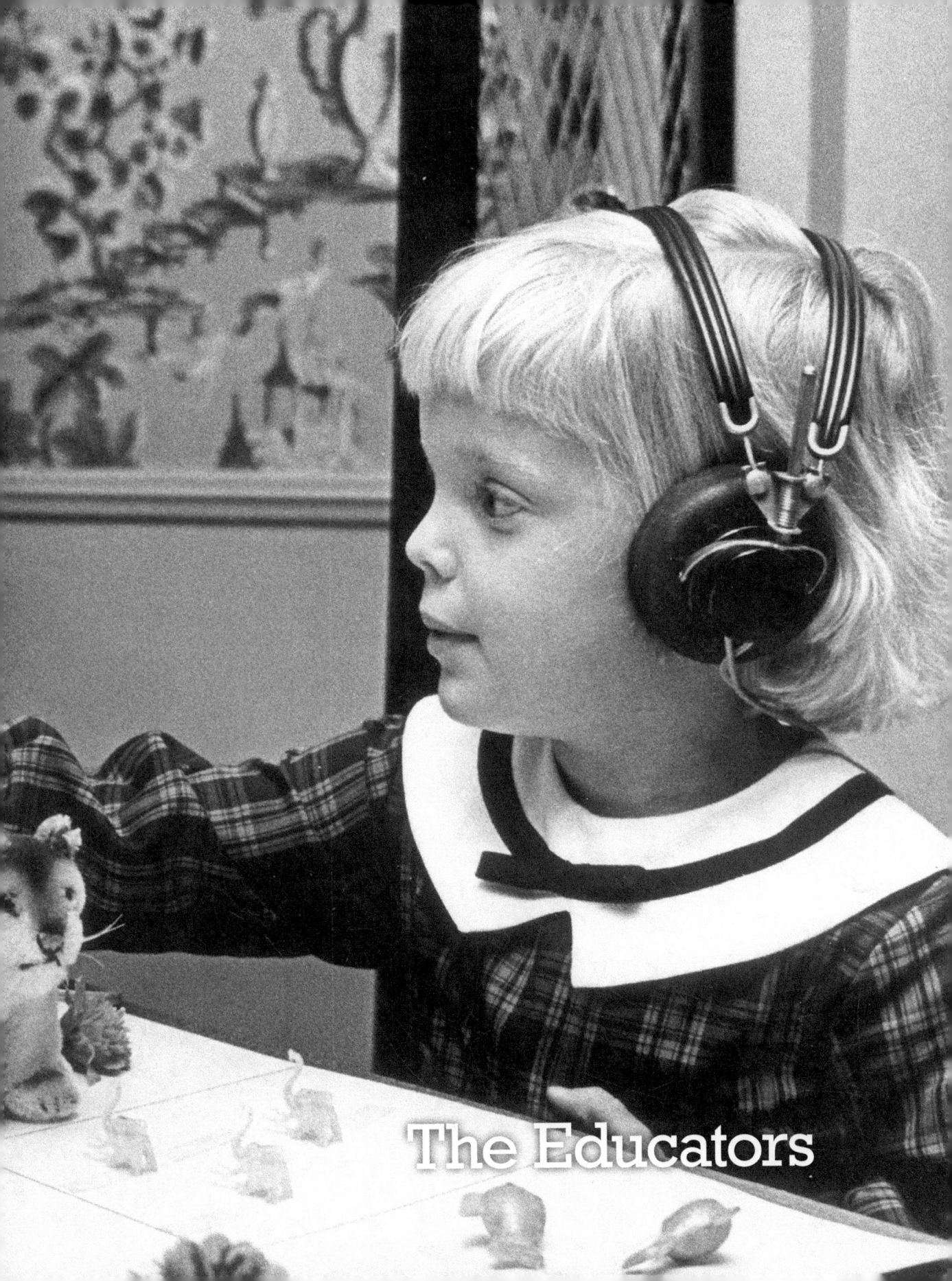

The Educators

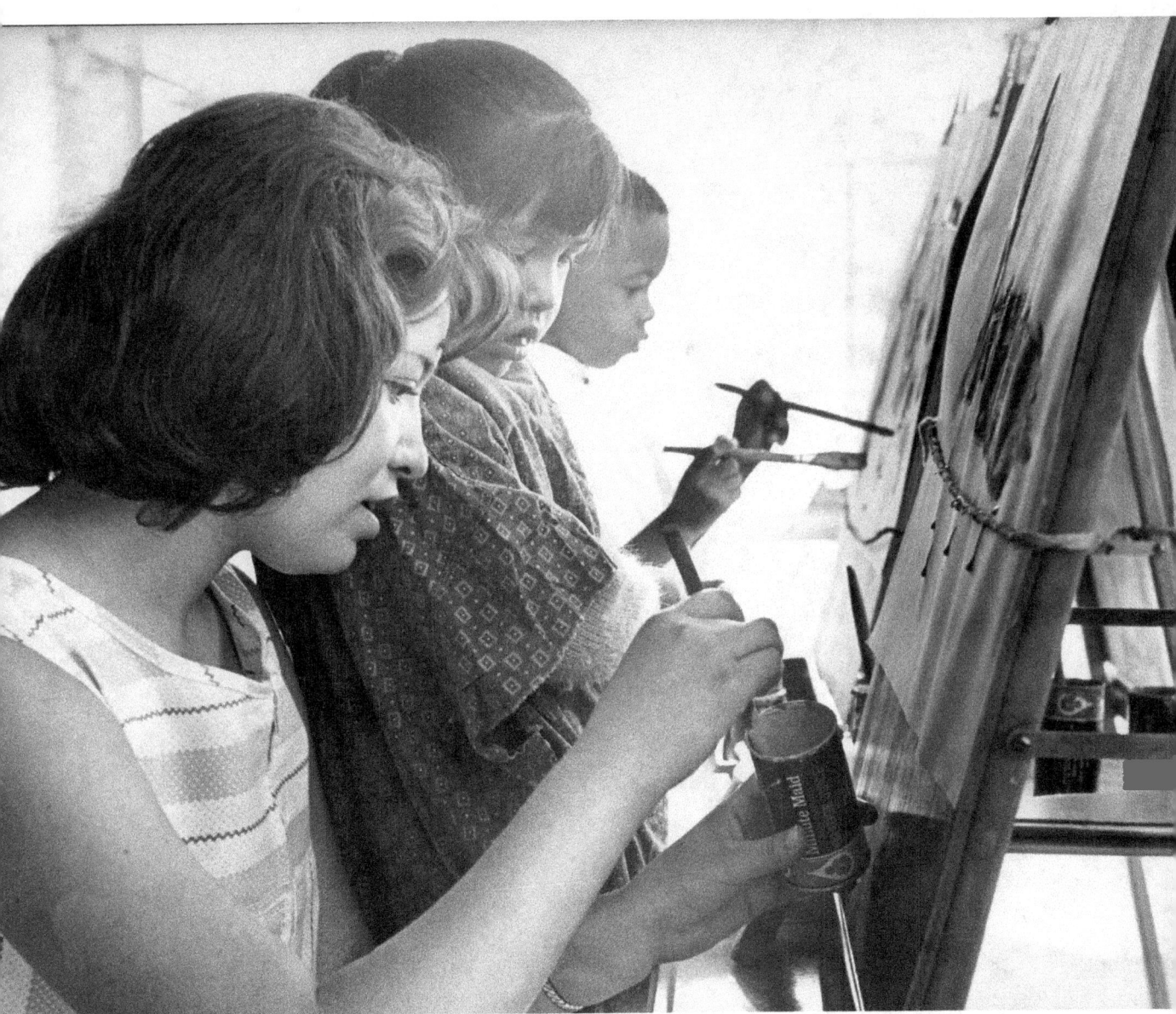

Neighborhood Youth Corps teacher aide Michelle Barrigan assists pre-schoolers as part of Operation Head Start.
1965. (George Brich)
(Order #00031553)

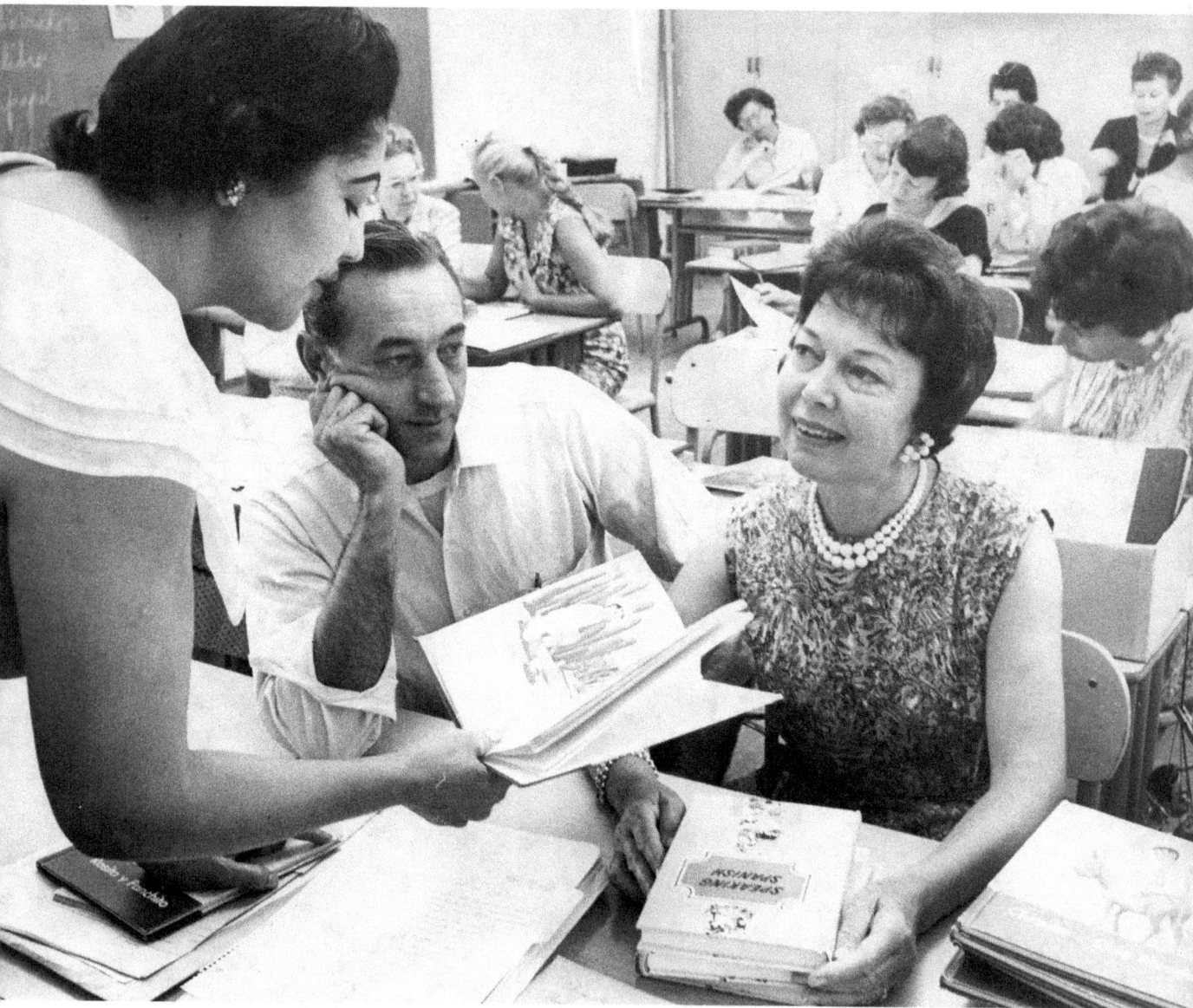

Los Angeles Unified School District teachers learn Spanish in order to offer it to elementary school children under a new district program, in which students in grades three through six would be offered language instruction. Here Fufina Chavez teaches Charles Downey and Florence Keats Spanish.
1961. (Order #00032191)

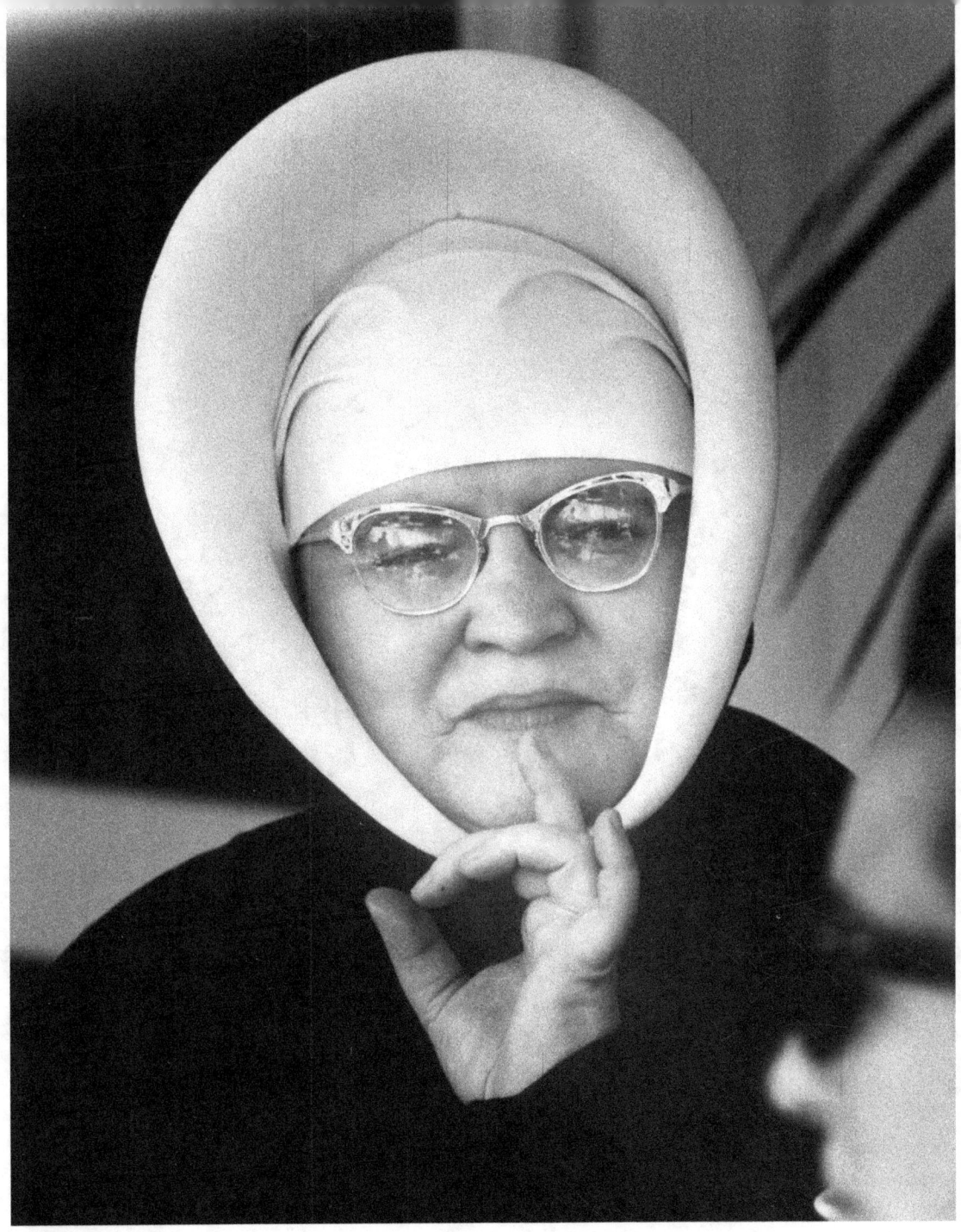

Mother Superior of Providence High School observes a Mother-Daughter fashion show at Bob Hope's Toluca Lake Estate. The fashion show and luncheon were held for the benefit of the Burbank school.
April 4, 1964. (George Brich)
(Order #00084147)

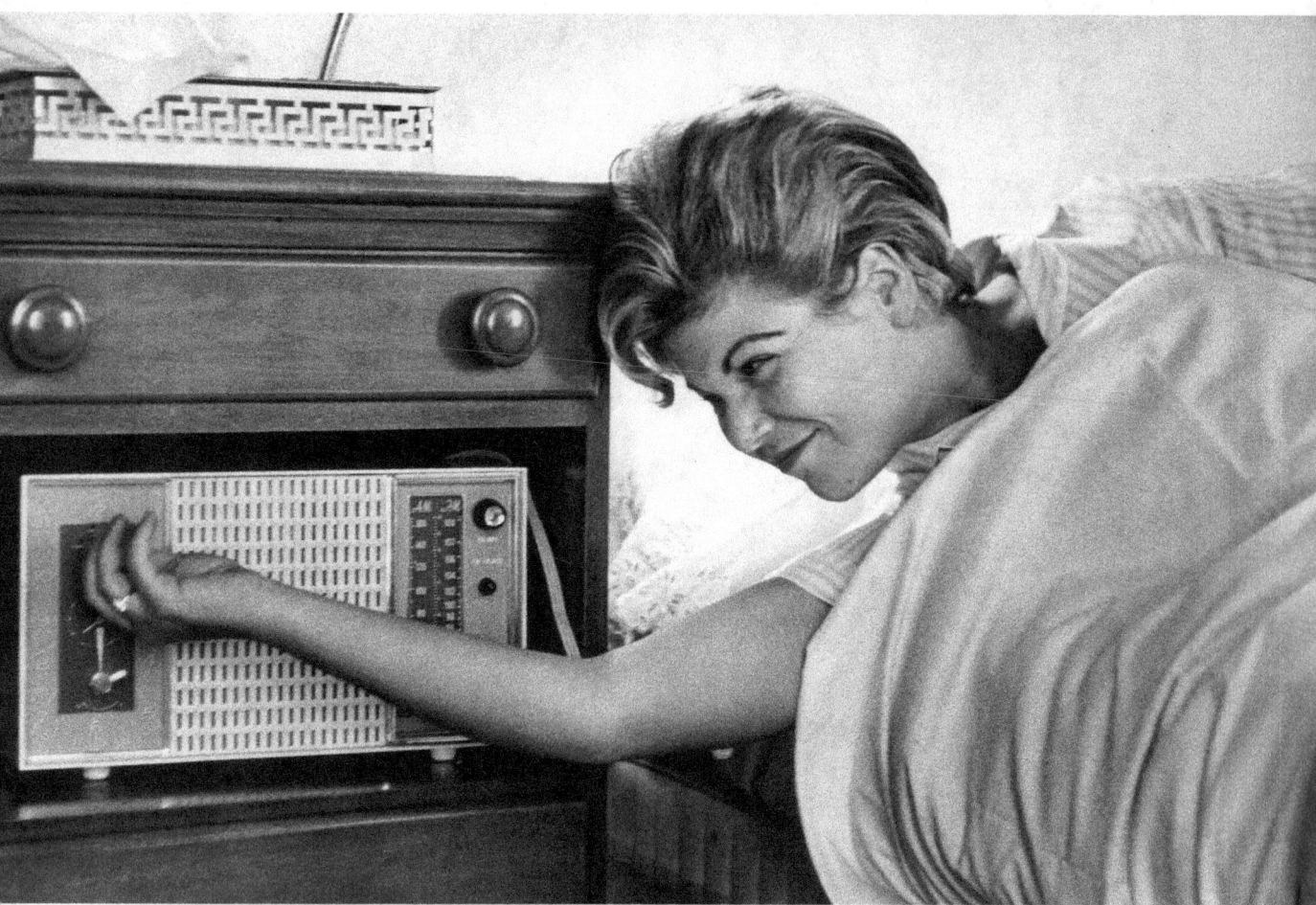

"Schoolteachers never seem to get away from the sounds of bells, and Mrs. Doris Segall of Sherman Oaks is no exception. The first bell is that of her alarm clock, which tells her it's time to get out of bed and get ready for the more than 30 students who will enter her B3 classroom Monday at Herrick Avenue School in Sylmar. There are name cards to fill out and lessons and bulletin boards to prepare. There's the momentary quiet of an empty classroom, which will soon be shattered when school bells ring and tell some 227,000 Los Angeles City School District pupils in the Valley that summer vacation is over and it's time to get back to work." September 14, 1962. (George Brich)

(Order #00084499 & 00084501)

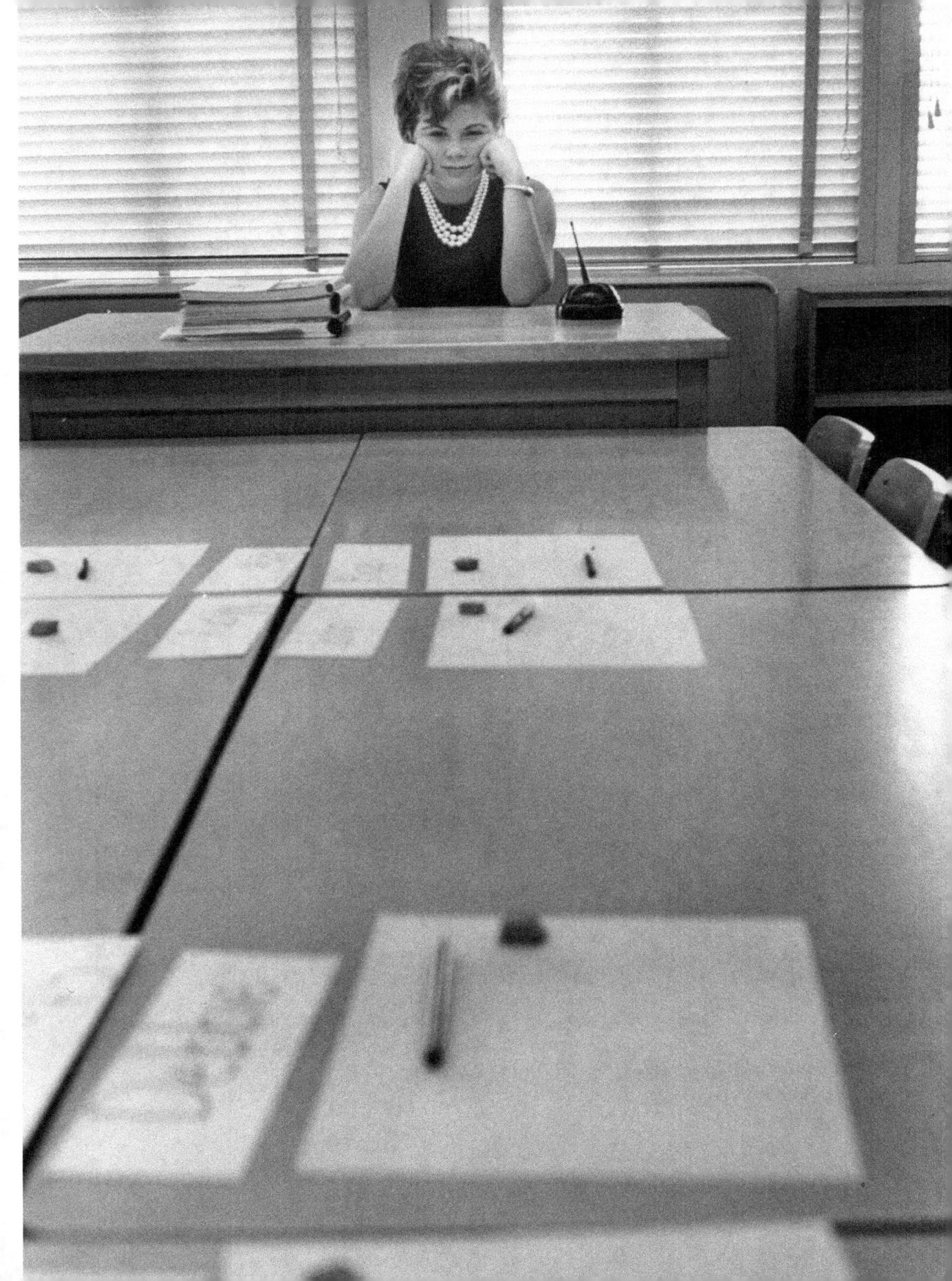

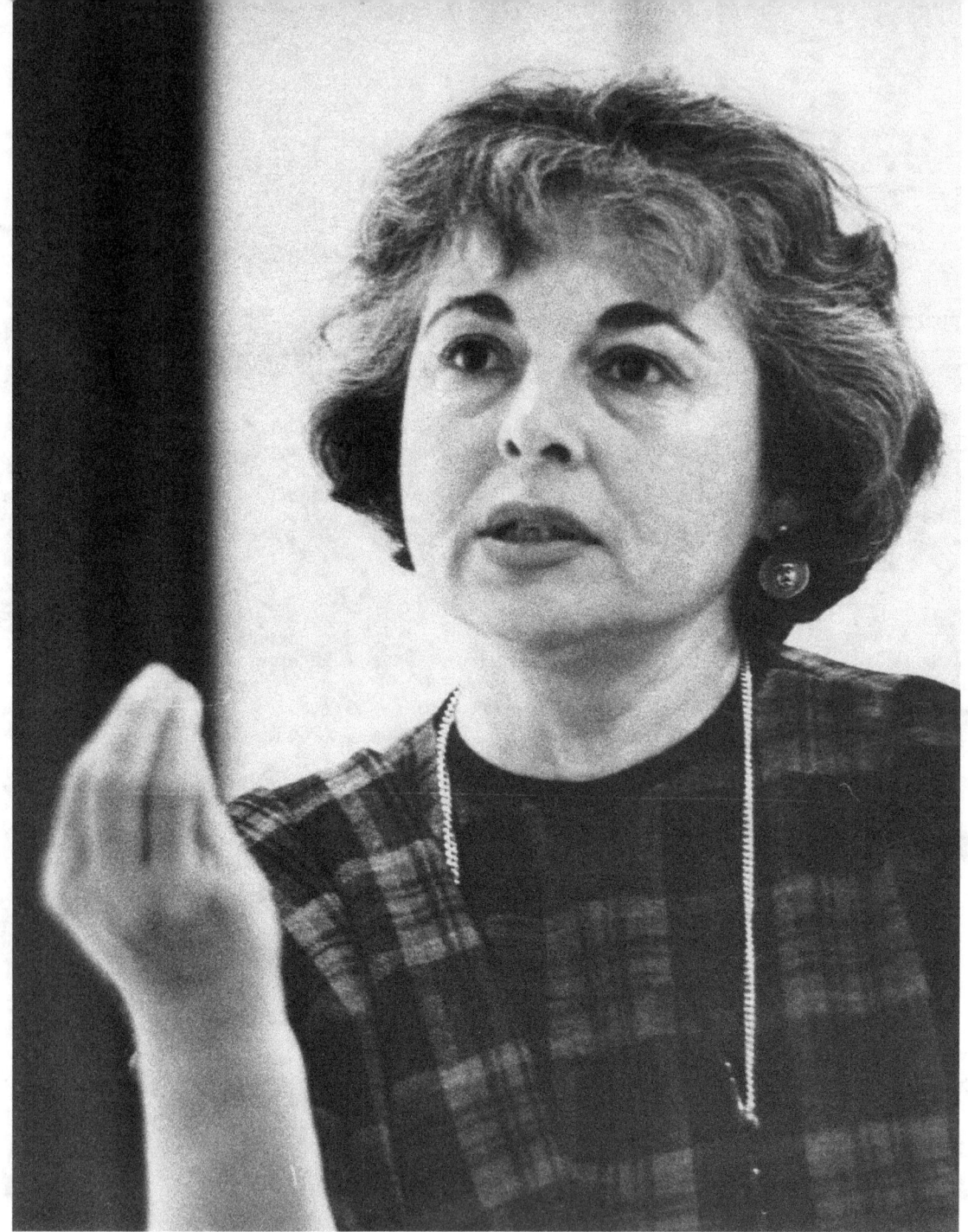

Mrs. Rodna Wisham, drama teacher at Grant High School and director of the school's production of *Ah, Wilderness* by Eugene O'Neill prompts one of her students to apply more "emphasis and expression."
January 11, 1964. (George Brich)
(Order #00084474)

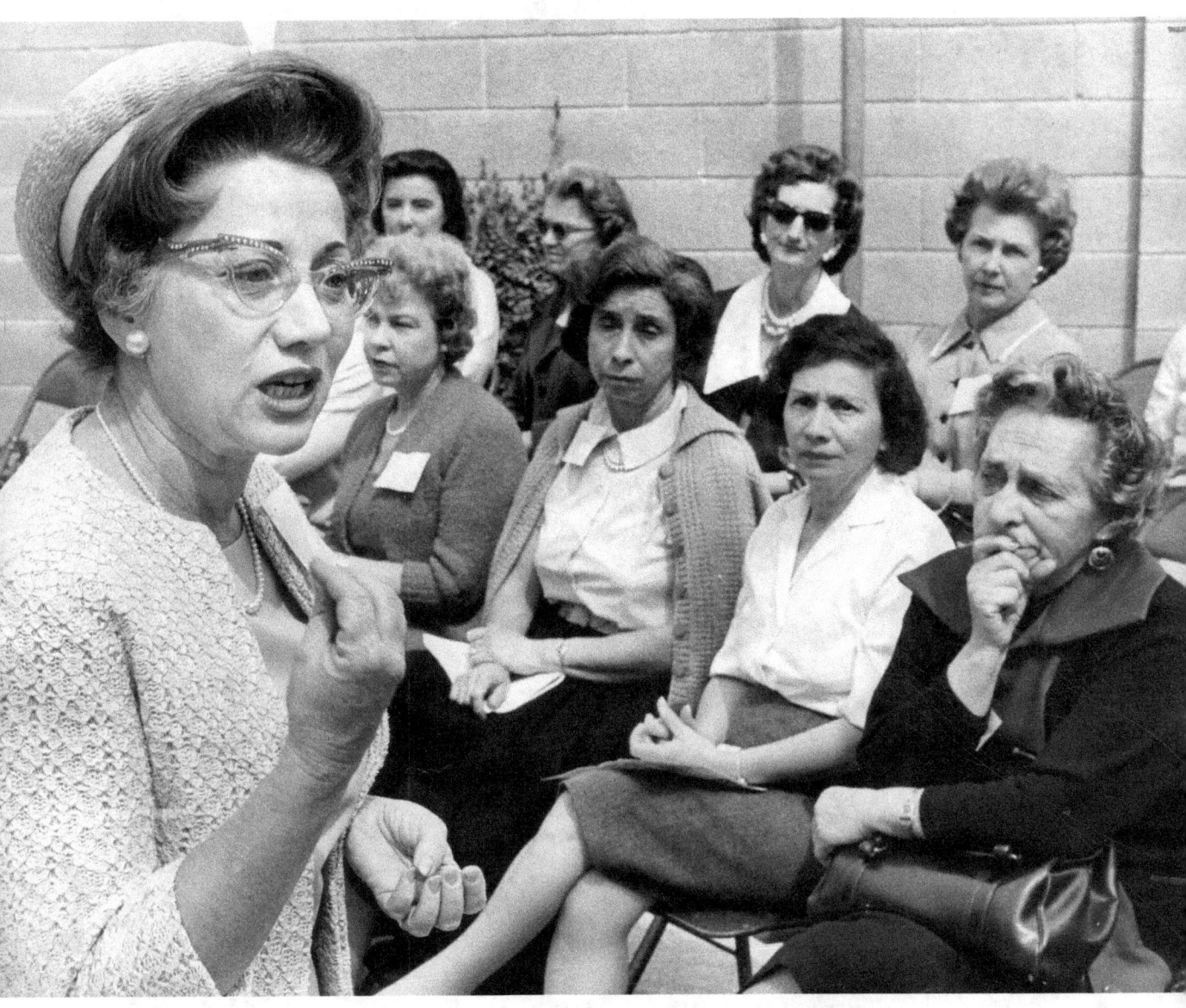

"Mrs. Marion Miller, Los Angeles City Board of Education candidate, Tuesday addressed a
neighborhood group of ladies at the home of Mrs. Doris Swink, 11333 Aqua Vista St., North
Hollywood. Mrs. Miller is a former teacher." Miller also infiltrated the Communist Party as a
spy for the FBI. Dubbed the "Poor Man's Mata Hari," Miller later recounted her experiences in
the memoir *I Was a Spy*.
April 1, 1965. (George Brich)
(Order #00085424)

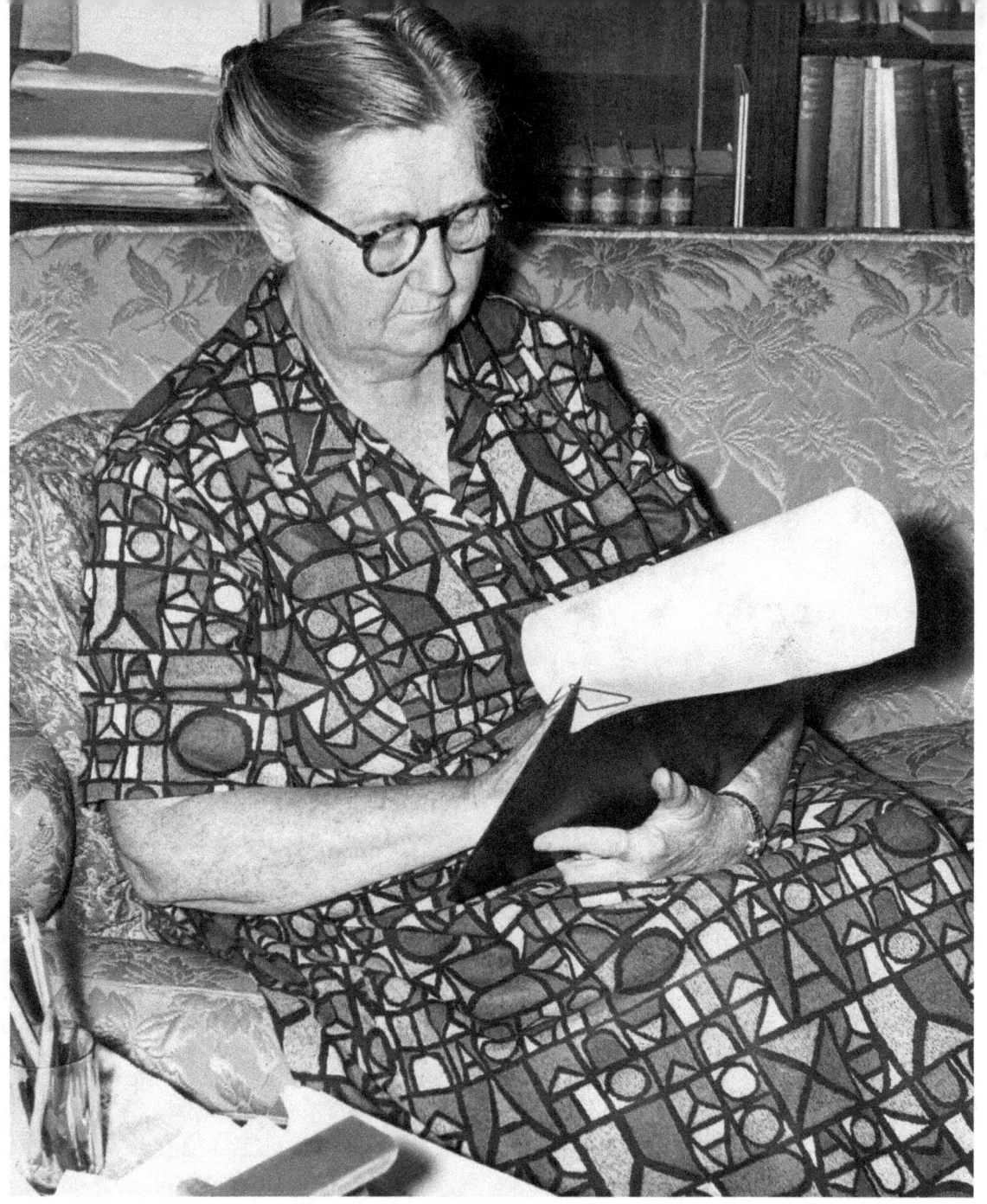

"Mrs. Jennie M. Zimmerman, Valley poet and teacher works on revision of Odyssey translation while she awaits publication of her own poetry." Zimmerman, who moved to the Valley in 1940, had worked as a proofreader, editor, taught verse writing at Van Nuys Evening School, and was co-founder of California Federation of Chaparral Poets.

December 3, 1959. (Order #00085855)

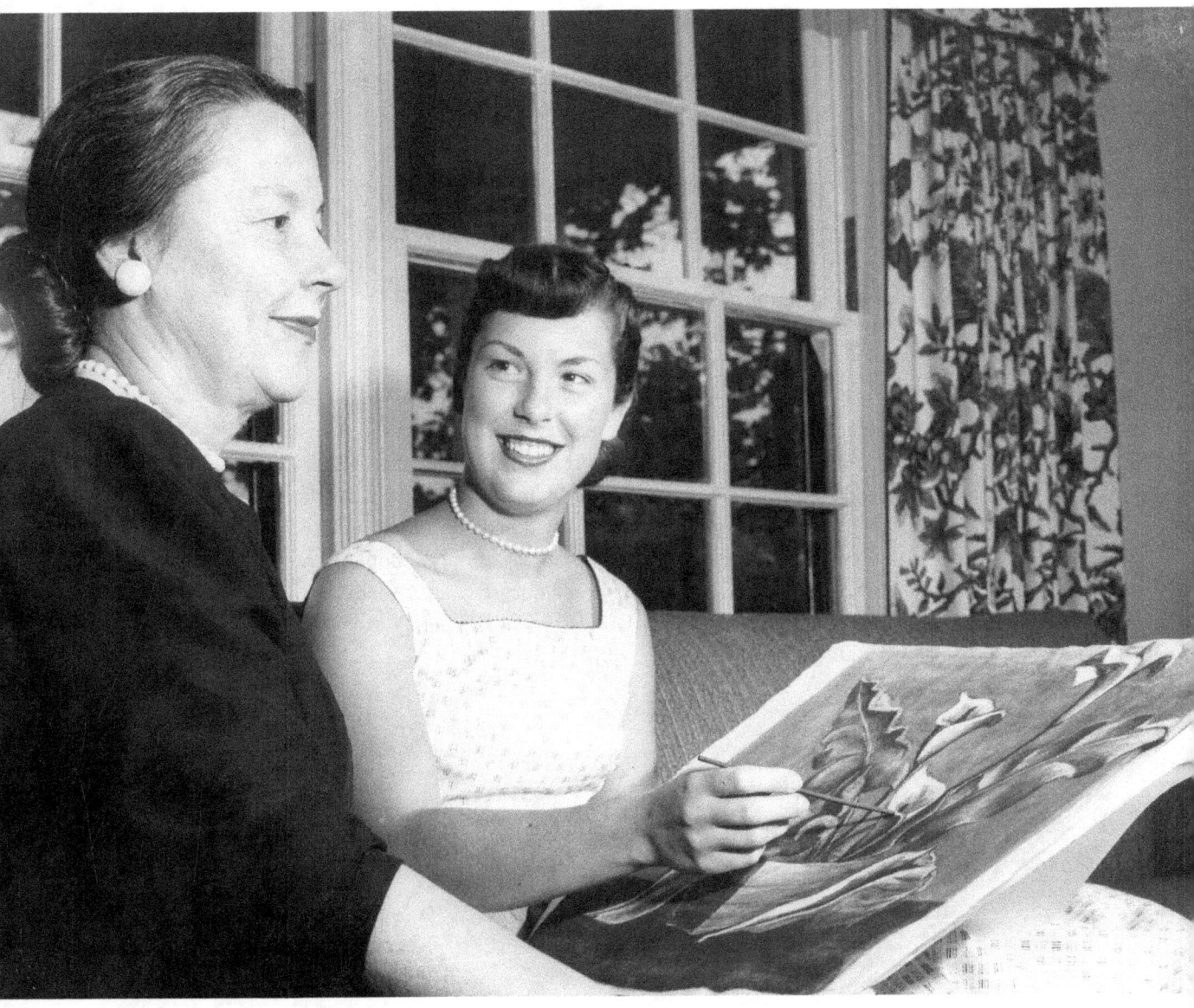

"Mrs. Edith K. Stafford of North Hollywood, newly elected president of Los Angeles Board of Education, offers suggestions to daughter Liz, 18, on charcoal drawing. Daughter admires mother's ability to be full time mother and school board member."
July 4, 1956. (Order #00108554)

"Terry (Joan) Hallet, an assistant professor of mathematics at Valley State College in Northridge confirms the supposition in President Eisenhower's recent report on higher education that an untapped source of 'manpower' to relieve the acute shortage of qualified university instructors is the female population whose members usually aim for careers in elementary or secondary schools. Terry, who instructs algebra, calculus and some courses for non-specialists, believes that teaching on the college level is an ideal profession for women."
October 13, 1960. (George Brich)
(Order #00109469)

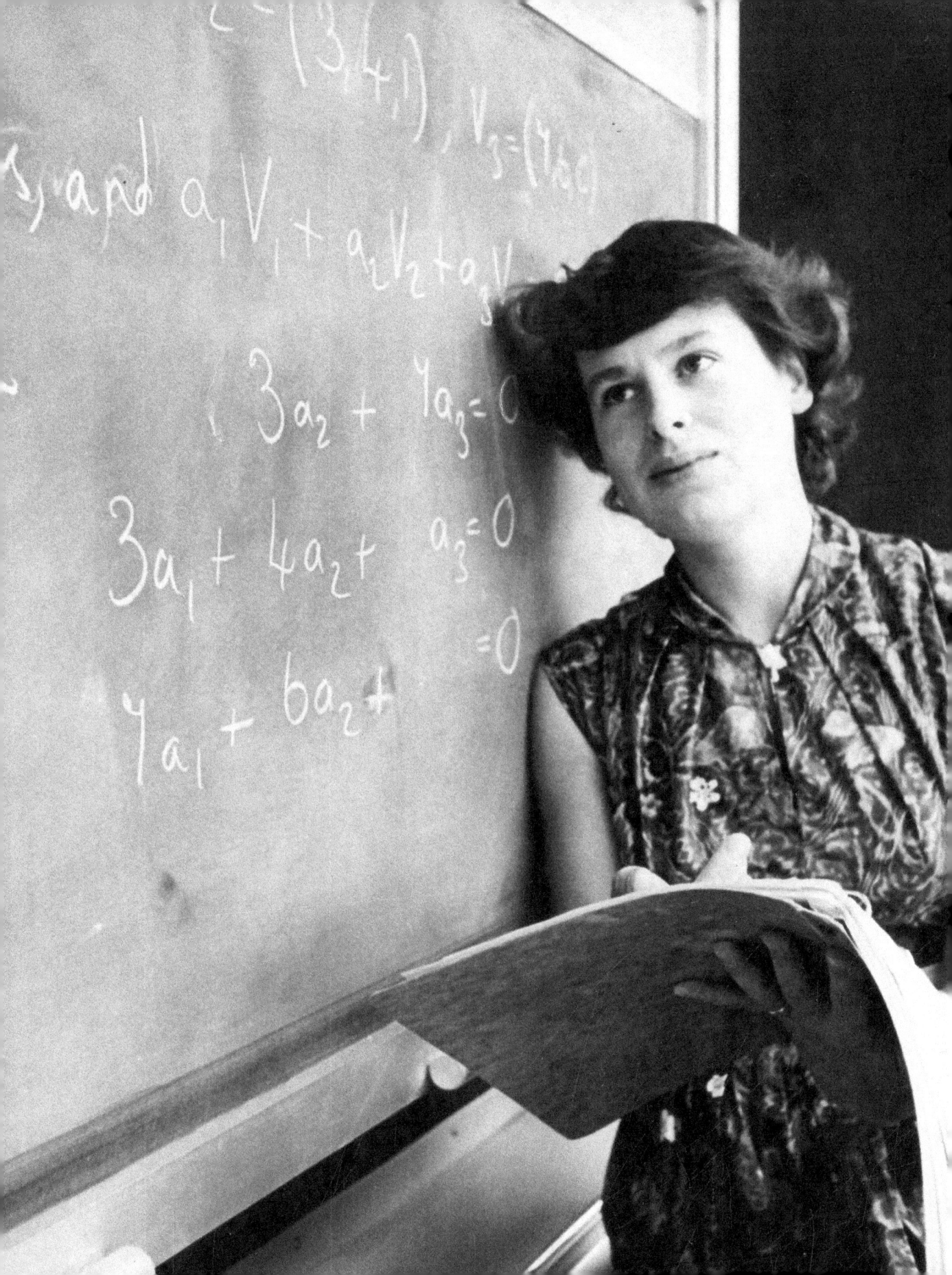

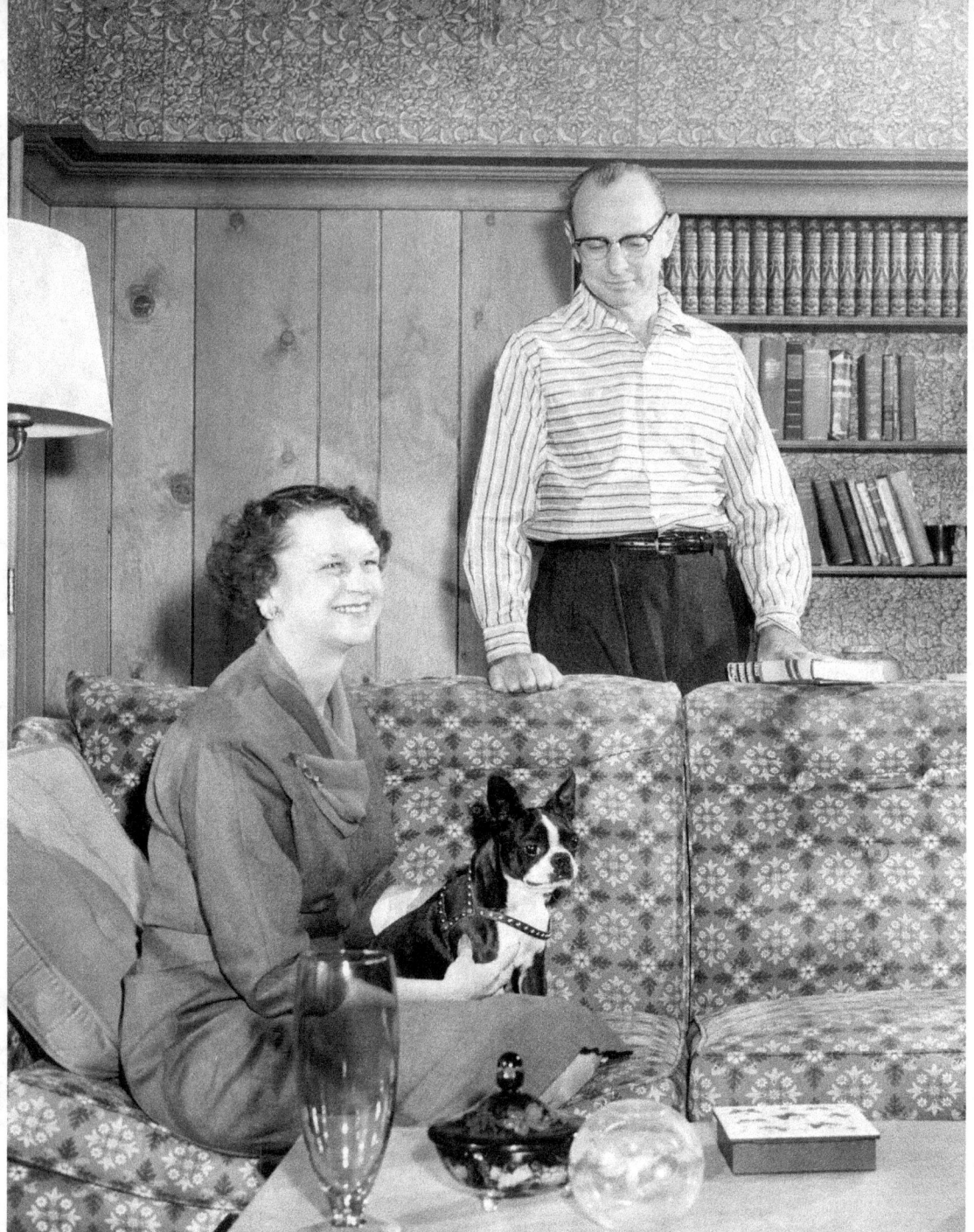

"Dr. Louise Wood Seyler, 49, new deputy superintendent of Los Angeles city schools, chats with husband Henry at Studio City home. With them is Boston bull Bummie." Seyler who would serve as the LAUSD deputy superintendent until 1967 was the first woman to earn a doctorate in education from UCLA. November 20, 1956. (Order #00108562)

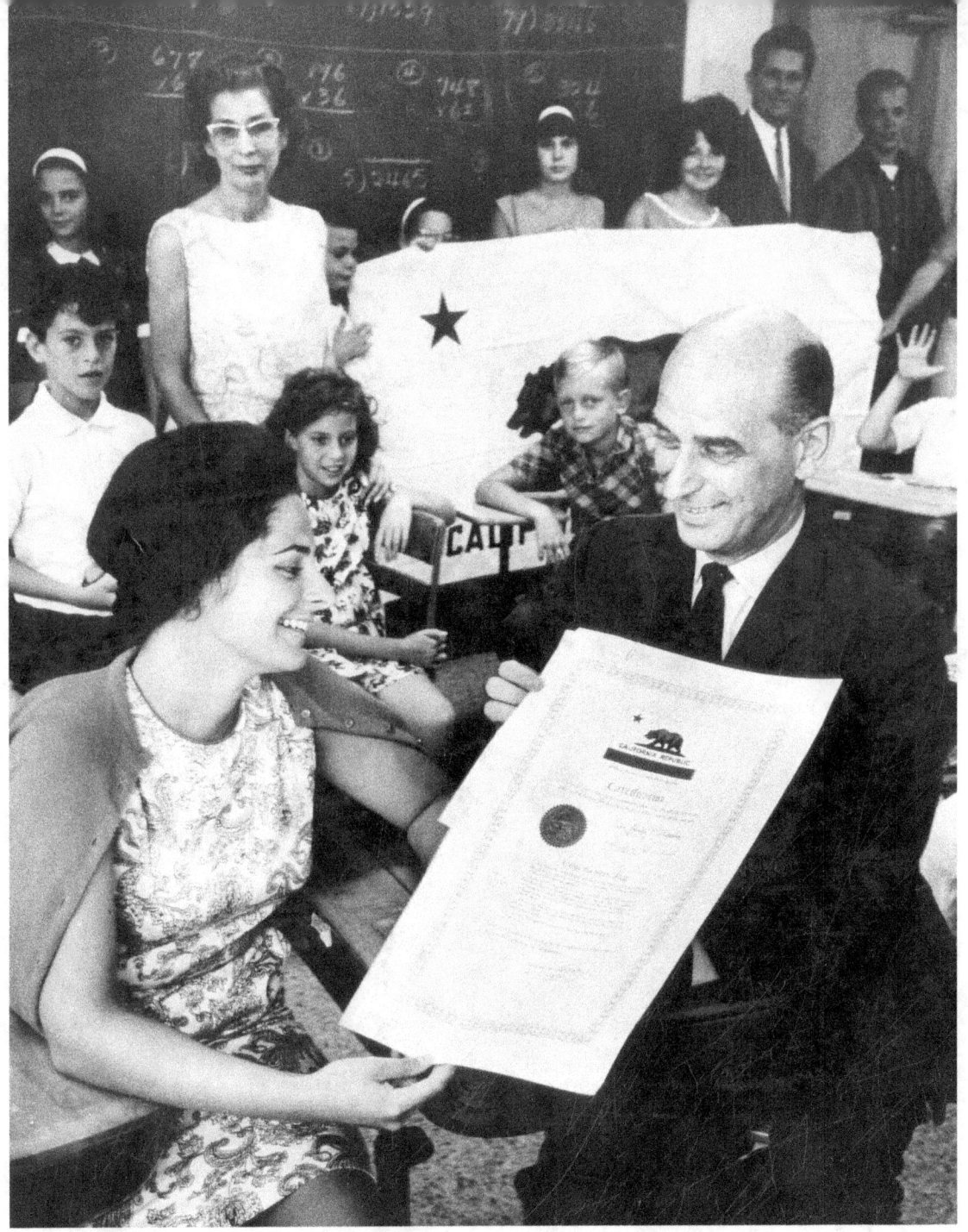

"Mrs. Janet Reynolds, principal at Harridge School, Northridge, accepts certificate for school's new state flag from Assemblyman Lou Cusanovich (R-Van Nuys). Mrs. Ruby Everell and her class examine flag in background at the presentation."
August 29, 1964. (George Brich)
(Order #00109432)

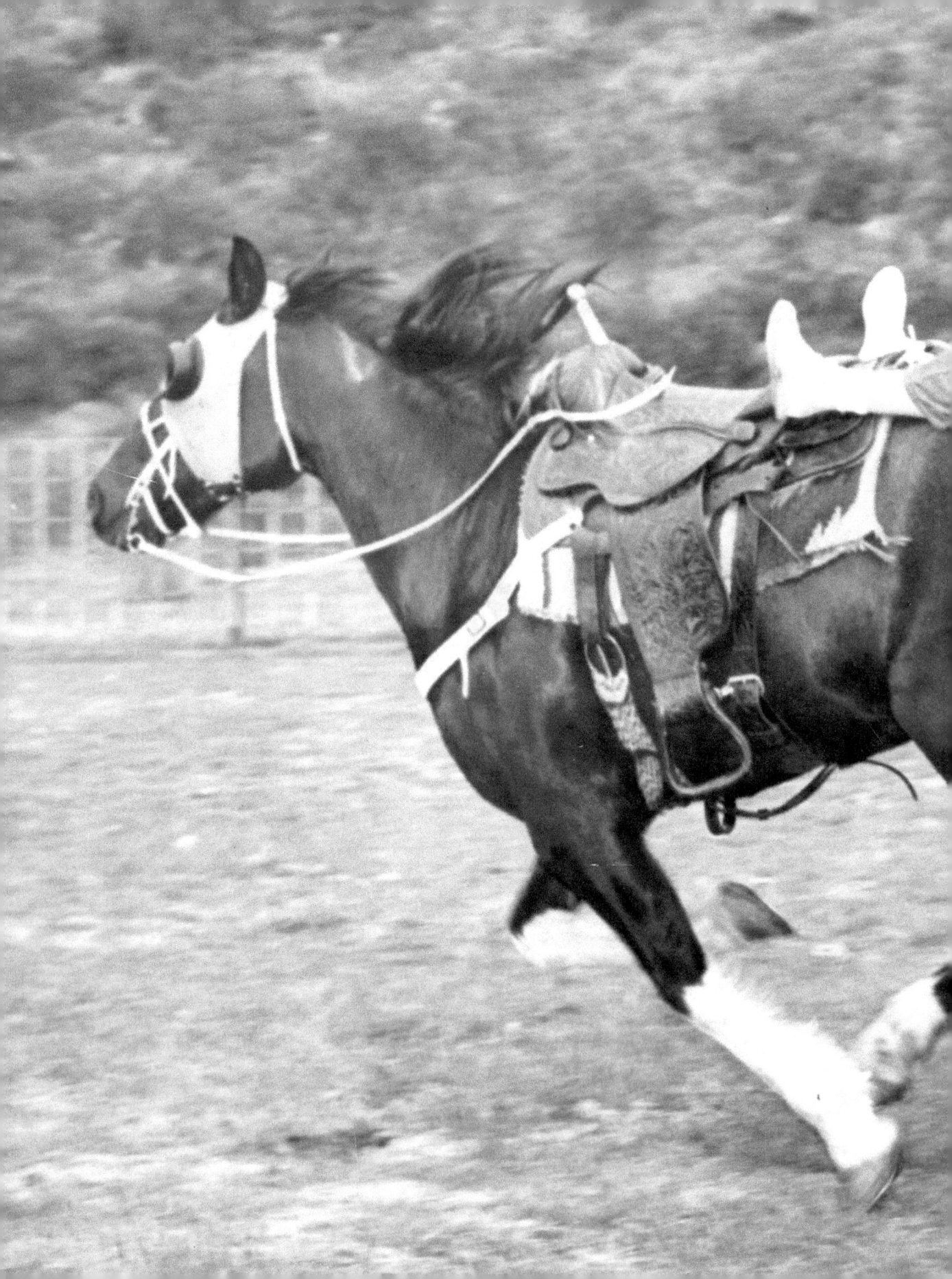

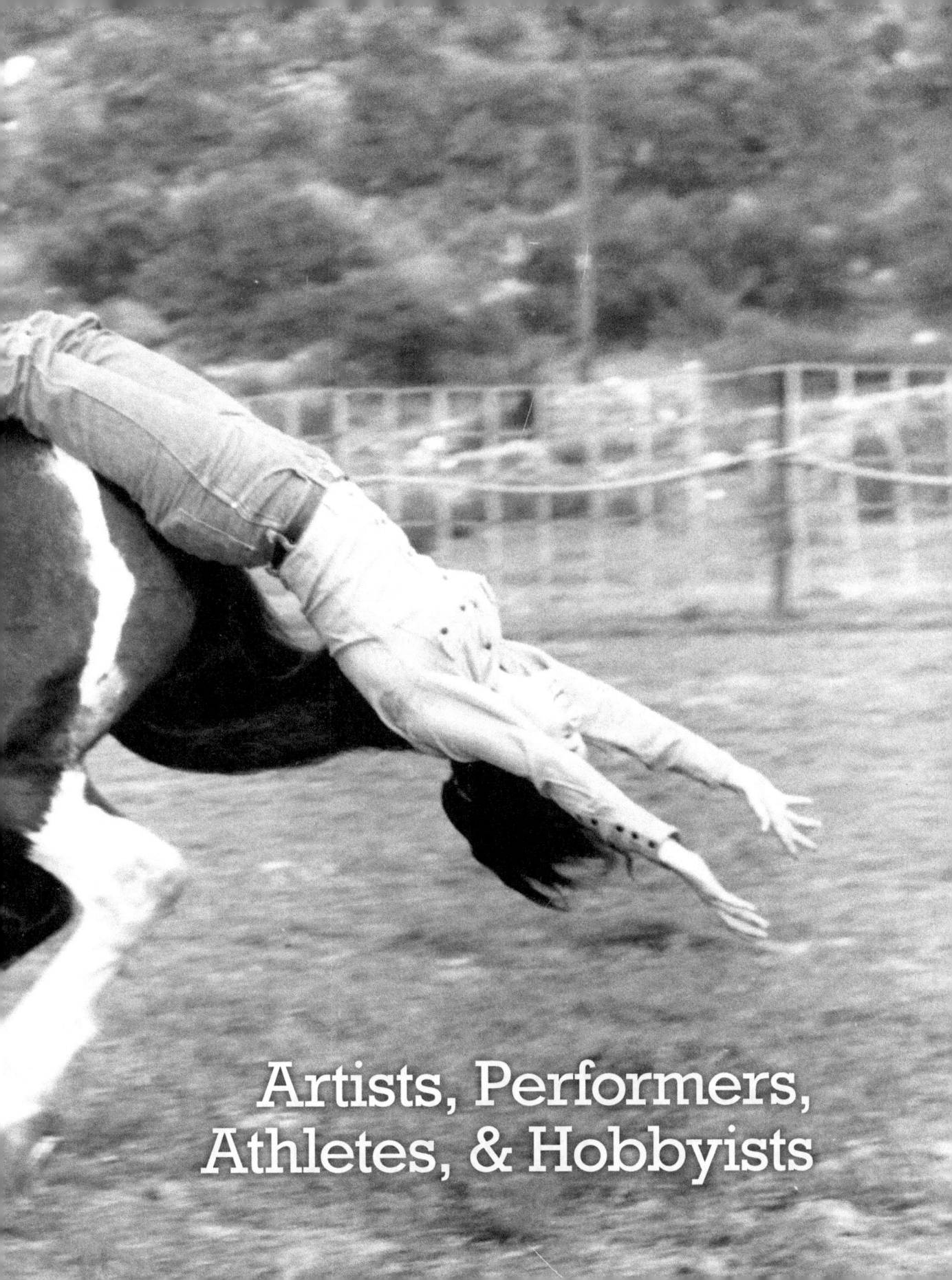

Artists, Performers,
Athletes, & Hobbyists

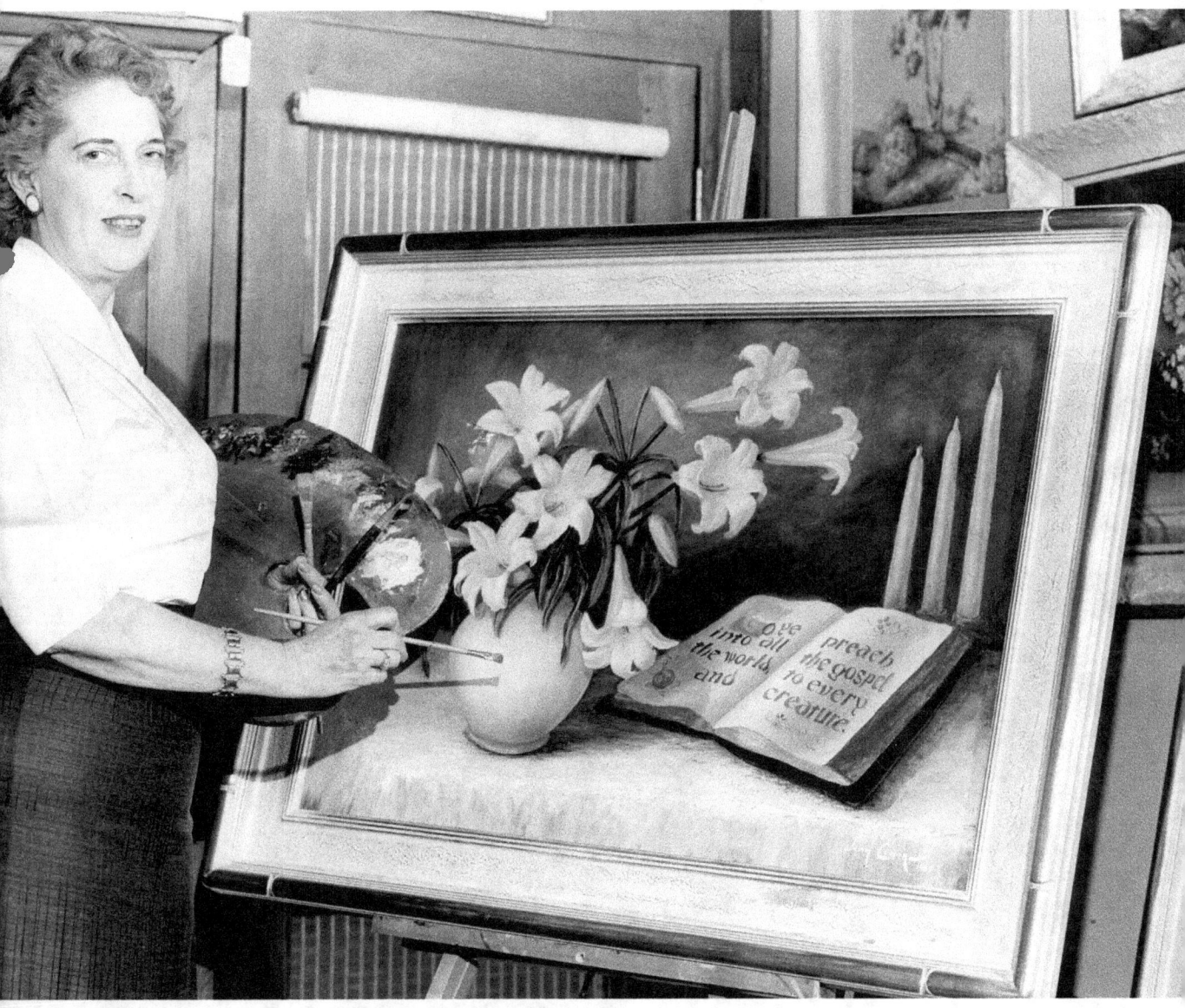

"Mrs. Jewell Cooper, Valley artist and art show winner, stands at easel in her home, 11610 Archwood St., North Hollywood, with a religious painting she presented to her church, First Presbyterian of North Hollywood. A member of Valley Artists Guild and active in church and community affairs, she painted two oils that hang in Fireside Room of First Presbyterian. Painting's biblical quotation reads: 'Go ye into the world and preach the Gospel to every creature.'"

October 31, 1959. (Order #00085580)

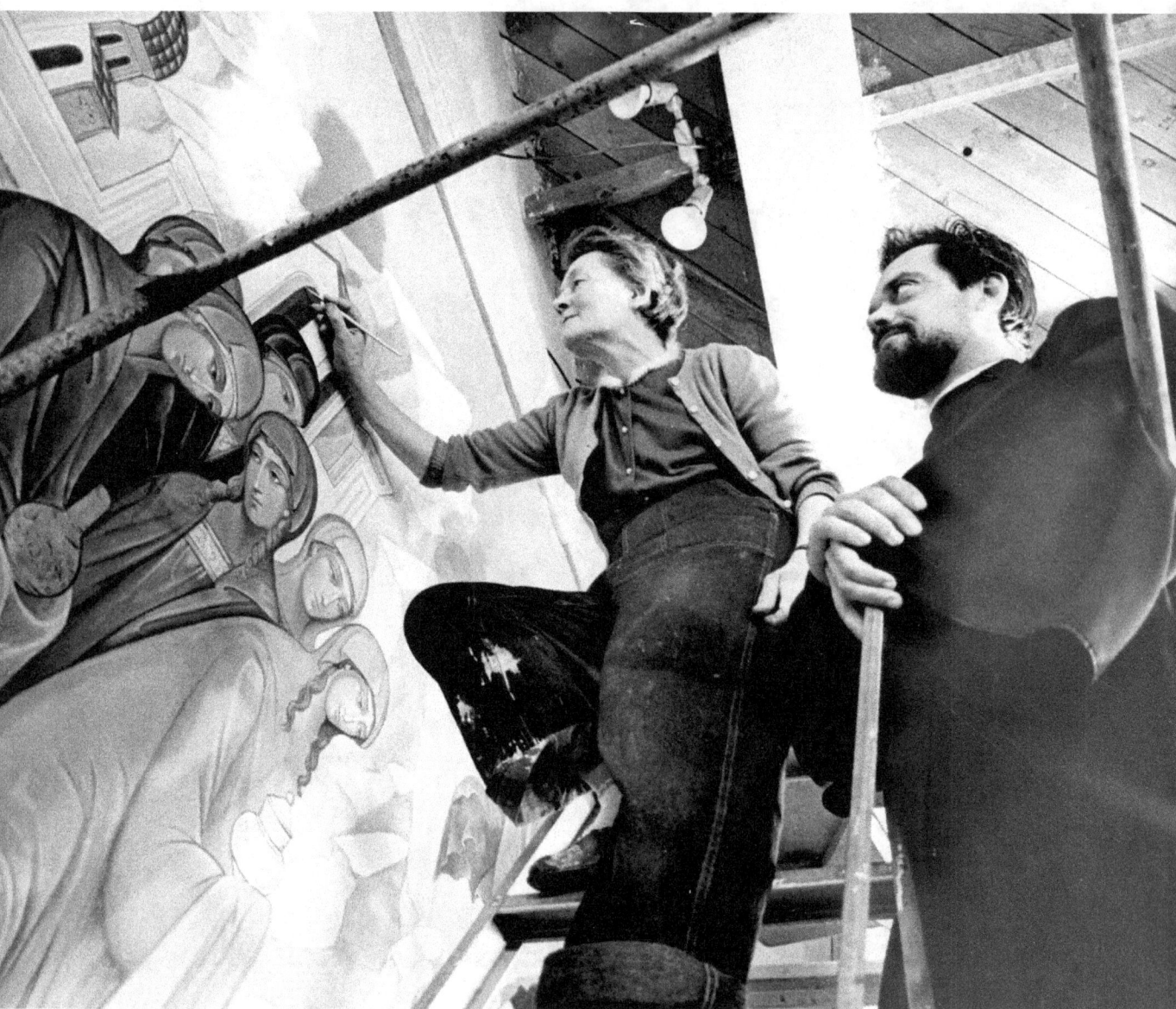

"Artist Tamara Lysloff paints Byzantine-style icons at St. Innocent Eastern Orthodox Church as
Father Sergei Glagolev looks on. The five icons, that have the Eucharist as the central theme,
will be blessed in a ceremony June 4 conducted by the Rt. Rev. John Shahovsky, Eastern
Orthodox Bishop of San Francisco."
January 9, 1961. (George Brich)
(Order #00082697)

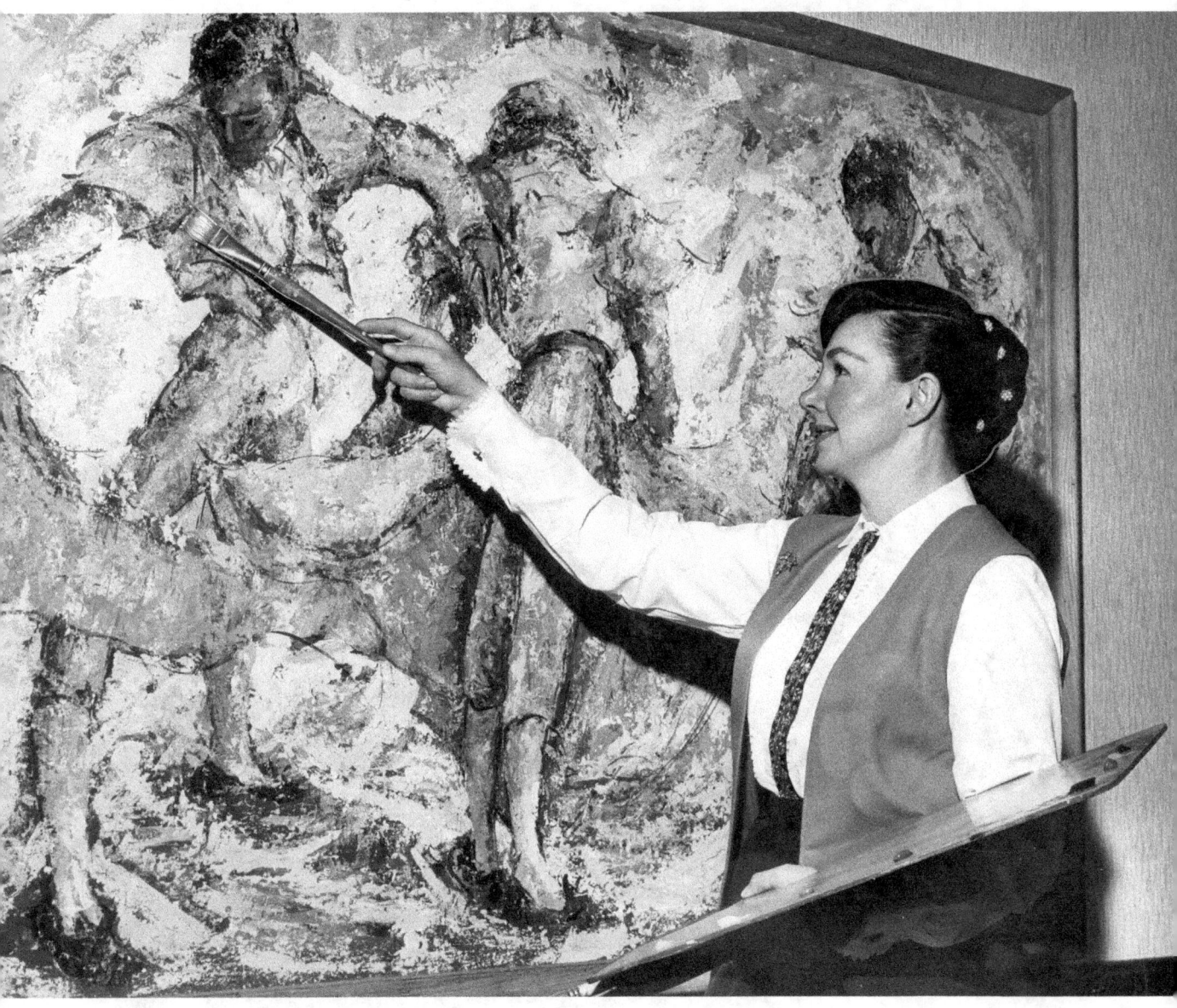

"Eve Jensen, above, is a successful taurine artist who acquires inspiration for canvasses by facing animals in arena." A resident of Studio City, Jensen's painting were exhibited at the Laguna Art Gallery, Los Angeles City Hall, Barnsdall Park, and the Greek Theatre.
September 8, 1960. (Alan Hyde)

(Order #00111044)

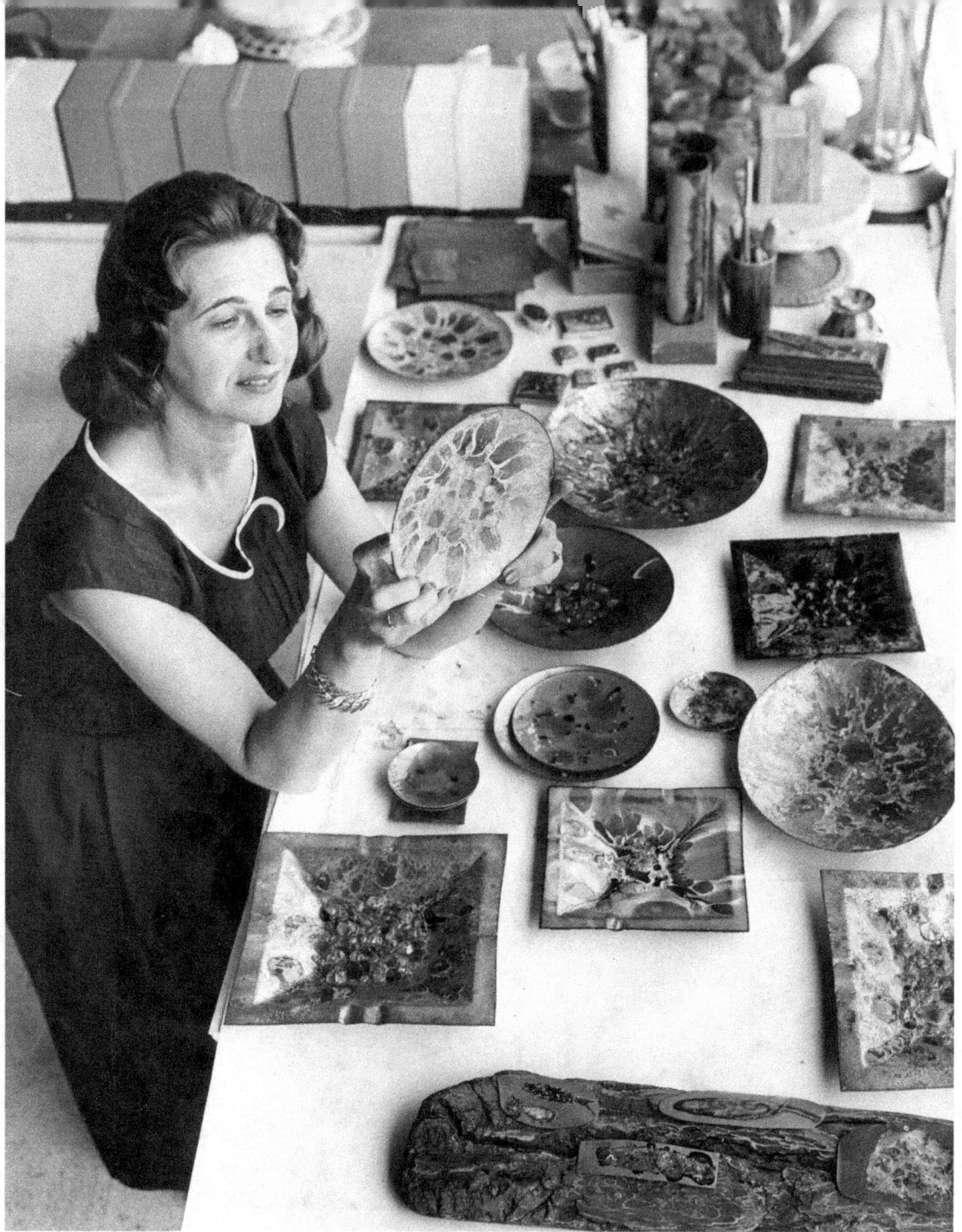

Artist Myrna Eaton displays some of her unique works of art including a lamp whose base is covered with copper sheets enameled in bright decorator colors, and dishes, bowls, plates and ash trays which she designs and distributes through hotel shops and gift stores.
September 5, 1960. (Order #00111041 & 00111042)

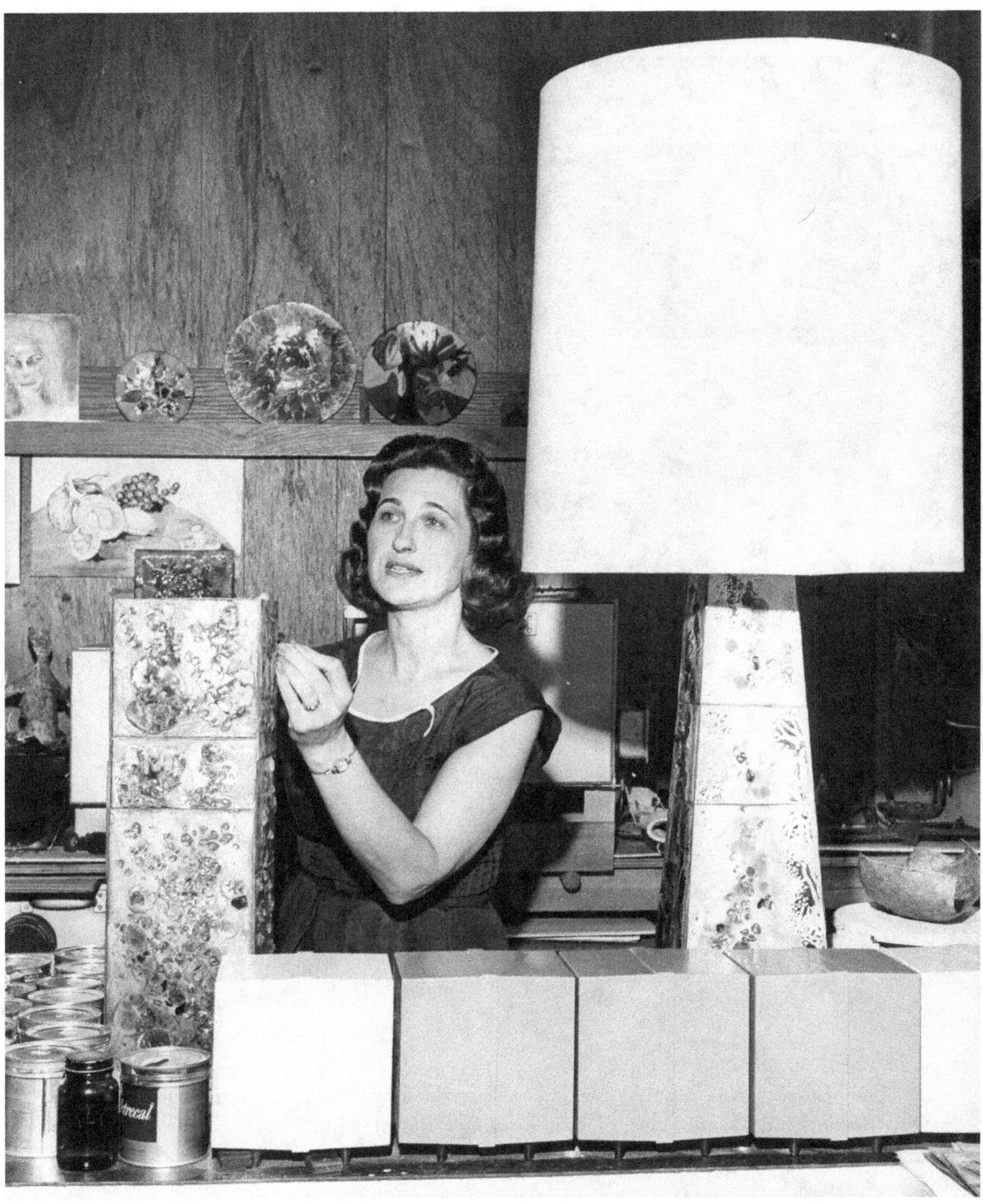

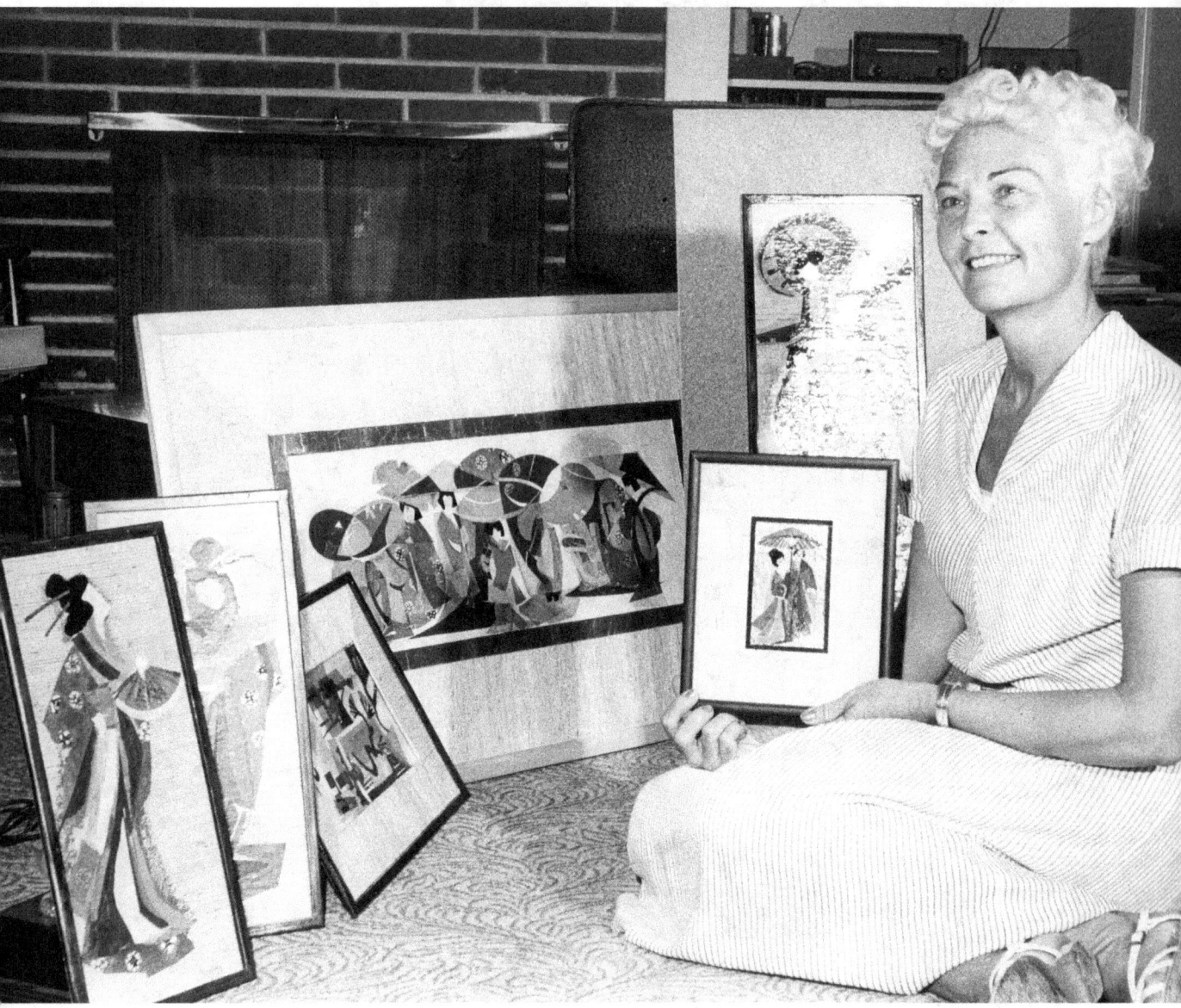

"Lorna Duncan displays examples of her art works created by overlapping vari-colored tissues to create patterns and pictures, most of them carrying Oriental theme."
August 5, 1960. (Jon Woods)
(Order #00108957)

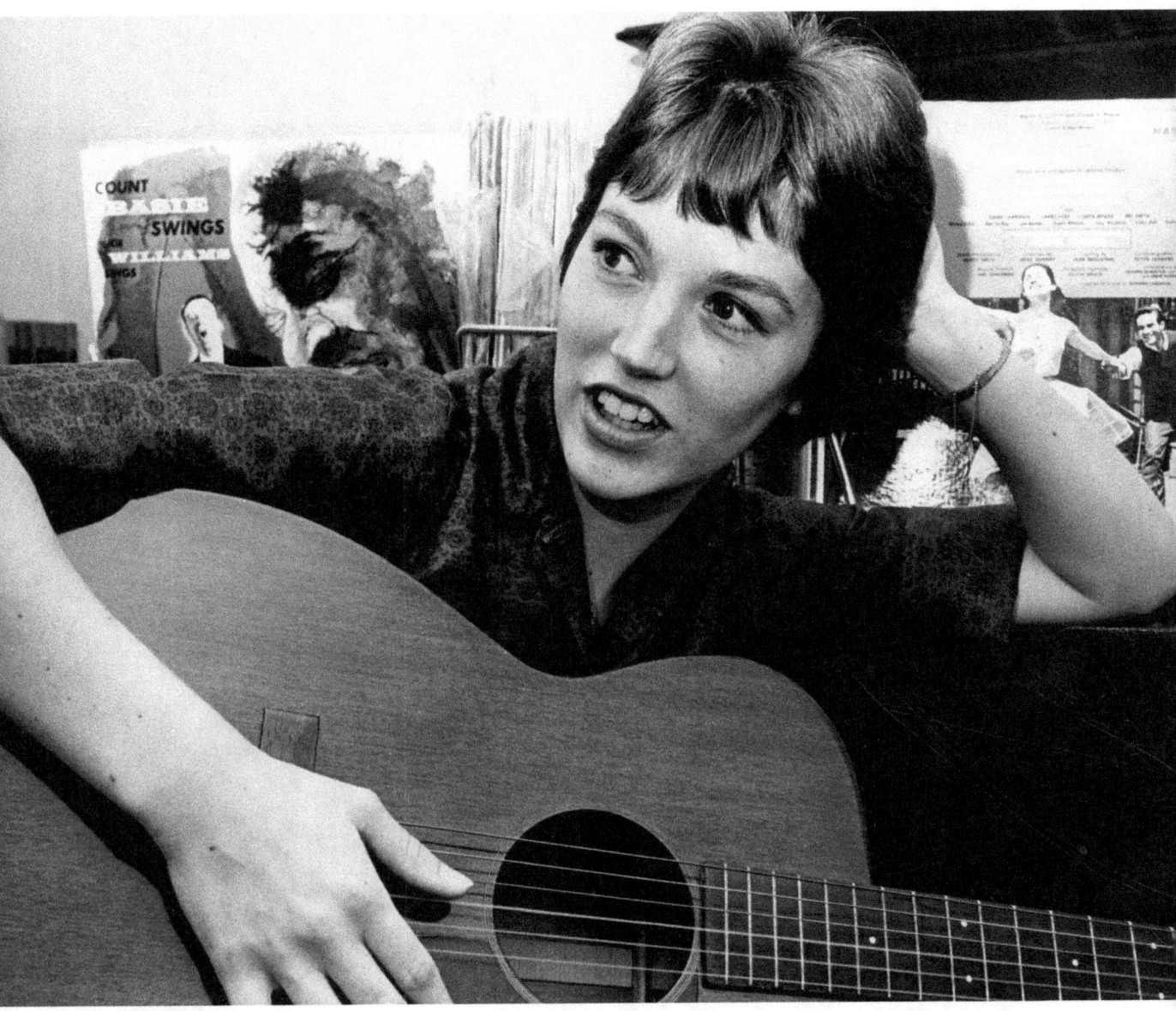

Shelby Flint, 21-year-old Valley resident and graduate of Birmingham High School in Van Nuys is shown strumming her guitar. Her recording of "Angel on My Shoulder" had recently hit the top 10.
February 6, 1961. (Jon Woods)
(Order #00084453)

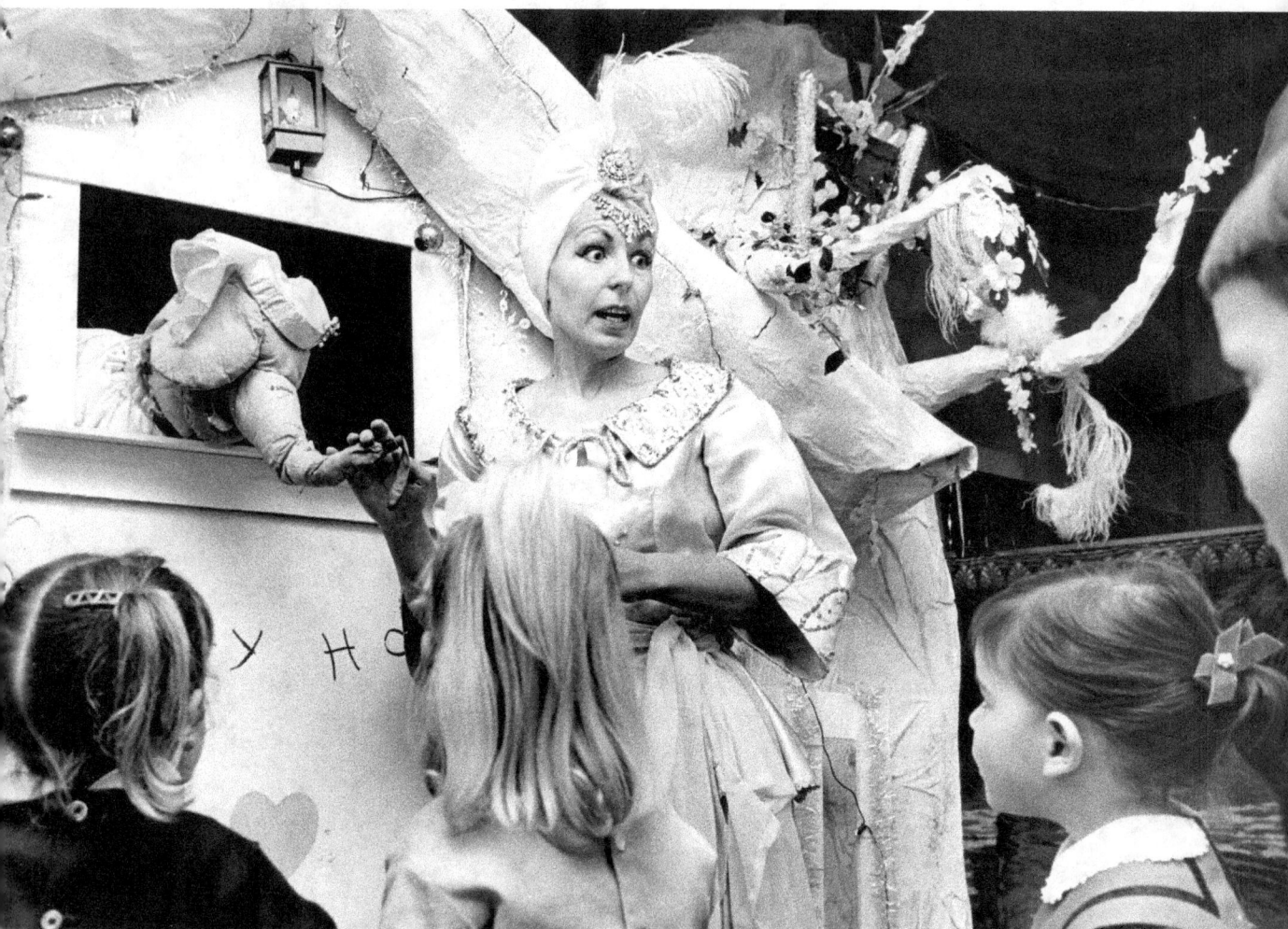

Youngsters visiting Geniiland cluster around Jean "Genii" Cease, as "Bubbles" the pink elephant enters the party scene. Geniiland at 14507 Dickens St. in Sherman Oaks was founded by Case in the late 1950s and operated for 18 years as a venue for children's parties.
January 6, 1961. (George Brich)
(Order #00085822)

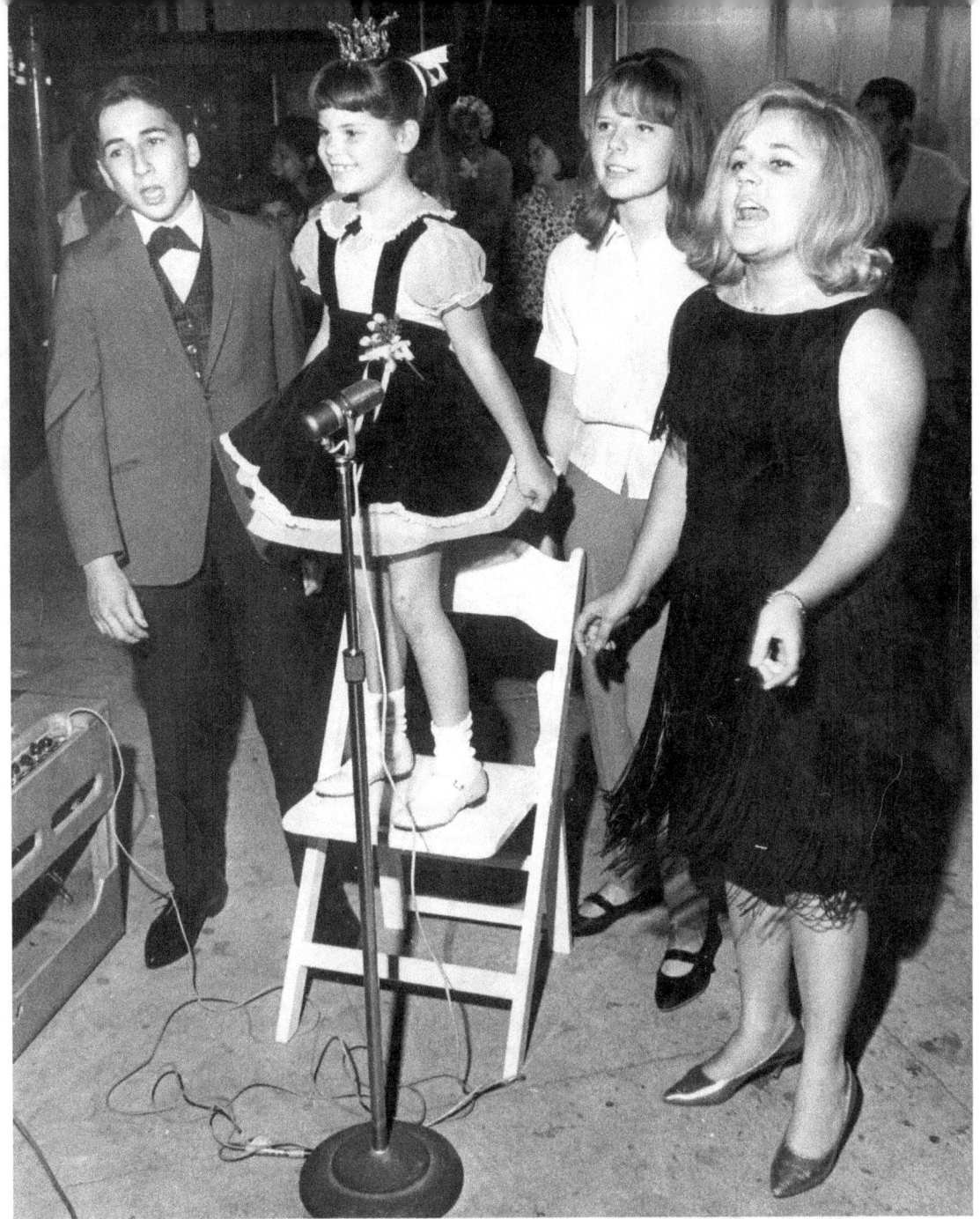

"In the new teenage singing group the Castle Stars little swinger Kimberly Nicholson is a standout attraction. She twists and solos her way into her teen-age audiences' good graces just as well as the big girls. Not on the chair, from left, are David Pavelka, Carole Lothmann and Pamela Castle, organizer of the group."
December 5, 1964. (Bob Martin)
(Order #00112280)

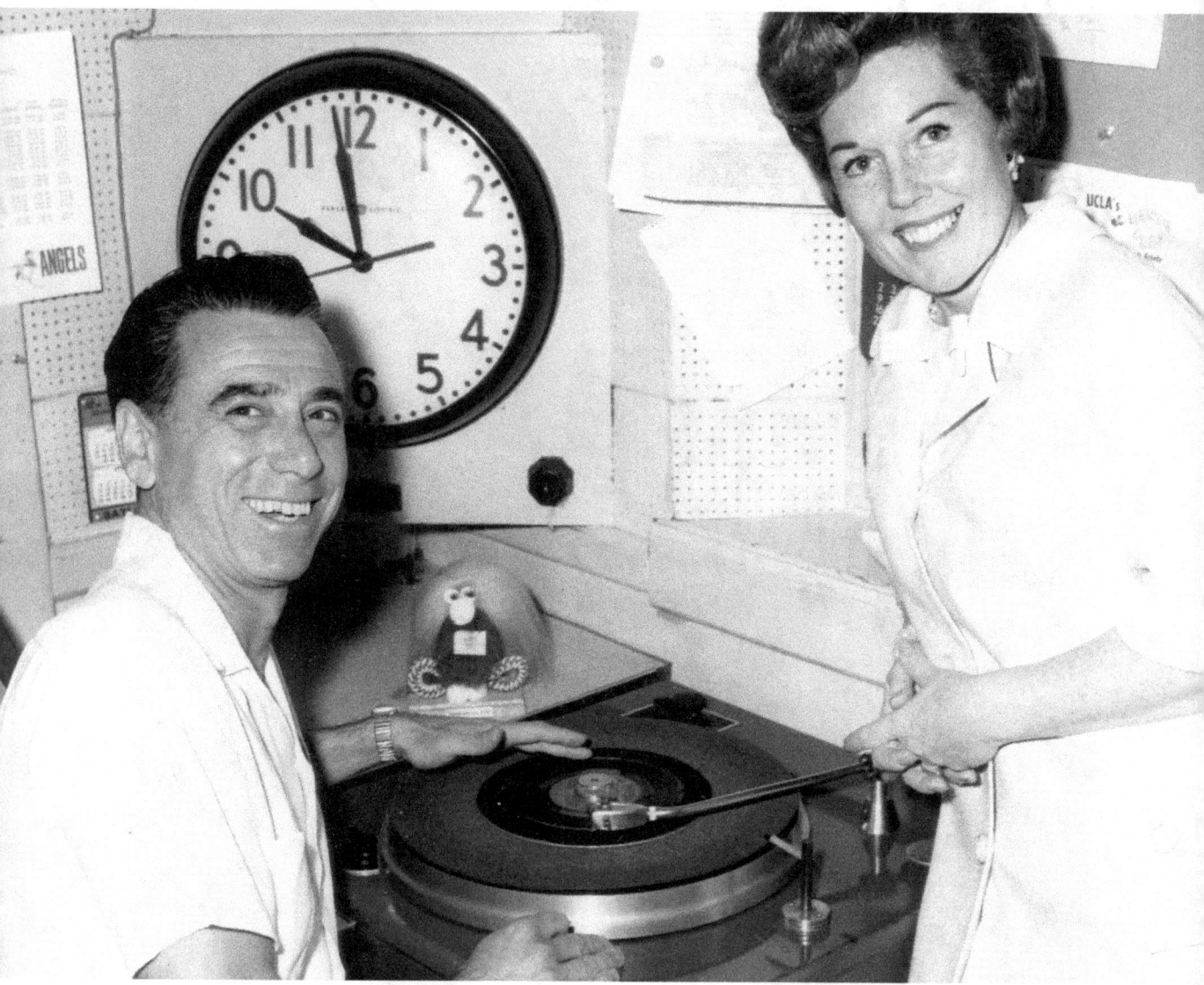

"Becca (Rebecca) Adler, North Hollywood, stands next to Ira Cook's turntable at KMPC radio station. Her first recording, an interpretation of Burke-Van Heusen's 'Personality' on Pieces of Eight label, became a hit platter. Ira Cook was the first disc jockey to play the record." June 9, 1965. (Order #00083088)

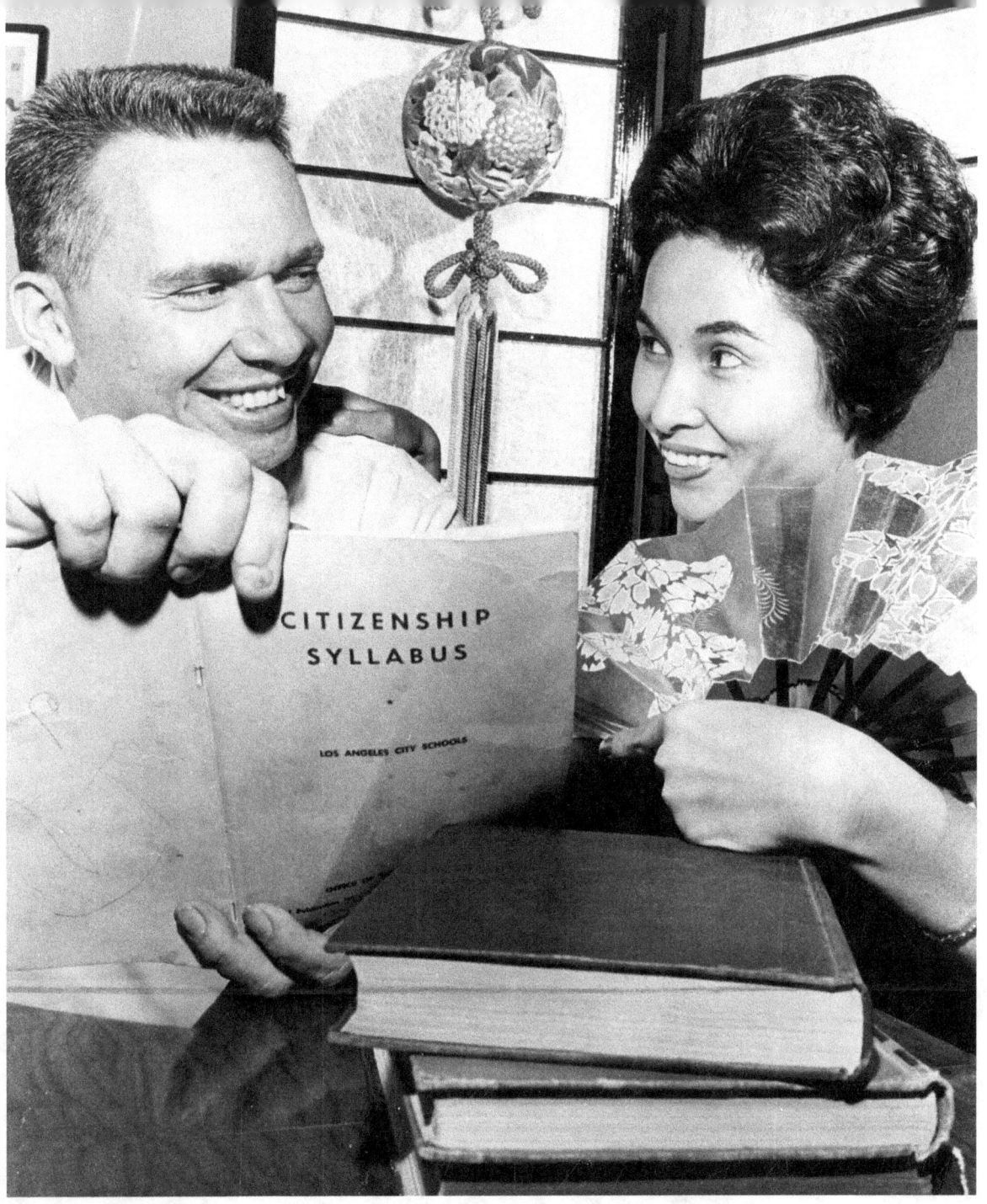

"One of Japan's first woman radio announcers becomes a U.S. citizen today. She's Mrs. Earl T. Paulson [pictured with Mr. Paulson], 20118 Labrador St., Chatsworth, who in the early 1950s sold Kiss Me lipstick over Radio Tokyo as Akiko Hirano."
August 19, 1960. (George Brich)
(Order #00109006)

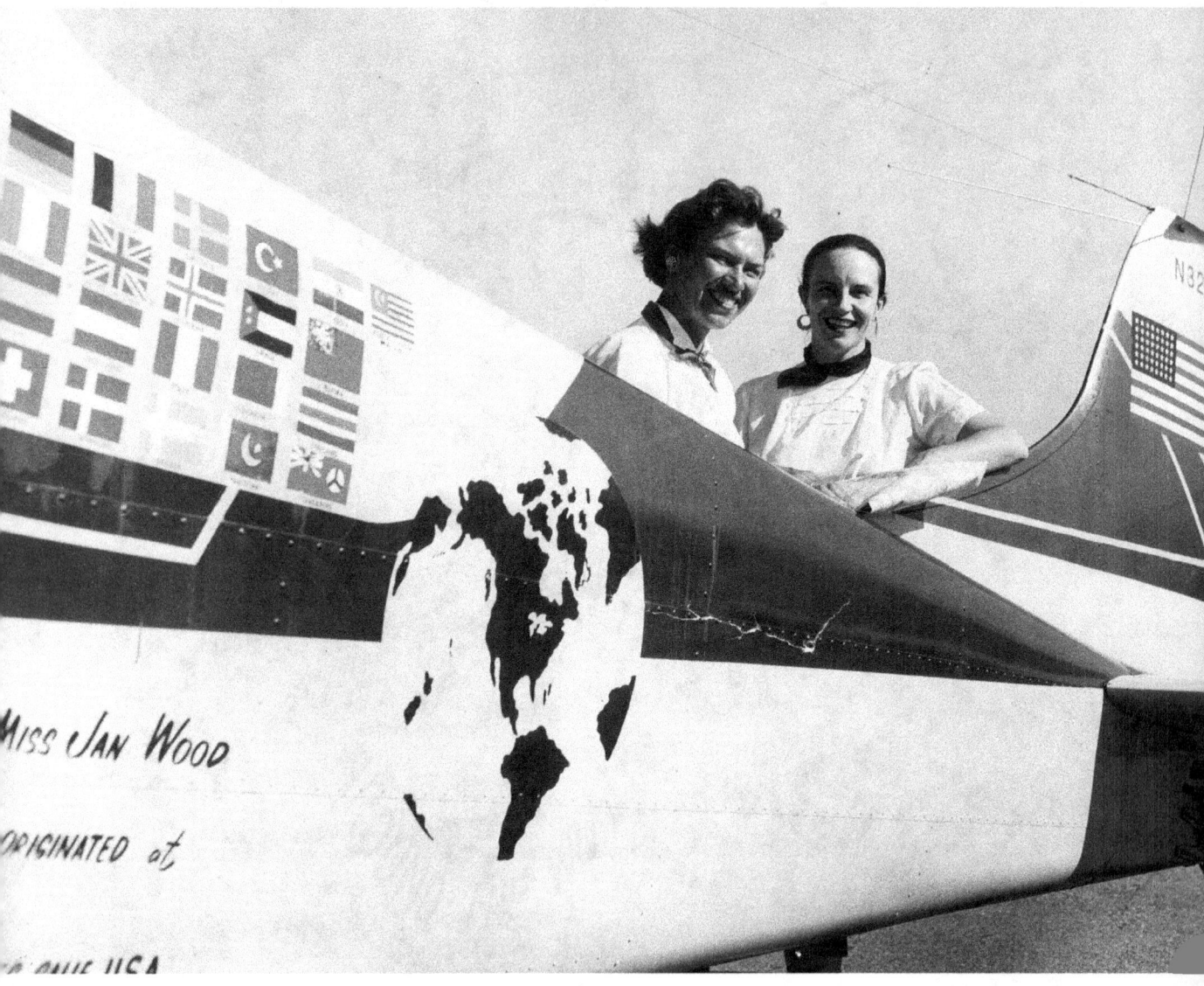

"Jan Wood, left, Reseda's flying school teacher, and her co-pilot Mrs. Trixie Ann Schubert of Glendale, talk over flight plans for 12th annual Powder Puff Derby. They will enter 'Little Yellow Cloud' Miss Wood's light aircraft in 2,177 mile race from San Diego to South Carolina. Race is scheduled July 4-8."
May 29, 1958. (Order #00108785)

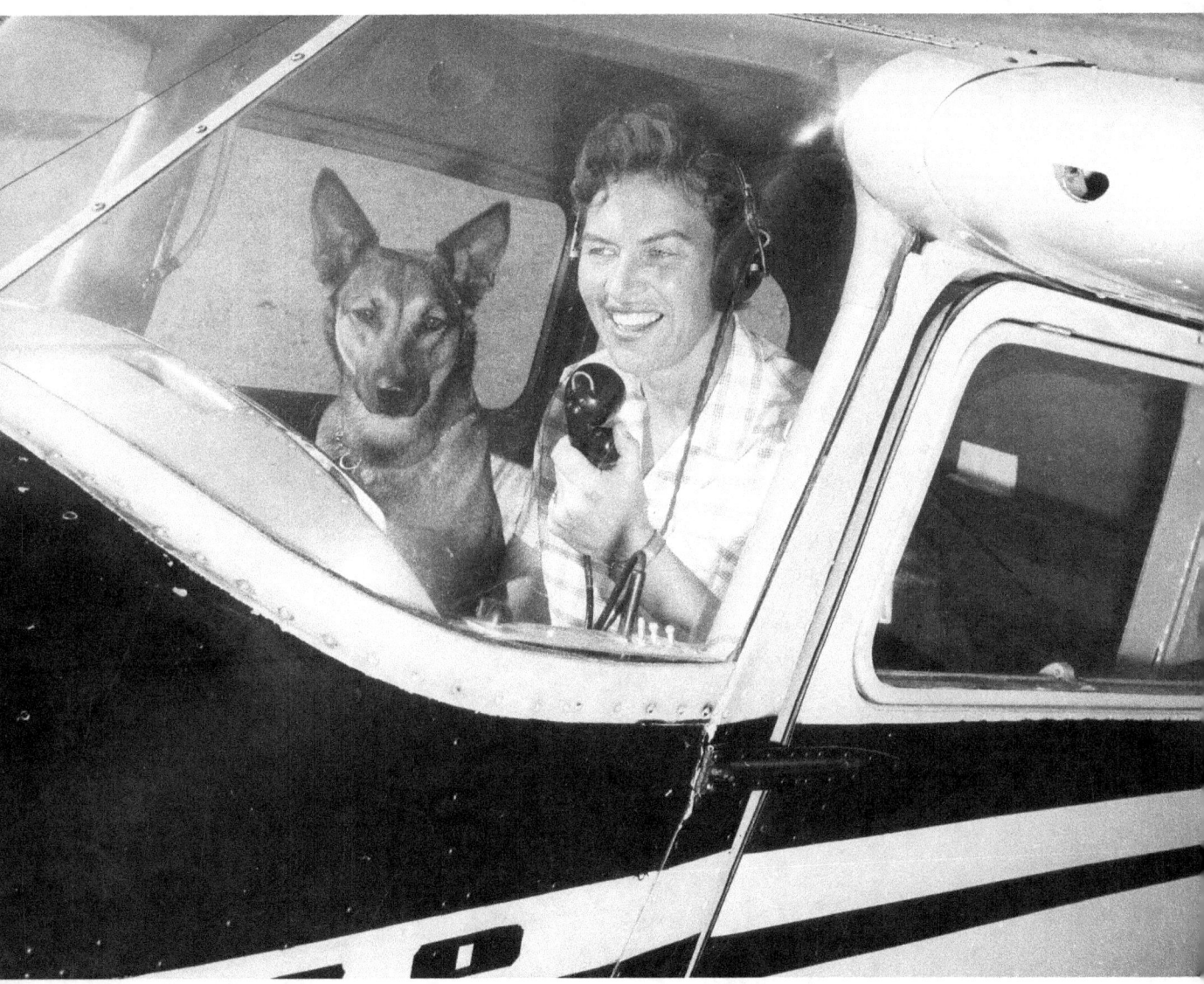

"Jan Wood, flying school teacher from Birmingham High School, tests her small Cessna 170 she will fly in annual 'Powder Puff Derby' July 4. With her is 'Cindy,' who started out at Miss Wood's co-pilot when she attempted to circle globe last year in same plane." May 29, 1958. (Order #00108784)

"Lois Miles of Reseda, right, receives annual Woman Pilot of the Year trophy from Mrs. Audrey Schutte, vice chairman of the '99s' and first recipient of the award four years ago. The '99s,' an international group of licensed women pilots, held their award banquet Saturday at the Sportsmen's Lodge in Studio City."
March 23, 1964. (Bob Martin)
(Order #00108787)

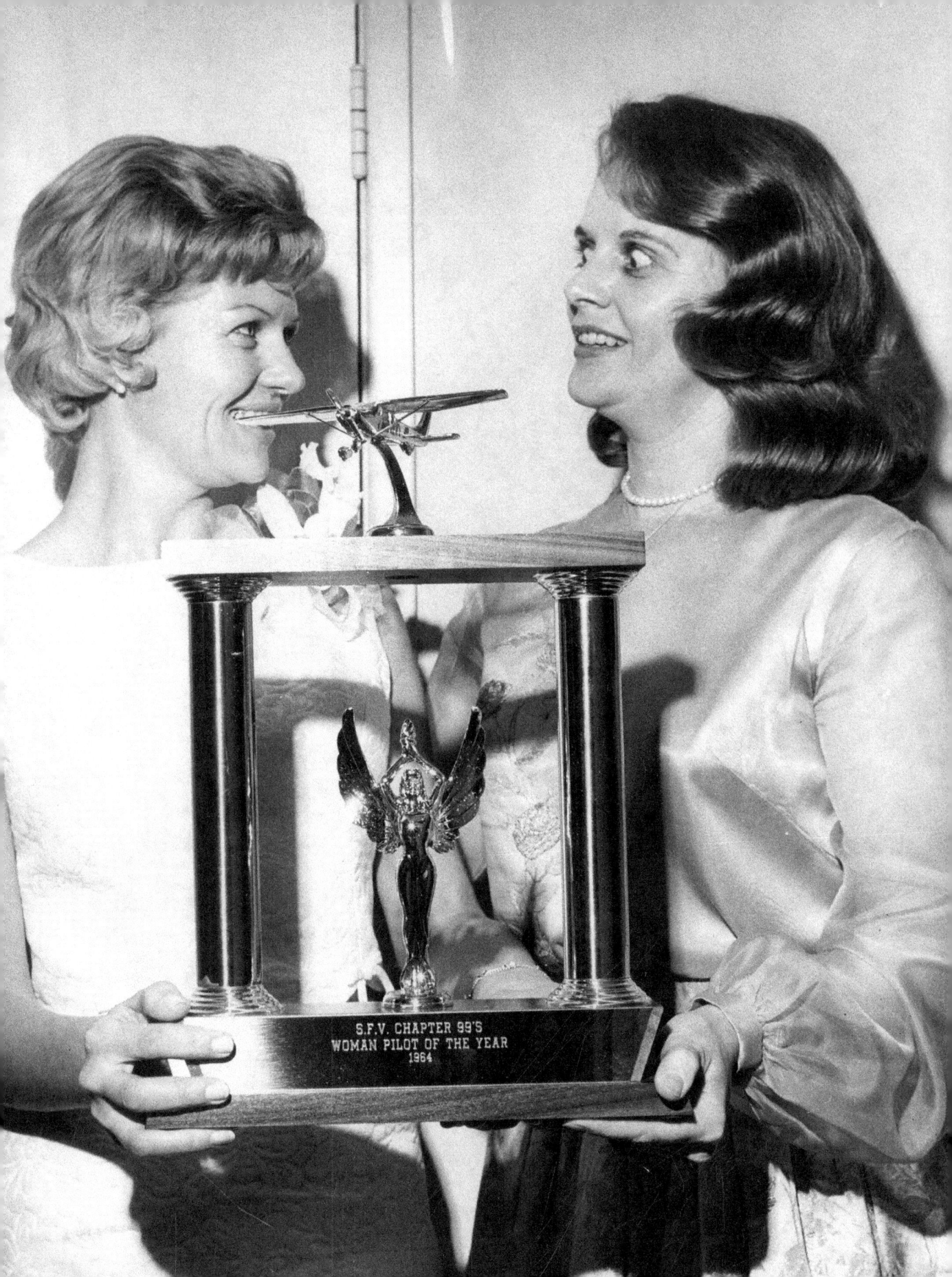

S.F.V. CHAPTER 99'S
WOMAN PILOT OF THE YEAR
1964

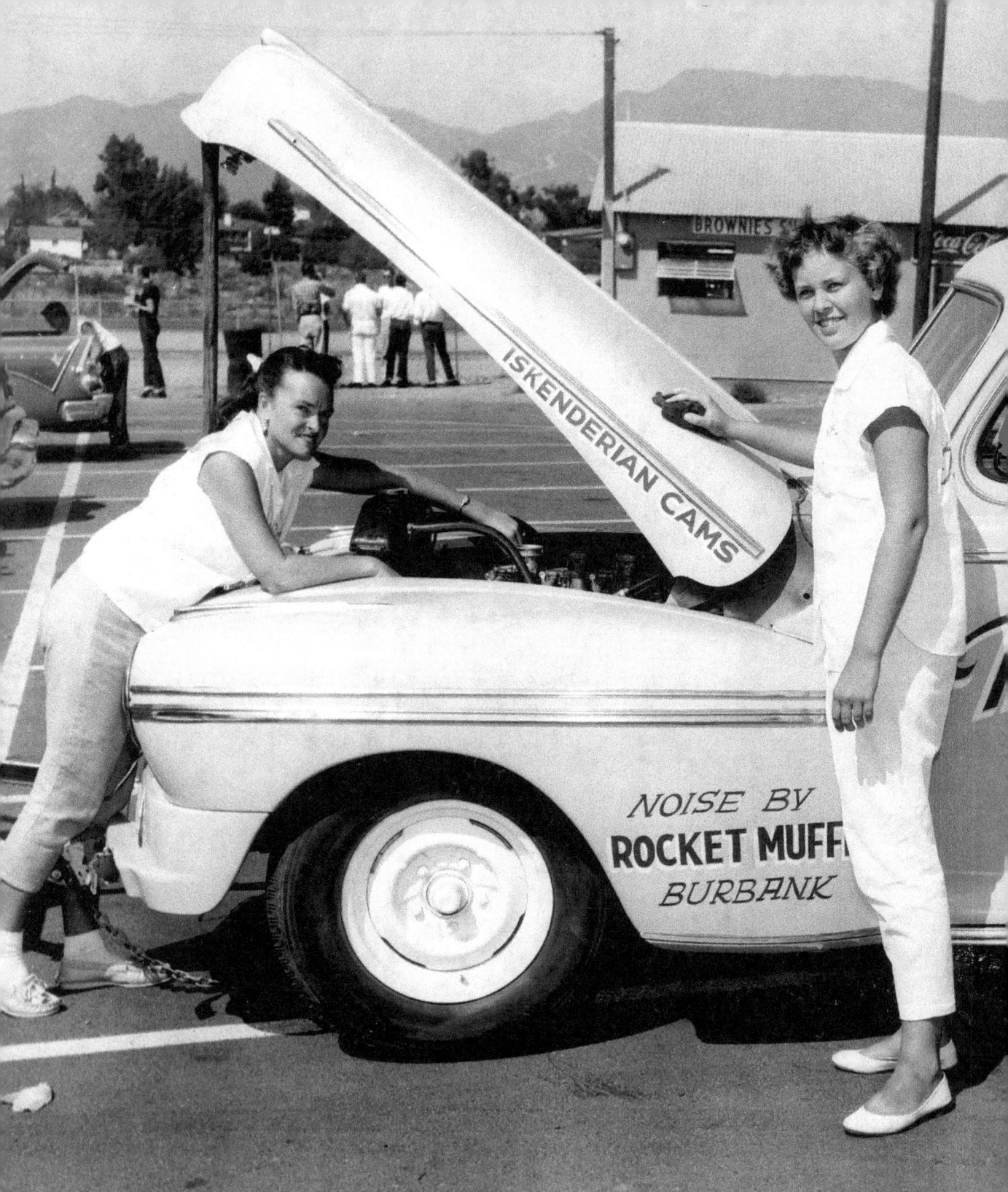

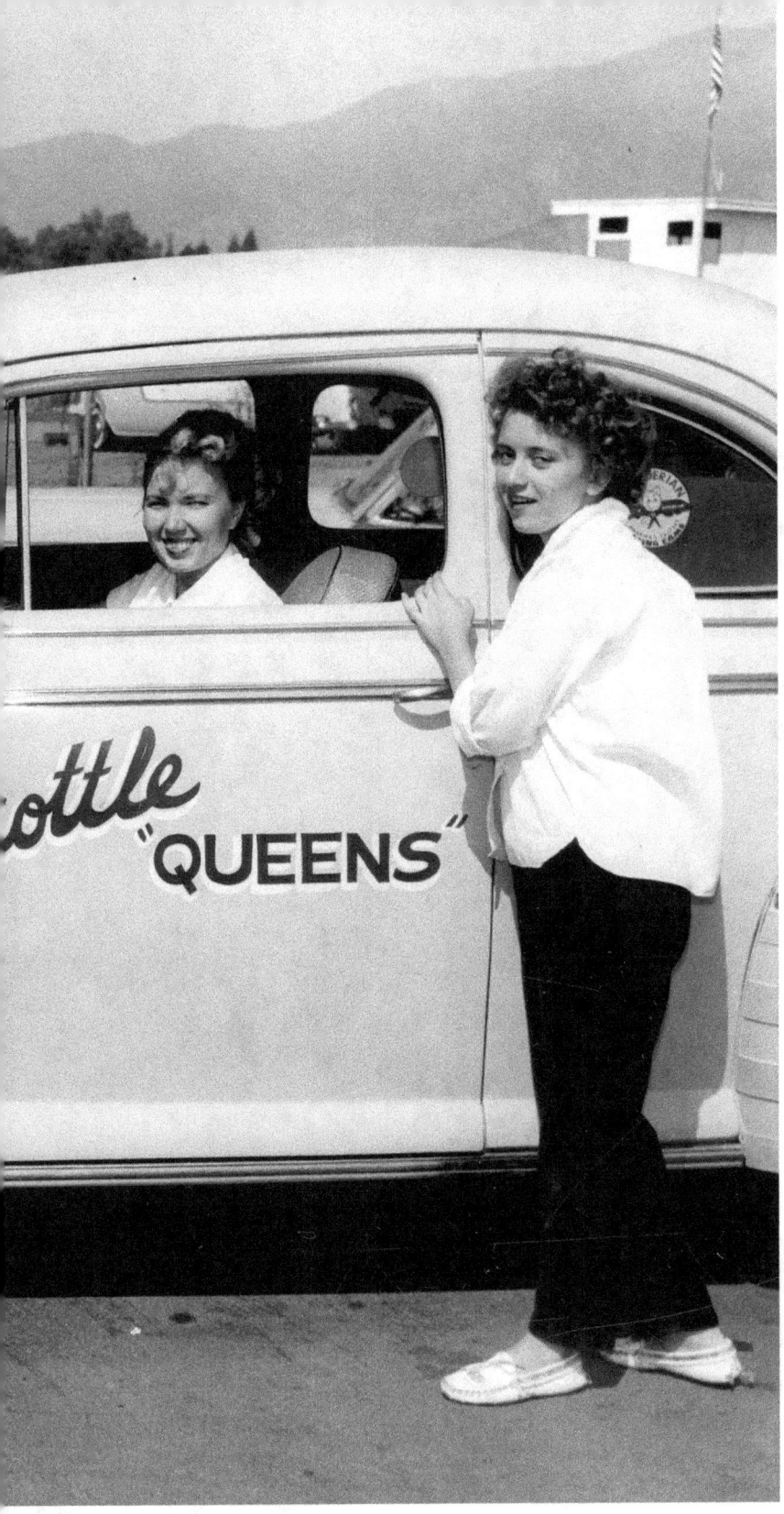

"Members of 'Throttle Queens' put last touches to their pride and joy, club coupe which will compete against male-driven car at the San Fernando Drag Strip. From left are Wilma Brown, Pat Marian, Pat Field, the driver, and June Minnich. Car hit 97 miles per hour and won trophy in its division." October 9, 1956.
(Order #00082875)

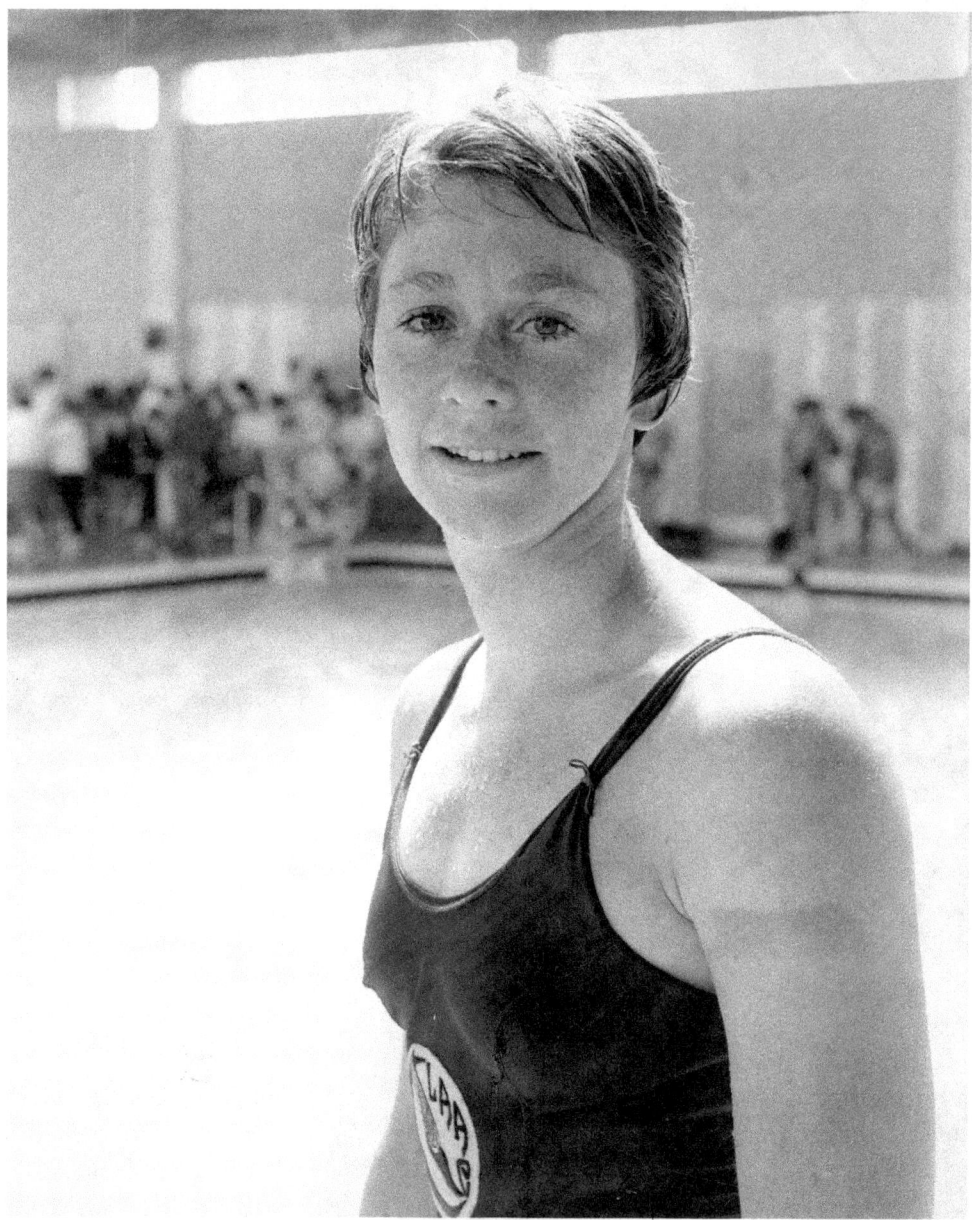

"Cathy Ferguson, 16-year-old Burbank High School student who won two gold medals at the 1964 Olympic Games, is one of stars entered in the National AAU Women's Swimming Championships, scheduled April 8-11 at the City of Commerce Aquatorium."
March 22, 1965. (Order #00055916)

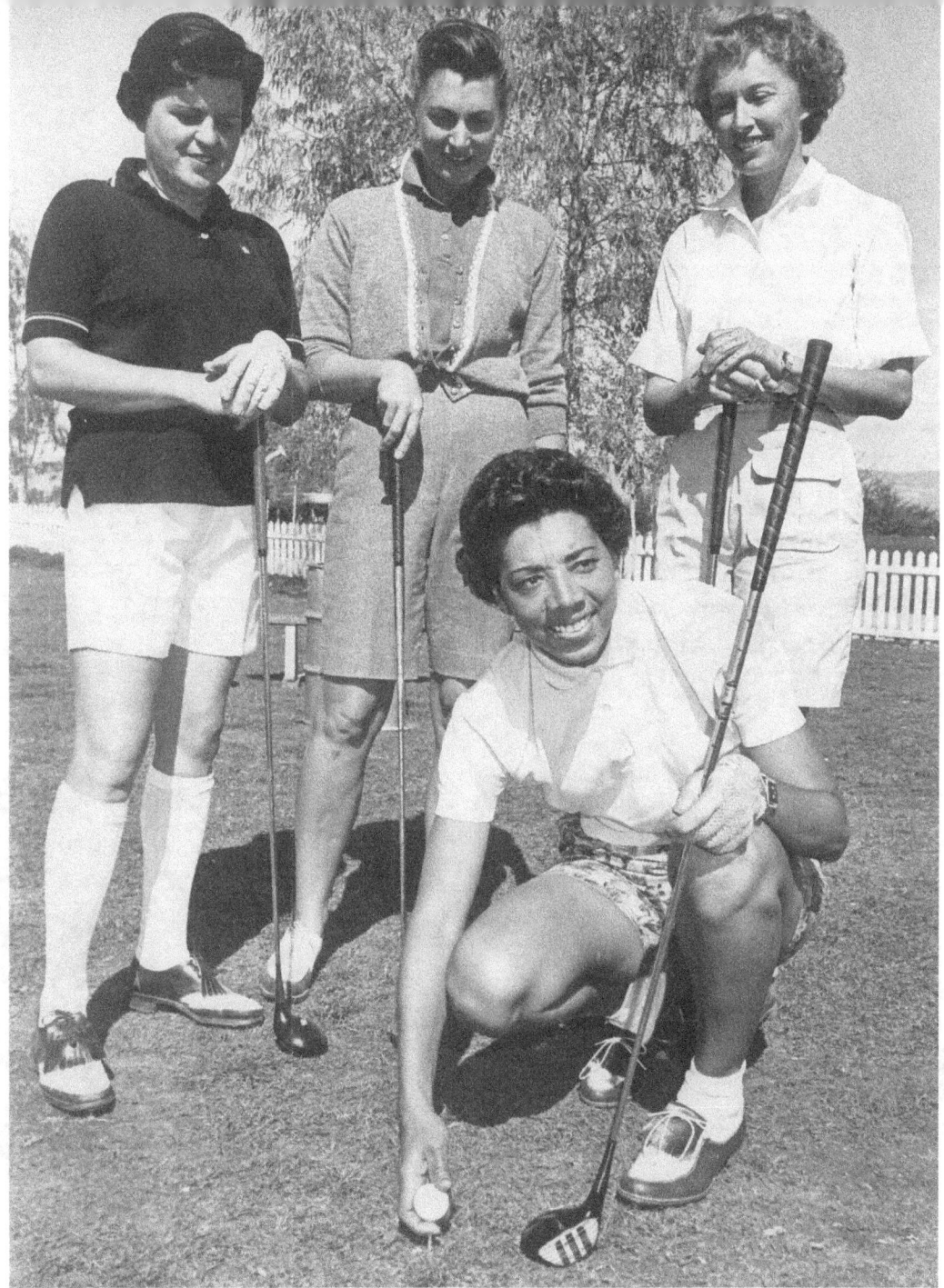

"Althea Gibson, former world's amateur tennis champion, has turned to the fairways and is shown teeing off at Sepulveda Golf course recently. Joining her is Alyve Goens, Nina Curtis and Connie Roeca, all of Sepulveda Golf Course Women's Club."
March 20, 1961 (Jon Woods)
(Order #00048887)

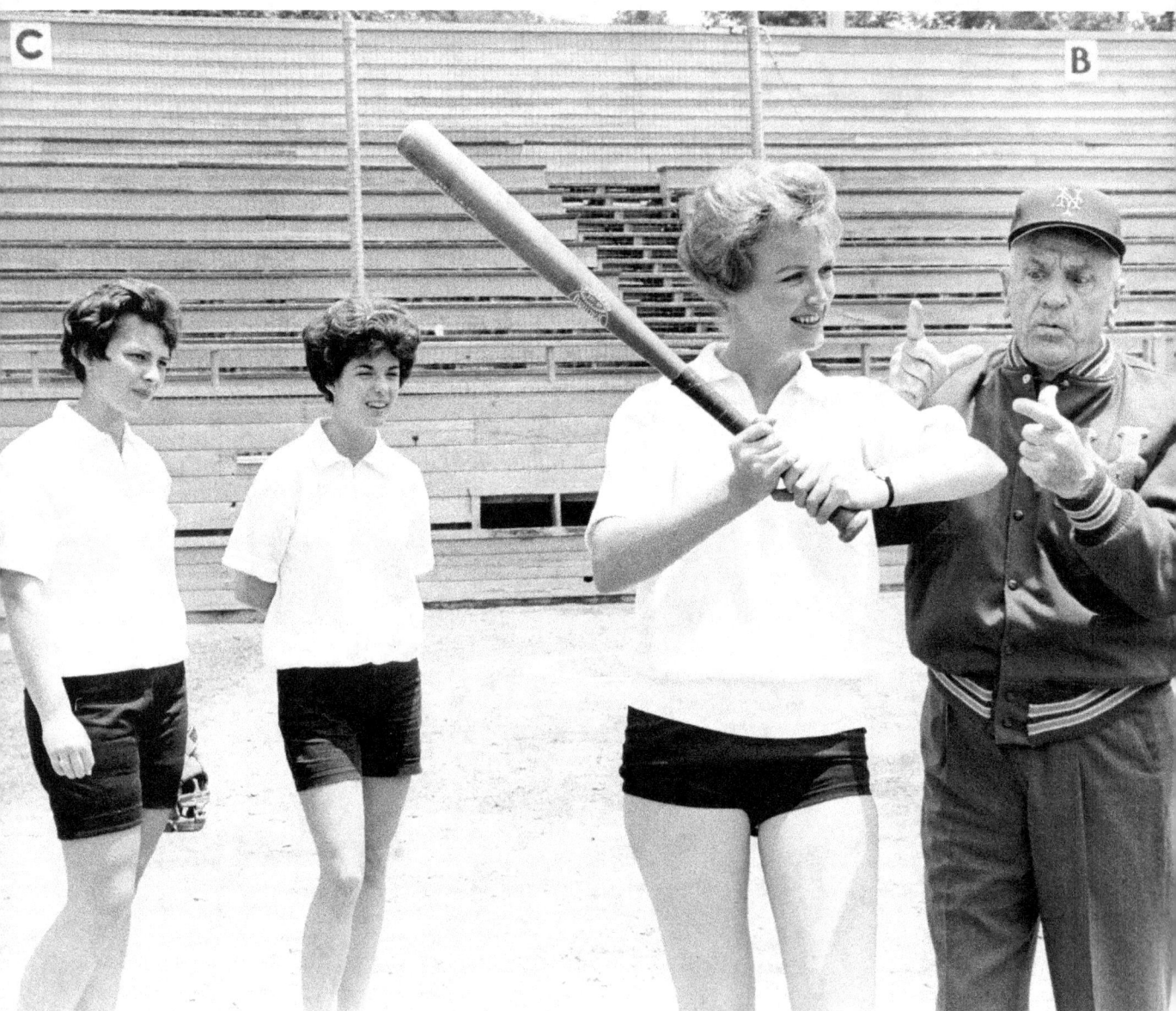

"Maggie Dreyer, Burbank Braids Manager and players Jane Widdersheim, left, and Gayle LaPask get advice from Casey Stengel, manager of New York Mets."
July 2, 1962. (Gordon Dean)
(Order #00085491)

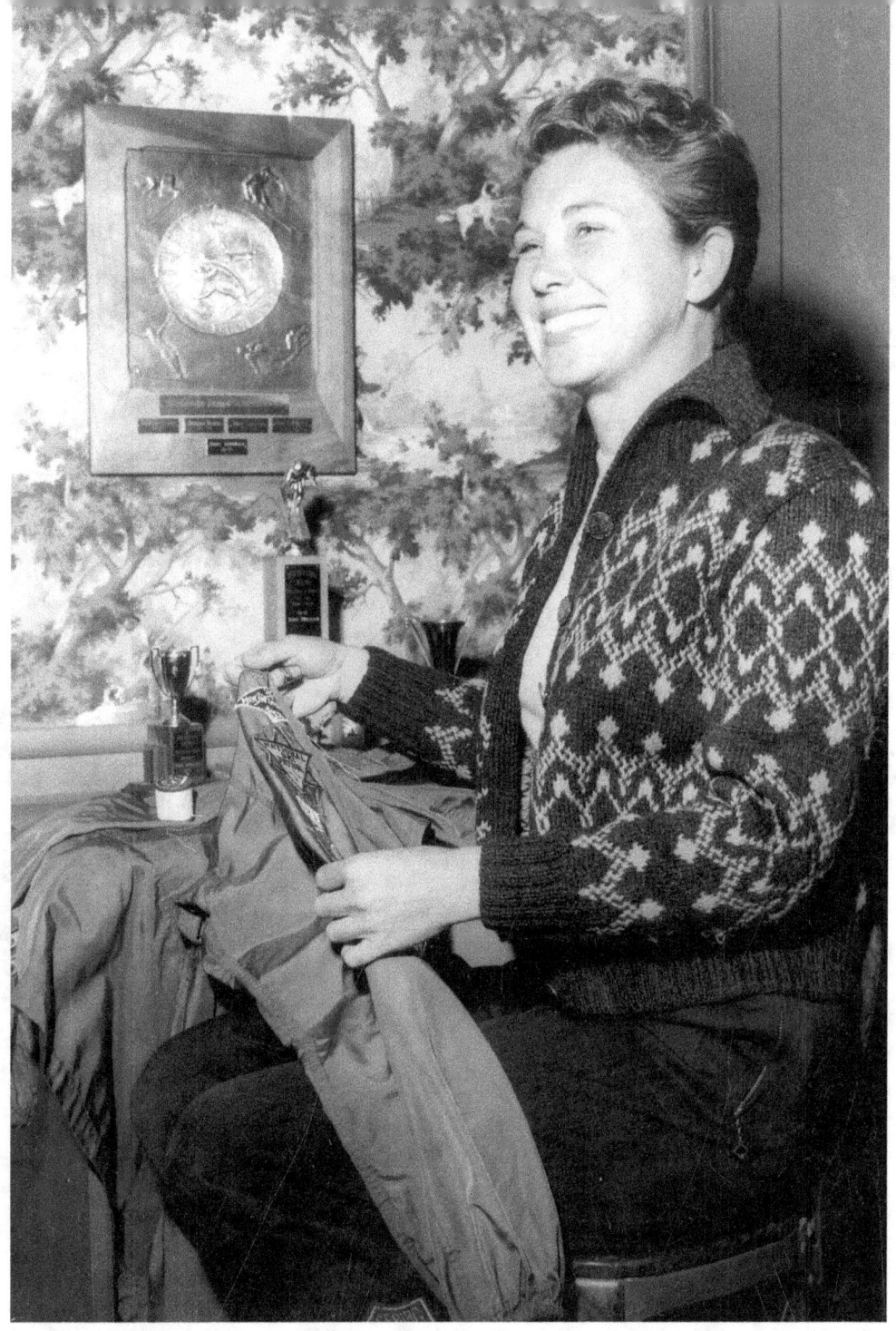

"Mrs. Bobbe Rumbaugh, 17601 Lemay Pl., Van Nuys, is elated as she sews National Ski Patrolwoman badge on parka. She is one of 150 women in United States granted honor of title in National Ski Association of America."
October 14, 1957. (Order #00108650)

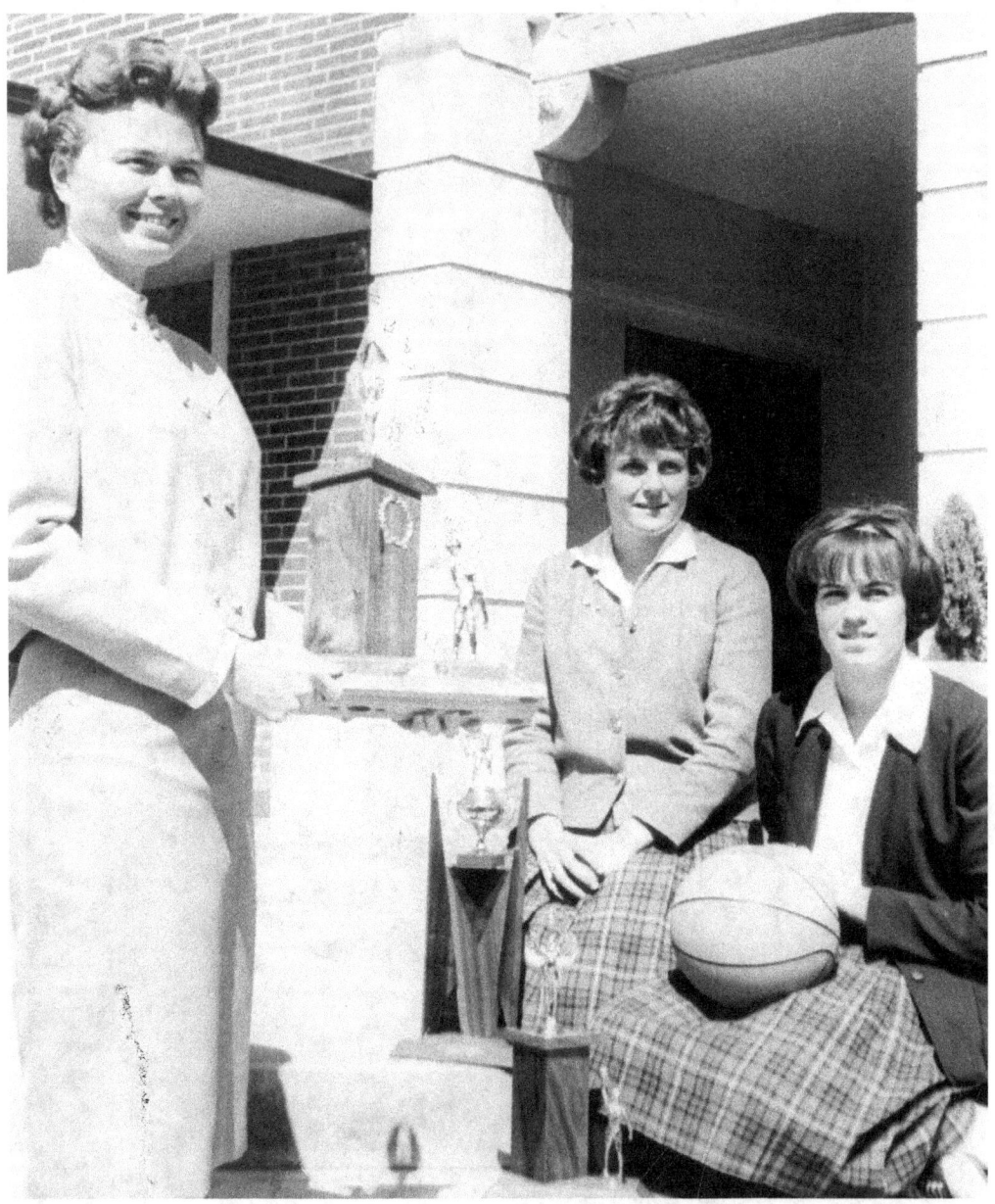

"Villa Cabrini girls' basketball coach Miss Judy Brown (left), and players Martha Sheedy (left) and Pat Fonseca, admire the trophy won recently by Miss Brown's team in competition in the Burbank area."
March 27, 1964. (Gordon Dean)
(Order #00108851)

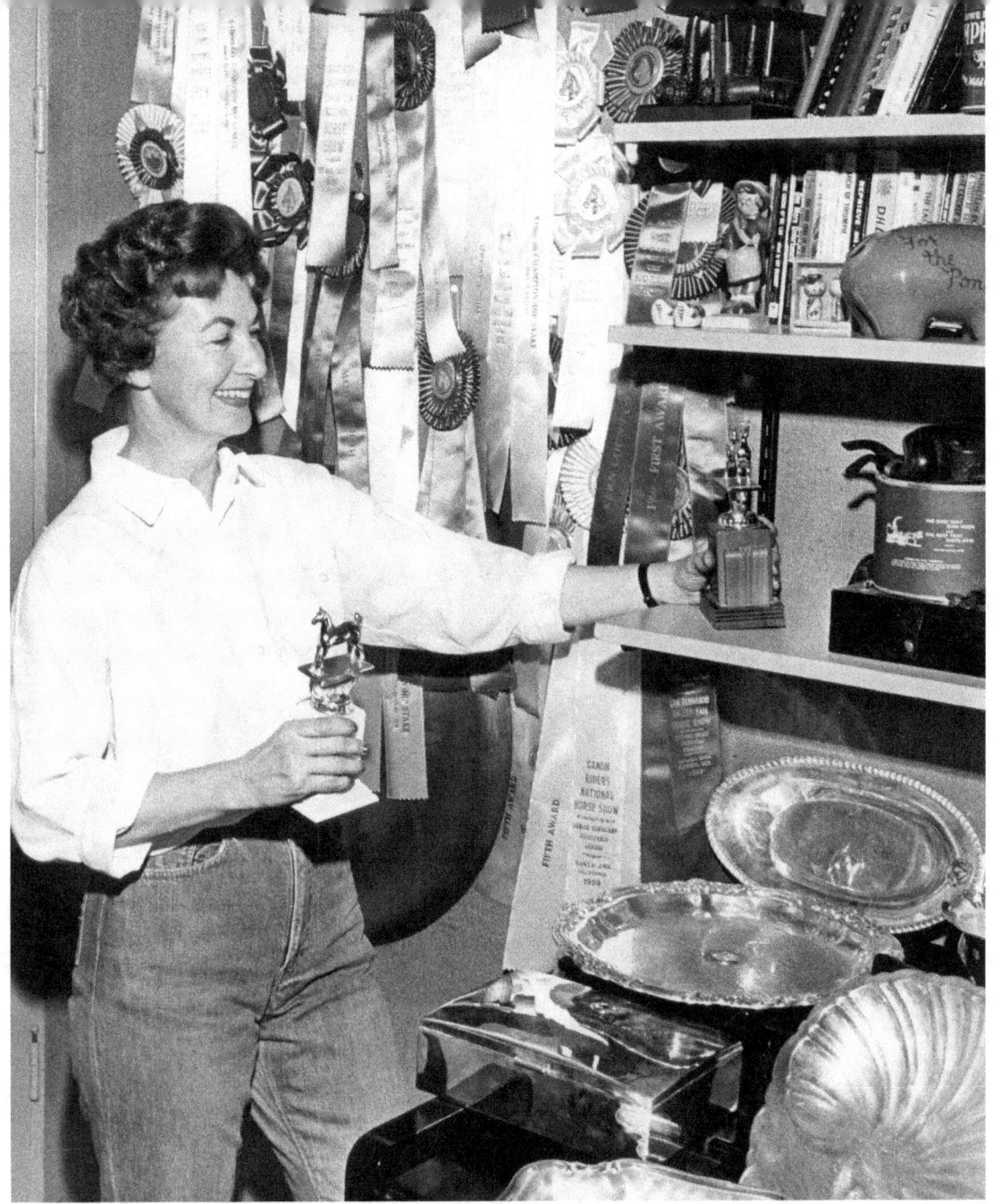

"Flip Manne stands before blue ribbons won last season throughout the state for classes in showing and training. One of the few amateurs who trains her own show horses, Flip has won many silver and gold trophies since she began traveling Western show circuit." Florence "Flip" Manne was a former Rockette in New York who later married jazz drummer Shelley Manne. As of 2014, she was serving as president of the Los Angeles Jazz Society.
February 2, 1961. (Alan Hyde)

(Order #00109016)

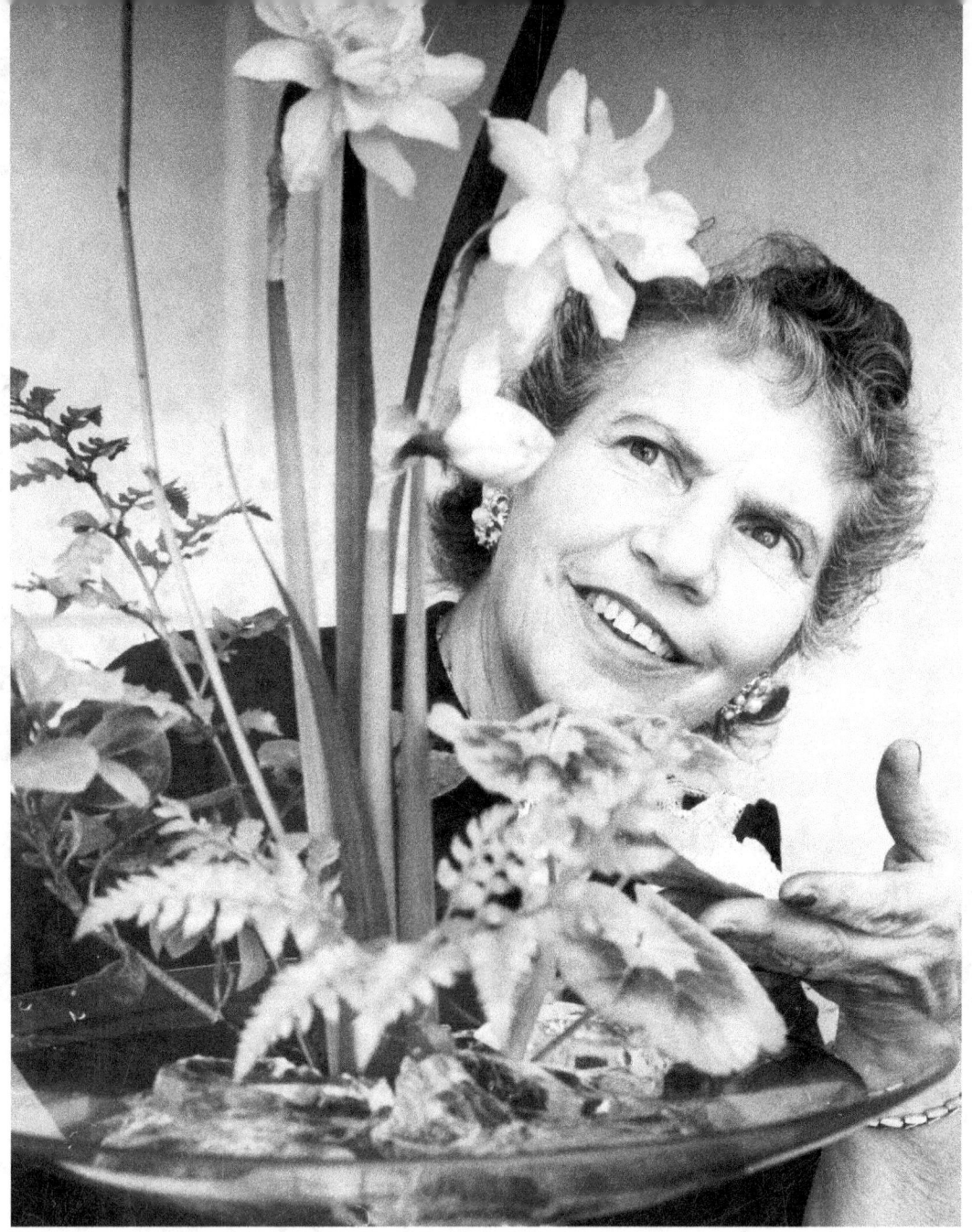

"North Hollywood's Jessie B. Black has been named Pacific region contestant to the only national flower arranging tournament. Mrs. Black who lives at 6406 Beck Ave., will join 13 other top floral designers this summer to compete in the seventh annual Sterling Bowl Tournament in Newark, N. J. One of the 14 will receive a $5,000 perpetual challenge silver trophy June 20 for being the nation's best flower arranger."
March 29, 1962. (George Brich)

(Order #00111776)

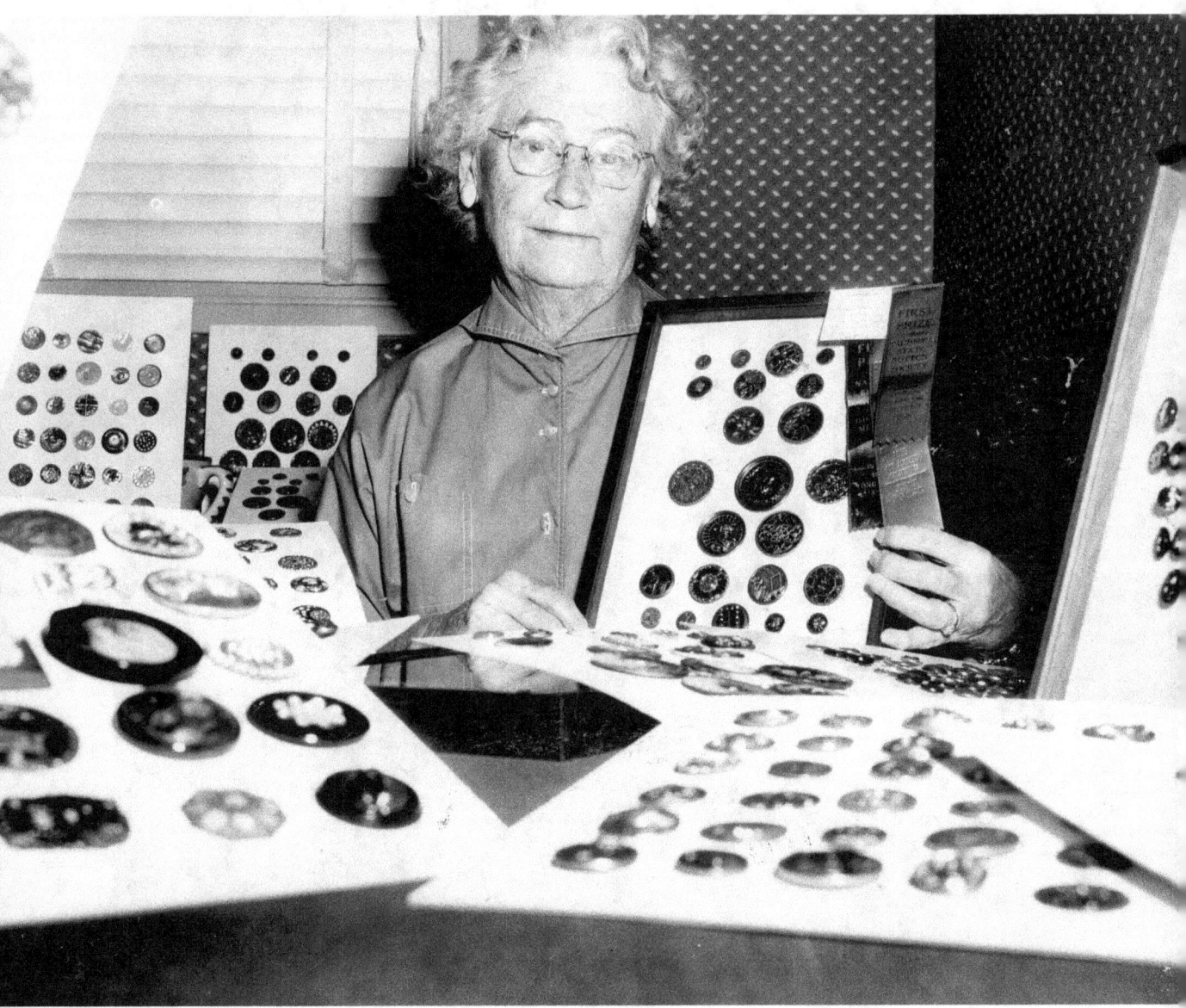

"Mrs. Frank E. Winkler of North Hollywood will exhibit her collection of 10,000 buttons to residents in Volunteers of America Sunland Home for Elderly Persons."
March 29, 1960. (Order #00093399)

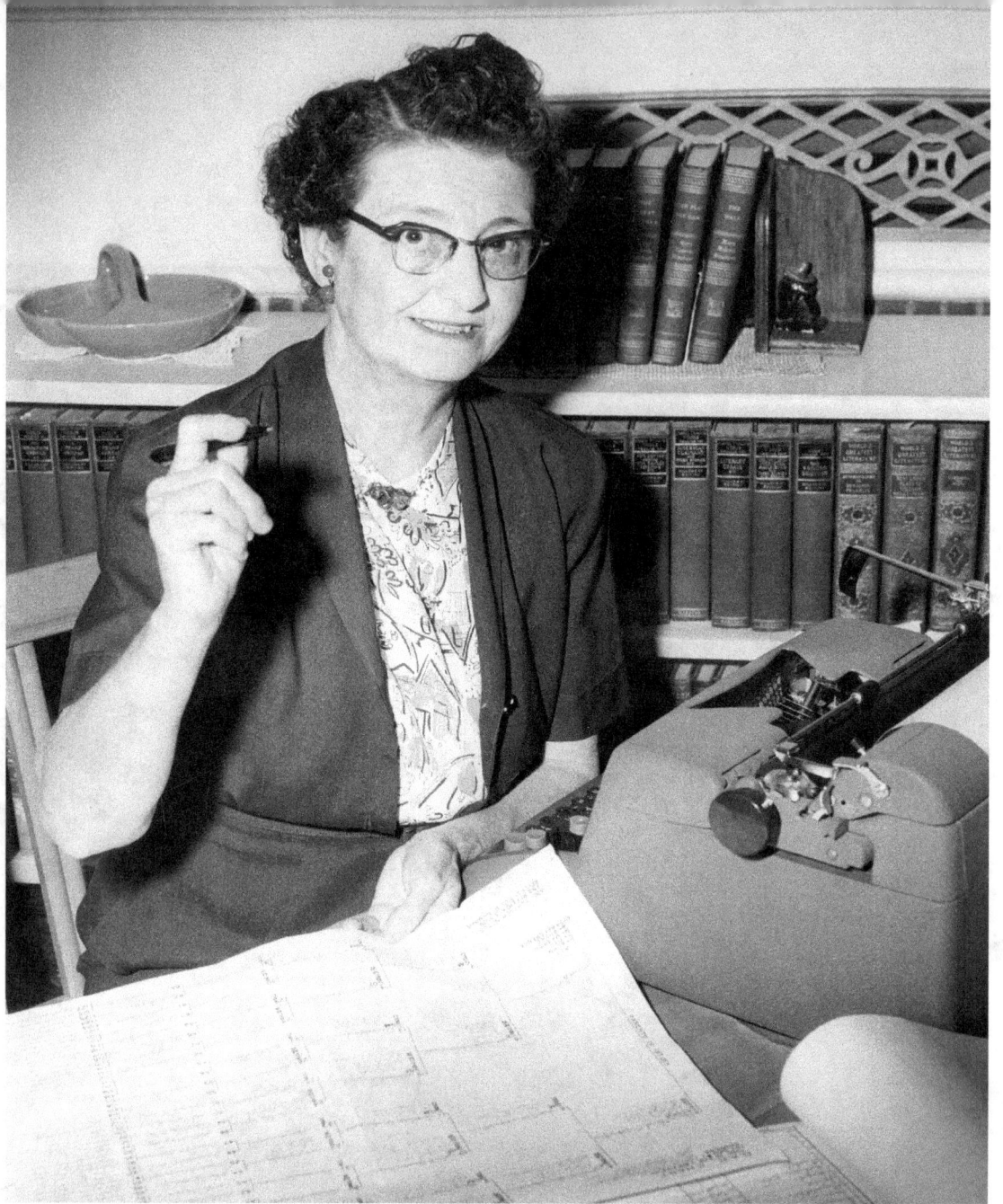

"Genealogy can be an expensive hobby or a frustrating profession, according to Mrs. John L. Quinn of Burbank, who until now has kept it in the former classification. After a 9,000-mile bus trip through Southern states last spring, Mrs. Quinn returned home to prepare the final draft of a book, 'Descendants of Governor Robert Gibbes of South Carolina.' More than 10,000 descendants of Gibbes, a Colonial governor in 1712-1714, are listed in the thick volume, which she expects to have published before the end of the year."
August 4, 1956. (Order #00108420)

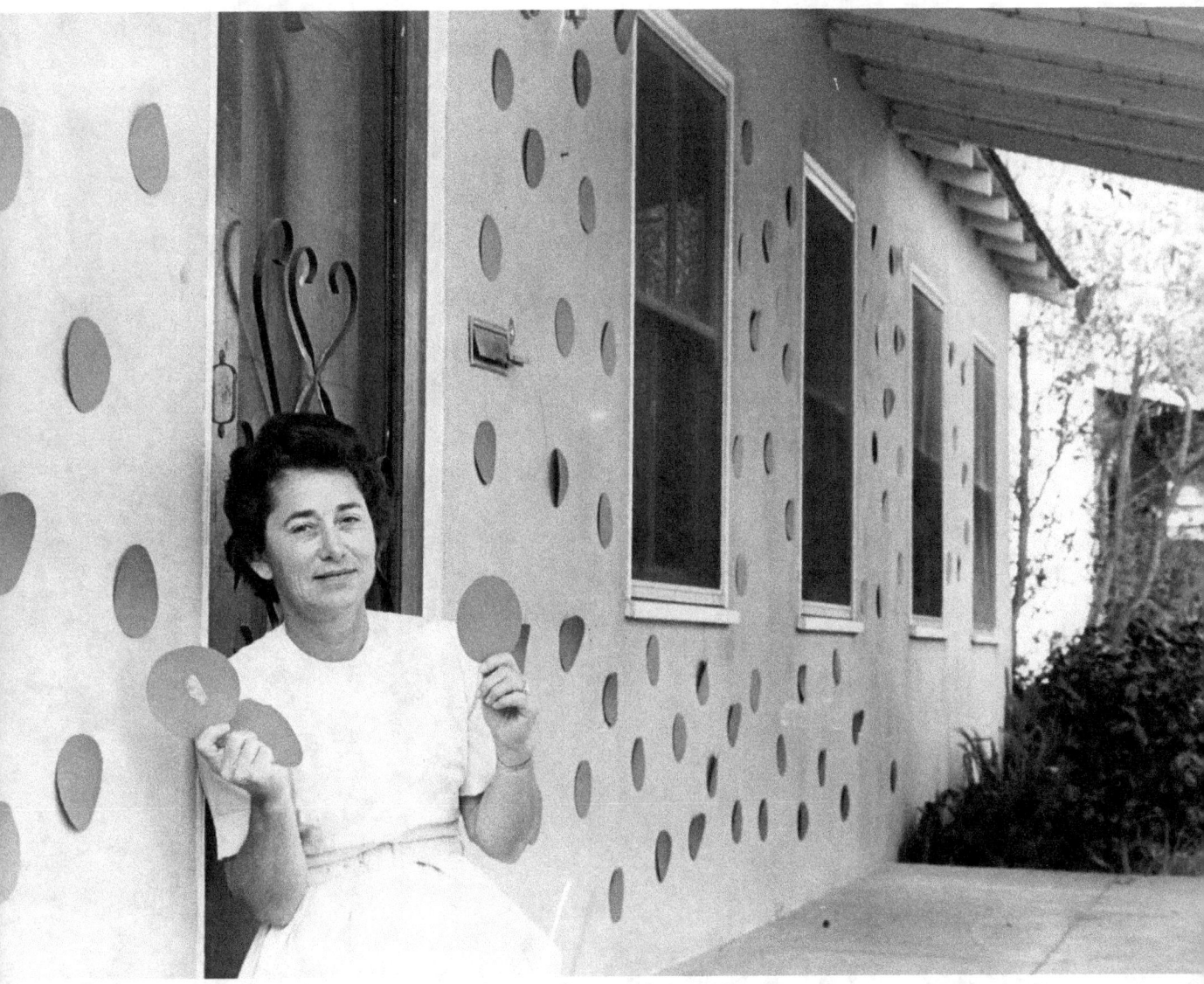

"Sun Valley house gets polka-dotted while owners vacation - Mrs. Arthur Wootton, holding two dots, is waiting retaliation."
October 11, 1962. (Gordon Dean)
(Order #00108937)

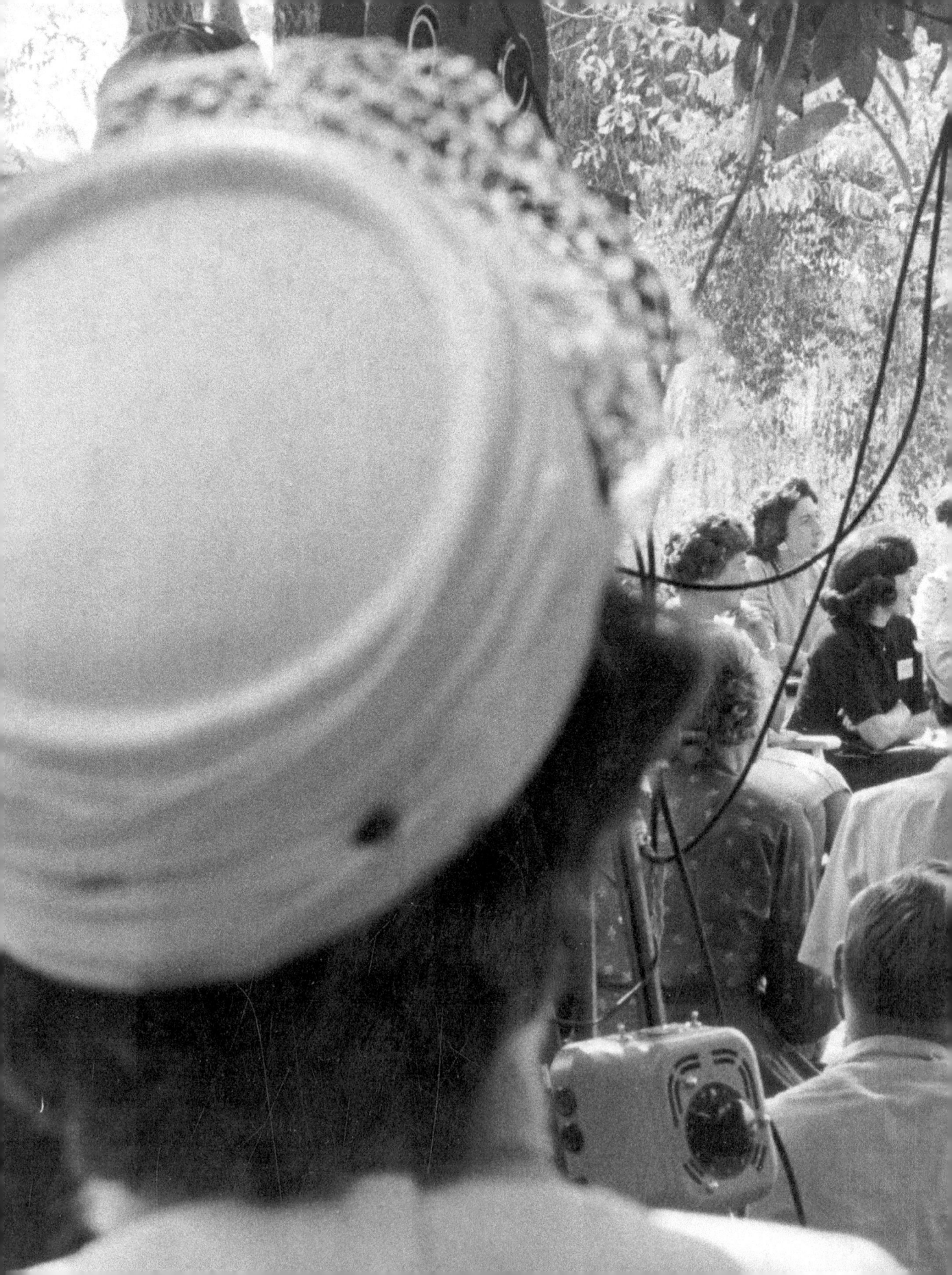

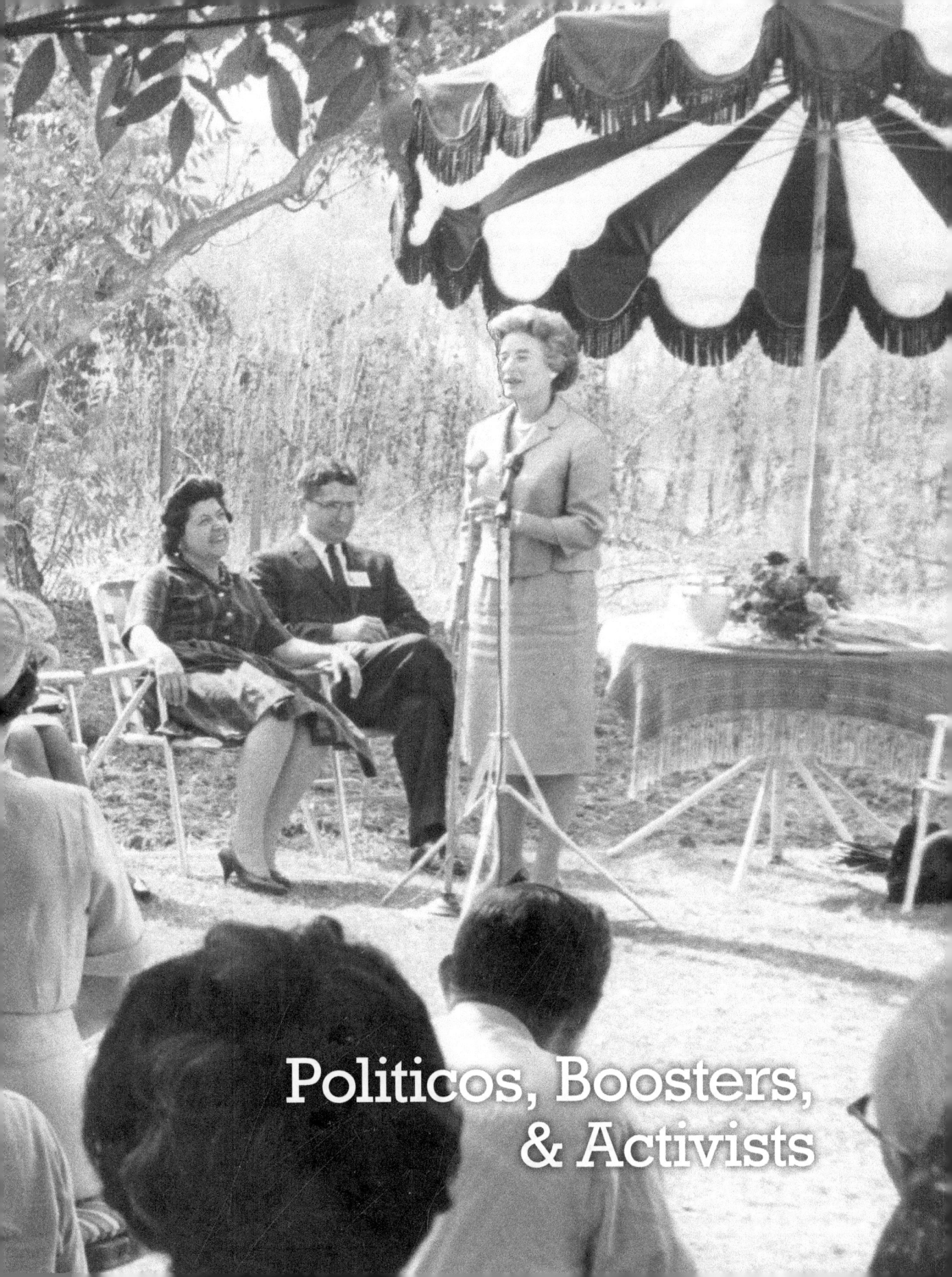

Politicos, Boosters,
& Activists

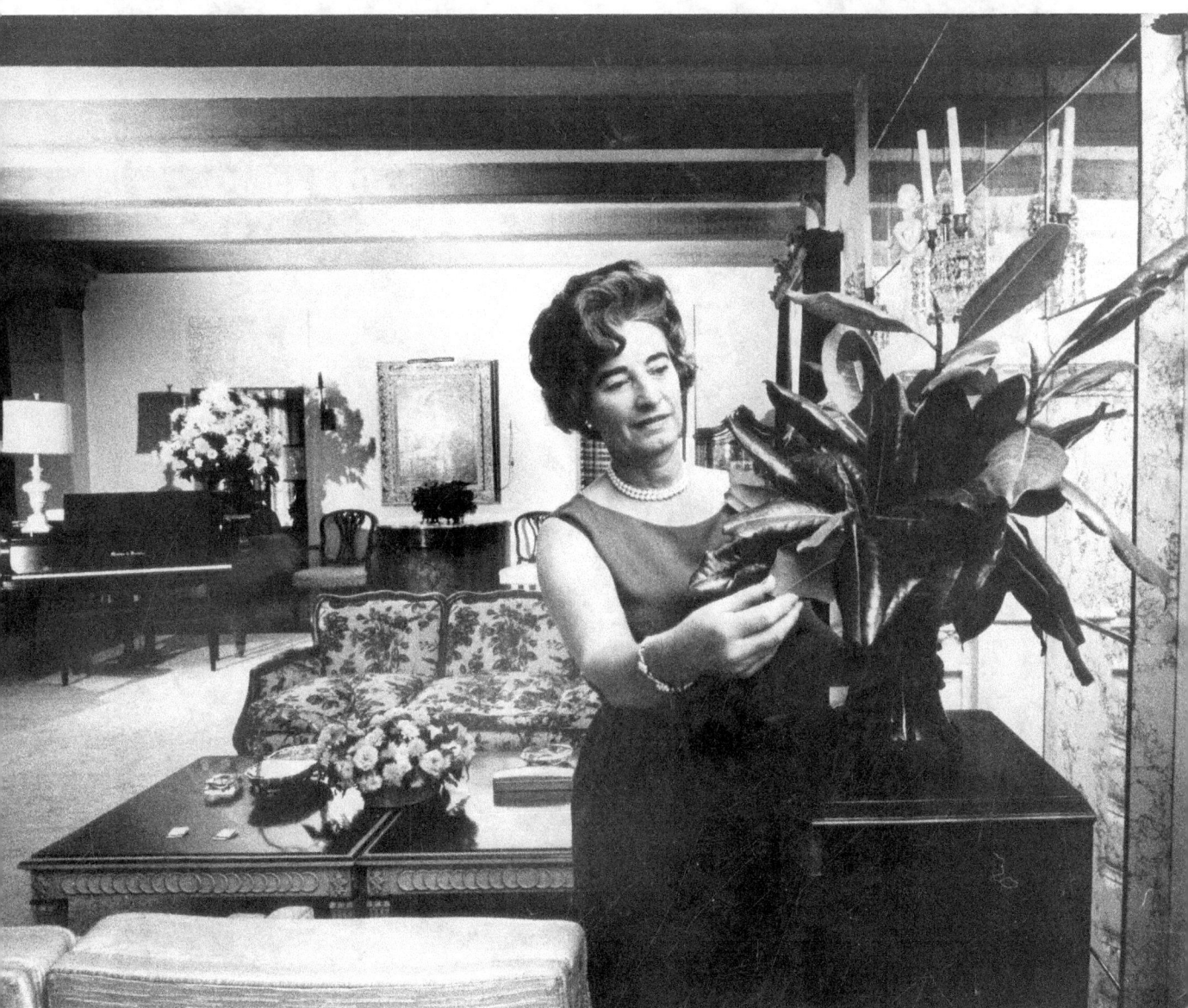

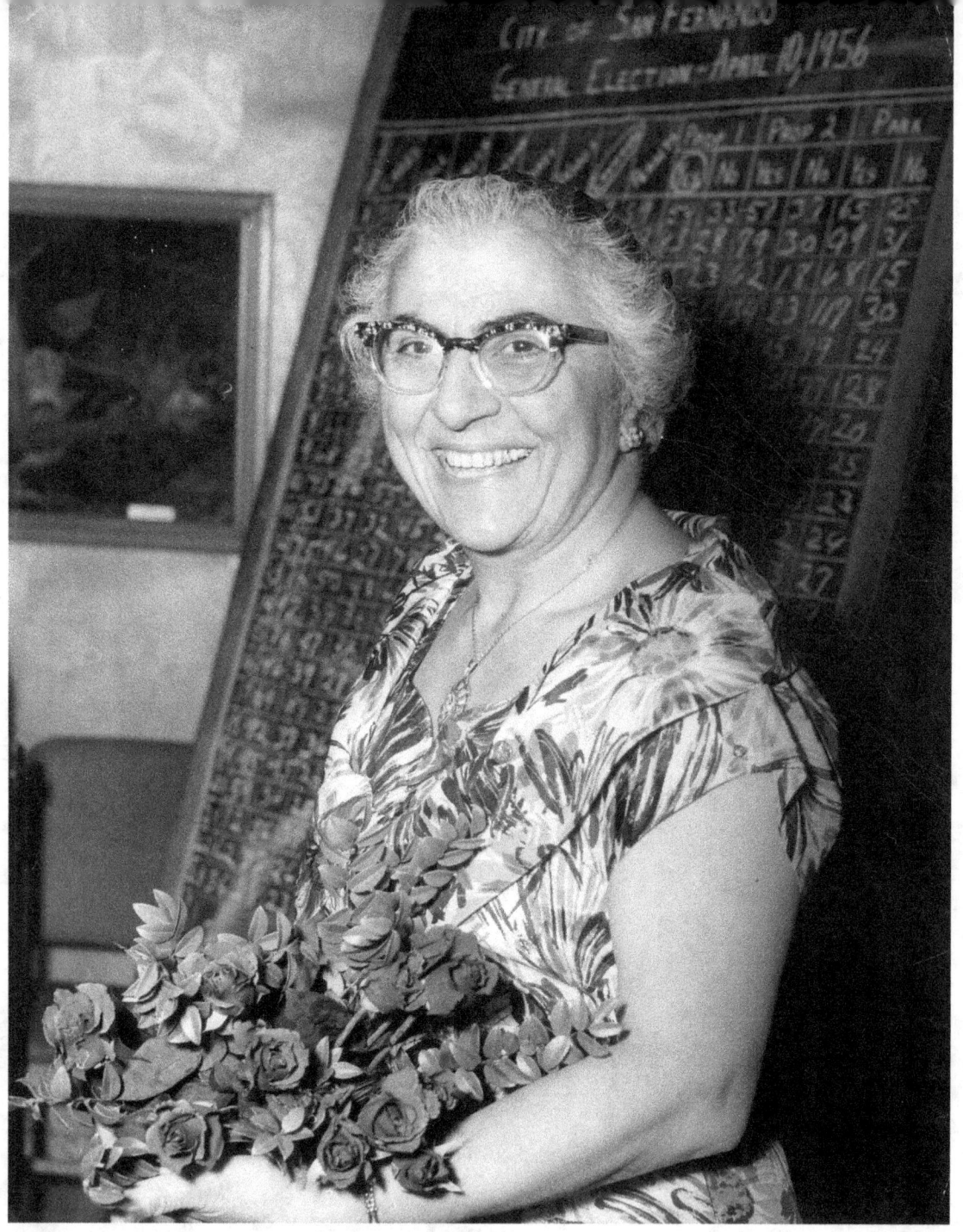

"Miss Gladys Moosekian, high school teacher who taught many who voted for her, shows winning smile and roses following her victory at polls. She is first woman elected to San Fernando City Council and takes office next Tuesday."
April 11, 1956. (Order #00083076)

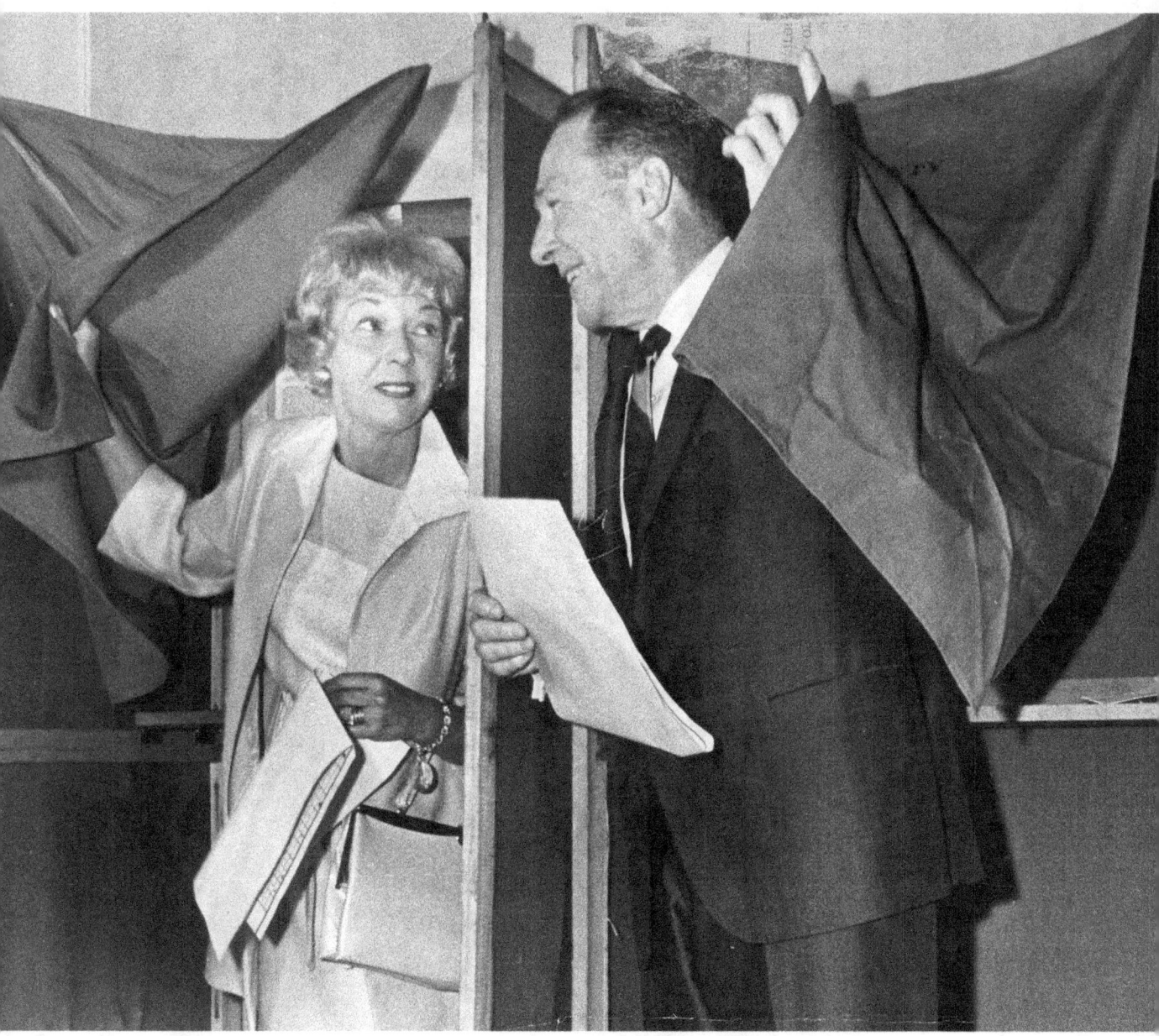

"Mayor Samuel Yorty and his wife, Betty, greet each other after voting today in the Studio City polling place. How the first family voted is strictly conjecture, but it is pointed out that Yorty is running for his second mayoralty term."
April 6, 1965. (George Brich)
(Order #00112166)

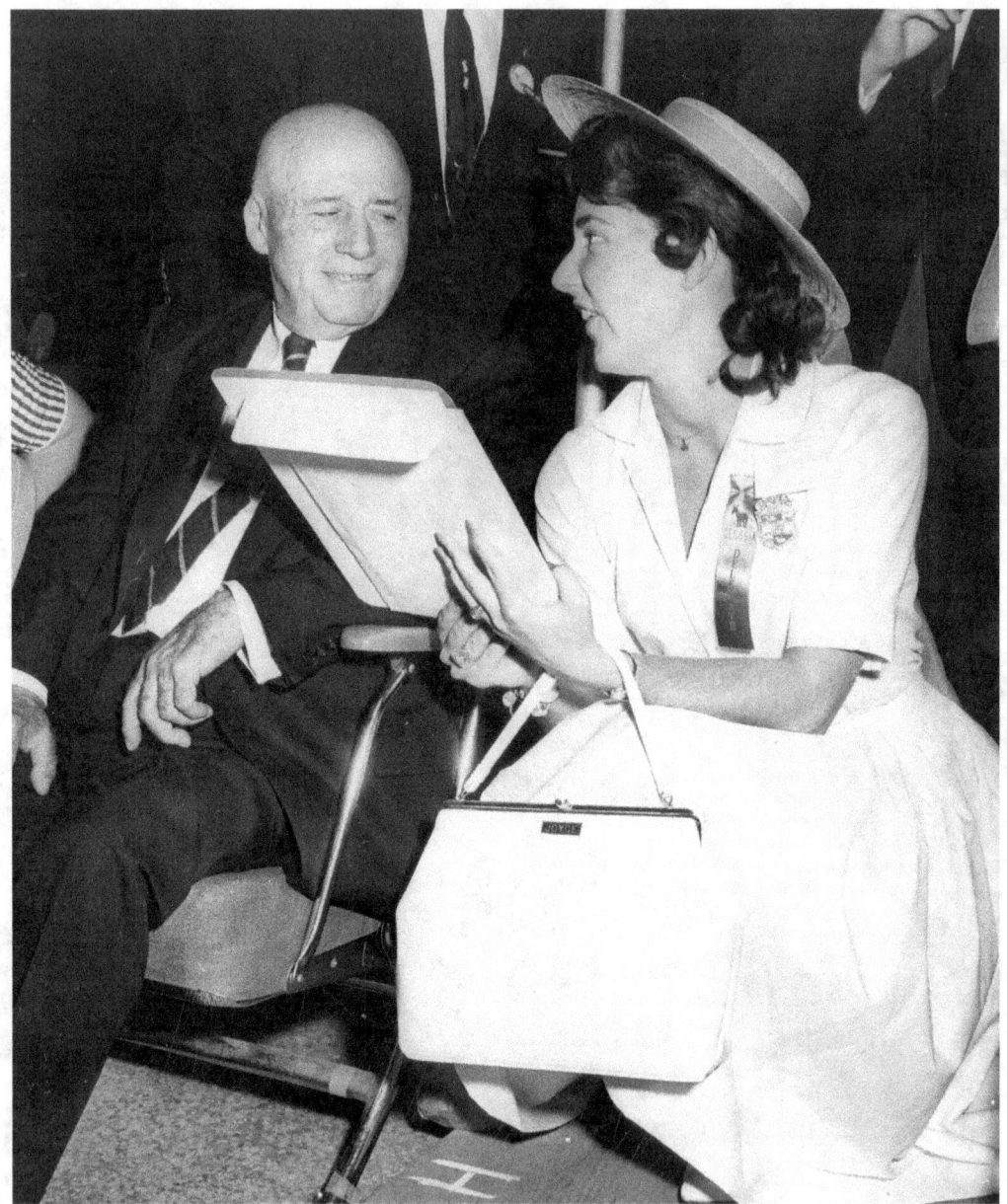

"*Valley Times* staff writer Joyce Lambeau takes time out from her duties as [Democratic National] convention Golden Girl hostess to buttonhole Sam Rayburn, speaker of the House, and quiz him on his candidate, Texas Sen. Lyndon B. Johnson."
July 19, 1960. (Gordon Dean)
(Order #00109134)

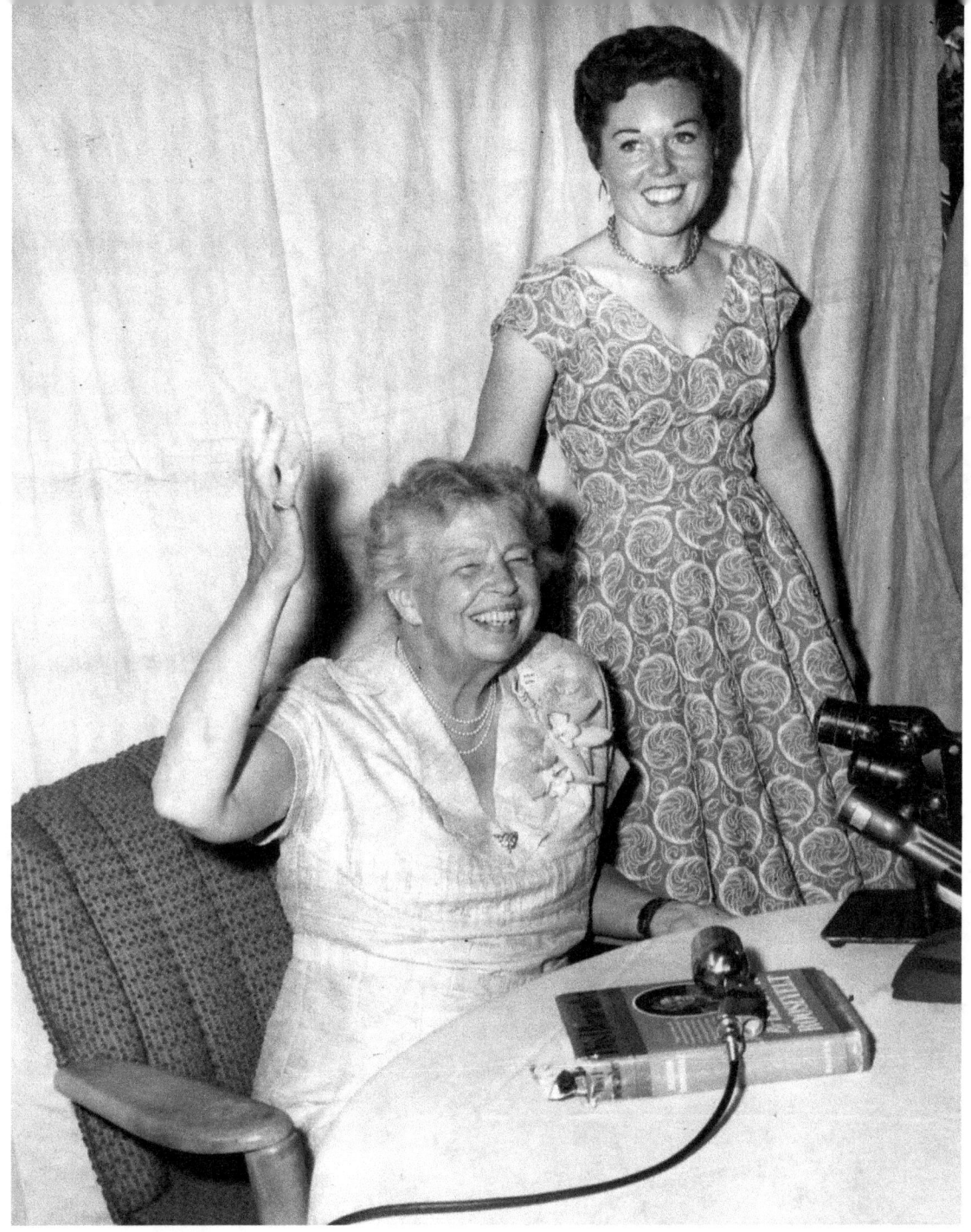

"Mrs. Eleanor Roosevelt waves to Valley Democratic women during appearance at Stevenson-Kefauver campaign reception at Studio City home of Mrs. Allen Adler, right. Mrs. Roosevelt accused Republicans of "drifting" in foreign policy."
September 29, 1956. (Order #00083664)

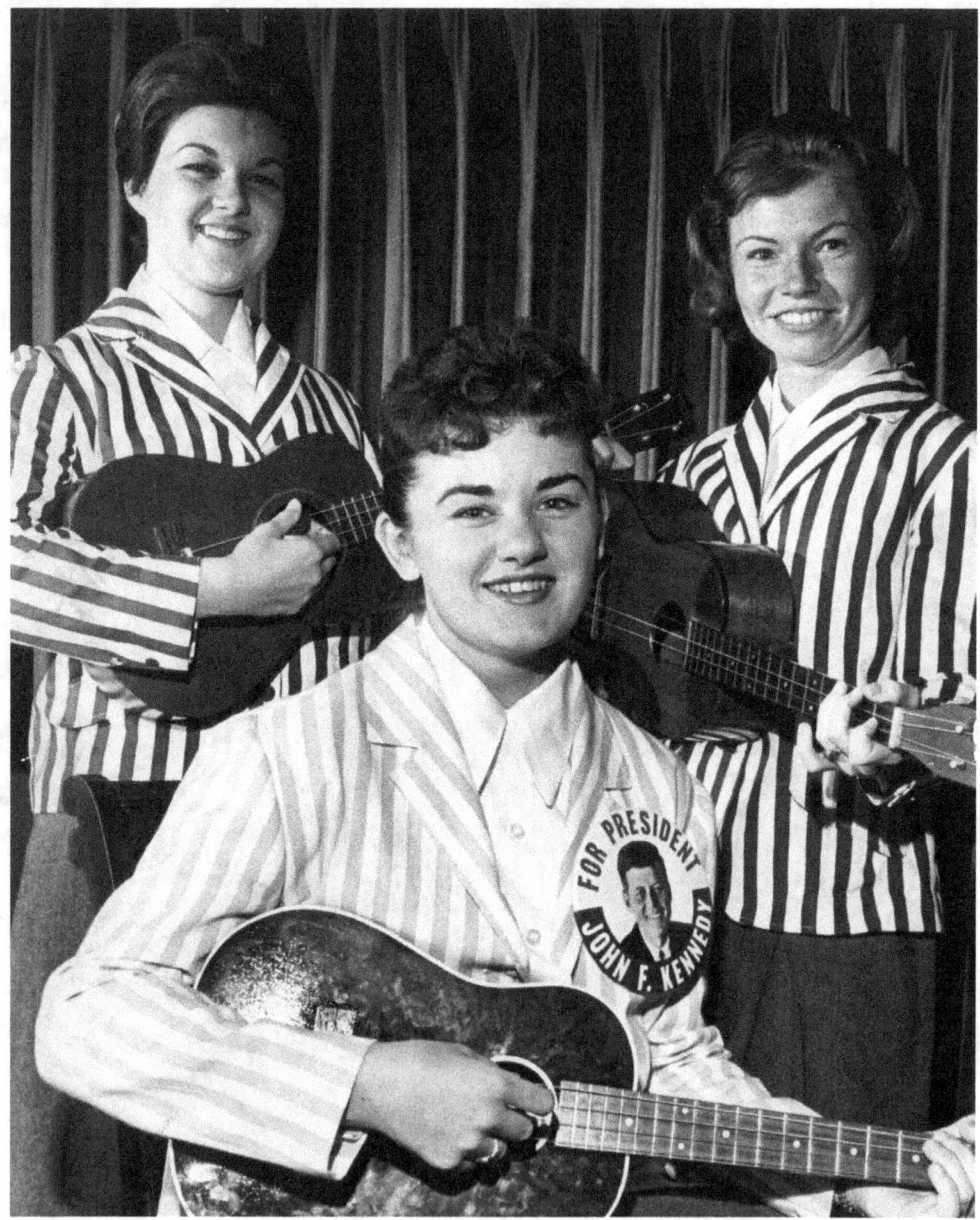

Three young women show their musical talents and support for John F. Kennedy during the 1960 presidential election.
1960 (Jon Woods)
(Order #00030098)

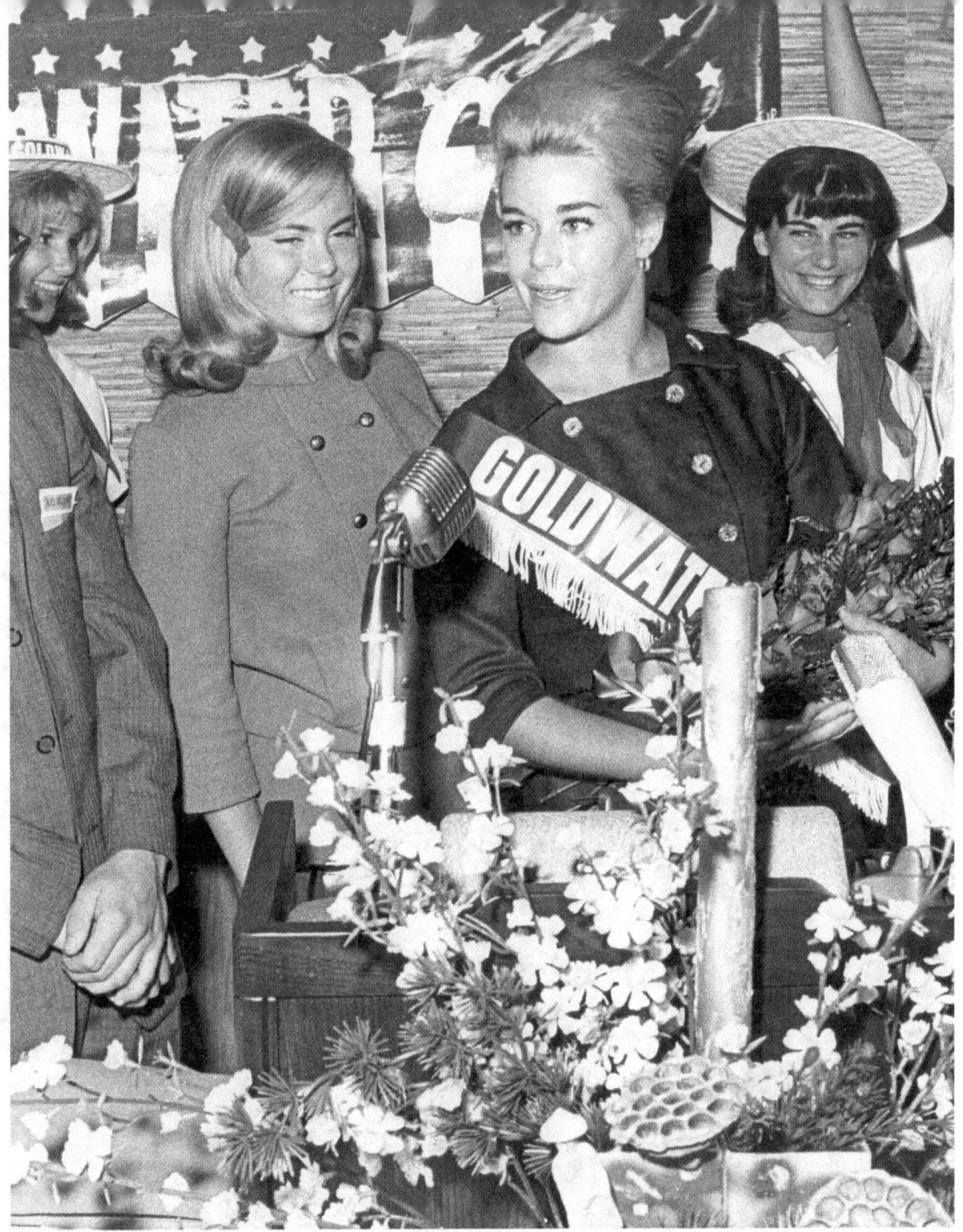

"Mrs. Peggy Goldwater Holt, right foreground, receives a bouquet of roses from Cherie Adams at the first meeting of Goldwater Girls at Phil Ahn's Moongate Restaurant in Panorama City. Several hundred Goldwater Girls, between 15 and 18 years of age attended."
September 24, 1964. (Steve Young)
(Order #00109776)

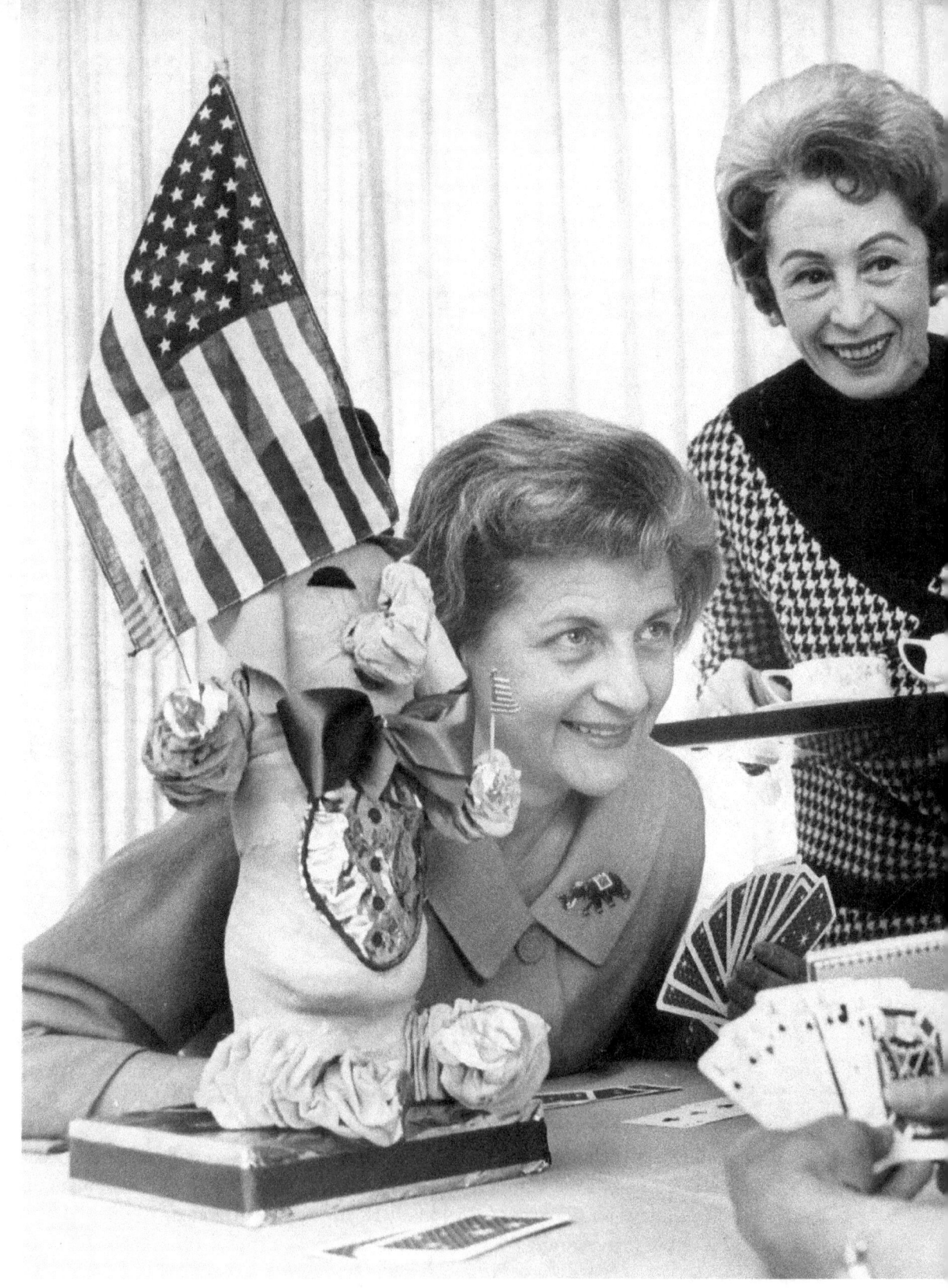

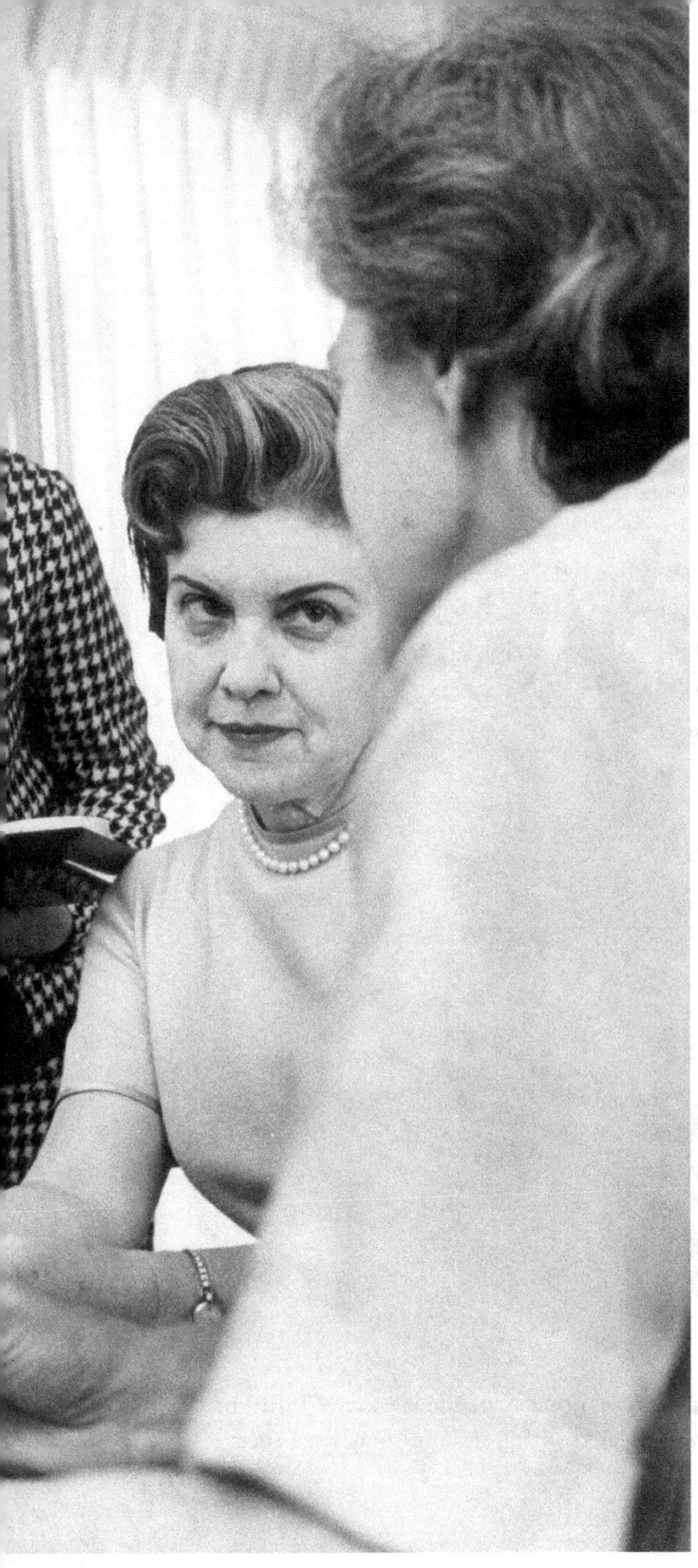

"Encino Republican Women's Club members make arrangements for their week-long fund-raising bridge week, which will begin March 22. From left are Mmes. Herman Voget, Sherman Oaks; William Hargrave, Encino, and O. A. Irving, also Sherman Oaks. The group's theme this year is 'Education.'"
March 12, 1965. (George Brich)
(Order #00109586)

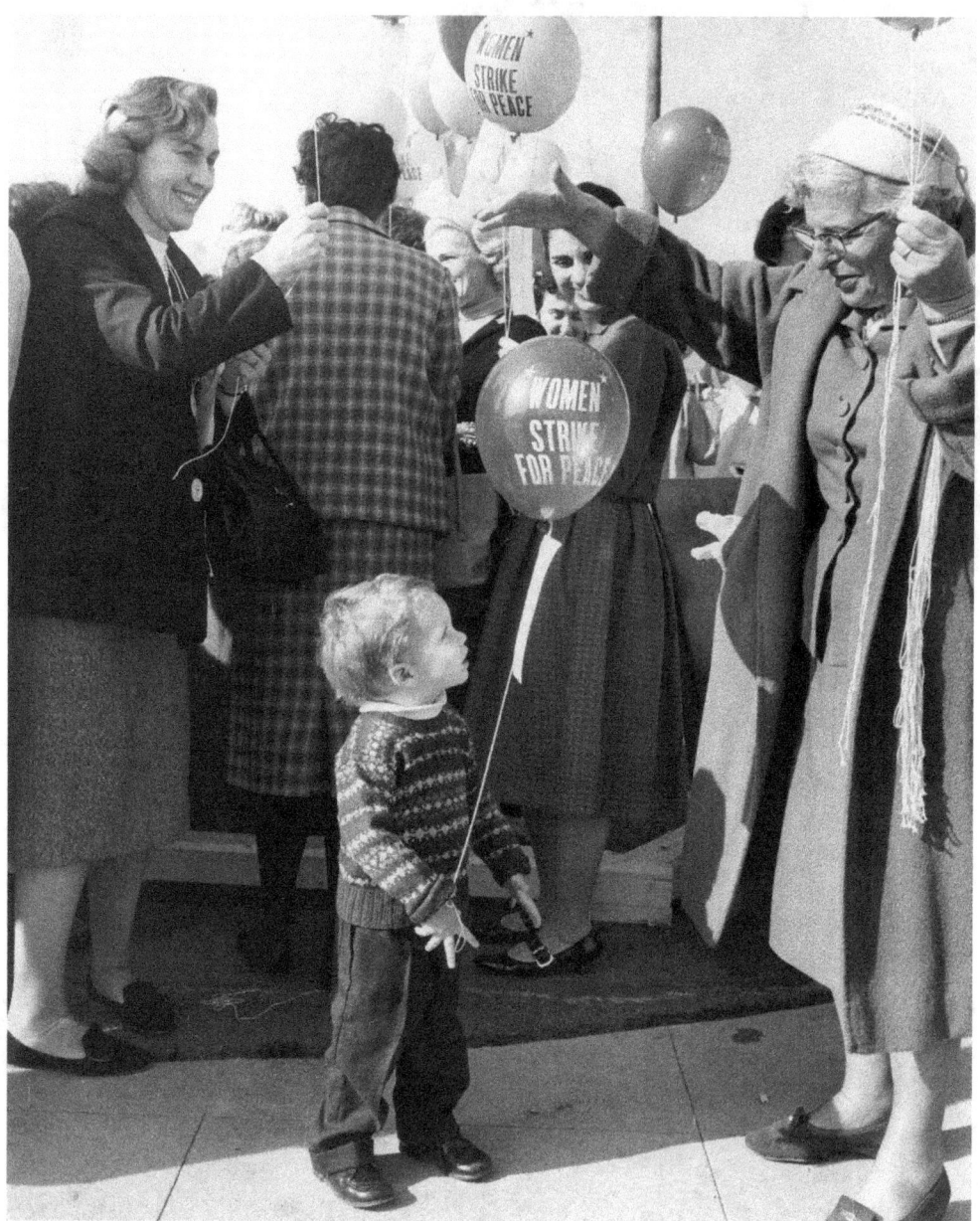

Valley residents participate in a Women's International Strike for Peace (WISFP) in Hancock Park where 4,000 balloons were released with notes outlining the beliefs of the WISFP.
January 15, 1962. (Gordon Dean)
(Order #00082906)

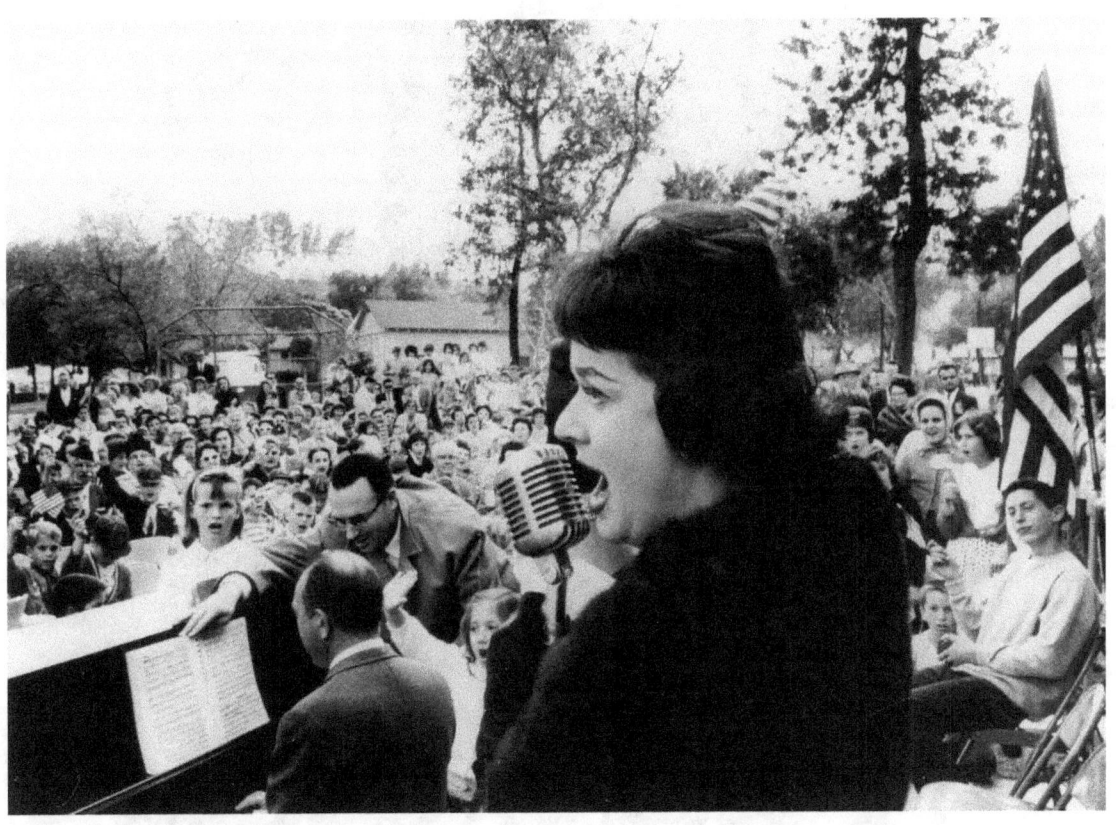

"Miss [Gisele] MacKenzie, honorary mayor of Encino, sings a pair of patriotic songs during an old-fashioned freedom rally in Encino Park in honor of Washington's birthday. More than 1,200 people attended the rally, sponsored jointly by Rotary, Kiwanis and Optimist Clubs, Chamber of Commerce, Community Center, Breakfast Club, Business and Professional Woman's Club Historical Society, American Legion, 4-H and Altrusa Clubs, Camp Fire Girls and Girl and Boy Scout units."
February 23, 1962. (George Brich)
(Order #00021814)

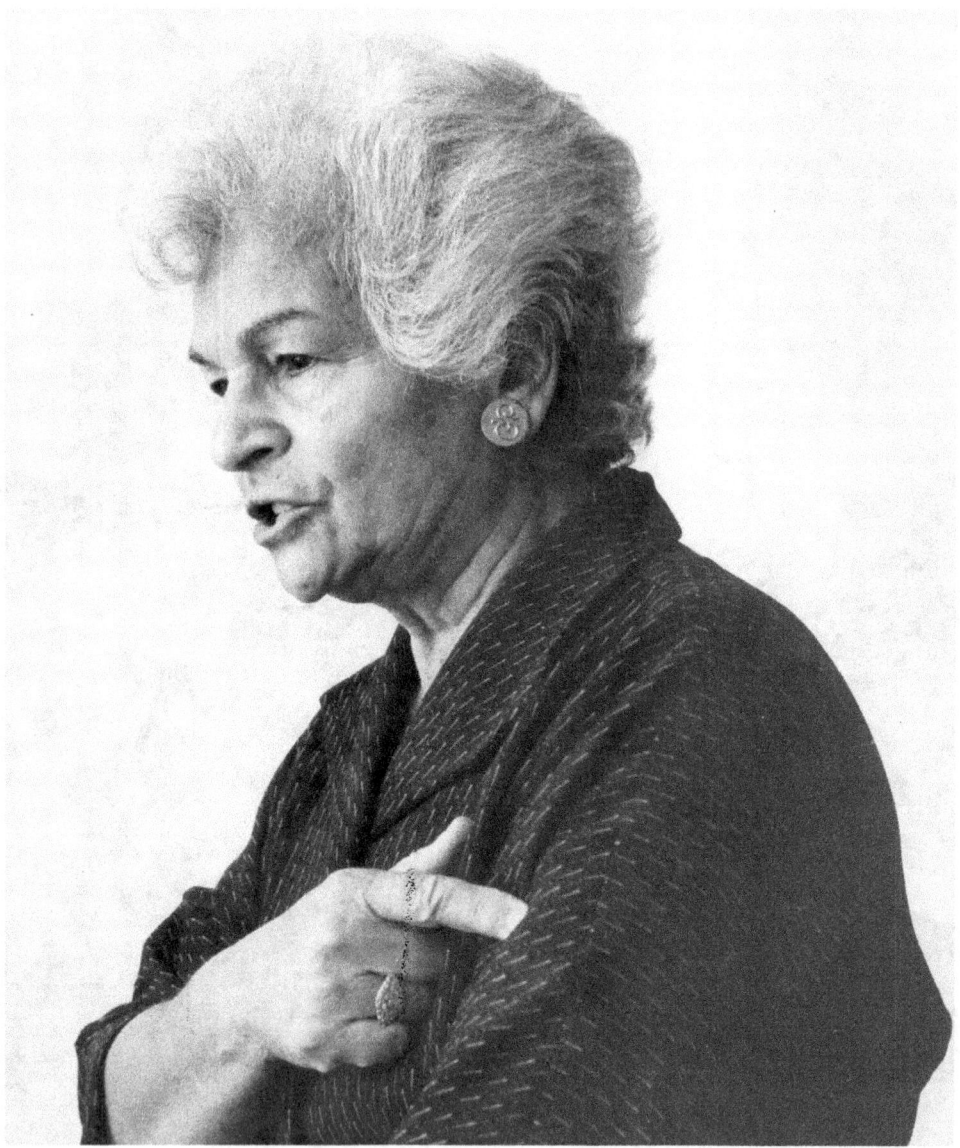

"Mrs. Sadie Weiss O'Sullivan points to her arm today as she related how she tore swastika arm band from shirt of American Nazi." O'Sullivan tore the armband from a man picketing a dinner for Democratic Congressman James Corman at the Sportsmen's Lodge in Studio City. "When I saw this guy in that uniform with that swastika, my blood just boiled. I saw red."
October 21, 1964. (George Brich)

(Order #00111797)

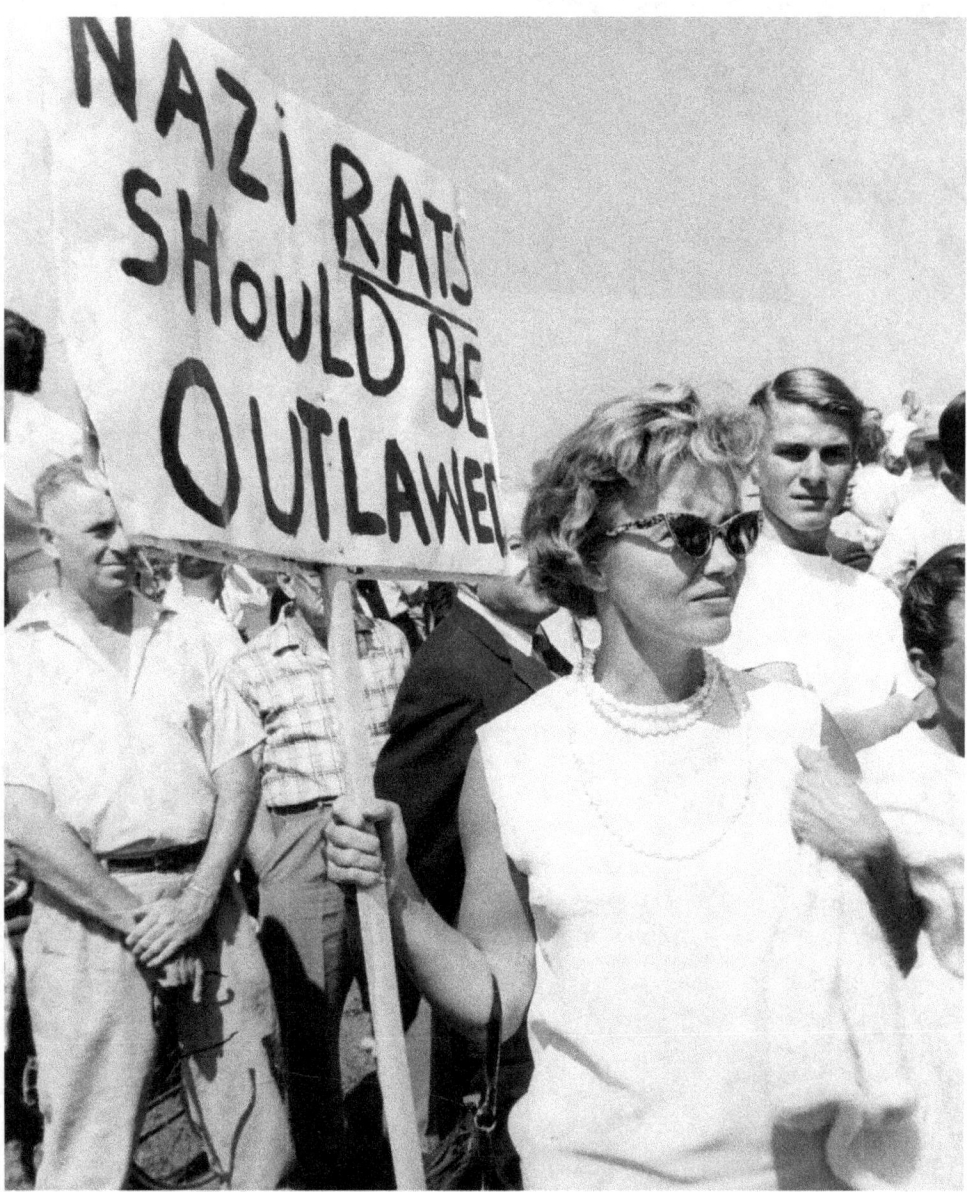

Mrs. Lillian Needleman is one of 125 people protesting a rally lead by Ralph P. Forbes of the American Nazi Party at McCambridge Park in Burbank. Forbes originally intended to hold the rally on the steps of Burbank City Hall, but was denied access and instead received a permit for the park instead.
August 1963. (Gordon Dean)

(Order #00082899)

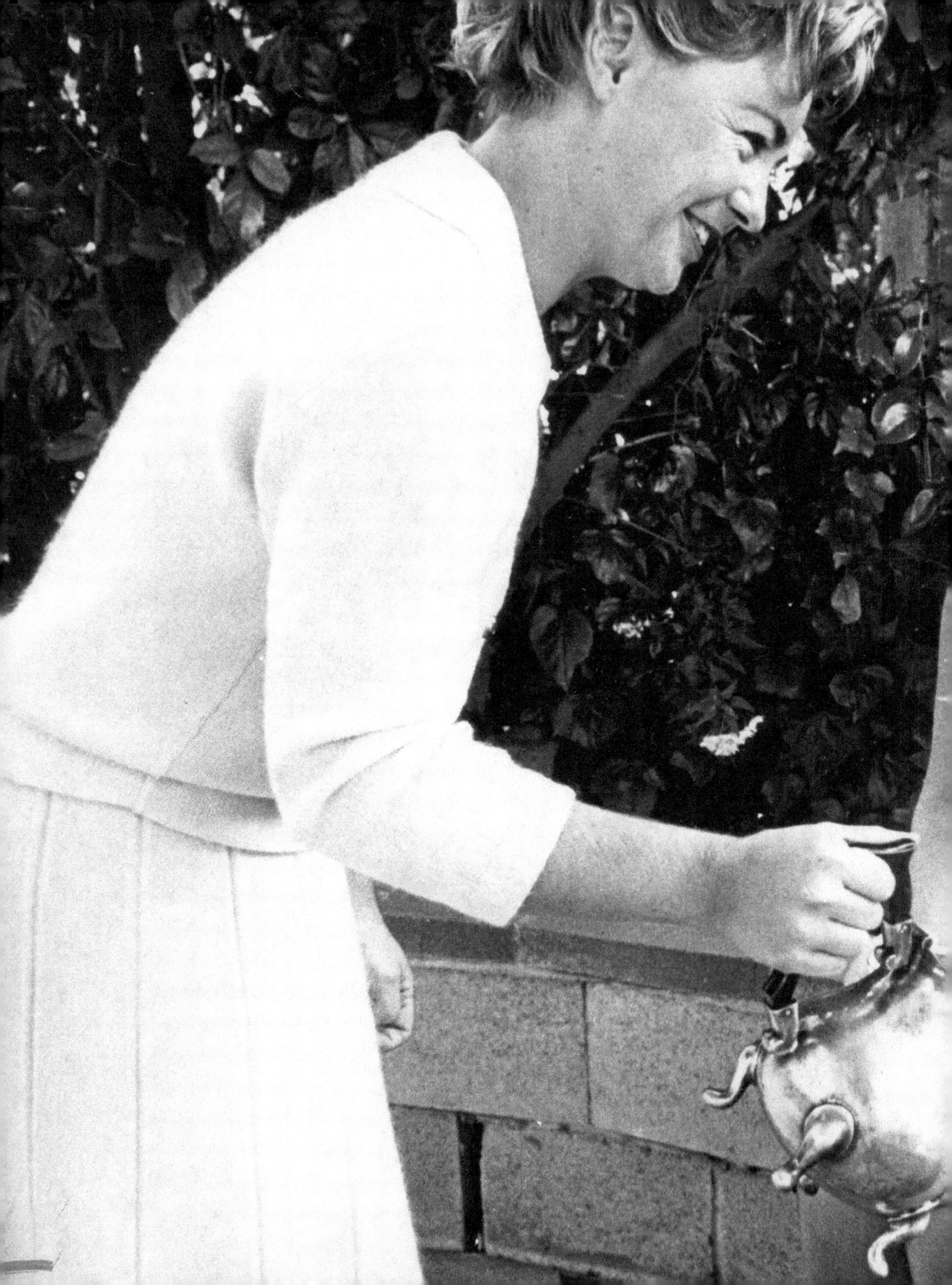

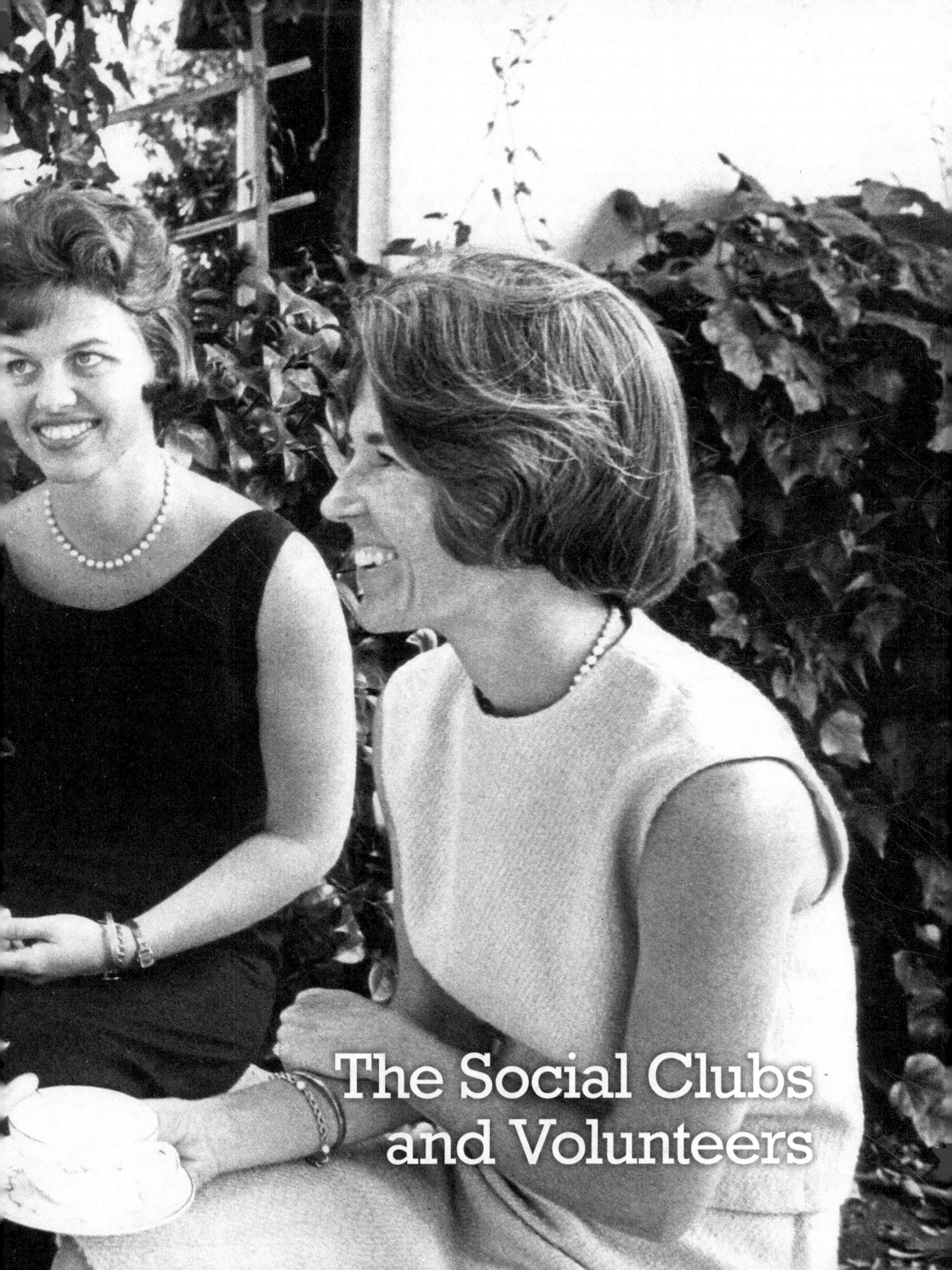

The Social Clubs
and Volunteers

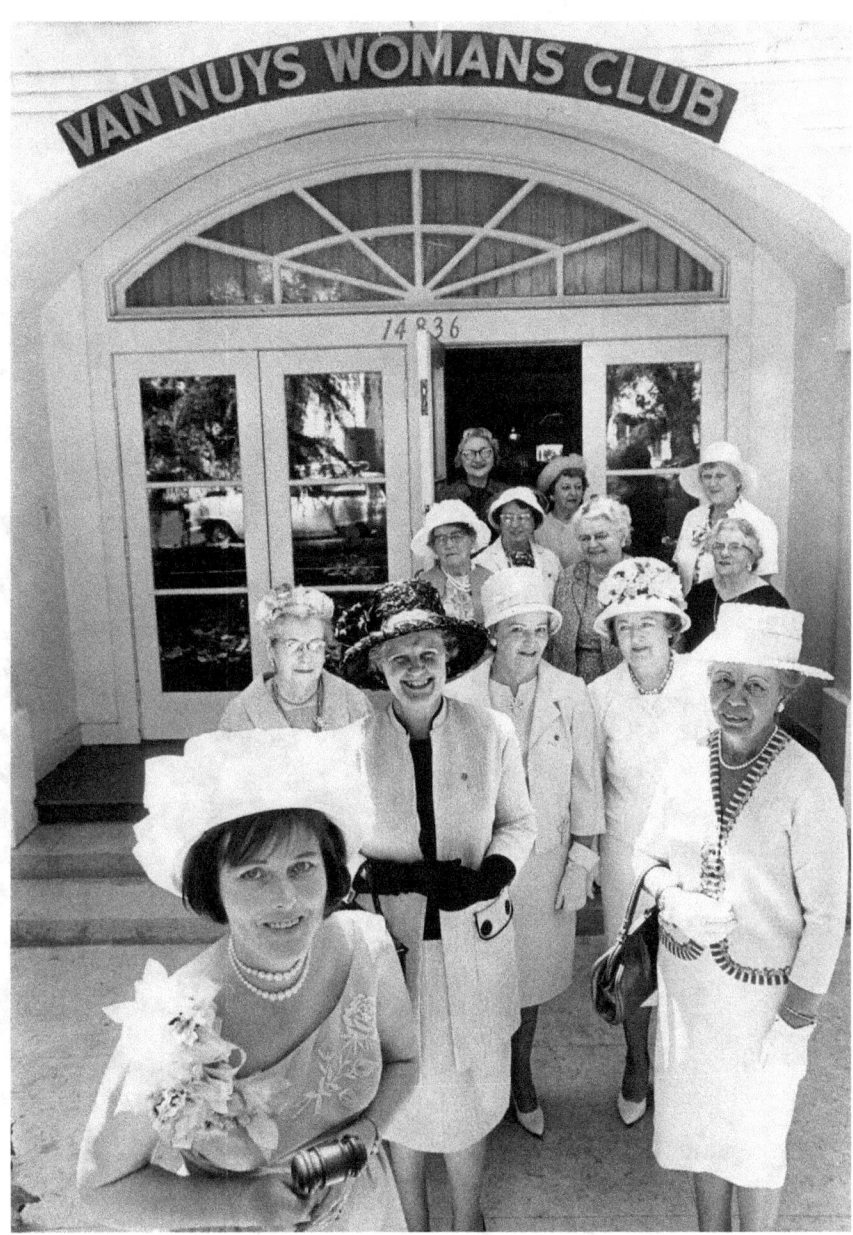

The Van Nuys Woman's Club honoring its past presidents at a recent charter day celebration. Club was organized on April 3, 1912, and federated in July of 1912.
1965. (George Brich)
(Order #00033930)

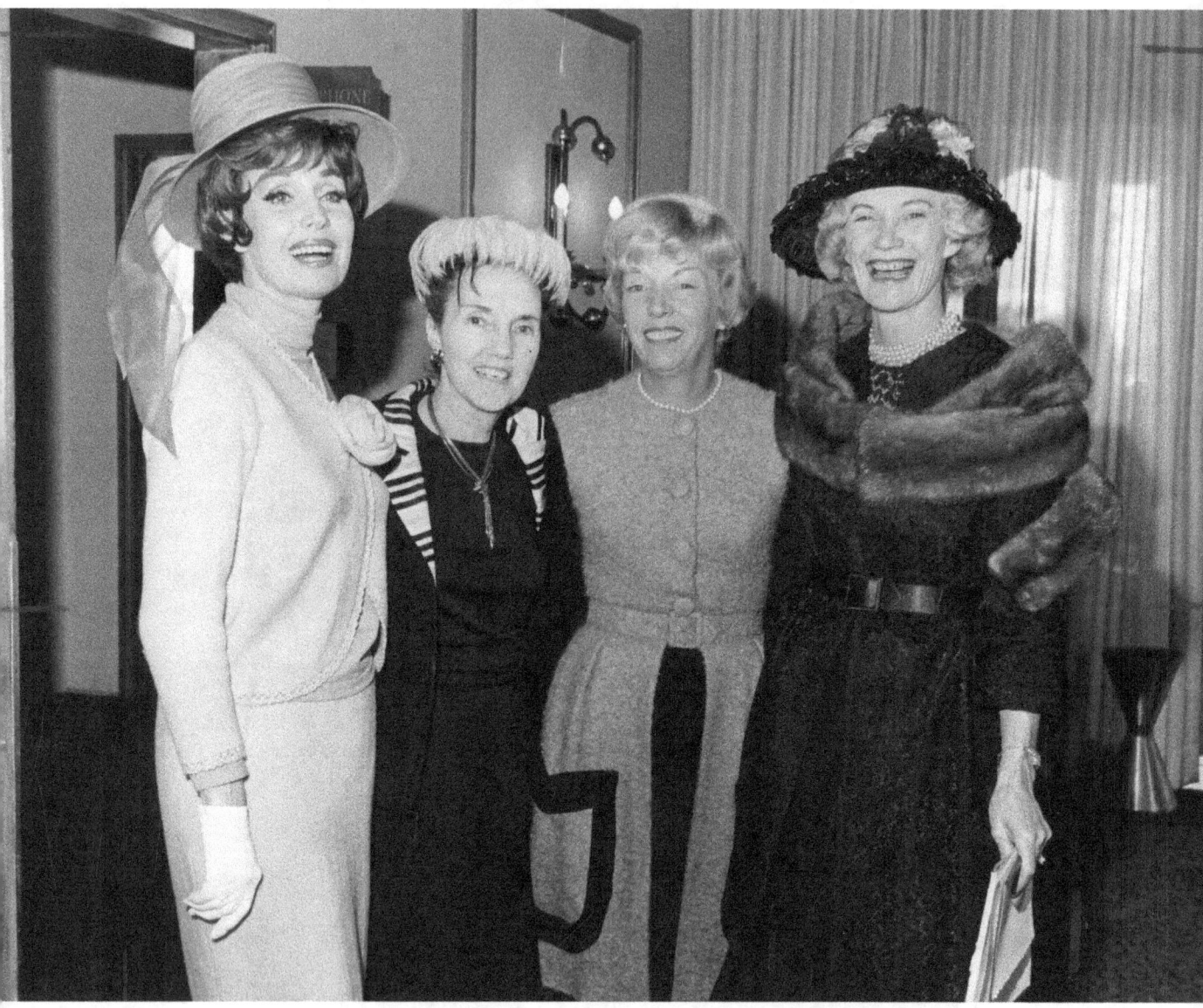

"Gathered at annual fashion-luncheon sponsored by the Sherman Oaks Chamber of Commerce Women's Division are, from left, Dorothy Shreve, fashion coordinator; Mrs. E.J. Turner, manager of the Sherman Oaks Chamber of Commerce; Mrs. Samuel W. Yorty, wife of Los Angeles mayor, and Mrs. Richard R. Roe, Women's Division president. The event, themed 'Round the Clock Fashions,' was held Tuesday at the Sportmen's Lodge, Studio City." February 19, 1965. (Tom Kravitz)
(Order #00031111)

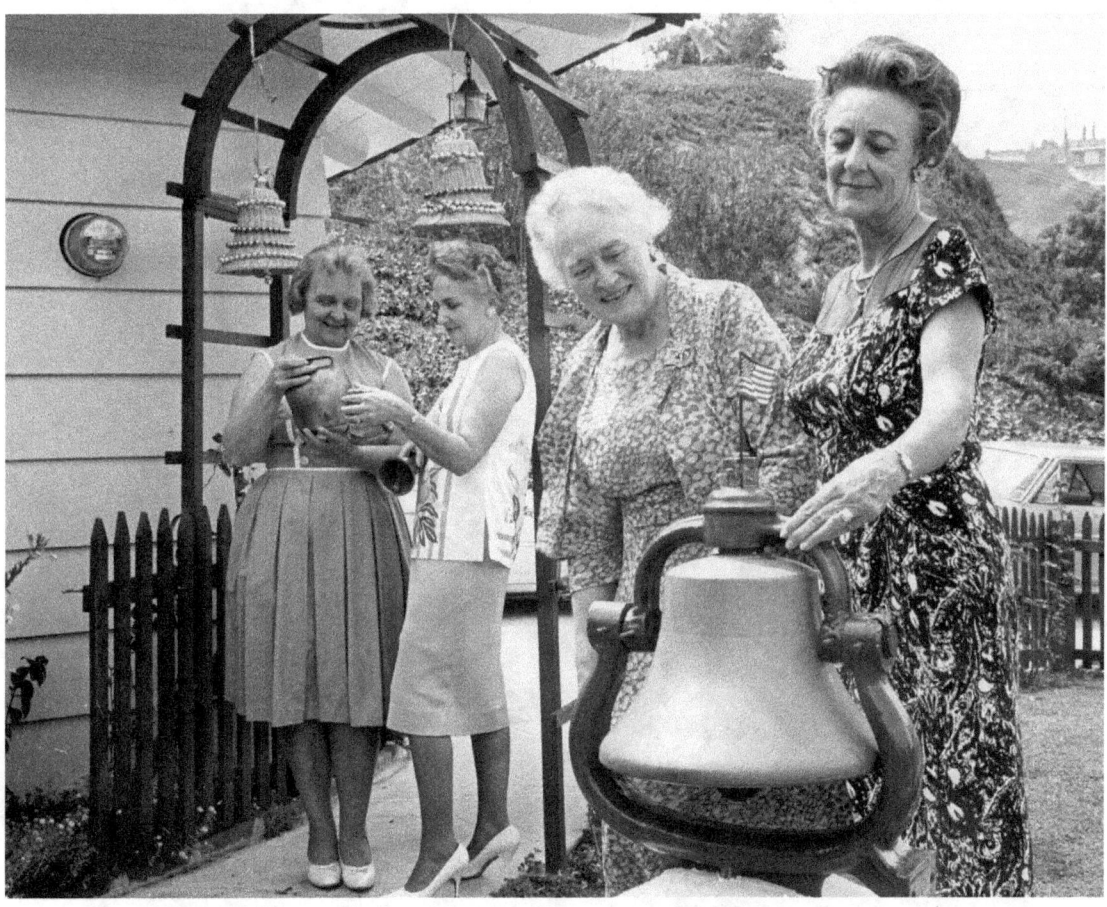

Sherman Oaks Women's Club members Mrs. Vivian McLorinan; left, Mrs. A.M. Beach; Mrs. Herbert H. Siddall; and, Mrs. Harry Loud, are assisting the California Federation of Women's Clubs in the federation's project to restore the bells along El Camino Real from Los Angeles to San Diego.
1965. (Gordon Dean)
(Order #00031119)

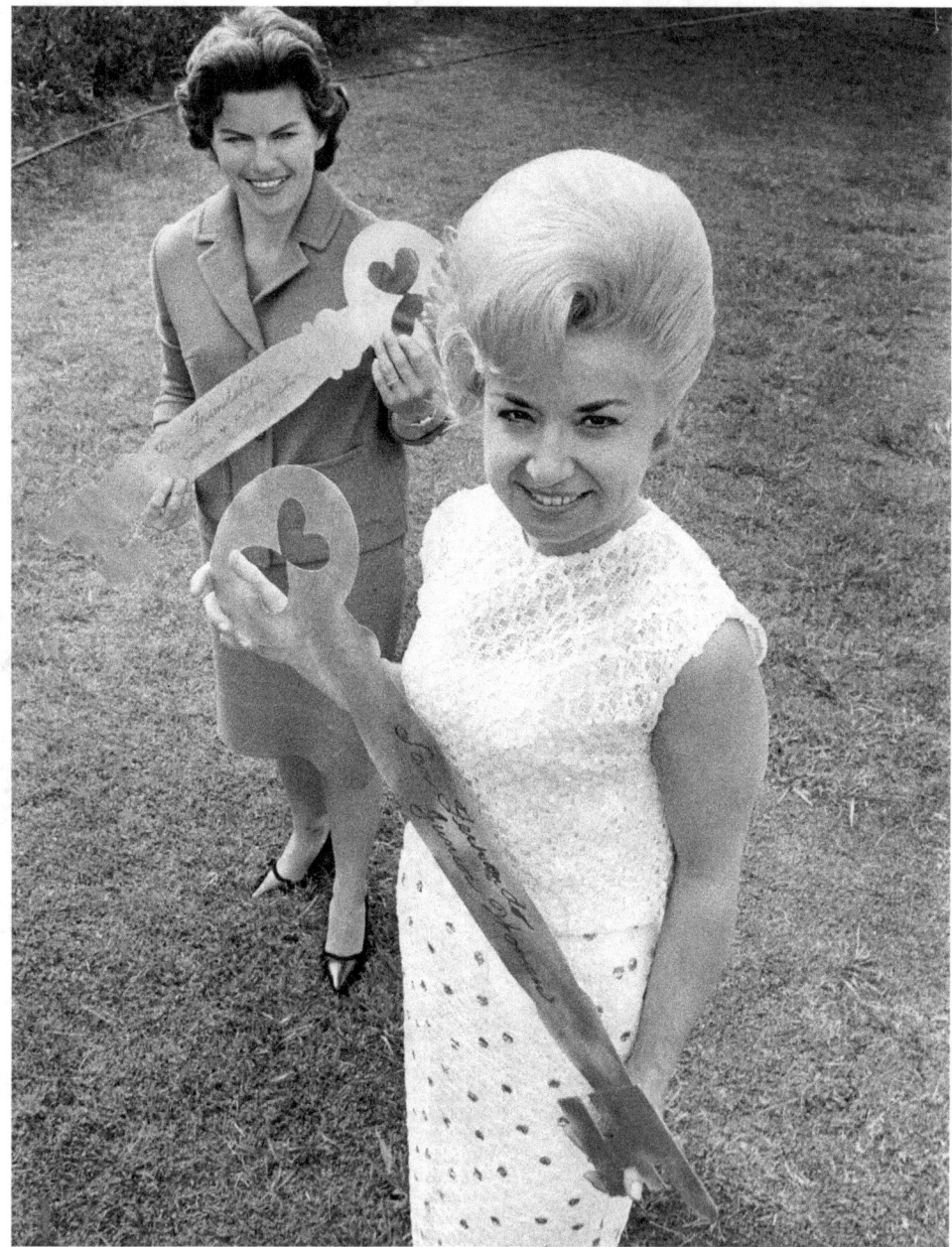

Mrs. Vern Allen, president, front, and Mrs. John Greenway, ways and means chairman of San Fernando Junior Women's Club, hold large gold keys spelling out the theme of a fall fashion show to be held as a fundraiser.
1964. (Order #00031509)

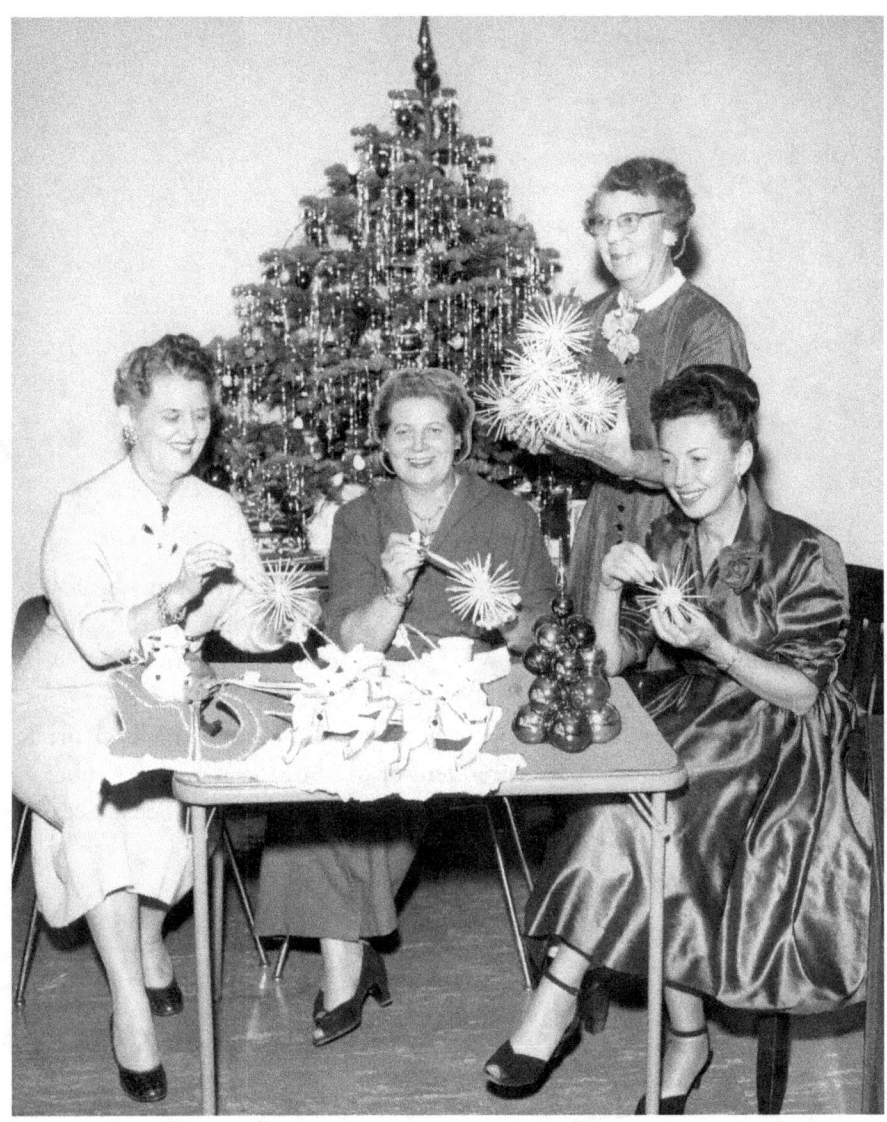

"Project chairman Mrs. Marvin Owen, seated, center, is busy with other
North Hollywood Zonta Club members in putting finishing touches
to items they are selling for benefit of Valley Youth Foundation. Club
president Lucille Raport, right, Dessie Miller, first vice president, and Mary
Hornaday, secretary, standing, represent membership which is donating
time and efforts to completing and delivering orders before the holidays."
December 14, 1955. (Justin Westerfield)

(Order #00082745)

"More than 500 Valley and Los Angeles women shared tea and pleasantries at Mayor Samuel Yorty's reception honoring Women Commissioners of the City of Los Angeles. Among prominent Valley women who took part, photo above, were Mrs. John Scully, Woodland Hills, president of the Valley Volunteer League, and standing, from left, Mmes. Irving Wieder, Sherman Oaks, arrangements chairman for the tea, Lou Holzer, Tarzana, vice president of the Tarzana Women's Club, and Joseph McKinstry, Sherman Oaks, member of the Los Angeles Social Service Commission."
May 16, 1964. (Order #00112154)

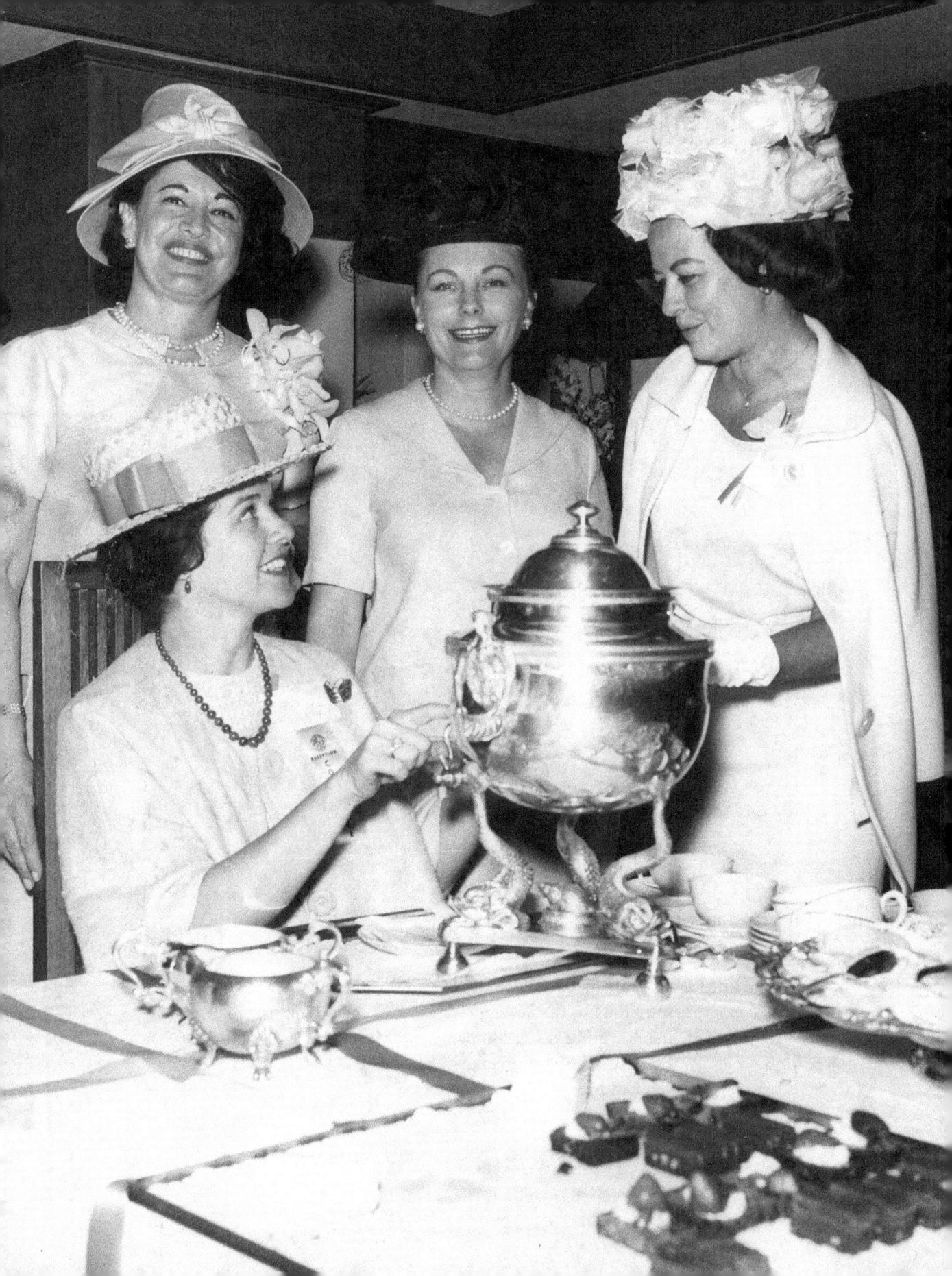

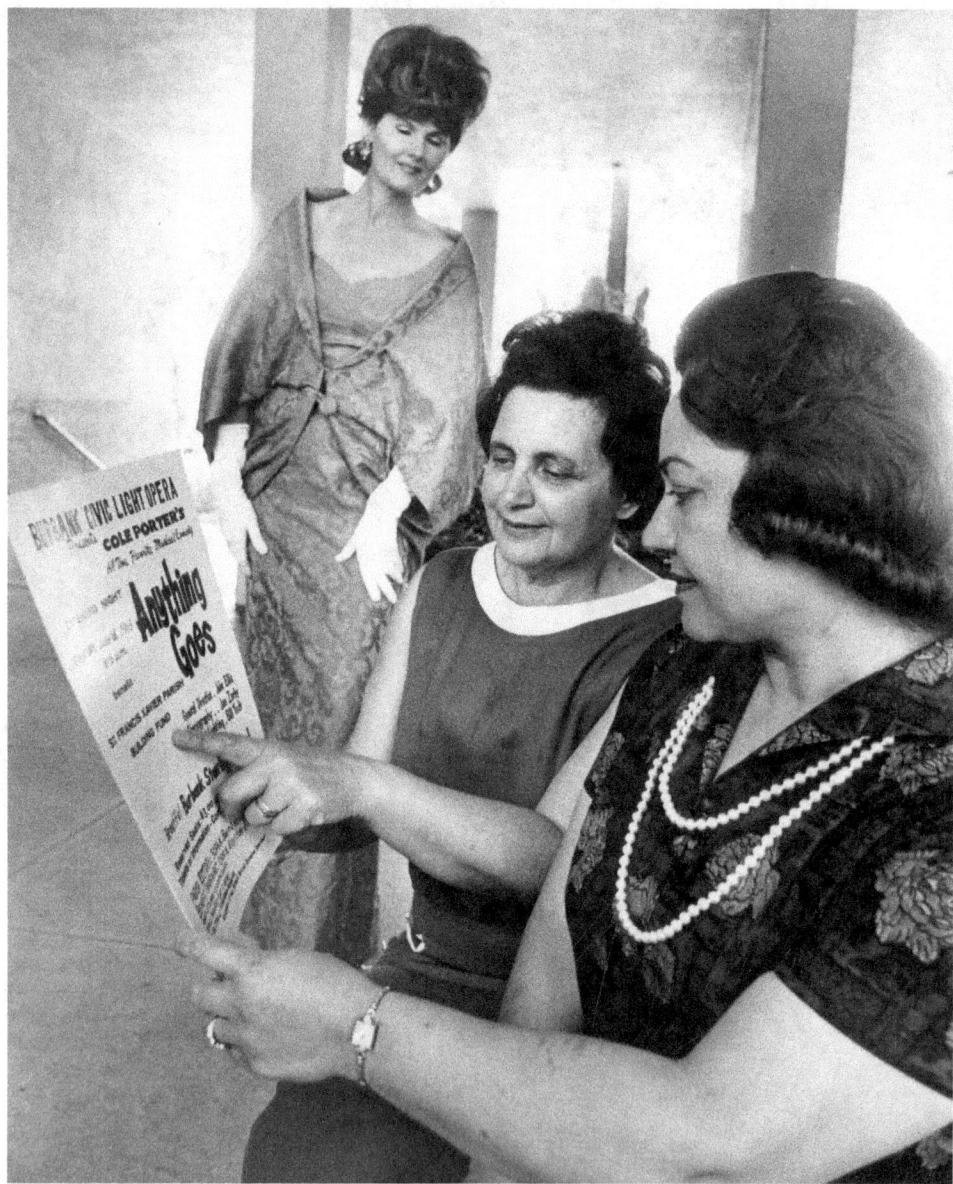

"Preparing for the Burbank Civic Light Opera production of Cole Porter's *Anything Goes* sponsored by the St. Francis Xavier Women's Council are, from left, Jane Hyland, member of the opera company; and Mmes. Vincent Orlando of Sun Valley and Warren Ettleman of Burbank."
July 2, 1965. (Jeff Goldwater)
(Order #00108699)

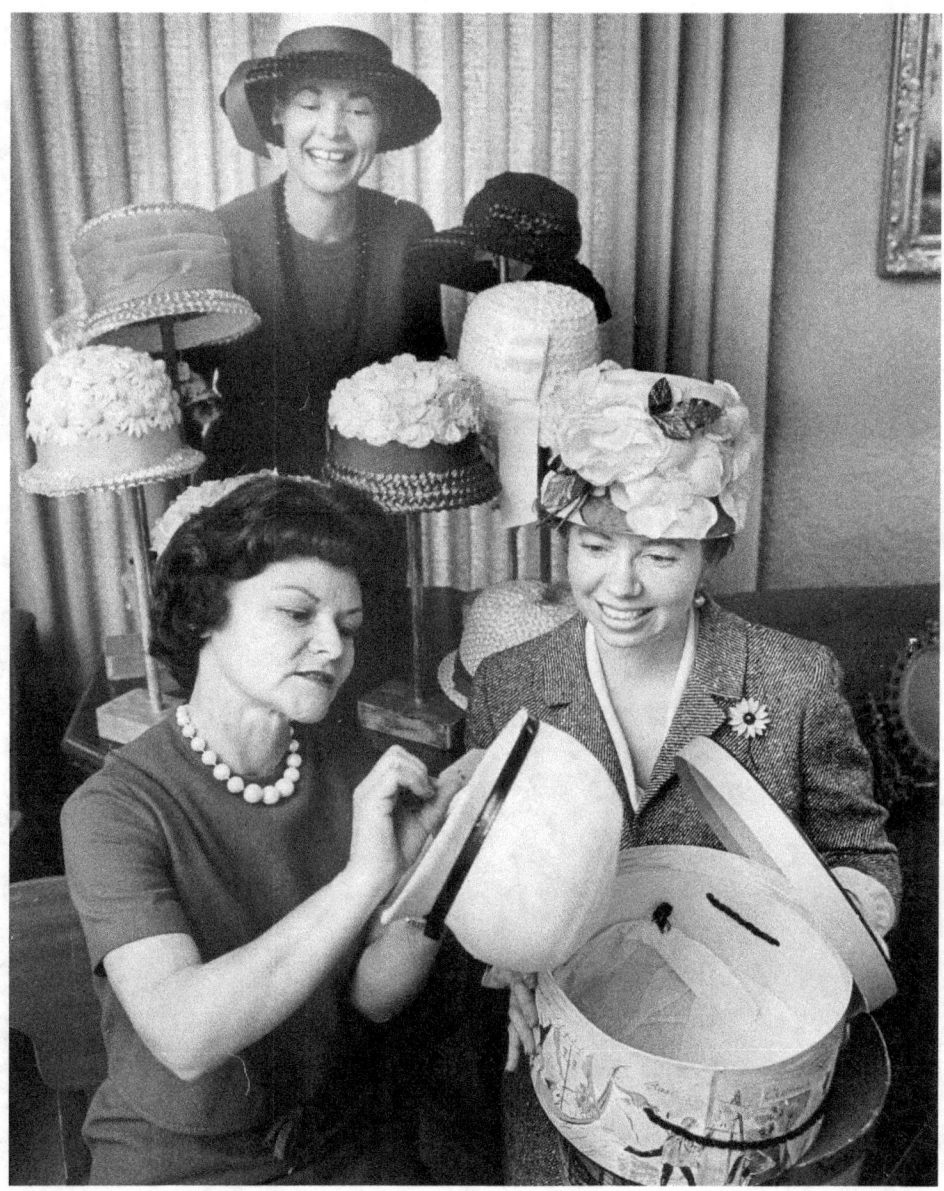

"Looking over hats for the St. Patrick's Day Spring Bonnet Brunch are members of the North Hollywood Woman's Club, Mmes. George Jacques, front left; Donald Villee and Robert Simgen, back, chairman. The event will be held at 10:30 a.m. March 17 at the clubhouse, 5629 Vineland Ave."
March 9, 1965. (George Brich)
(Order #00082771)

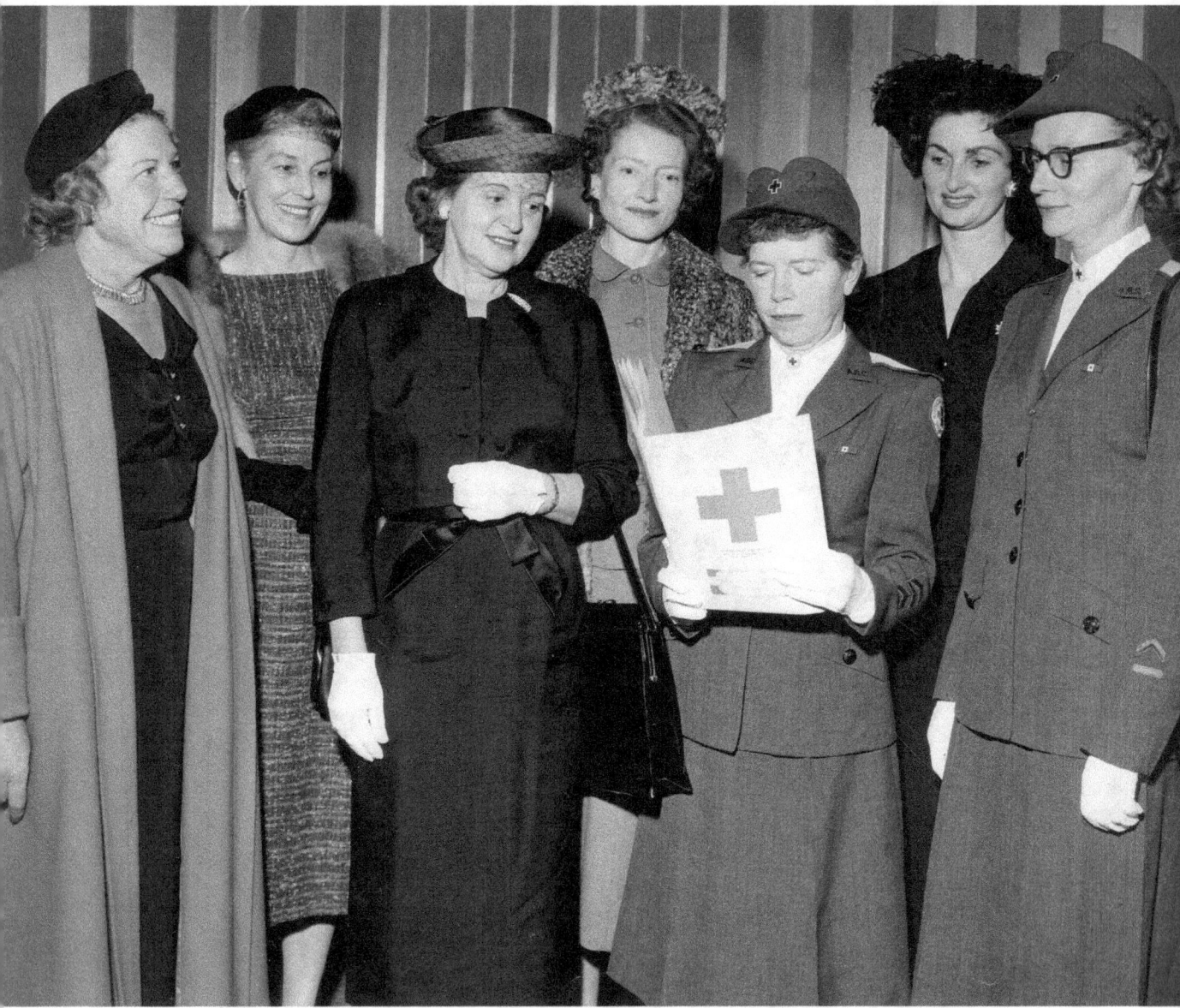

"Community volunteer workers for Valley Red Cross fund campaign hold meeting to formulate plans for forthcoming drive which will begin March 1 with Valleywide goal of $200,000. Workers, from left, are Mmes. A.L. Ethridge, Dean S Conklin, C. Paul Vogel, D.L. Haile and George S. Dudley, all of Studio City; Howard Hinig, North Hollywood, and R.L. Kisteler, West Van Nuys."

February 22, 1958. (Order #00084447)

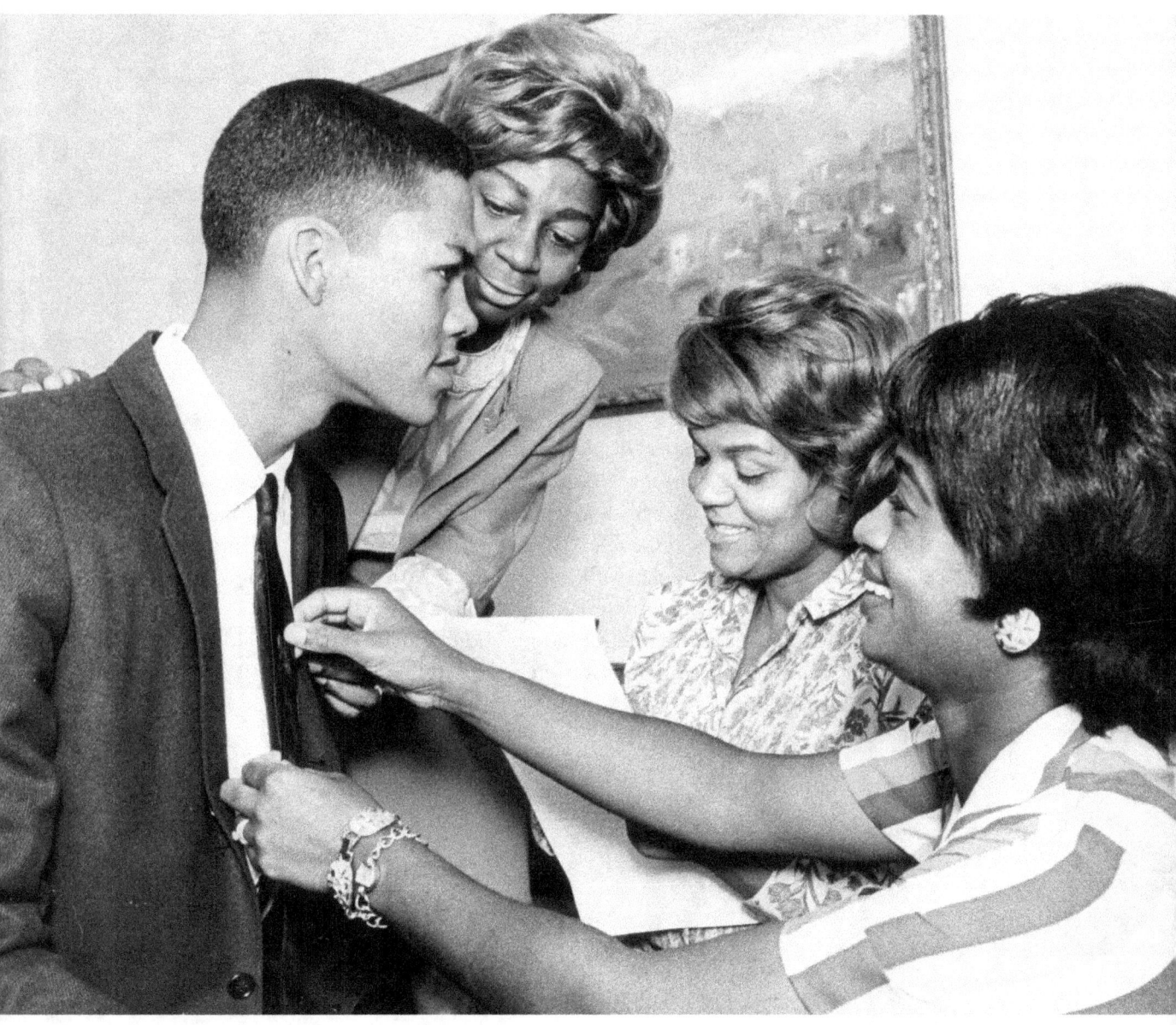

Lloyd Watson, 18, gets hints and confidence from founders of a North Valley group, Neighbors for Community Understanding dedicated to helping the Negro prepare for employment and community life. Women are, from left, Mmes Walter Dore, Ira Madison and Arthur C. Seiffert."
October 29, 1963. (George Brich)

(Offline image)

"Alpha Chi Omega Alumnae members display their favorite desserts. They are, front, Mrs. James A. Hawkins, Tarzana; second row, Mrs. Charles Borst, Canoga Park, president, left, and Mrs. James Shellaberger, Northridge, and last row, Mmes. Robert Laird, Northridge, left, and George T. Zinn and Ralph Phillips, Woodland Hills." Mrs. Charles G. Borst president of West Valley Alumnae of Alpha Chi Omega hosted a "Dessert Fun" at her first meeting. Each member brought a dessert then bite size samples where sold for 2 cents and dessert recipes were sold for 10 cents. The club's fund raising went to Cerebral Palsy charities.
May 27, 1964. (George Brich)
(Order #00085522)

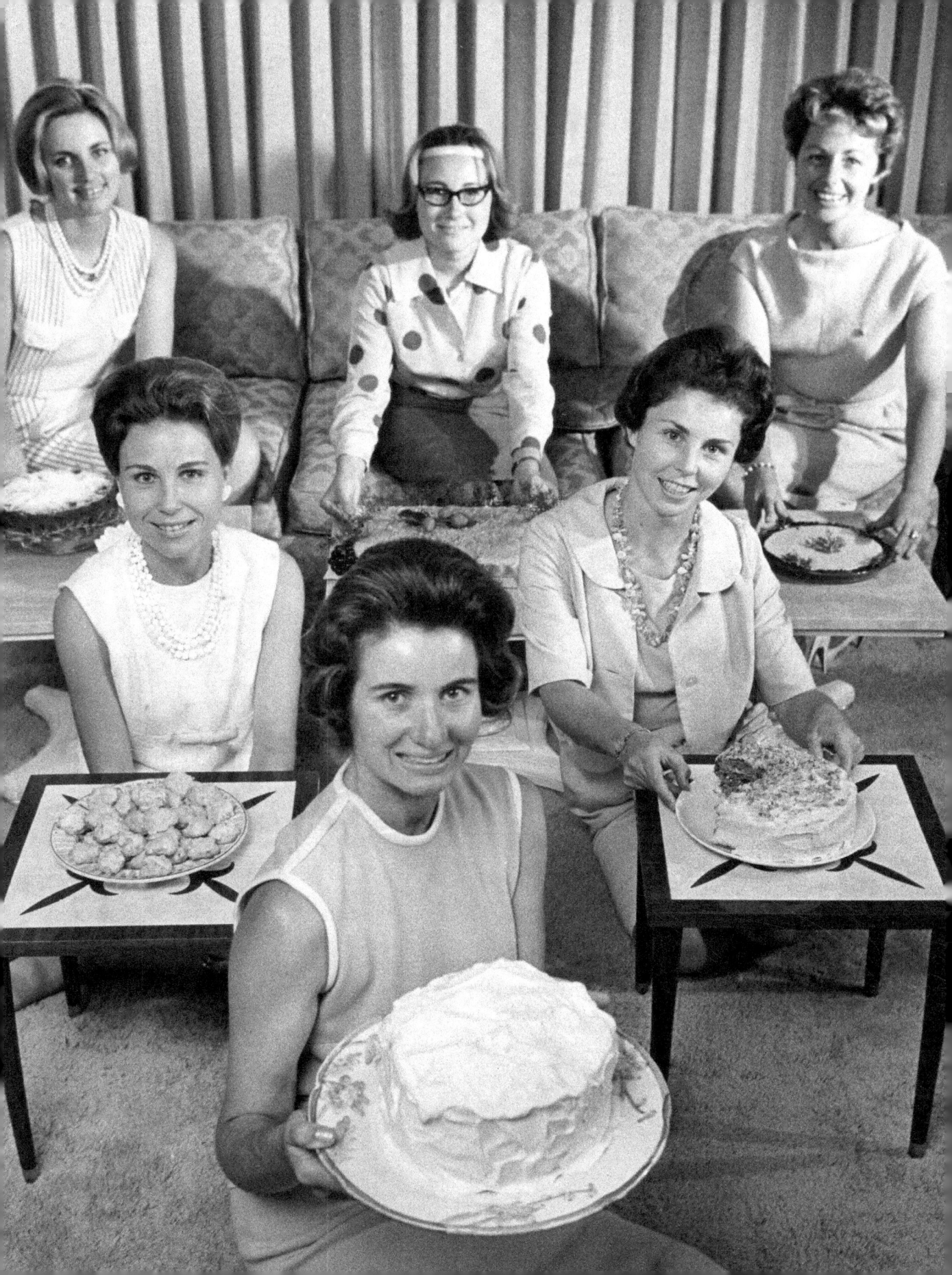

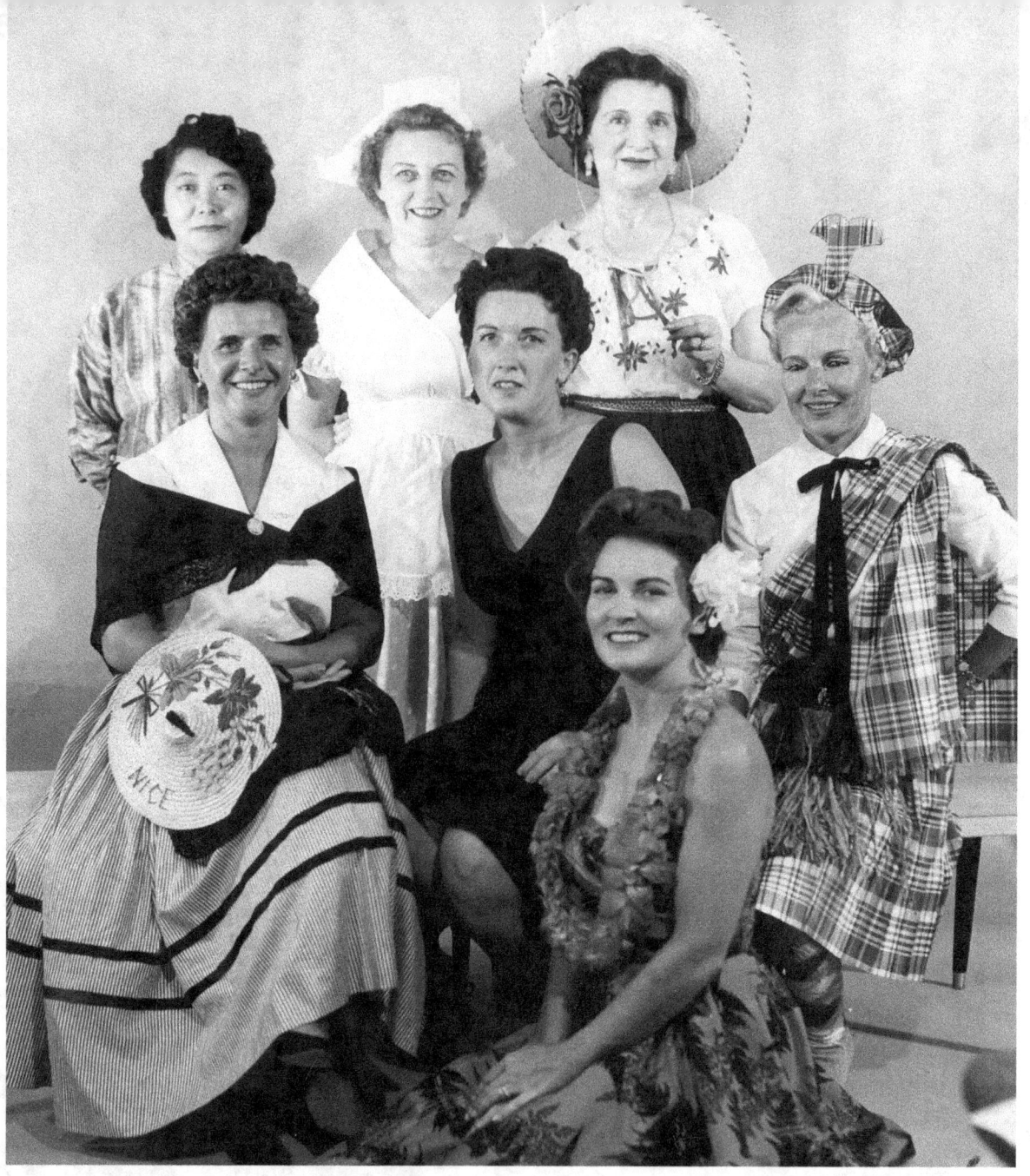

"Members of Tarzana Business and Professional Women's Club are planning for tonight's dinner meeting which is to carry out club's year theme 'International Relations.' Assisting with program will be, back row from left, Sally Gohata, Alma Berndston, Theresa Fro Morris; center from left, Marie Louise Spencer, president, Eileen Morgan, Marion H. Burbridge; front, Donajean Fishwick."
February 4, 1960. (Bob Anderson)
(Order #00111978)

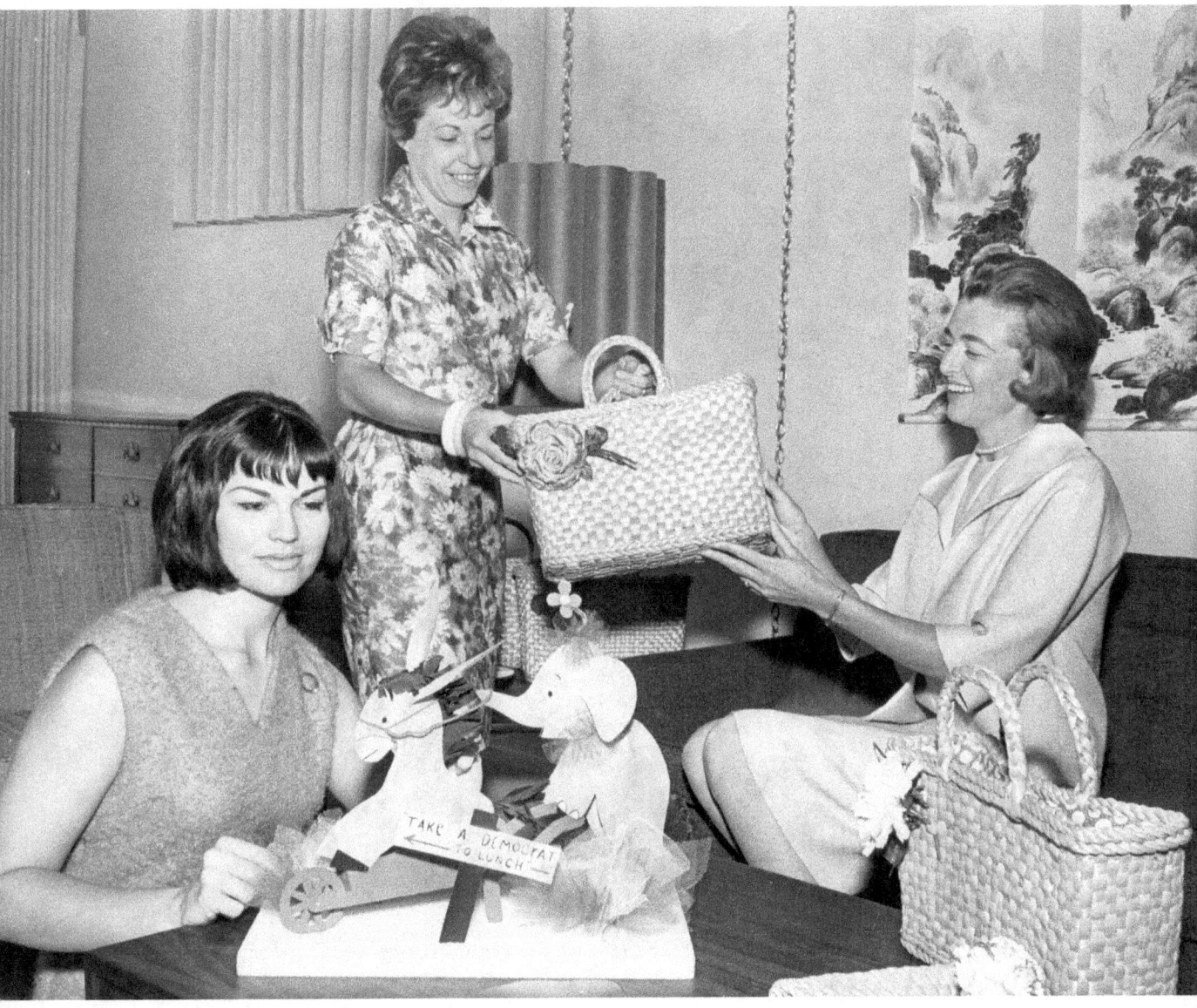

"Canoga Park Republican Women's Club members make plans for 'Take a Democrat to Lunch' event. From left are Mmes. James Johnson, Walter Greenawald and Robert Gourlay, event chairman. The 'strictly social' affair will be held on June 4 at the Canoga Park Women's Club."
May 28, 1965. (Gordon Dean)
(Order #00109822)

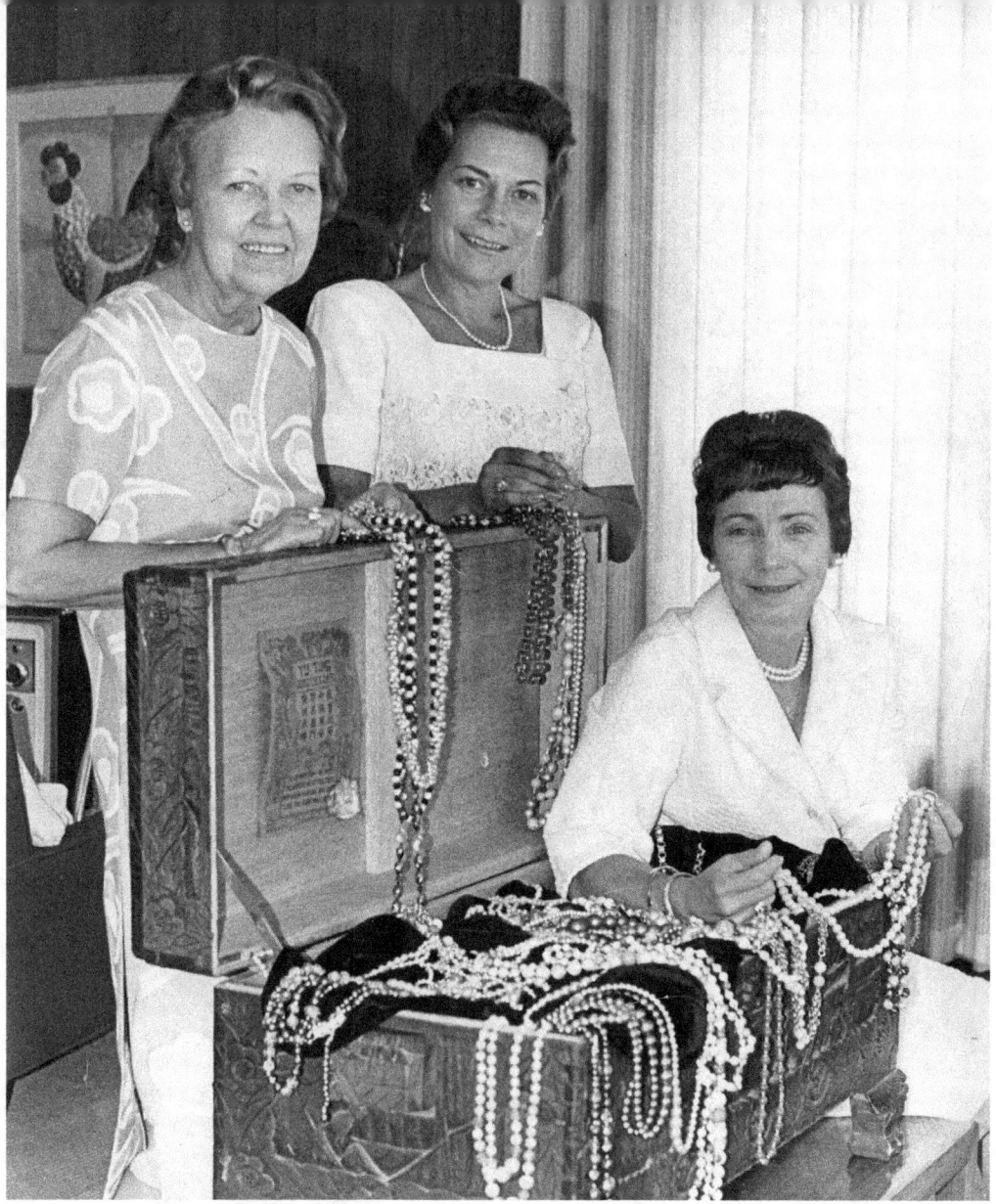

"The Friendly Hand Foundation will benefit from a dinner-dance sponsored by the Pandoras Sept. 26 at Lakeside Country Club in Toluca Lake. Social hour will begin at 7 p.m. Opening Pandora's Box as a symbol of the evening's theme of 'Hope' are Mmes. Roma Barto, left, and Victor McLeod, event chairman, both of Toluca lake, and Sheila Bartlett, reservations chairman, Brentwood. Mrs. McLeod explained that legend says that when Pandora opened the box she found Hope at the bottom. The Friendly Hand Foundation operates Friendly House, 347 S. Normandie Ave., Los Angeles, a home for alcoholic women."

September 11, 1964. (Steve Young)

(Order #00111037)

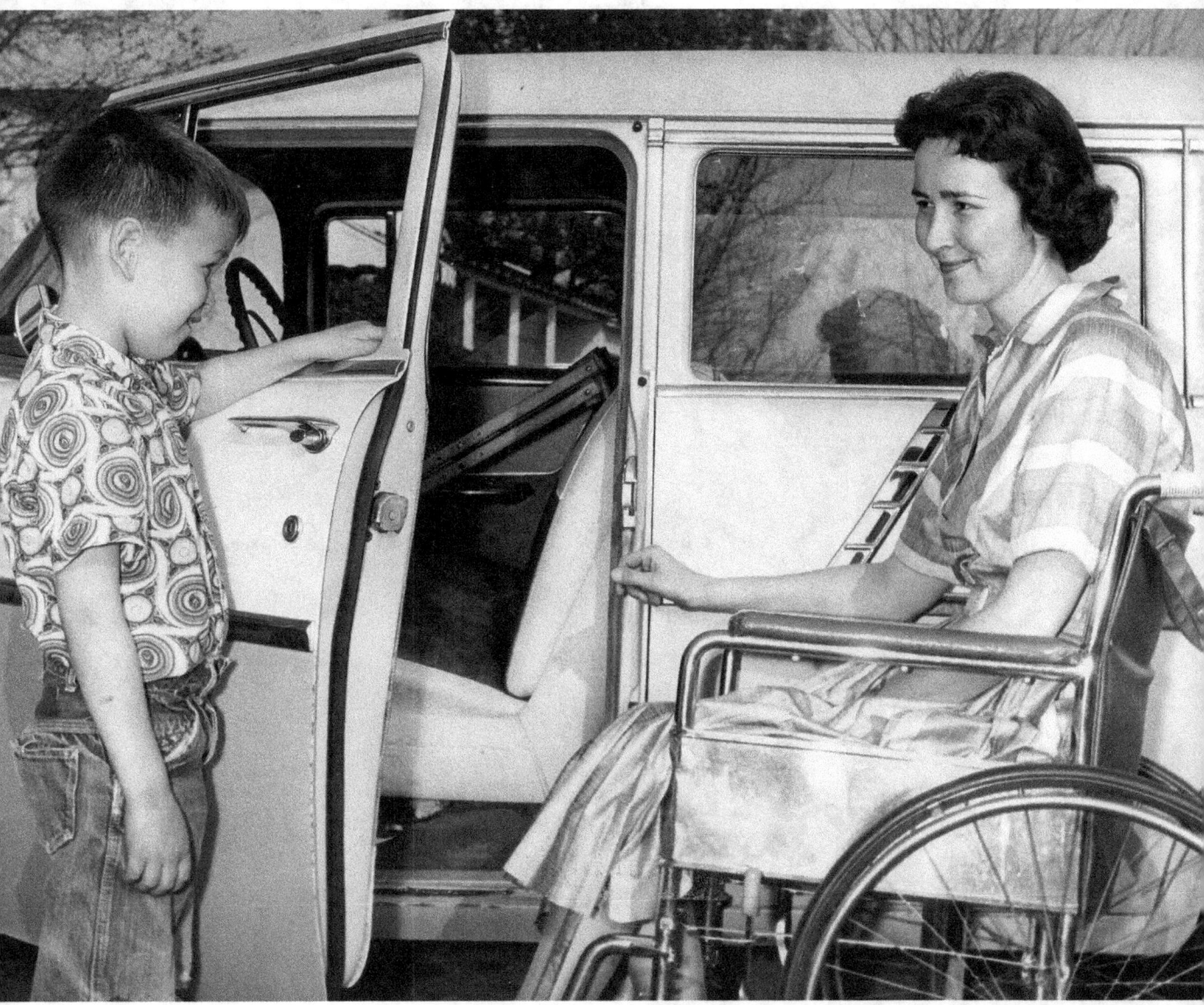

"Mrs. Billie Clinger, Reseda Division 1 chairman of Red Cross drive which opens tomorrow, prepares to enter car with aid of son, Mark, 5. Mrs. Clinger, from her home at 19623 Lorne St., gives leadership to four section chairmen and block leaders who prepare for annual Red Cross fund campaign. Mrs. Clinger says she remembers that Red Cross aided her when she suffered polio attack six years ago and again when her son was born."
March 14, 1960. (Order #00092452)

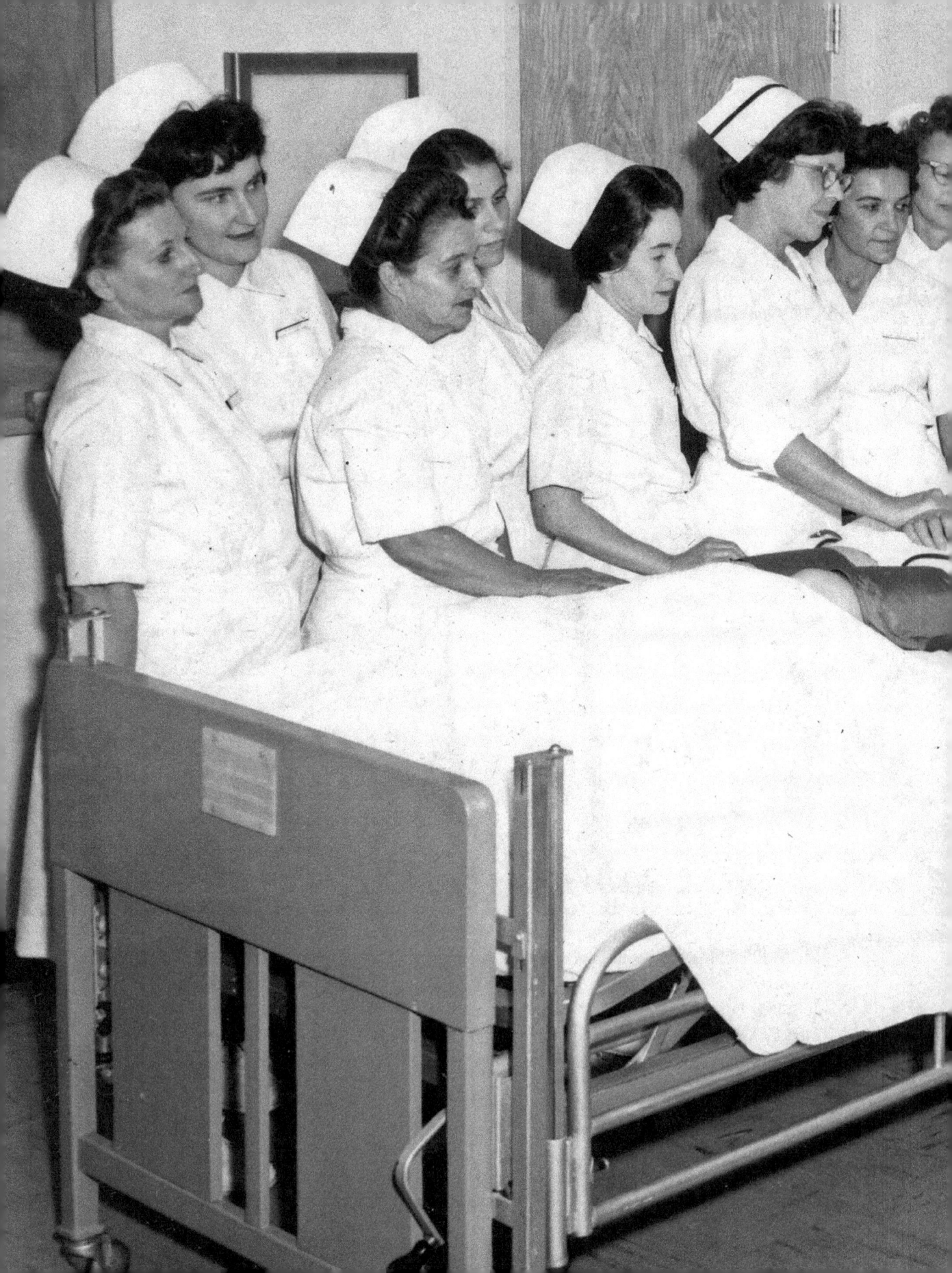

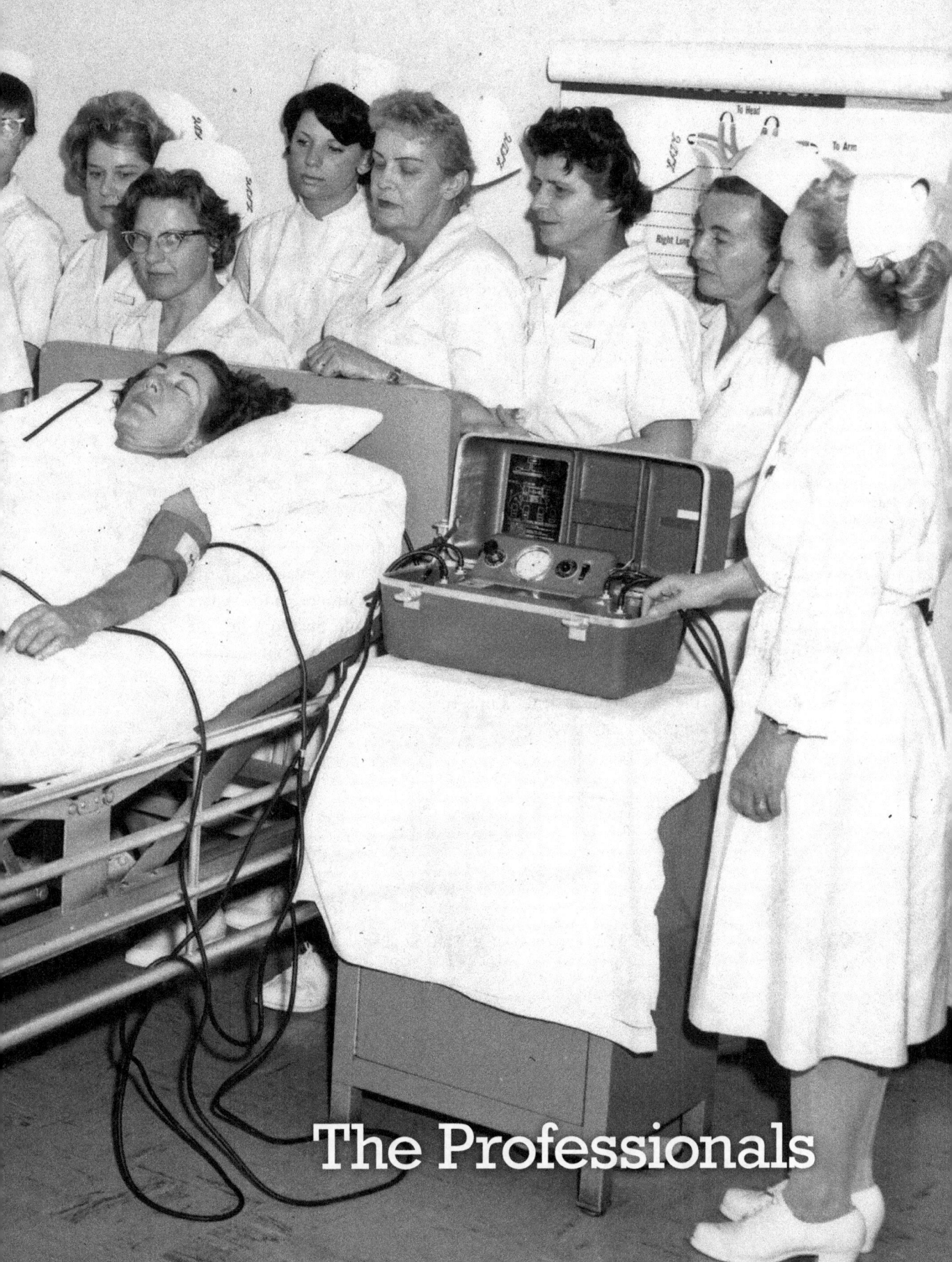

The Professionals

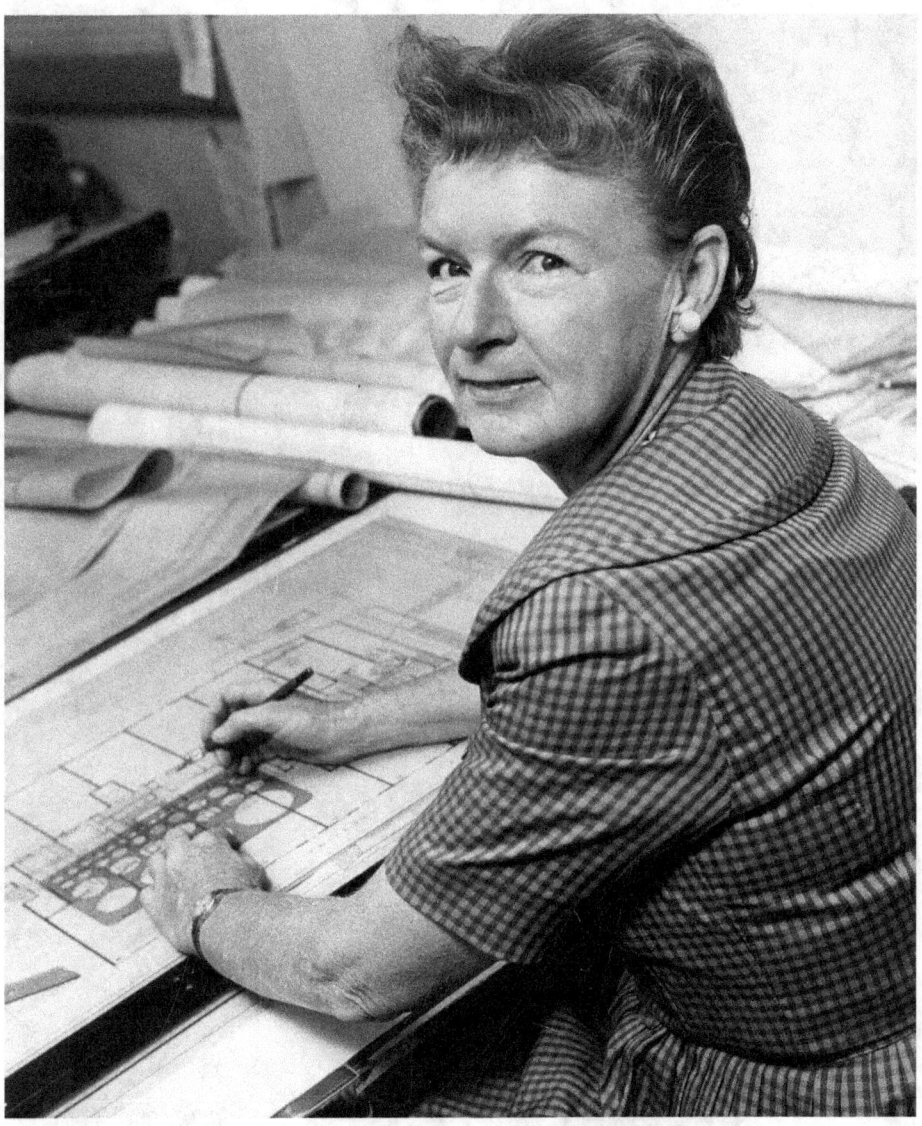

"The career of Jocelyn Domela, one of Los Angeles' ten top landscape architects, had its beginning as a hobby. Recent winner of Los Angeles Beautiful Award for the landscaping of Ralph C. Sutro Co. building on Wilshire Blvd., Mrs. Domela also has won cups for her work on the initial phase of NBC-TV studios in Burbank and an apartment building in Los Angeles. The trophies were given by Los Angeles Contractors Association."
August 15, 1960. (George Brich)

(Order #00108987)

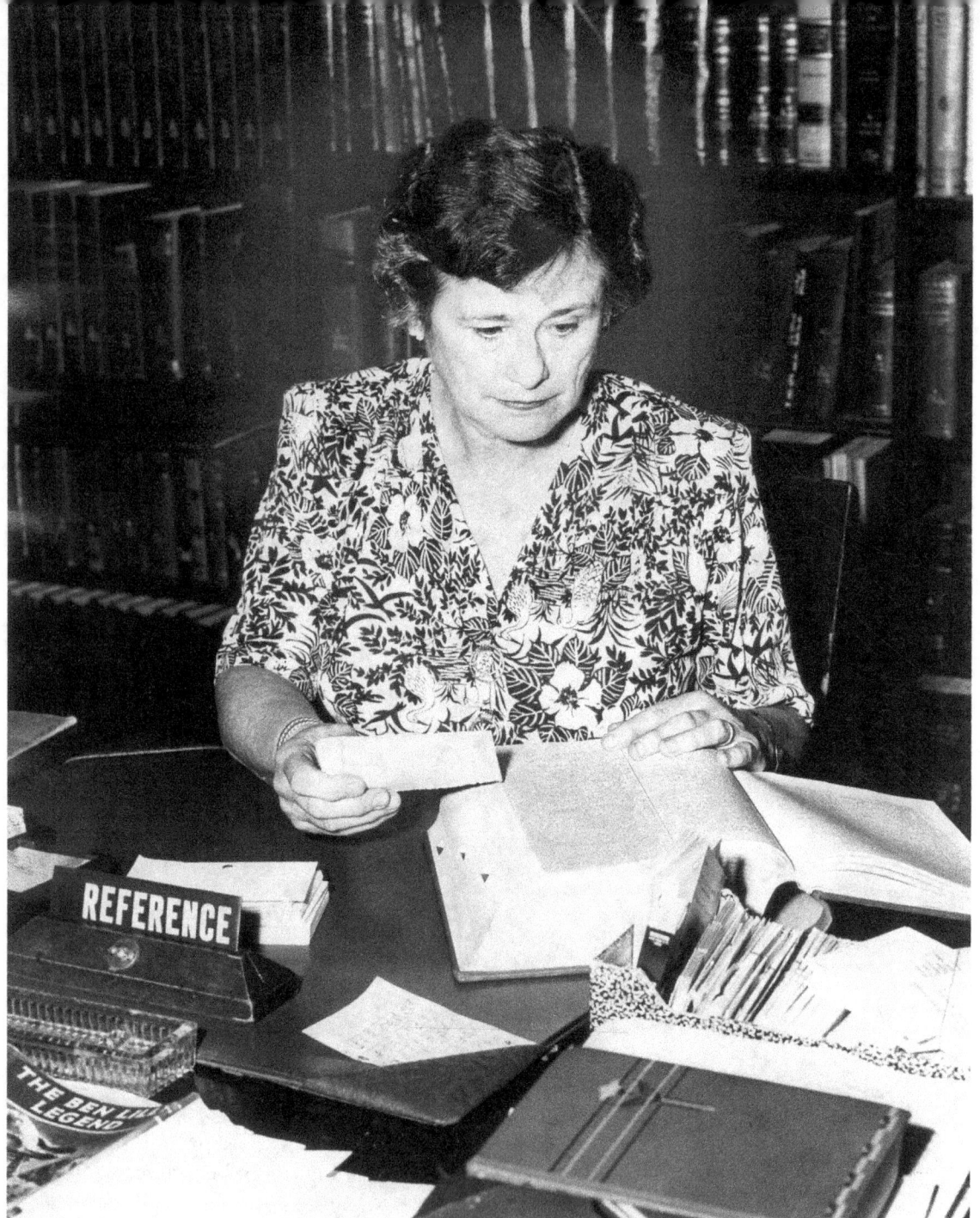

"Mrs. Helen Allen searches through a poetry reference book for the answer to a problem that worries a Valley resident. Fragments of poems can be traced and identified through careful searching in library research files." Allen was a librarian at the Los Angeles Public Library's North Hollywood branch.

July 11, 1950. (Order #00082688)

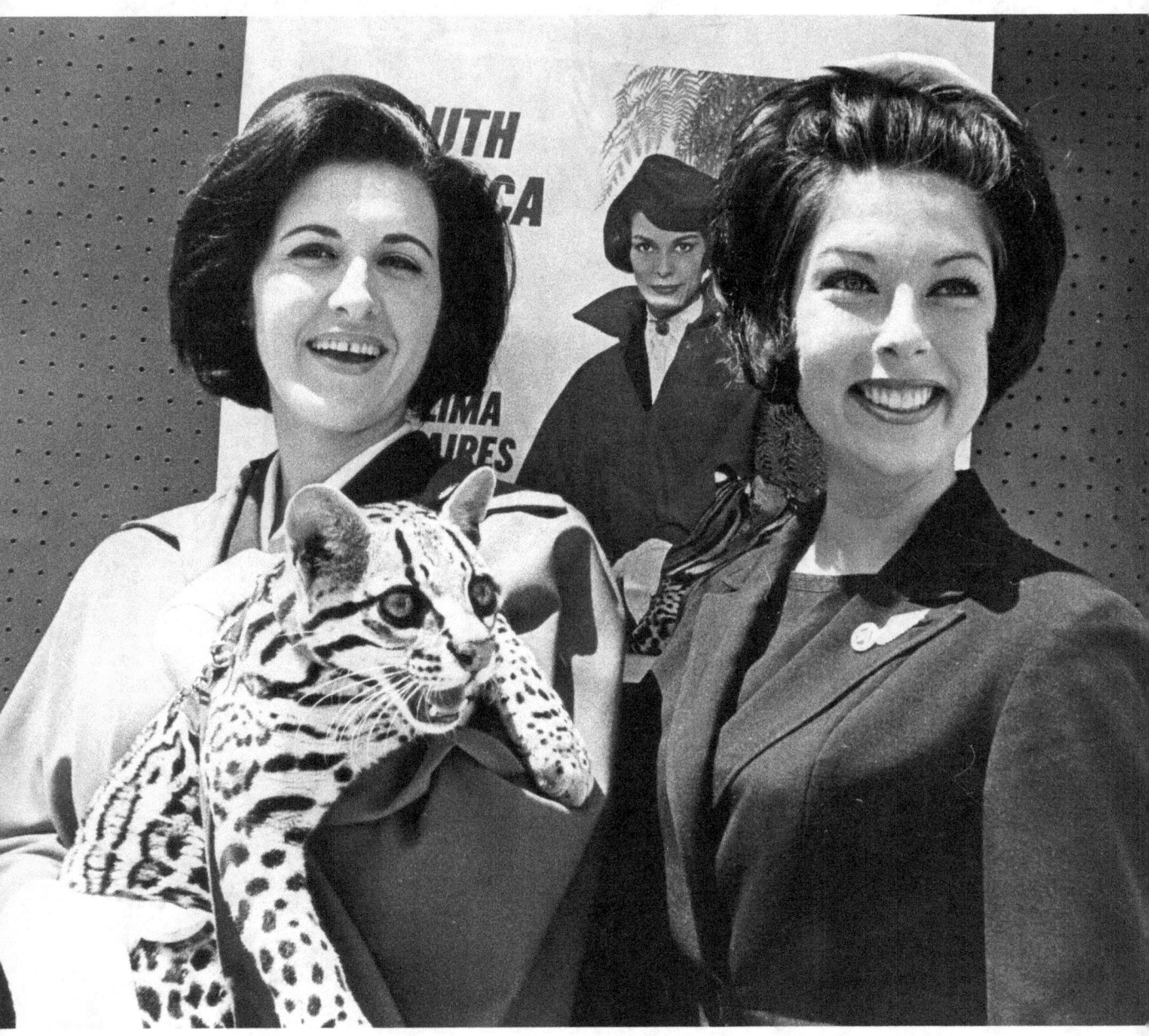

"Adela Santo Domingo, hostess for Avianca, Colombian airline, holds pet cheetah as she joins Linda Mandelstam, of National Airlines, Saturday, to mark second anniversary of Bullock's Fashion Square, Sherman Oaks."
August 17, 1964. (Bob Martin)
(Order #00084541)

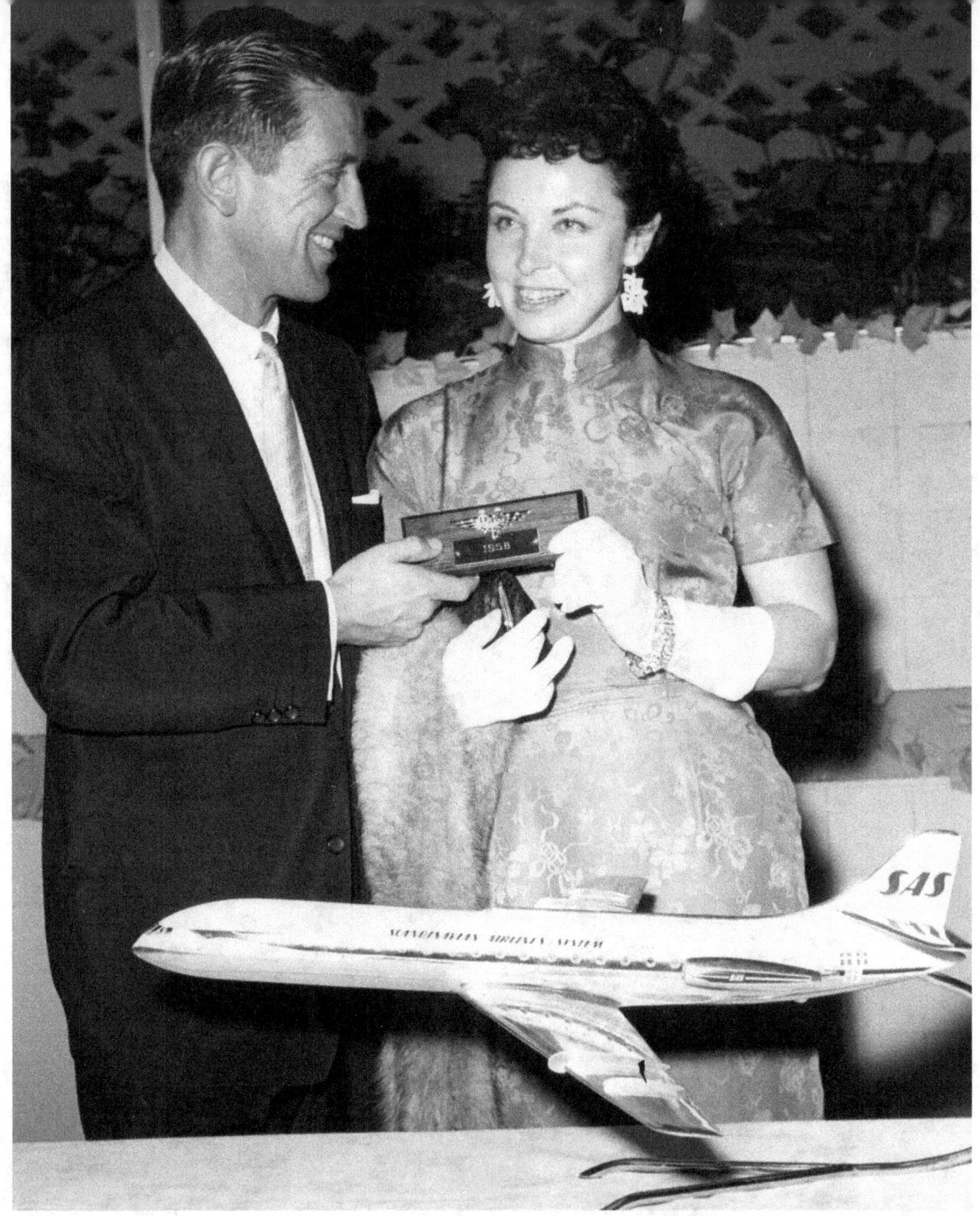

"Miss Meta Sherman, Meta Sherman Travel in Woodland Hills, receives congratulations from Kelly Palmer, district sales manager for Scandinavian Airlines System, on being named Royal Viking Agent for second year. Award was made at recent SAS banquet." Meta Sherman Travel was located at 21926 Constanso St., Woodland Hills.
March 10, 1959. (Order #00108008)

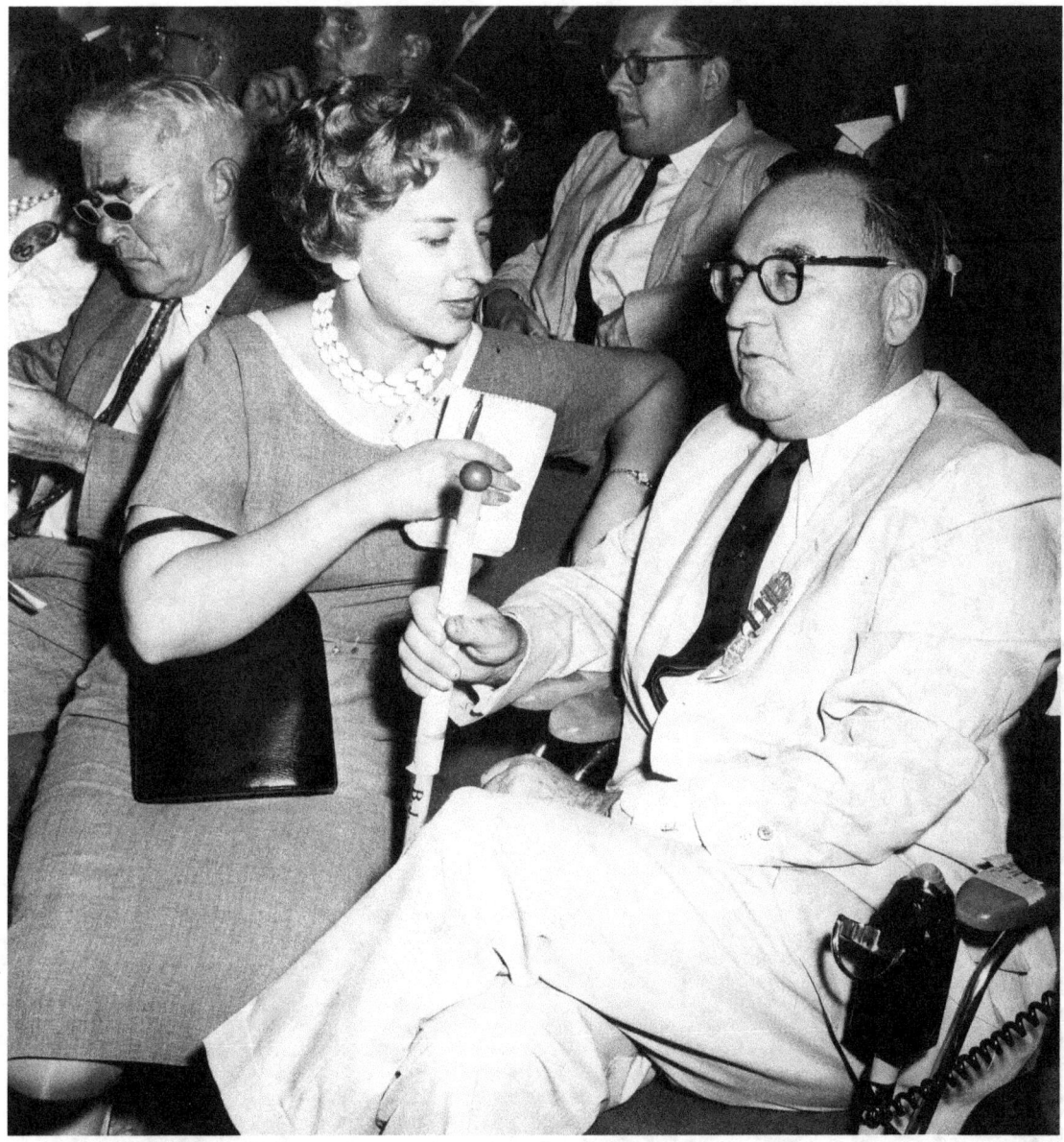

"Doris Klein, *Valley Times* reporter, questions California's Gov. Edmund G. 'Pat' Brown bringing out inside information on the controversial California delegation. Miss Klein was the first to tell the entire story of the sensational developments that split the delegates into two embittered camps, producing one of outstanding stories of the [Democratic National] convention."
July 19, 1960. (Gordon Dean)

(Order #00109135)

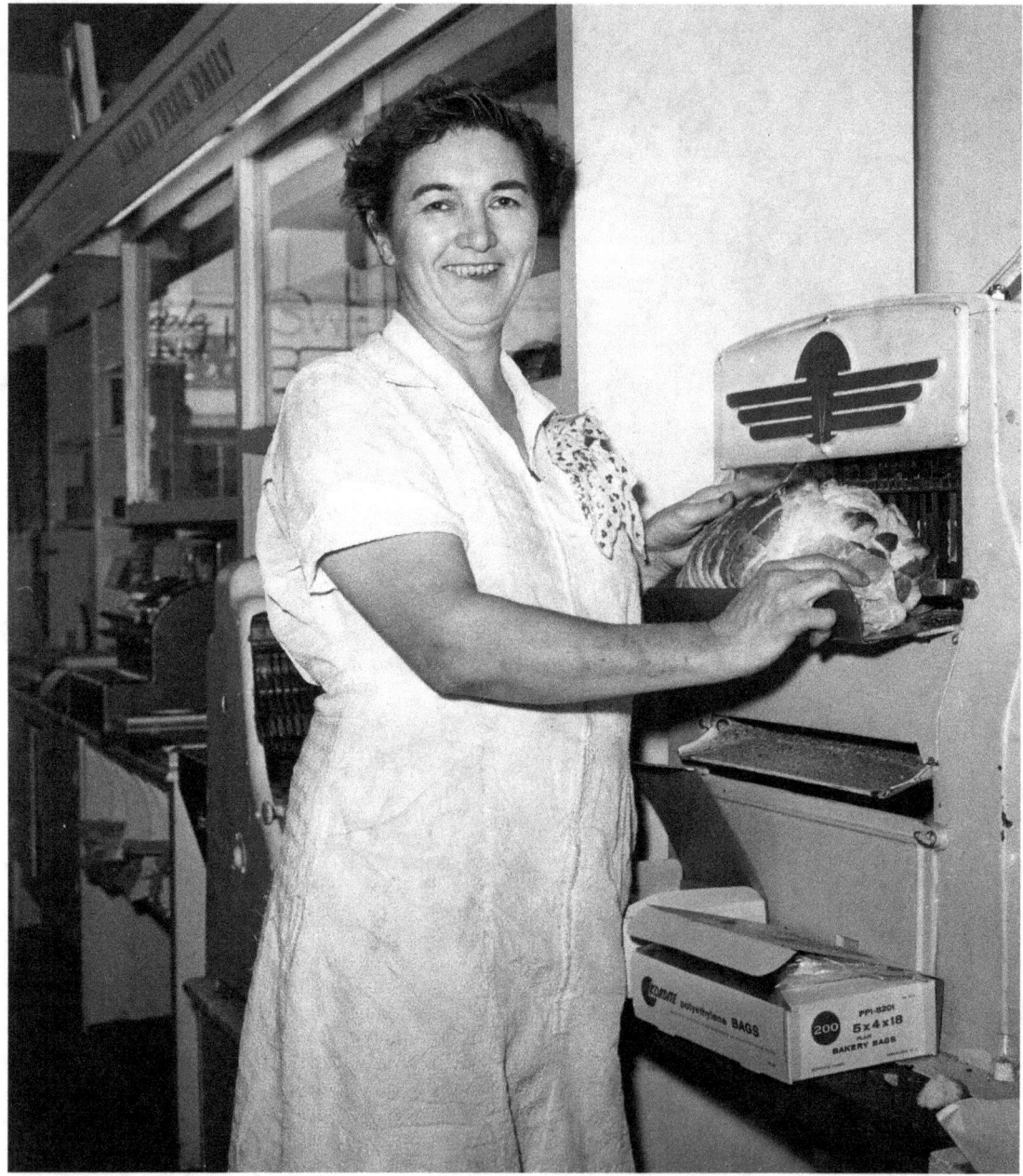

"From a tiny beginning by baking cookies in her own kitchen, Astrid Blomstrand now runs her own fine Swedish bakery in the Valley. Here she slices a loaf of her famous Sheepherder's bread." Astrid's Swedish Bakery was located at 4359 Tujunga.
August 6, 1959. (Order #00083731)

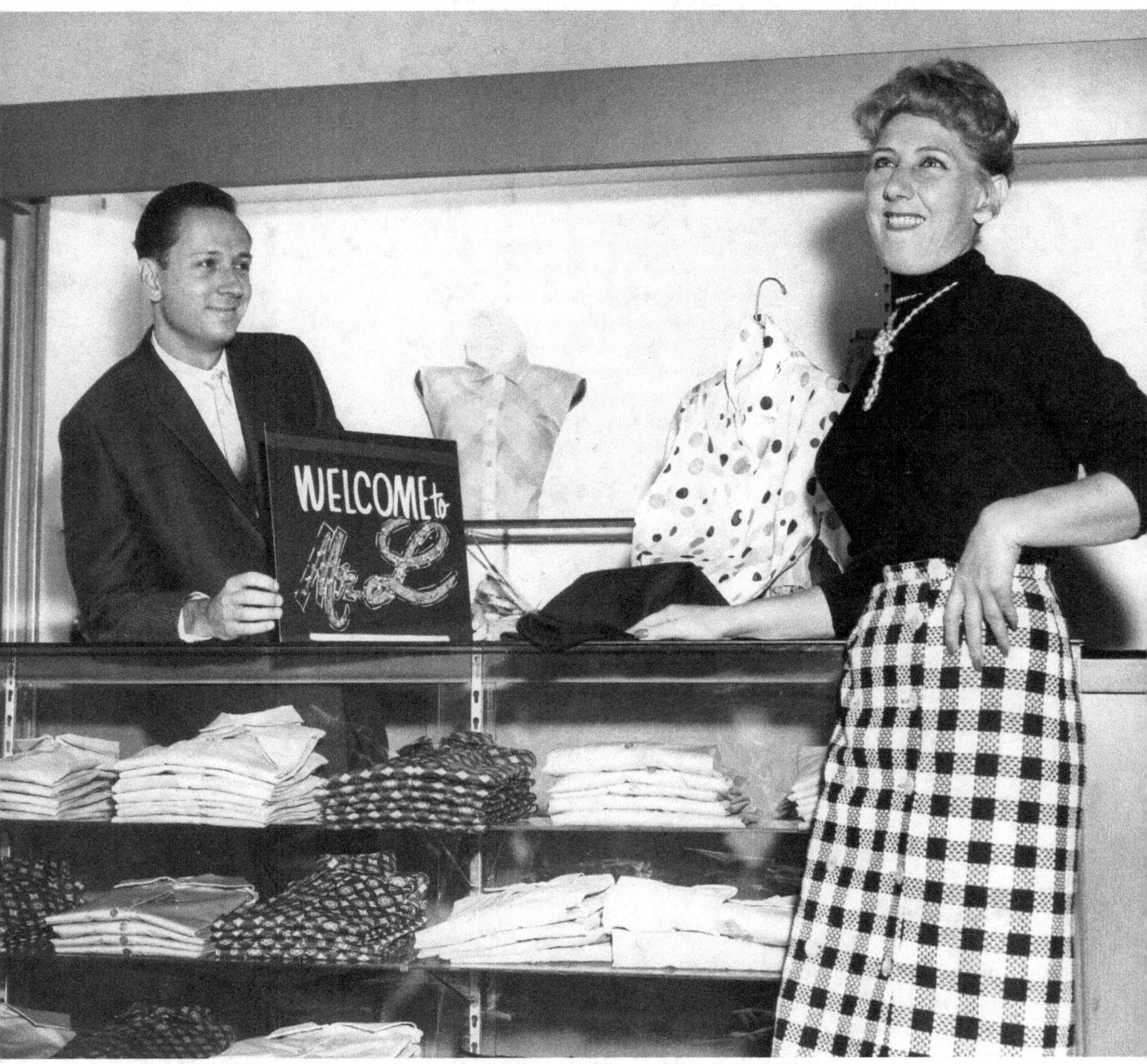

"Jack Shitlock, manager of Mr. L, Van Nuys new women's sportswear shop, welcomes Anne Cwerman as fashion coordinator. The shop, keyed for college and career women, is at 6505 Van Nuys Blvd., Van Nuys."
May 24, 1959. (Order #00083058)

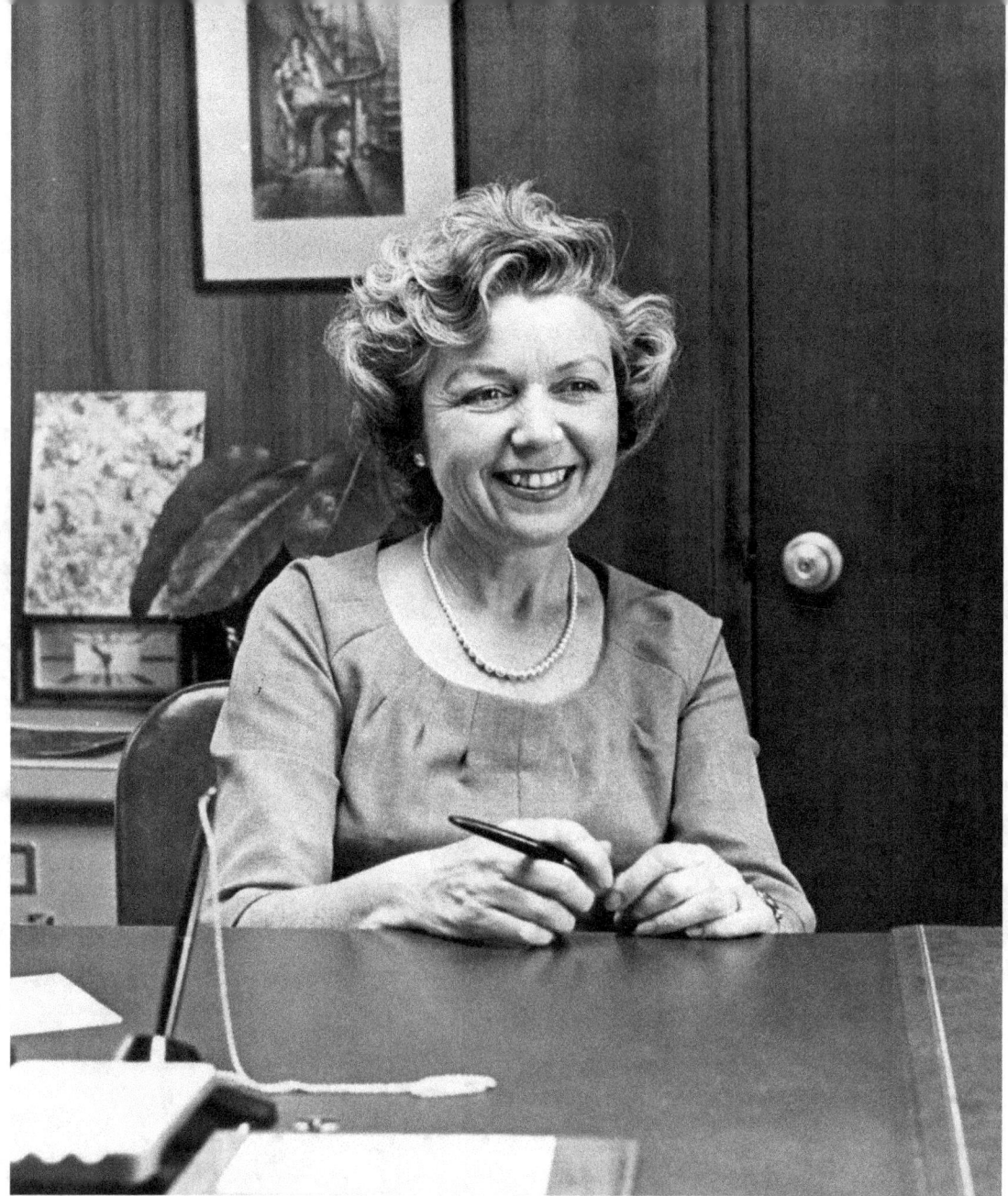

"Lauretta Savory, registered broker of Van Nuys, is now in her third successful career. She was formerly a dancer in motion pictures then a flight instructor. Mrs. Savory is associated with Dempsey-Tegeler and Co. in Studio City." Of her decision to switch careers from flight instructor to stock broker, Savory said, "Flying is fun, but a woman who does it professionally runs into a great deal of resentment from men co-workers. But men appreciate and encourage women in the investment business.
March 14, 1961. (Alan Hyde).

(Order #00108530)

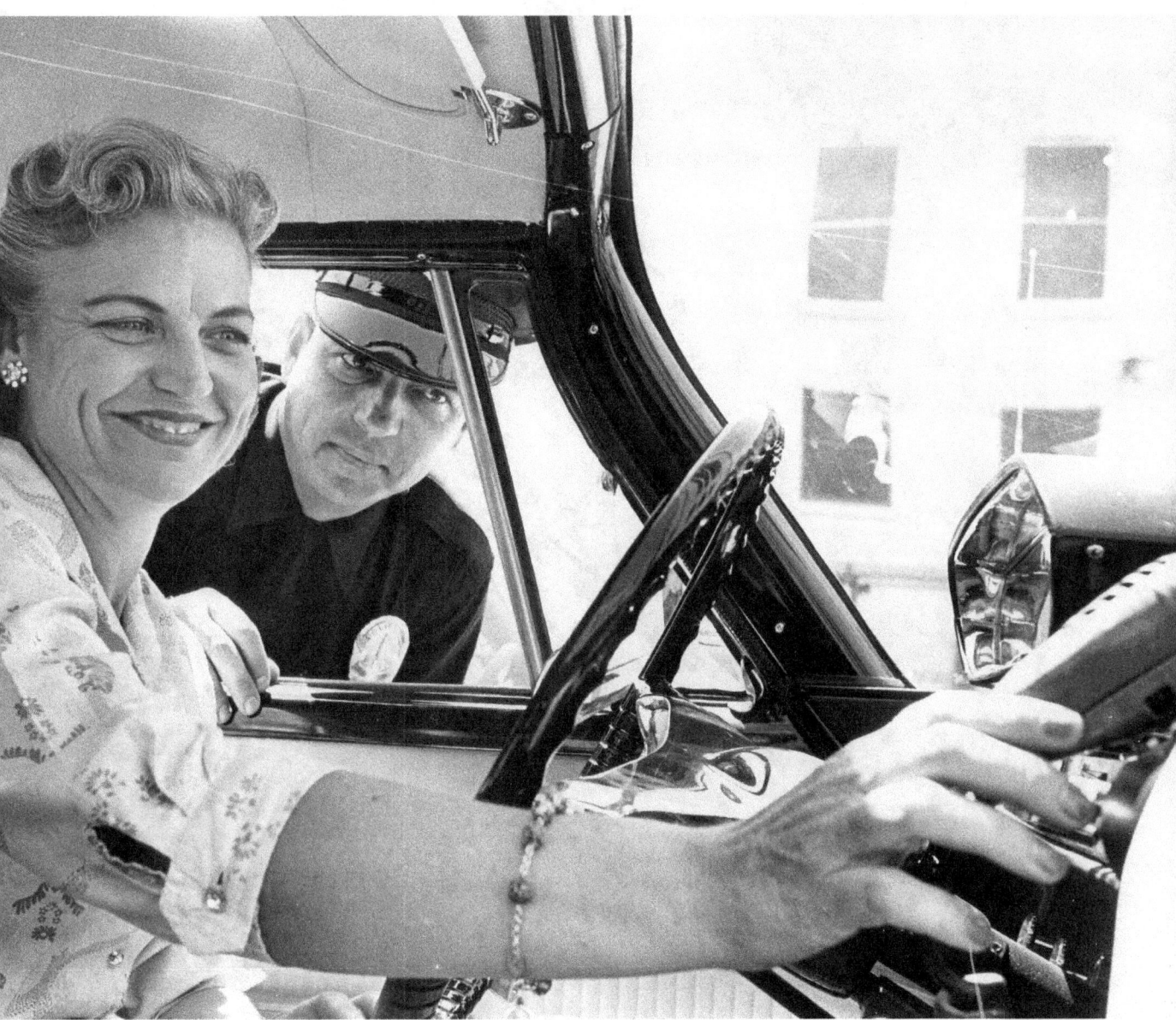

"Sgt. Paul S. Hospodar looks on as a smiling Sgt. Genevieve Hauck, who works in the Juvenile Division of the Van Nuys Police Department, reaches over to the hand-held radio inside a police car." Hauck joined the LAPD in 1947, was promoted to Sergeant in 1958 and assigned to the Juvenile Division the following year where she served until her retirement in 1975. August 11, 1960. (George Brich)

(Order #00108971)

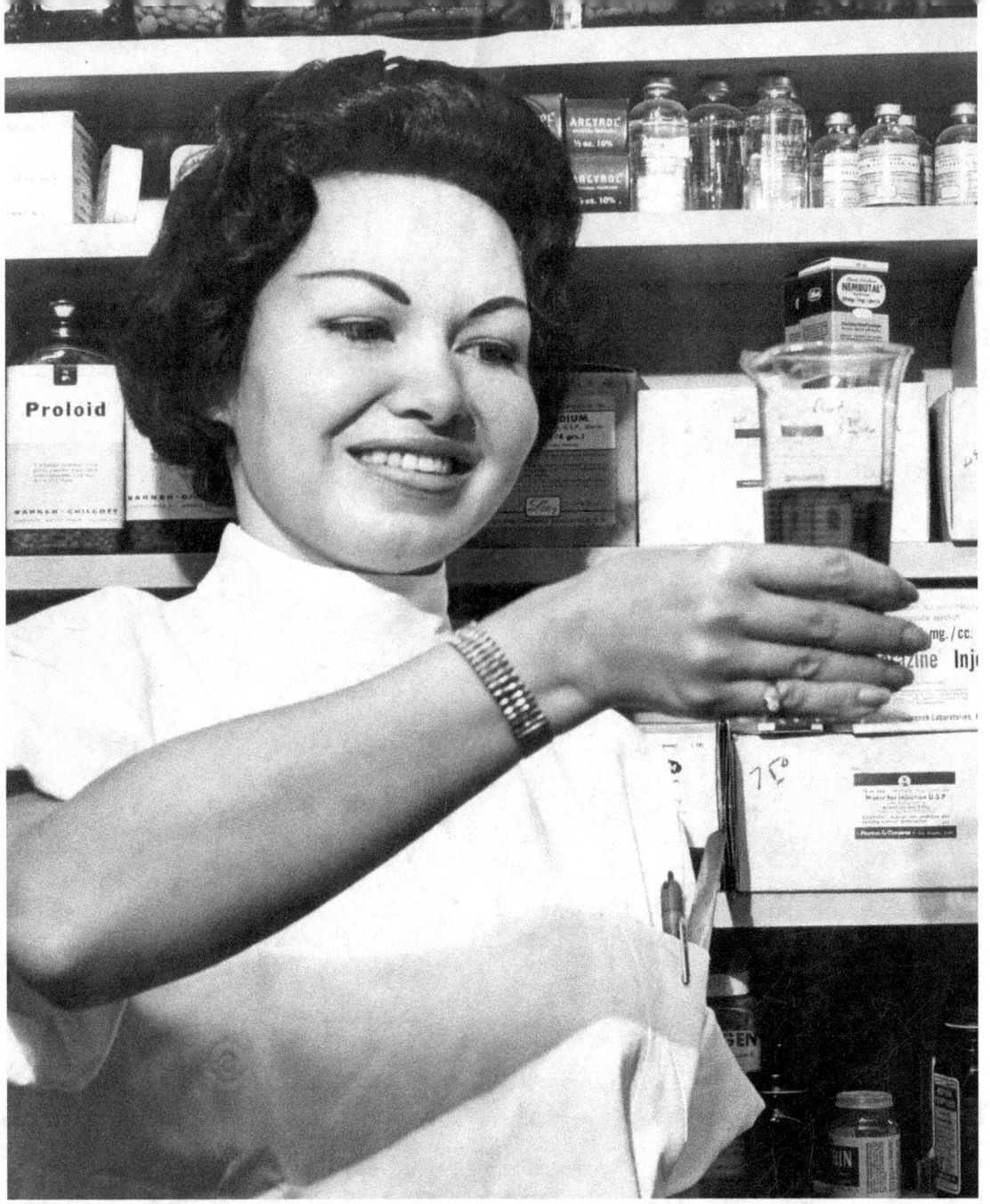

"Pharmacist Lois Kyffin of Van Nuys claims that, though few women enter the field of preparing and dispensing medicines, it is a profession particularly suitable to their natural talents. Mrs. Kyffin entered the field of pharmacy because a scientific course appealed to her. She particularly liked chemistry, but did not want to do work which confined her to a laboratory. Pharmacy afforded her the opportunity to come in contact with many types of people."
August 17, 1960. (William E. McCullough)

(Order #00108994)

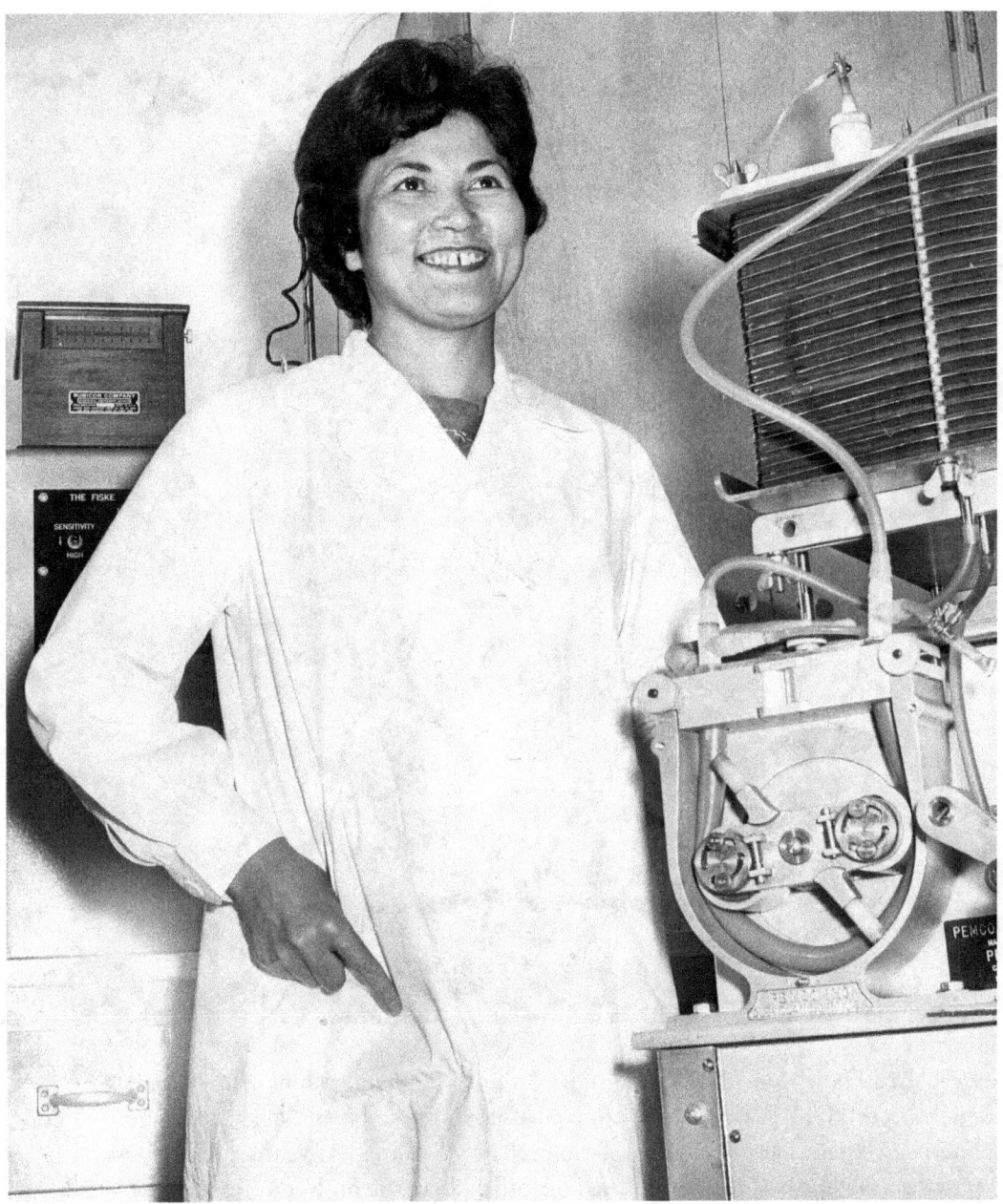

Dr. Kimiko Katsahara, Japanese heart specialist studying at St. Joseph Hospital stands by artificial kidney, heart-lung machine.
August 17, 1960. (Gordon Dean)
(Order #00108993)

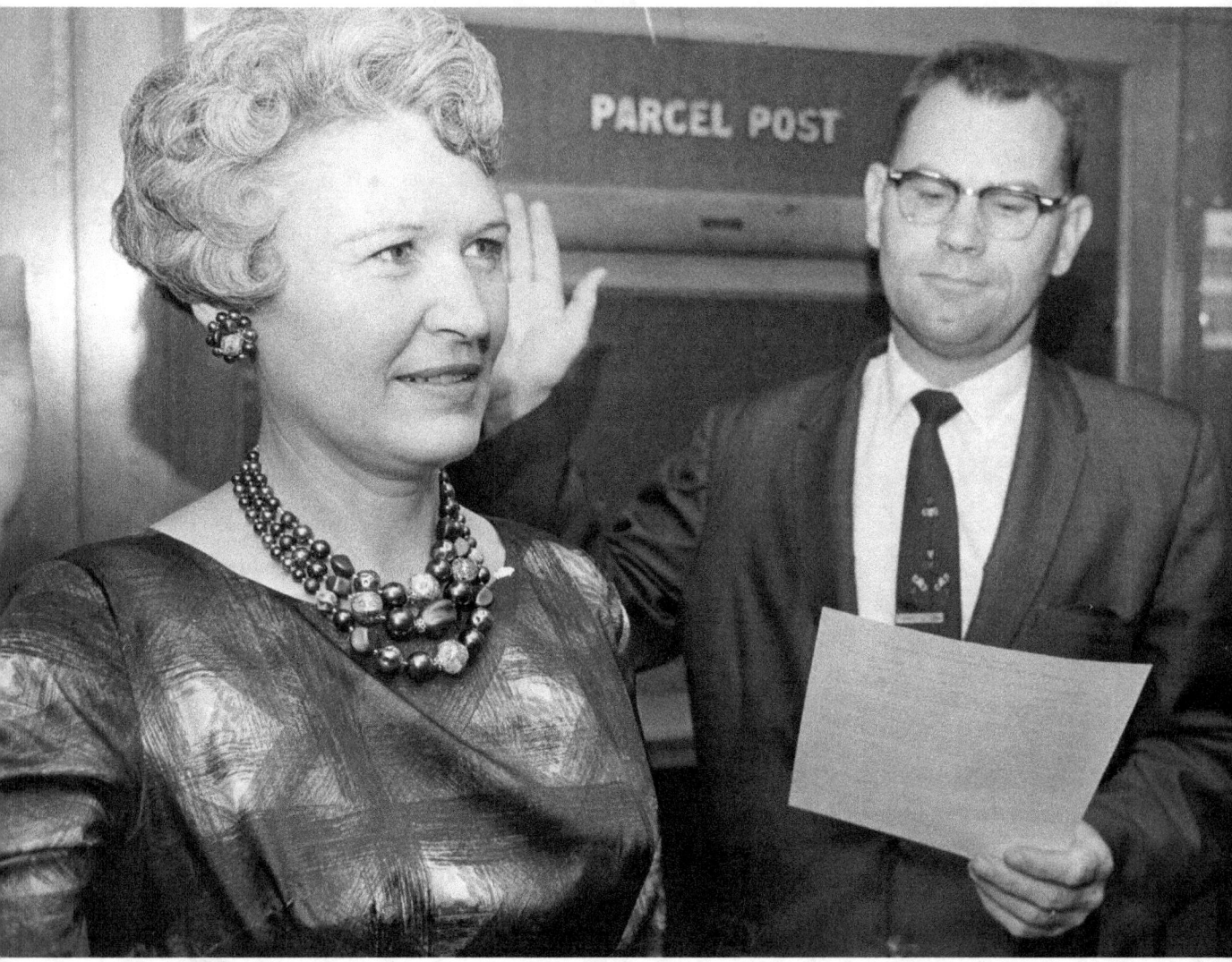

"Mrs. Mildred Hudelson, 7321 Valmont St., Tujunga, took an oath of office Monday from
Postal Inspector S. H. Jensen and became postmaster of the North Valley community. The
ceremonies were held at the Tujunga station, 10105 Commerce Ave. Her job as boss of
29 postal employees is her first with the post office department, but not with the federal
government. Formerly employed by the State Department of Motor Vehicles and Employment,
she was campaign manager in 1952 for Assemblyman Tom Bane in his first and successful drive
for the 42nd District seat."
October 3, 1961. (Don Michel)

(Order #00108447)

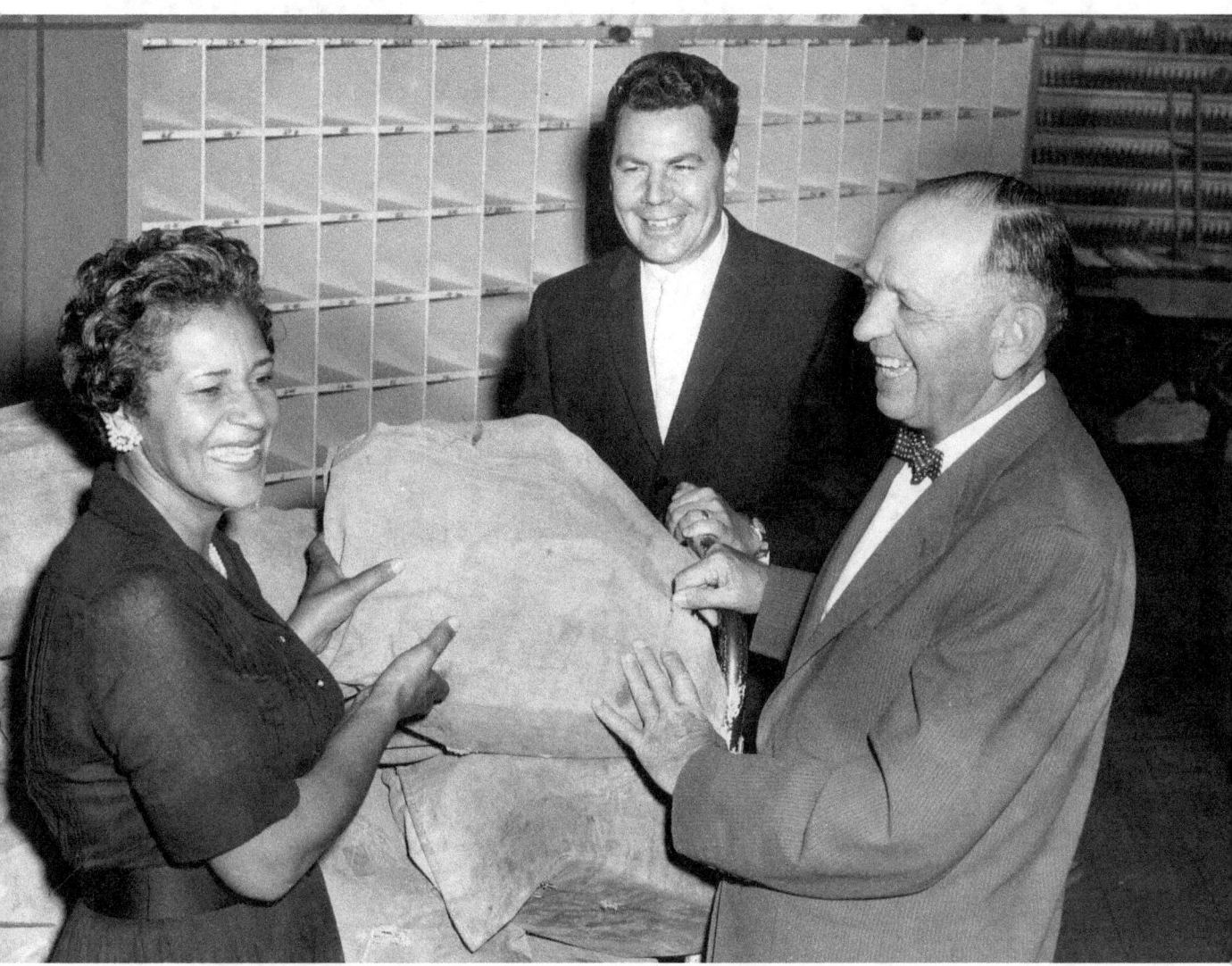

"Mrs. James Avery was installed acting postmaster of Pacoima Friday to become the first Negro to be selected as postmaster of a major office in California. Mrs. Avery, 42, 11501 Herrick Ave., receives congratulations after the ceremony from John DeRoo Jr., Granada Hills, 41st Assembly District Democratic delegation chairman, center, and Tom C. Carrell, Assemblyman from the 41st District." Nancy Avery was appointed to her post by President John F. Kennedy and remained in the position until 1984. She was once quoted as saying, "The Democratic Party wanted to do something that had never been done before. I was the token."
October 2, 1961. (Alan Hyde)

(Order #00086205)

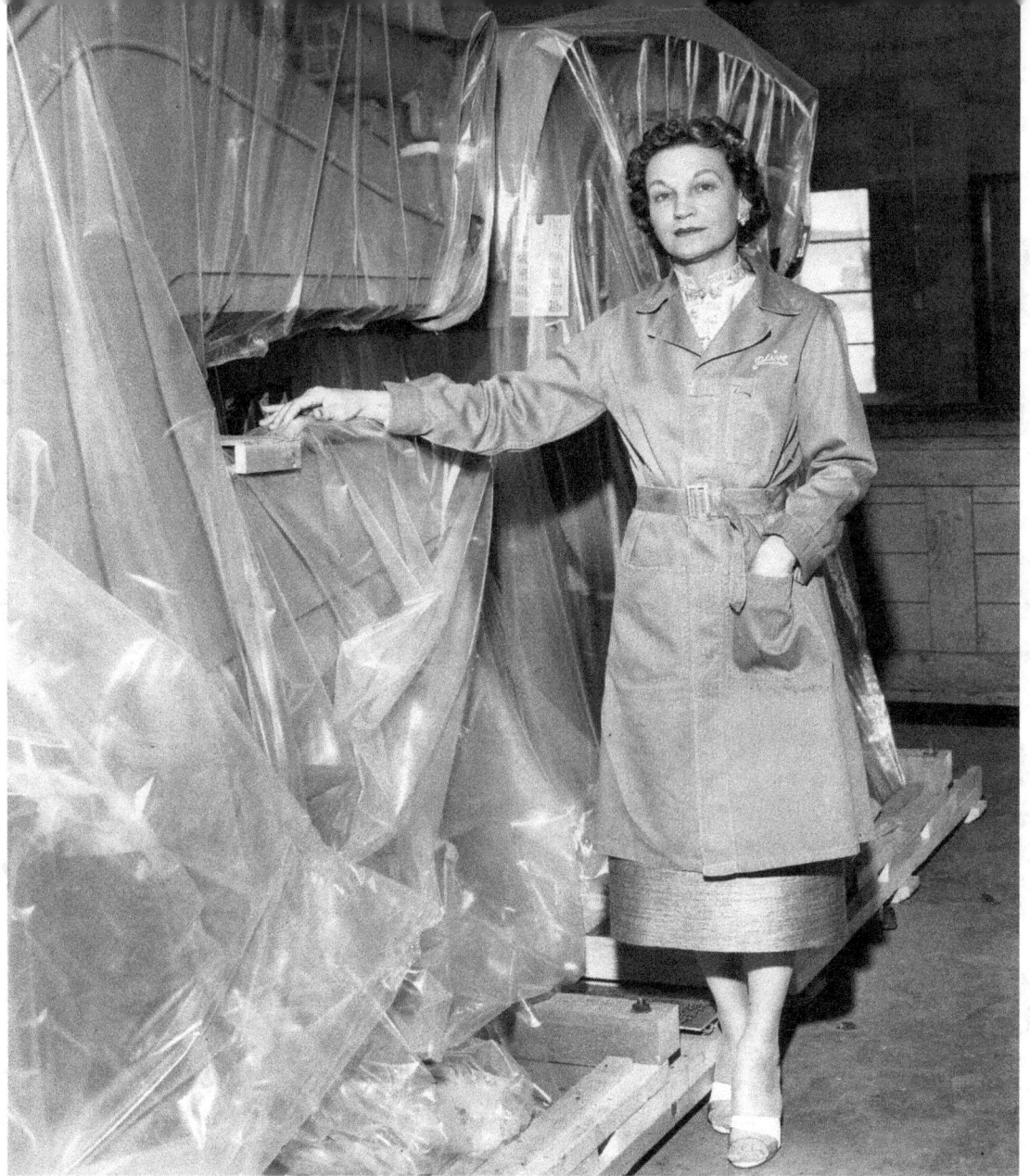

"Mrs. Olive Salembier, one of only two women presidents in National Security Industrial Association, inspects packaging job done at SPEC [Specification Packaging Engineering Corp.] Packaging, North Hollywood. Polyethylene plastic hood guards paint and reserving agents on machine, and in turn will be protected by crate overstructure still to be attached to package." Salembier, a packaging engineer who later moved her operation to Arizona worked by the motto, "If you want your packaging by noon yesterday, you have to get it here by at least tomorrow." She served as president of the Society of Women Engineers and now has a memorial scholarship named after her to encourage women to enter the field of engineering. April 23, 1959. (Order #00082924)

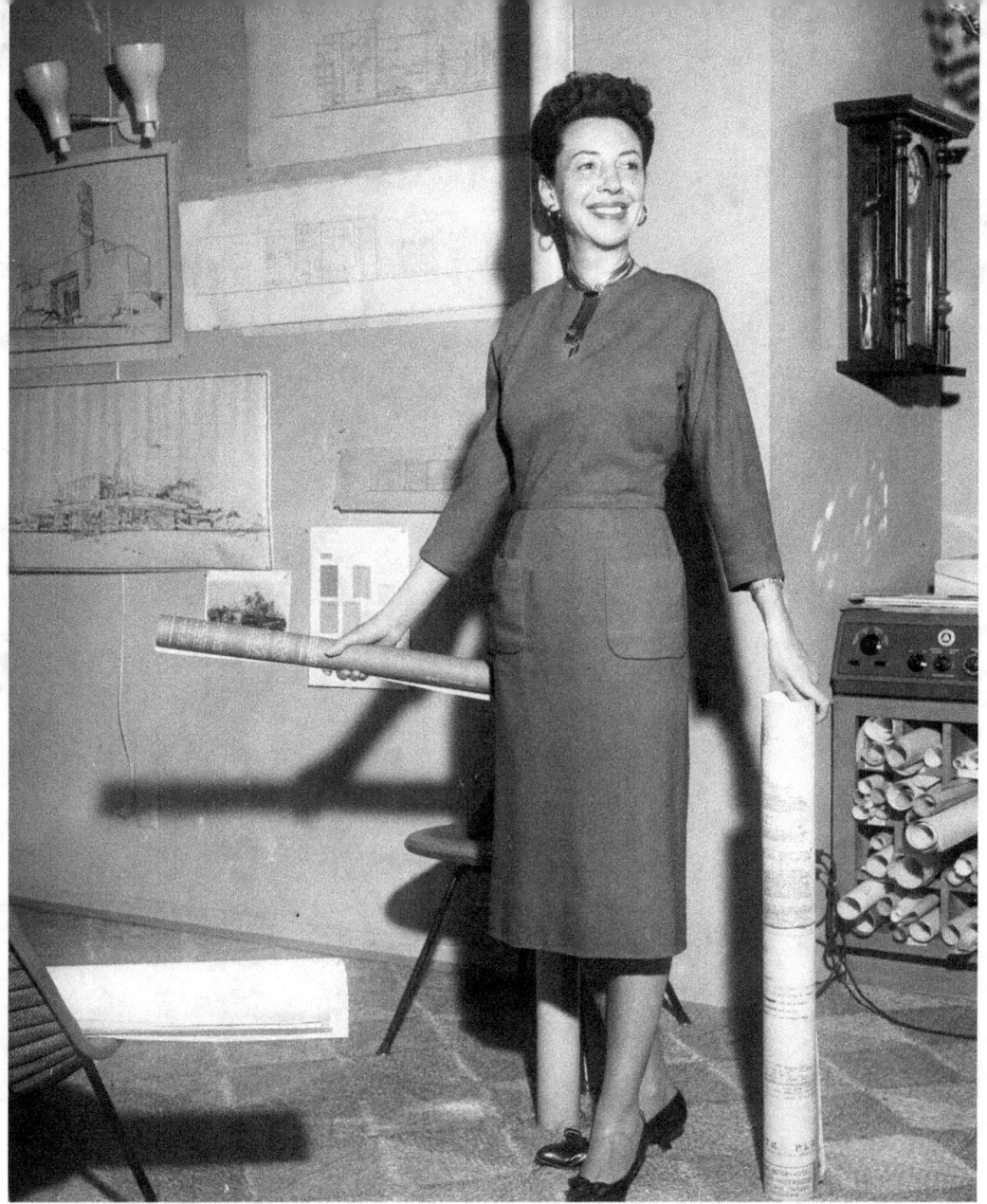

"North Hollywood architect Lucille Raport is one of the 350 licensed women in her profession in the United States." Rapport, a graduate of the University of Kansas launched her career as an architect in Kansas City during the War, and relocated her firm to North Hollywood in 1946. She designed residential, commercial, and public buildings including Oakwood Elementary School in Moorpark and the Building Contractors' Association building in Los Angeles. Raport's advice for working in a predominately male profession was, "Look like a girl, think like a man, act like a lady and work like a dog."

March 15, 1961. (Order #00082744)

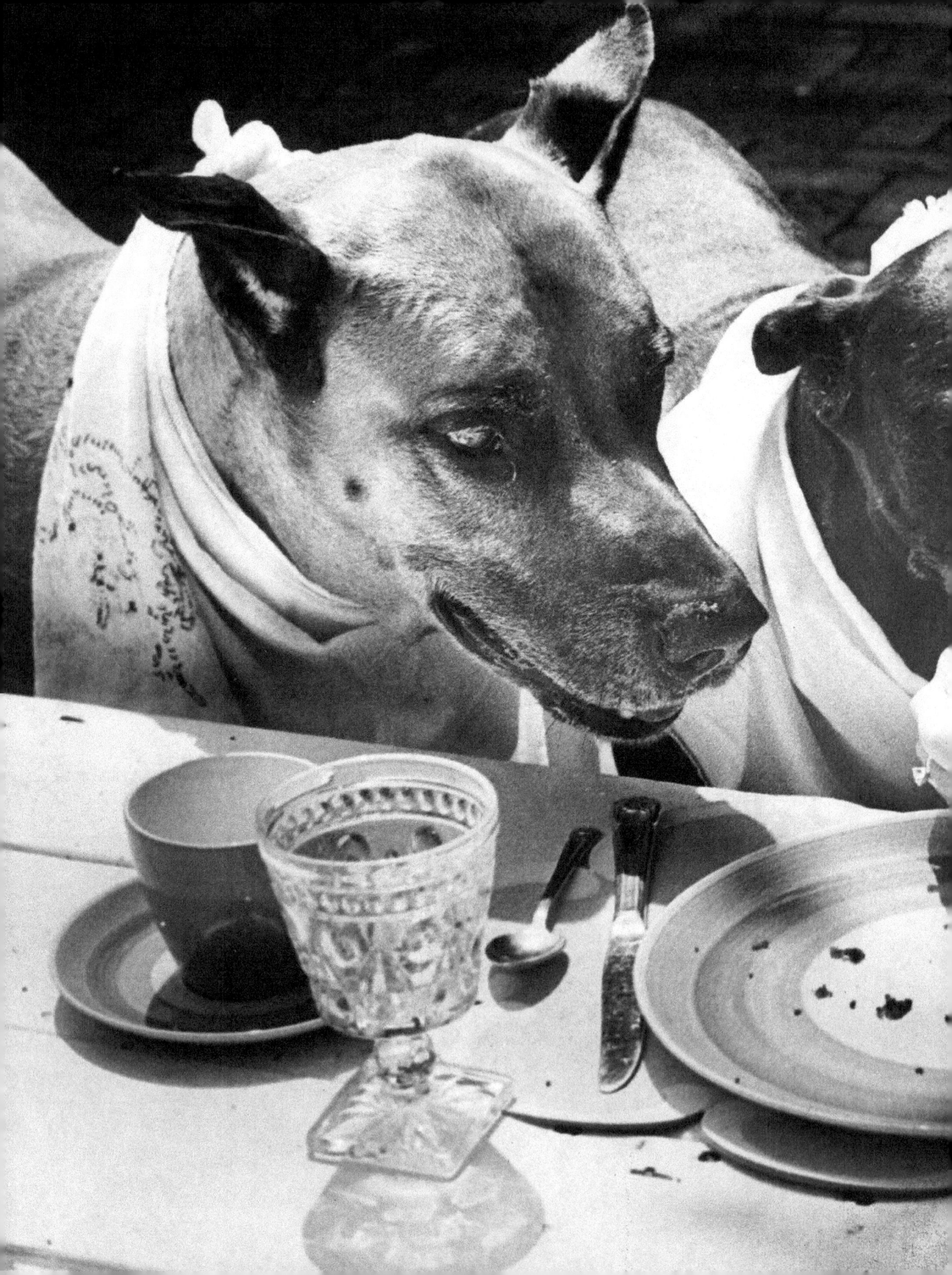

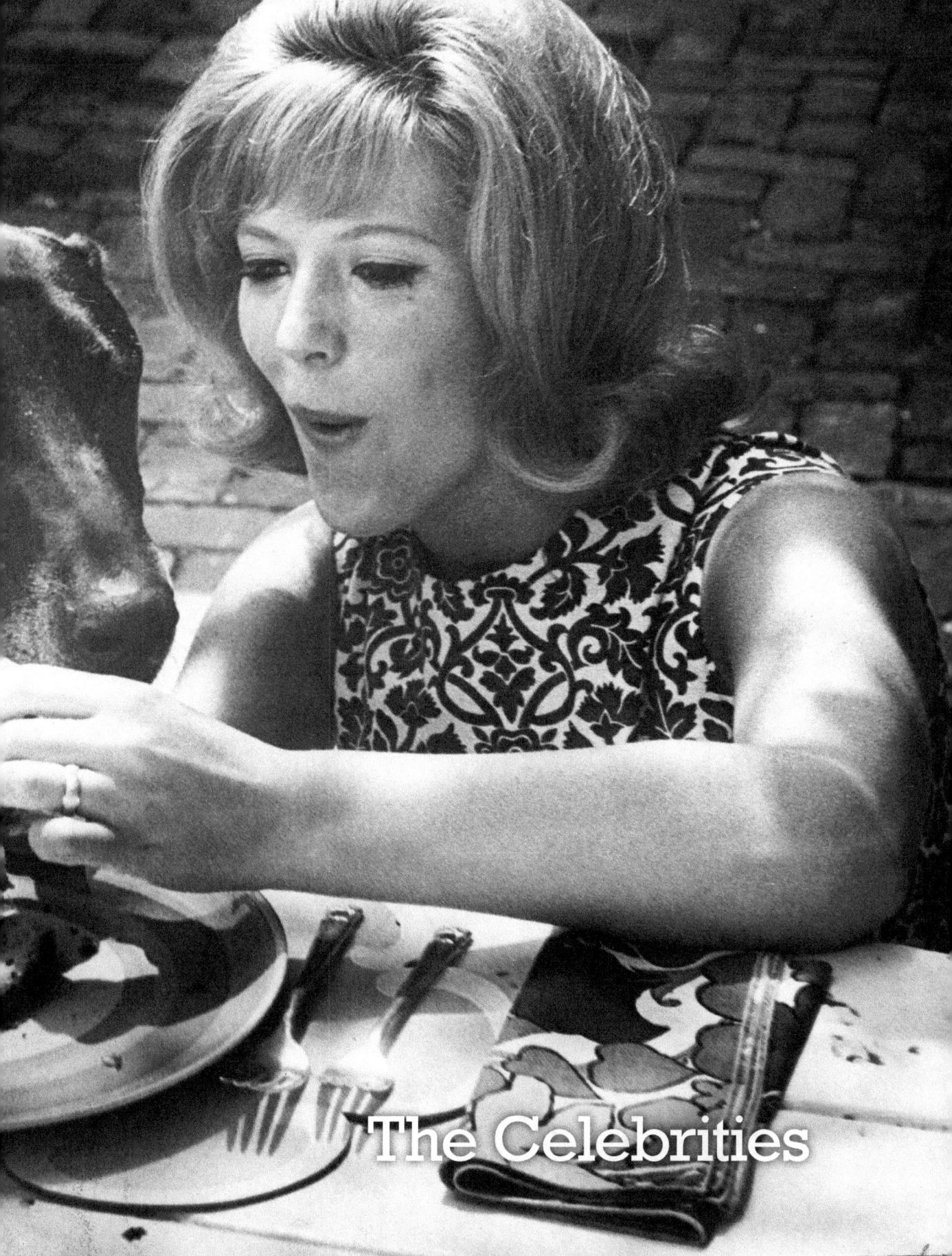

The Celebrities

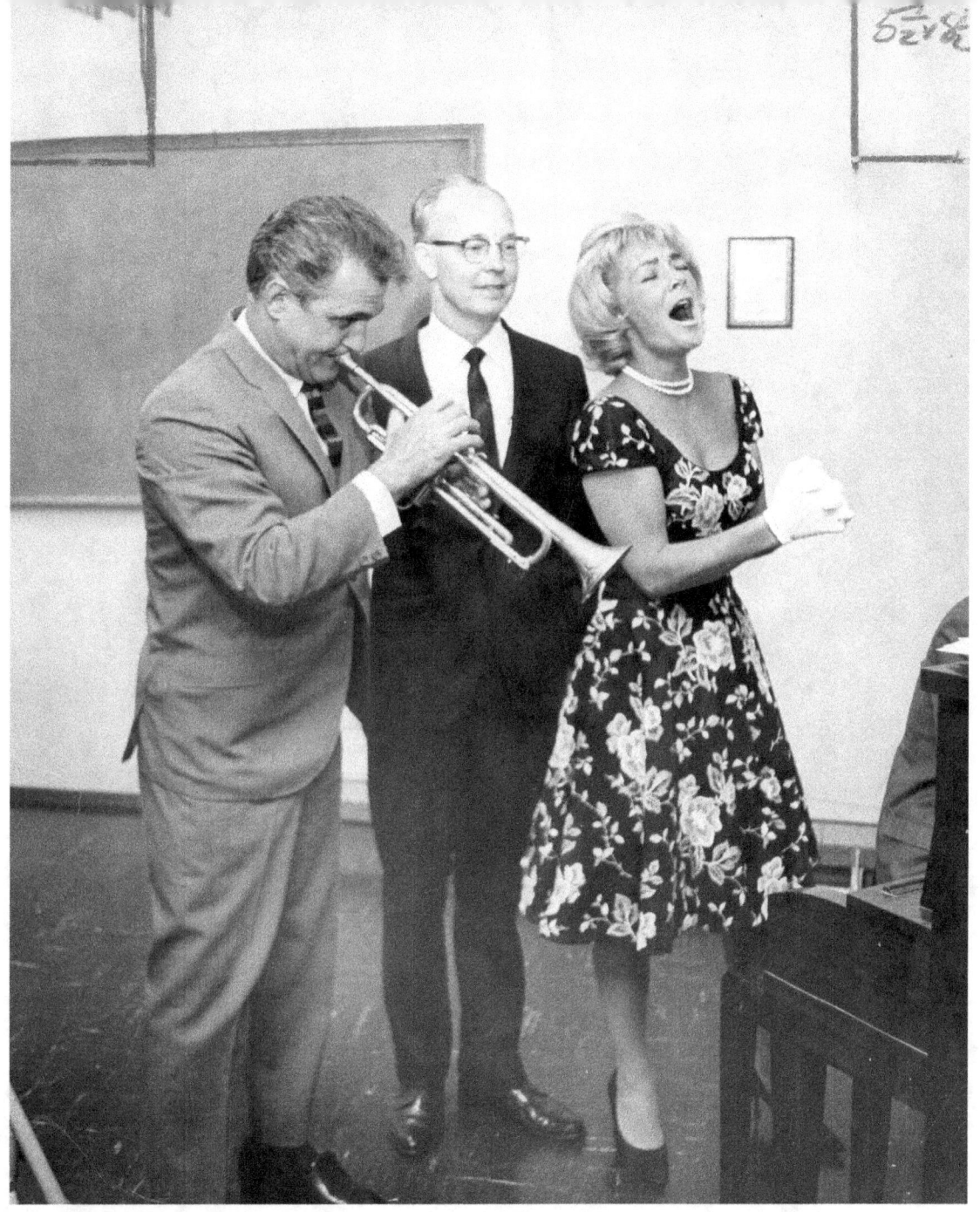

"Actress Betty Hutton and her musician husband Peter Condoli follow the course taken by a number of Hollywood stars over the years as they turn to testimony for Christ. They sang and played recently at the First Assembly of God, 11455 Burbank Blvd., North Hollywood, as part of a southland evangelical mission. With them is church music director Jerry Eskelin."
June 5, 1965. (Tom Kravitz)

(Order #00109693)

Actress Jayne Mansfield holds 35-day-old daughter Mariska while surrounded by the rest of the family, from left; Jayne Marie, Mickey Jr., Mickey Sr. and Zoltan. As the photo was being taken, Hargitay asked his wife, "Don't you feel like Mother Goose?"
February 28, 1964. (George Brich)
(Order #00091585)

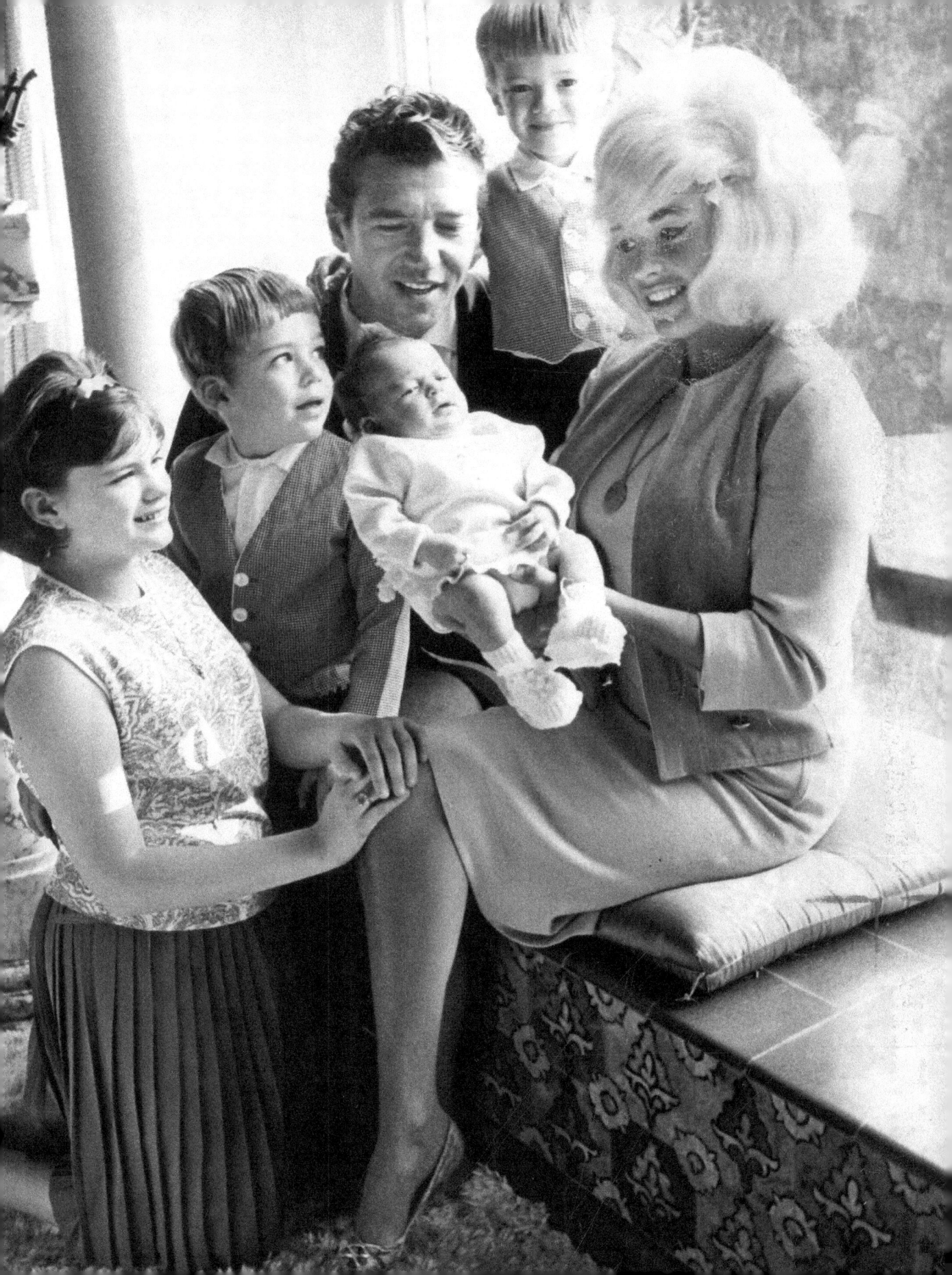

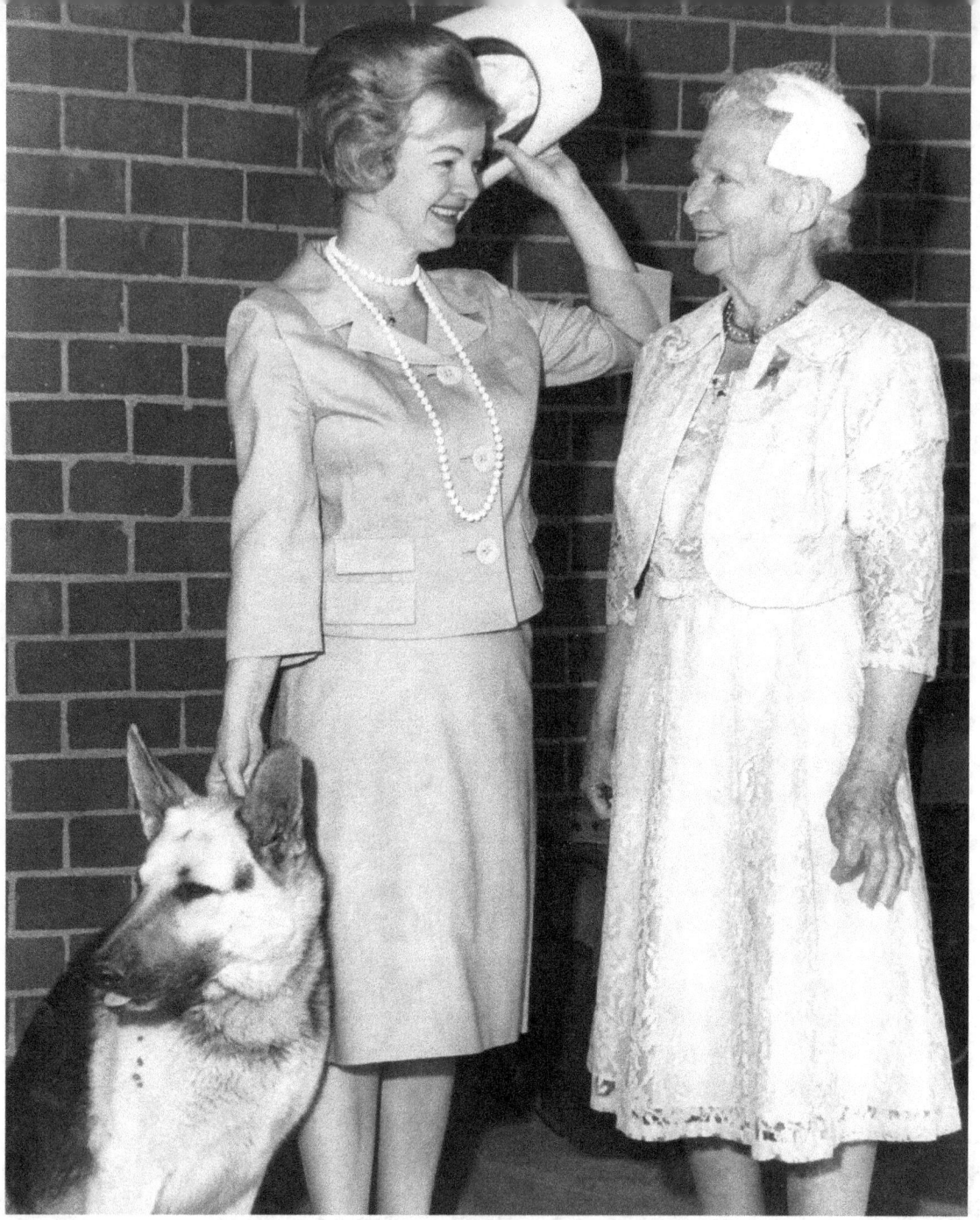

"Movie cowgirl and longtime Chatsworth resident Dale Evans (Mrs. Roy Rogers), left, discusses plans to save the Valley's oldest Protestant church with Mrs. Minnie Palmer, 77, newest member of the Chatsworth Historical Society. With them is the Rogers' famous dog, Bullet." May 27, 1964. (Jeff Robbins)

(Order #00053022)

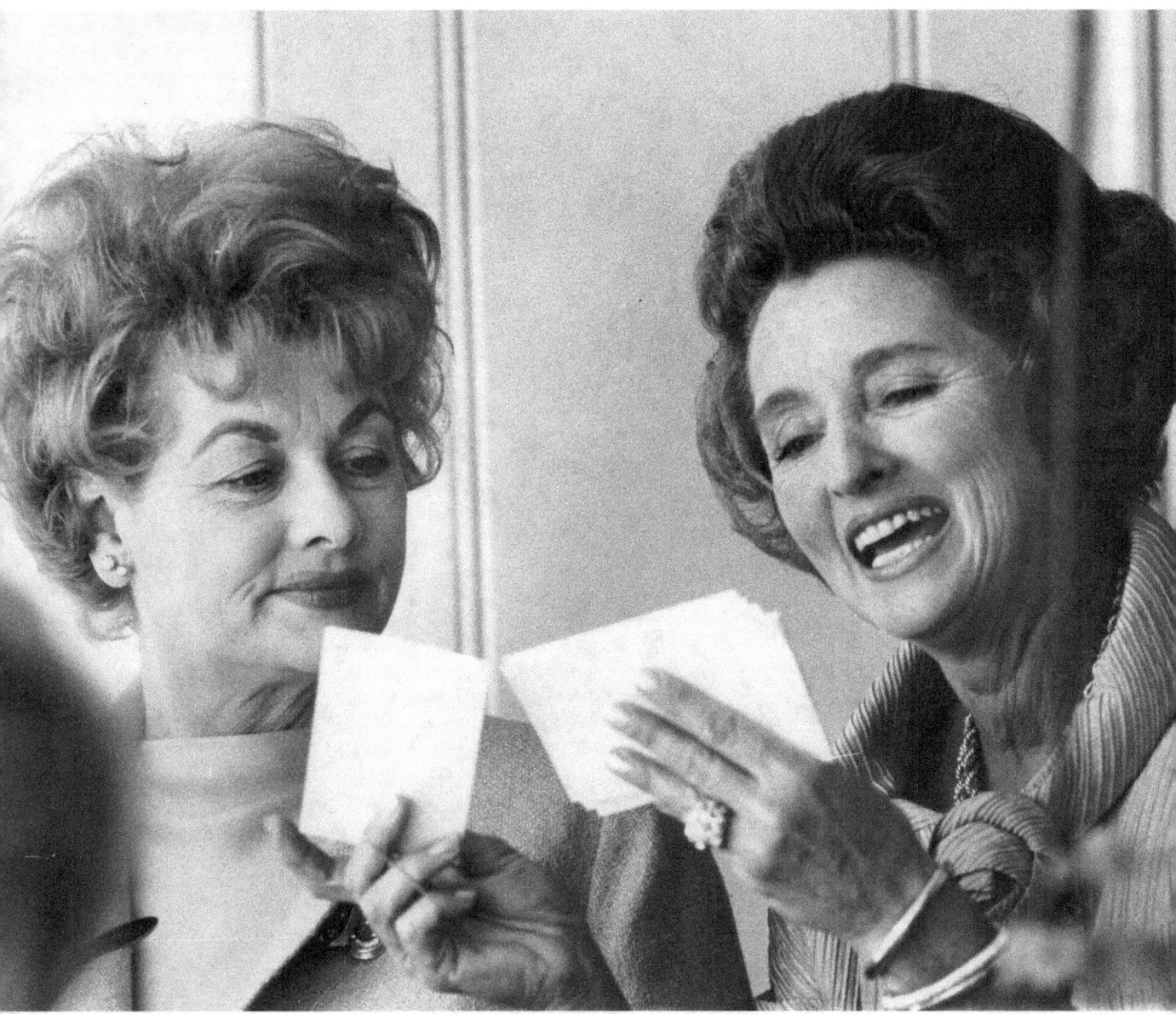

Actress Lucille Ball, left, and Dolores Hope, wife of Bob Hope are shown at the Hope estate in Toluca Lake, which provided the setting for a Mother-Daughter fashion show and luncheon for the benefit of Providence High School in Burbank. Mrs. Hope was hostess and chairman for fashion show.

April 4, 1964. (George Brich)

(Order #00084146)

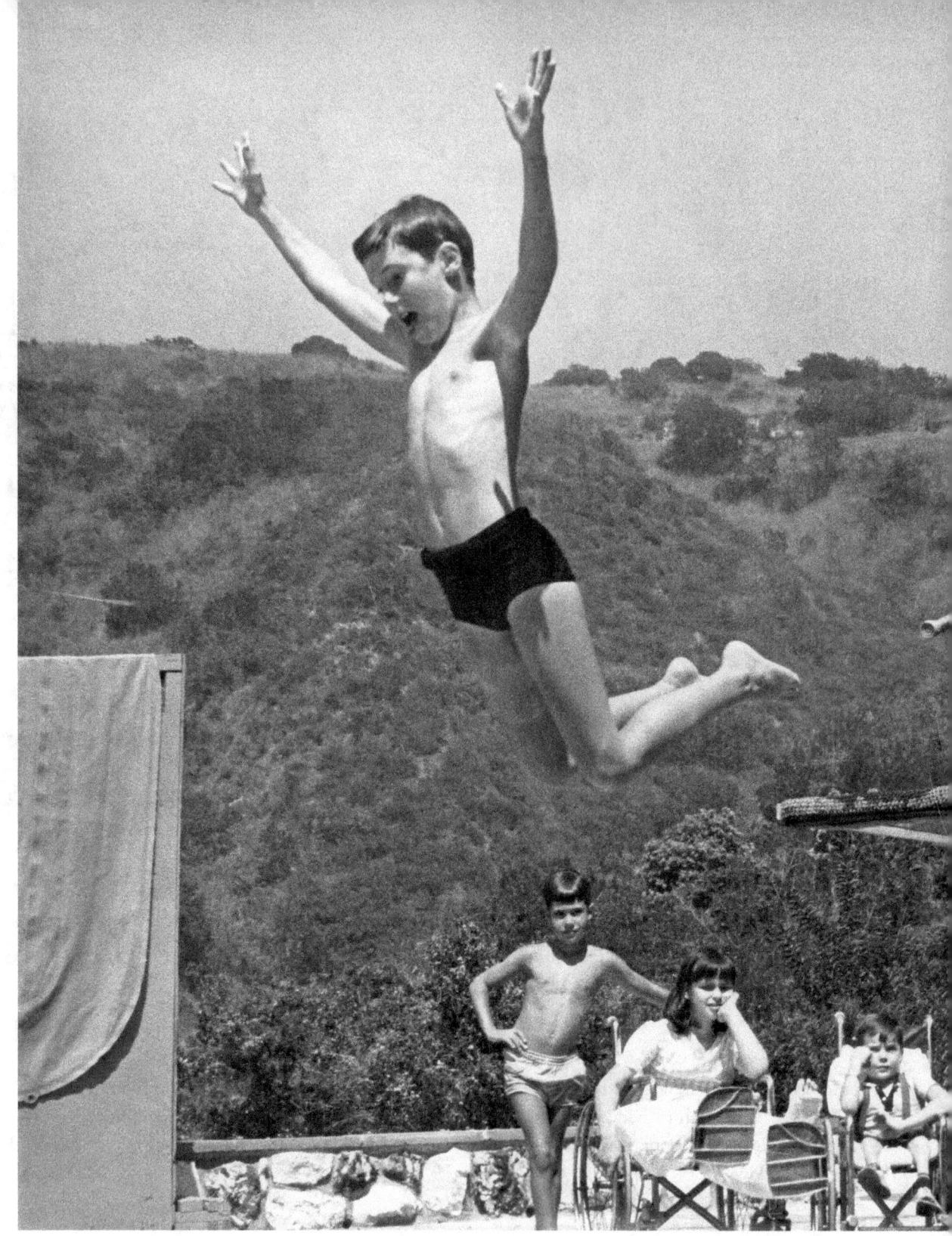

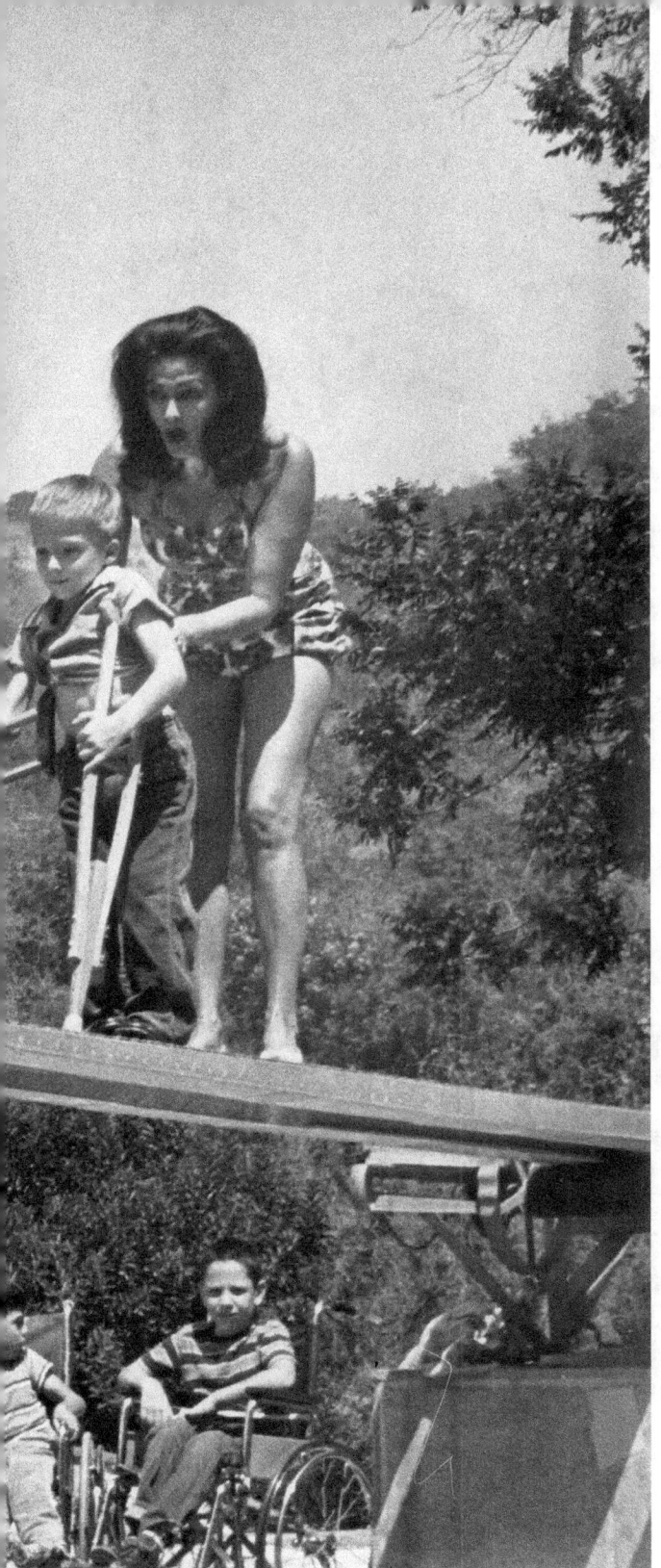

"Bruce Morgan, son of actress Yvonne de Carlo, celebrates his 11th birthday by a flying leap into pool at his Studio City home. Party guest Alan, 7, a patient at Casa Colina Rehabilitation Center in Pomona, observes flight from springboard with Miss de Carlo looking on. Poolside are more party guests, from left, Michael Morgan, Tracy, Dave, Teddy and David." De Carlo invited the children after learning of the benefits of swimming as an activity for the disabled. July 10, 1965. (Tom Kravitz)

(Order #00083637)

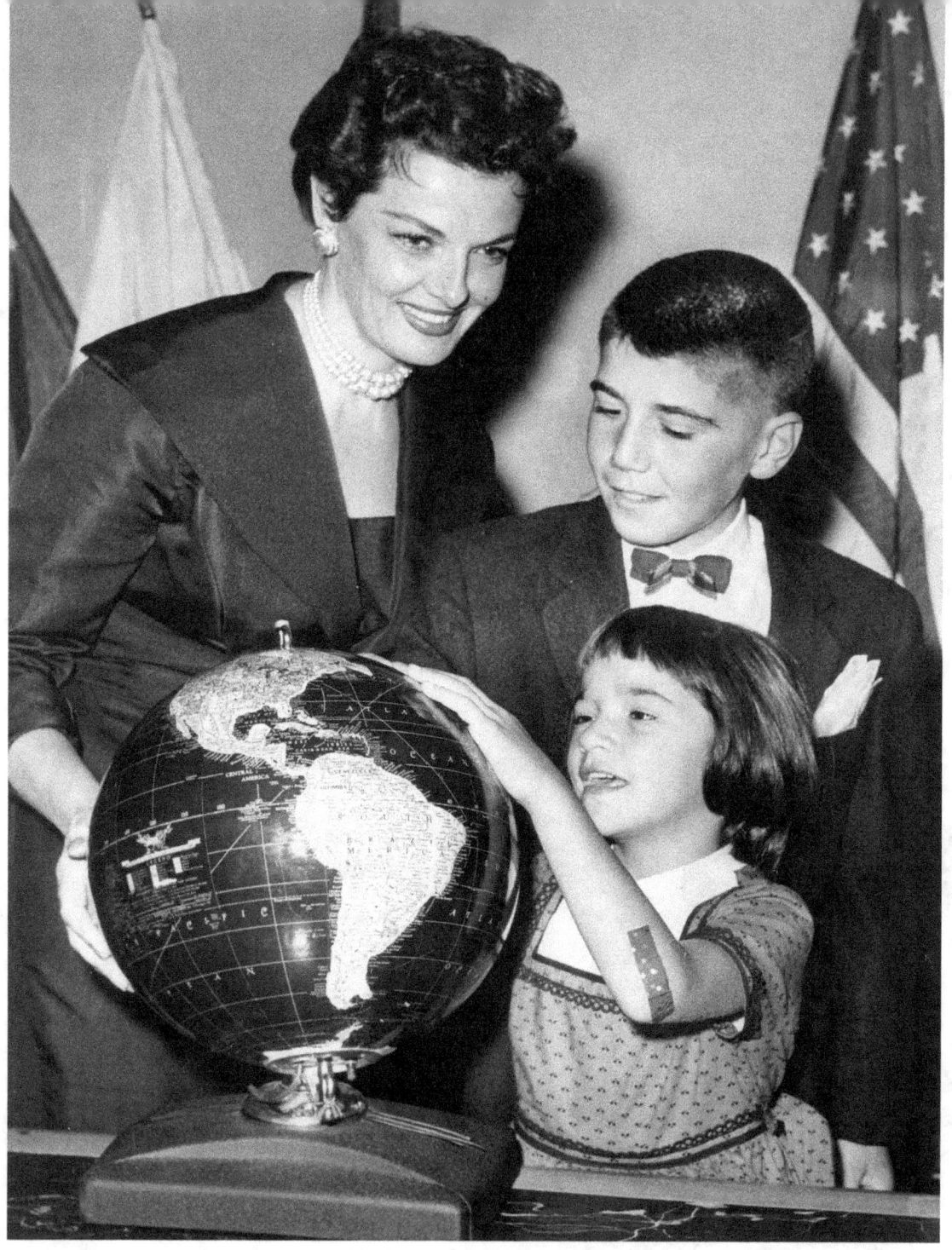

"Actress Jane Russell of Sherman Oaks shows Andrew Vinock, 11, and sister, Julia, 6, Greek children adopted by Pasadena couple, homelands of children who will benefit from WAIF Imperial Ball at Ambassador Nov. 7. Miss Russell is WAIF founder."
October 26, 1959. (Order #00082752)

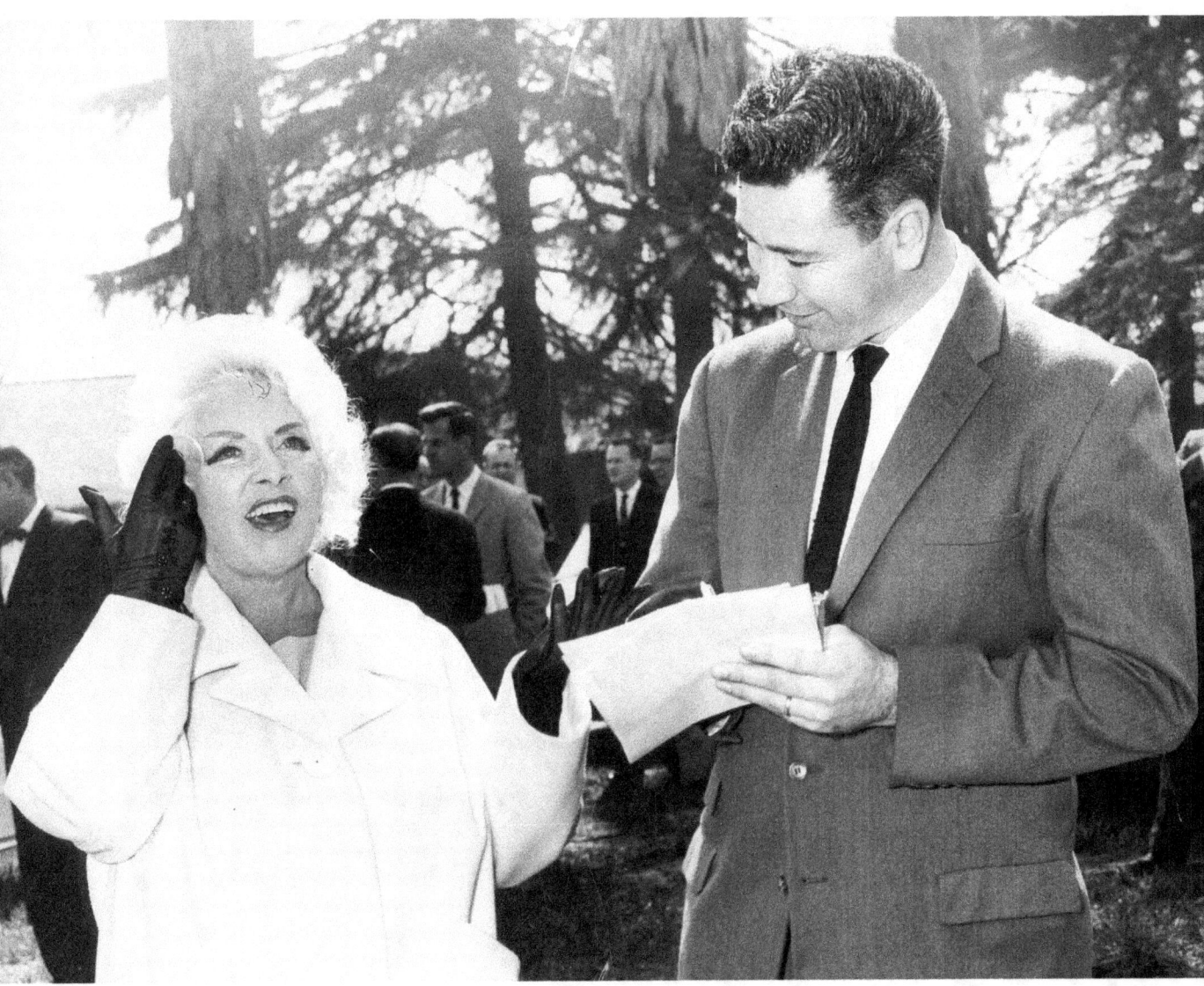

"Sultry actress Mae West tells *Valley Times* reporter she is looking for bids on property she owns in Valley. She attended the Ontra Cafeteria groundbreaking."
March 11, 1960. (Order #00086248)

"Academy Award-winning actress Bette Davis will be guest of honor tonight at the Valley Press Club's annual installation dinner-dance at the Sportsmen's Lodge. Disc jockey Bob Crane will serve as master of ceremonies."
March 14, 1964. (Order #00108634)

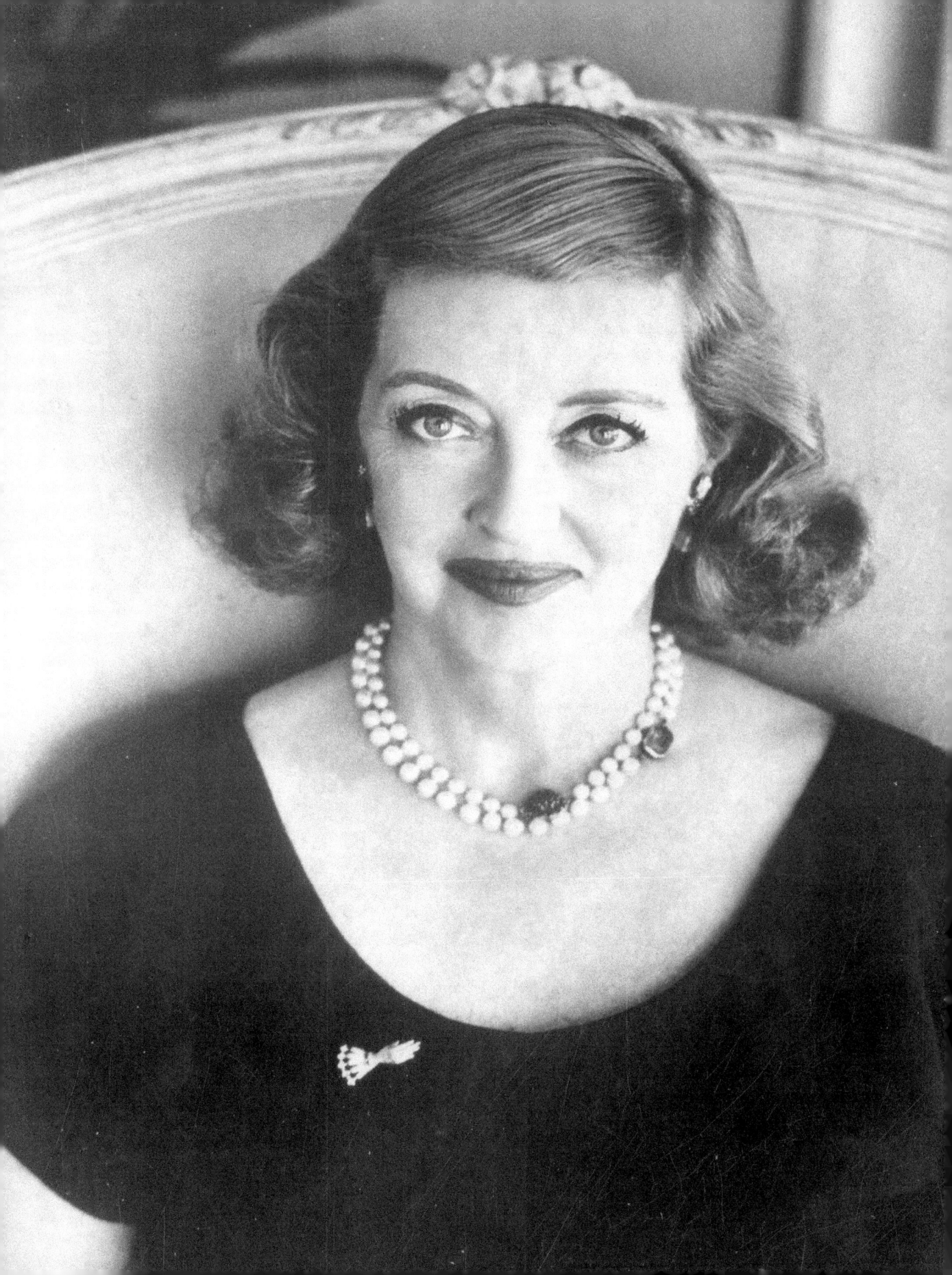

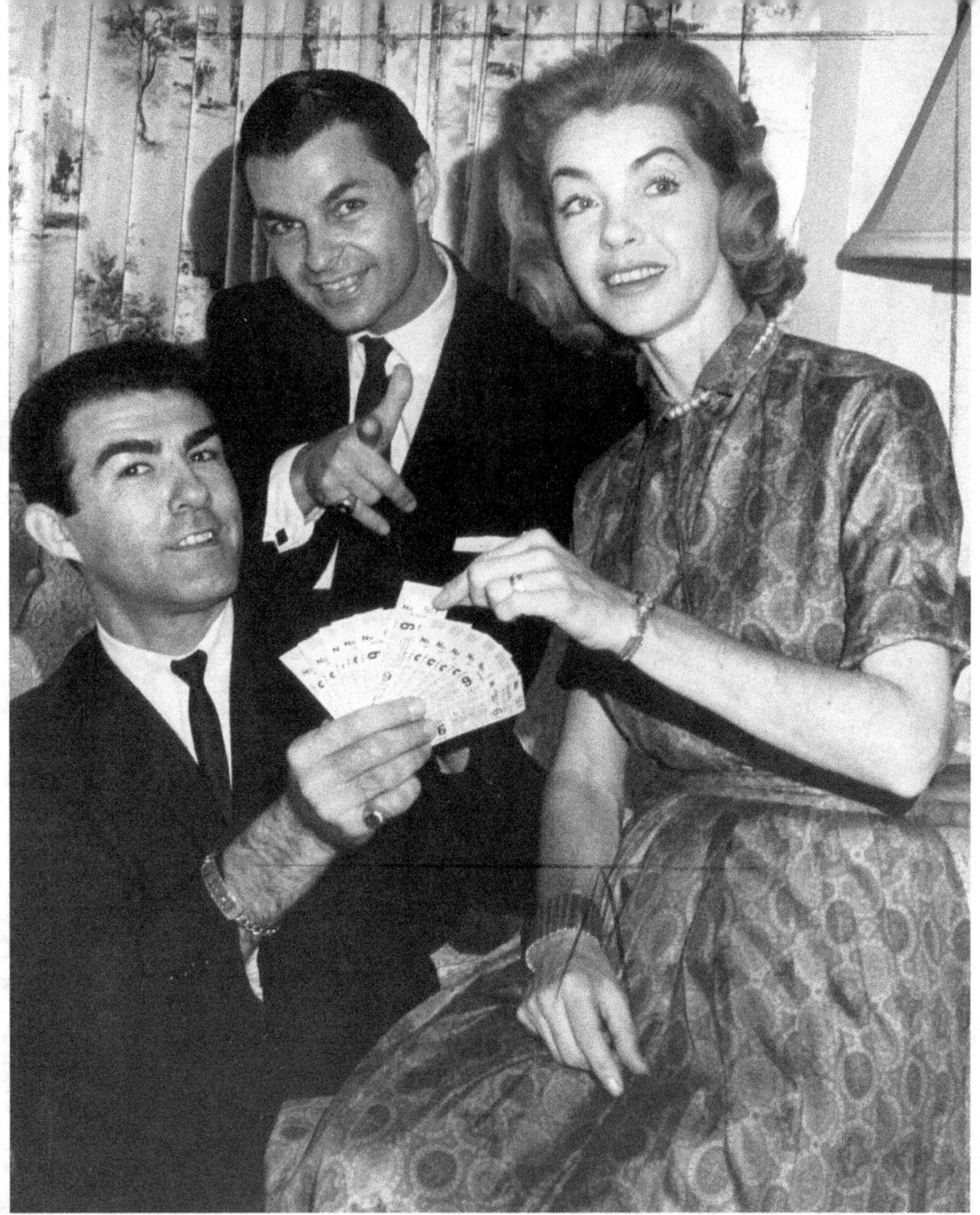

"Actress Marsha Hunt, president of the Valley Chapter of the American Association for the United Nations and board member of the U.S Committee for Refugees, accepts tickets to the Saturday performance of the Santa Monica Civic Ballet at Van Nuys High School from the ballet's director, Andrei Tremaine, sitting, and Paul Maure. The ballet has invited former refugees to be its guests that night."
May 3, 1961. (Order #00086252)

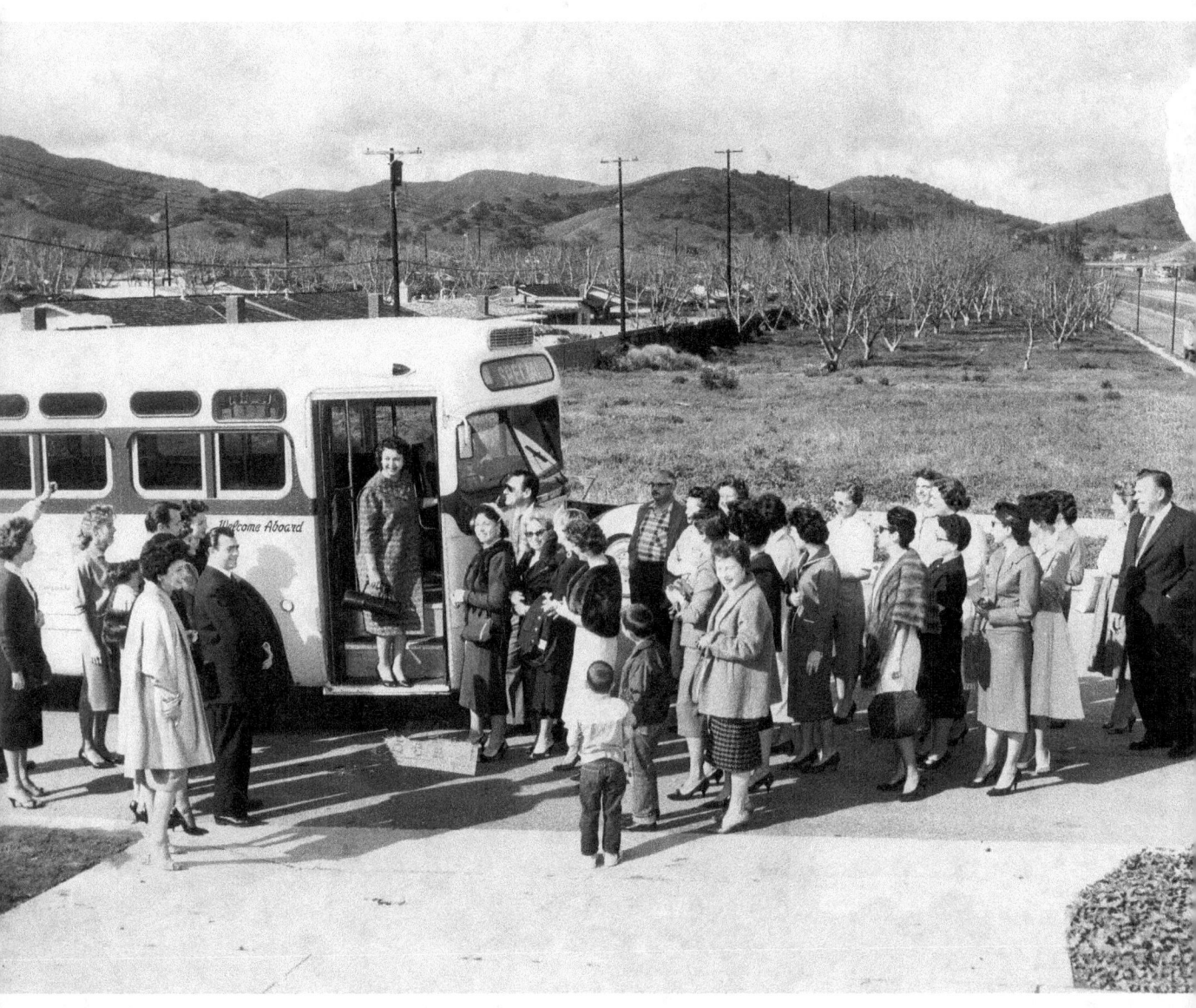

"Actress Jane Withers, on steps of bus, joins with Woodland Hills neighbors to help do fabled
"impossible"—fight City Hall. Residents are up in arms over apartment zoning for land visible
beyond charter bus which carried them downtown today. Homeowners say they bought homes
with understanding area would remain zoned for single family homes."
March 29, 1960. (Order #00093395)

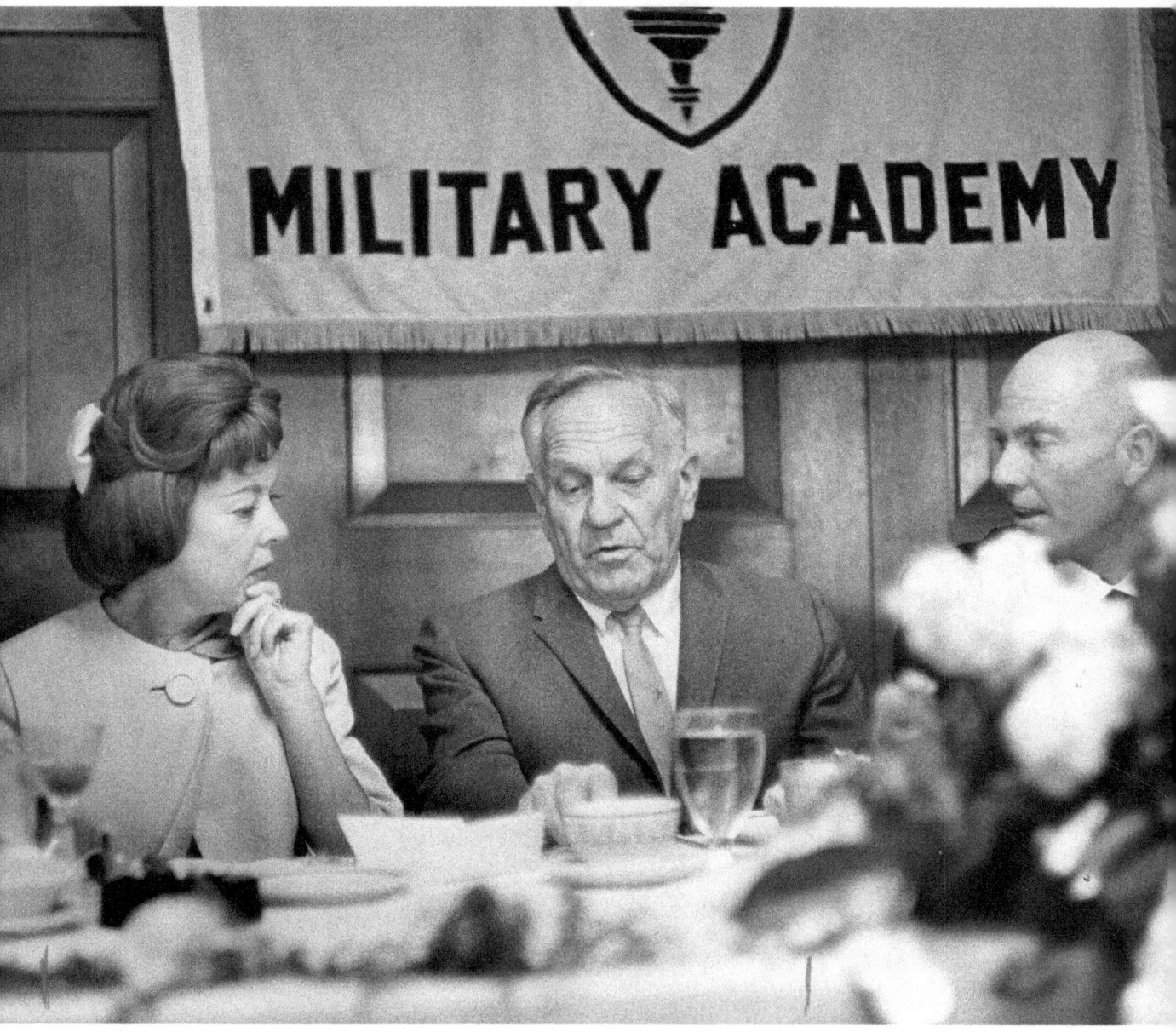

"Former Gov. Goodwin J. Knight talks to actress Ida Lupino at a luncheon Saturday for the Honorary Colonel's Club of Sepulveda Military Academy."
April 13, 1964. (George Brich)

(Order #00085325)

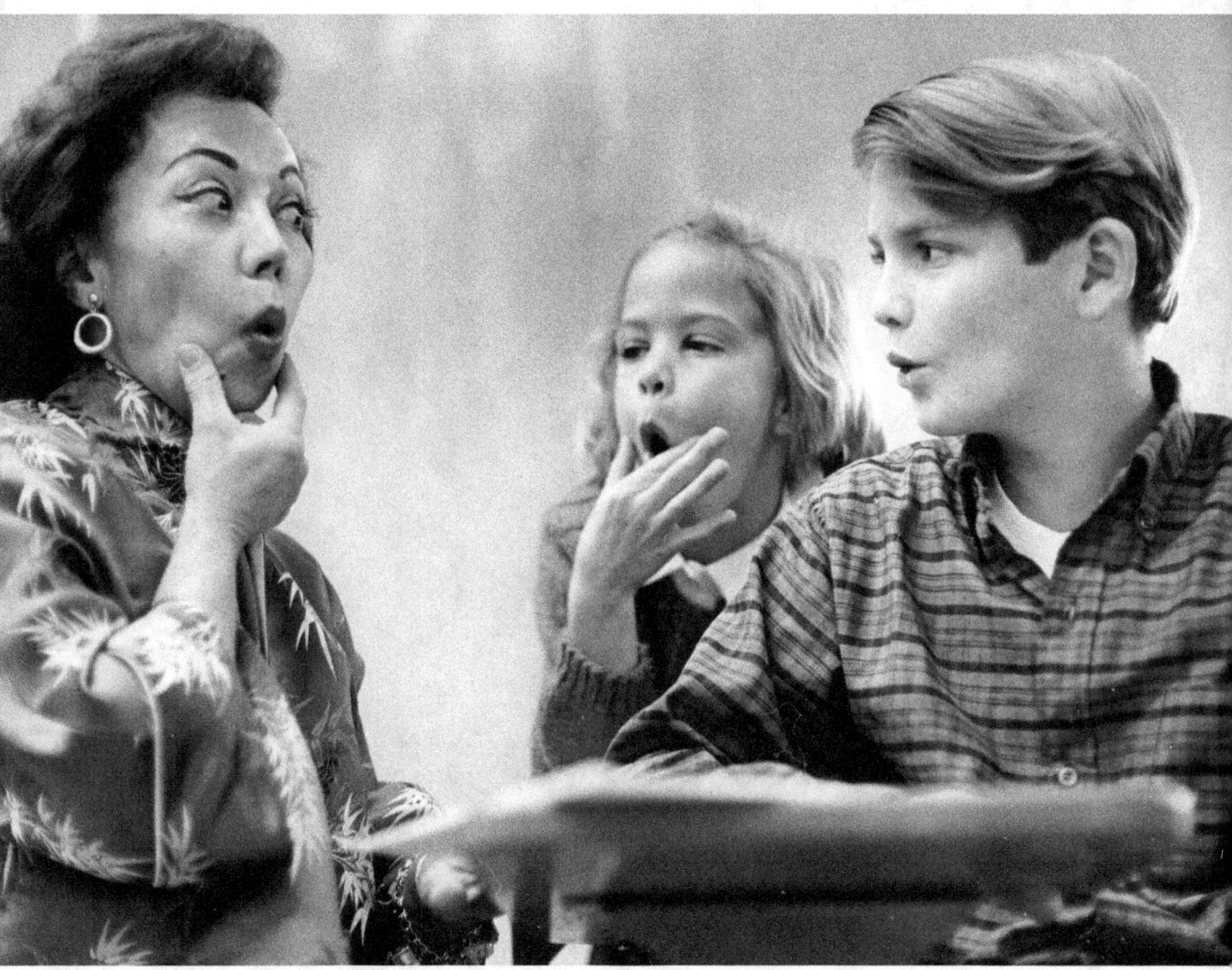

"June Foray shows youngsters Muriel Davis, 7, Northridge, and Tim Andreasen, 7, Northridge, how she achieves the pearly tones she uses in Bugs Bunny cartoons. It is part of a unique speech and drama class beginning March 15 at the Harridge Foundation."
February 15, 1965. (George Brich)

(Order #00109434)

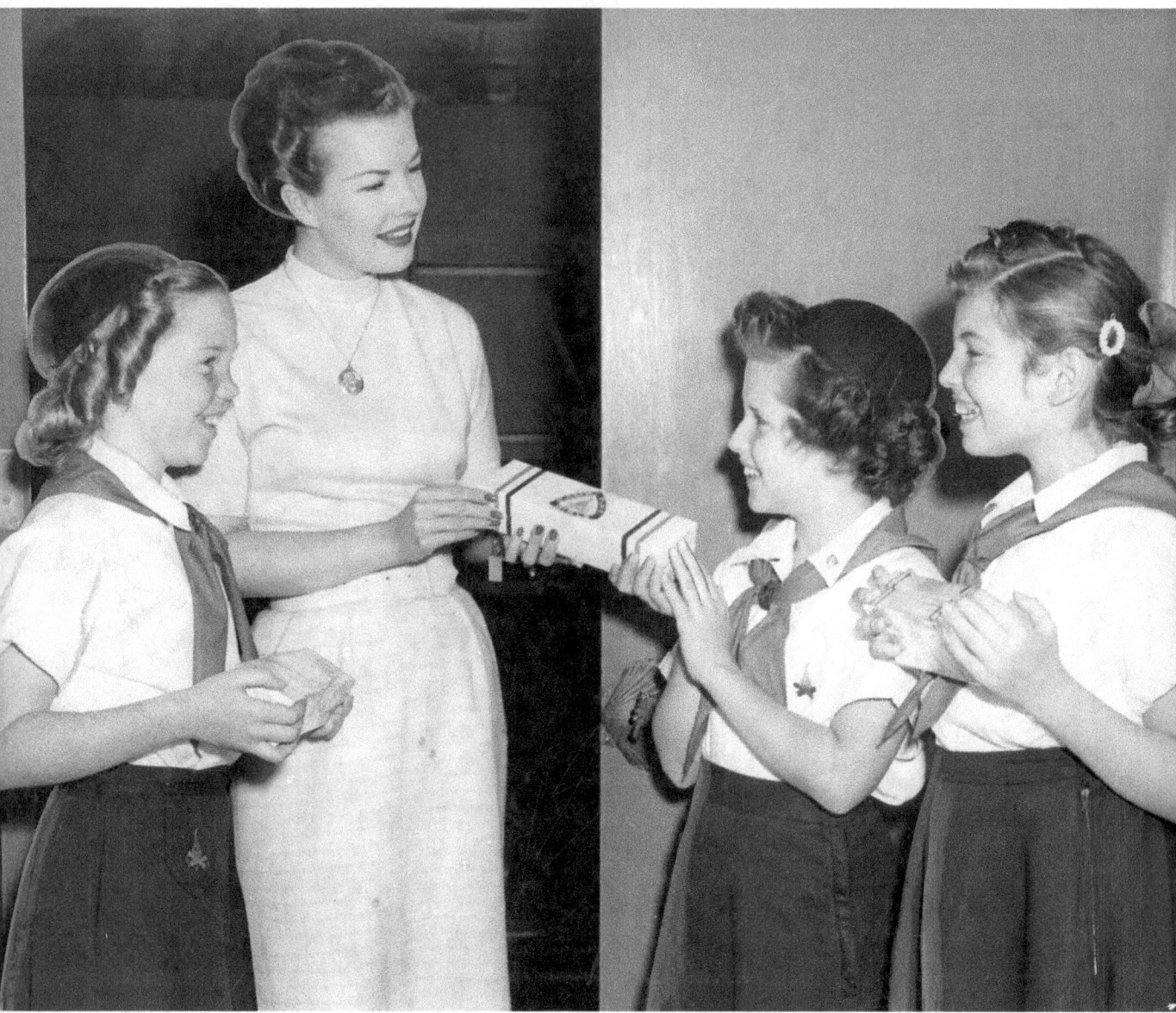

"'My Little Margie,' Gale Storm, center, buys Camp Fire Candy from Salesgirls, left to right, Sherry Caldwell, Mary Lou Giesler and Janice Robinson. Actress Gale Storm helps girls of O-Tan-Lo-Tin Group, sponsored by Valerio Elementary School, launch current Valley drive." April 5, 1955. (Order #00109684)

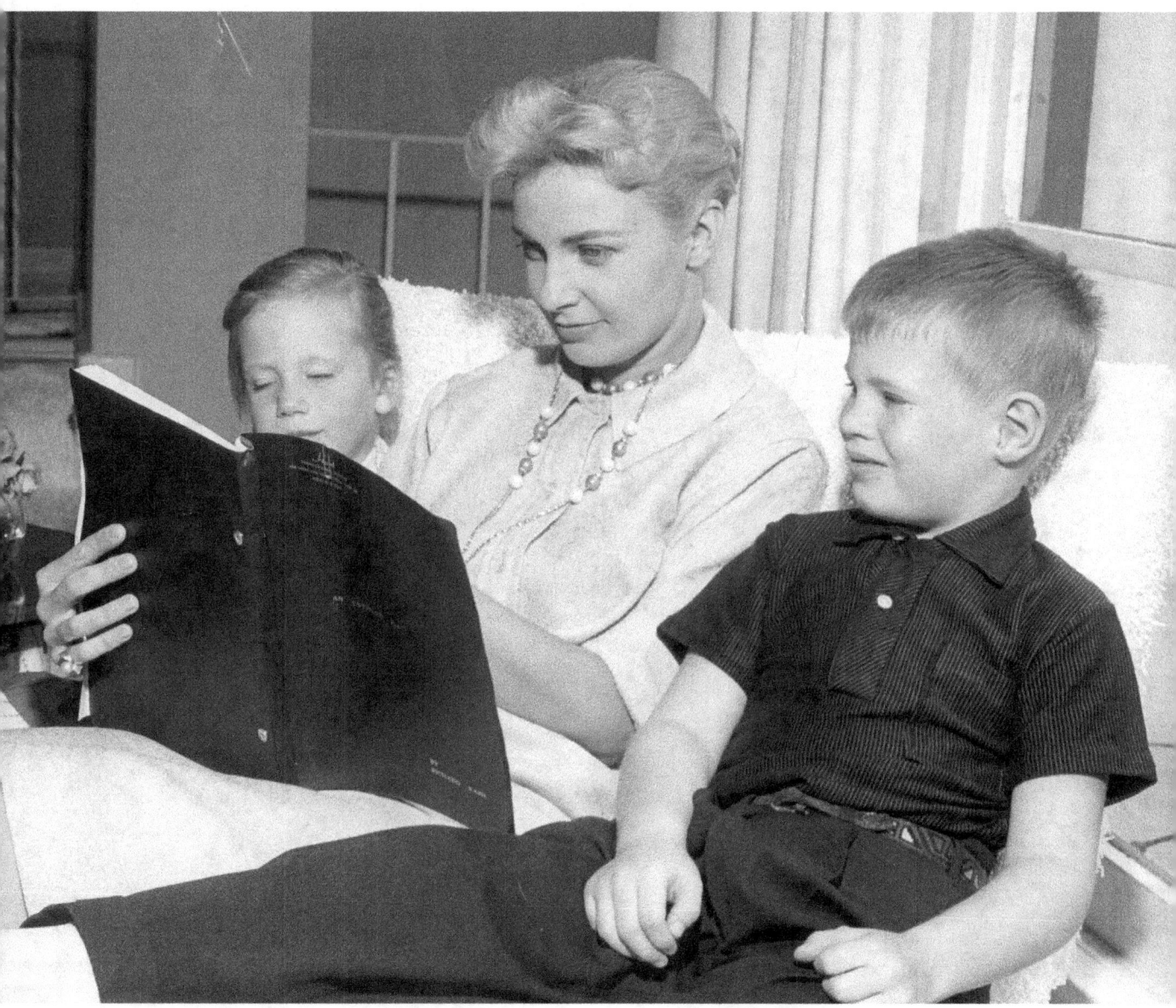

"Academy Award Winning actress Joanne Woodward reads to Tricia Reeve, 5, left, and
Kelly Smith, 7, at Speech Therapy Center, 4726 Libbit Ave., Encino. Miss Woodward is
one of number of movie personalities who have lent support to center which assists speech
handicapped children."
April 13, 1958. (Order #00109618)

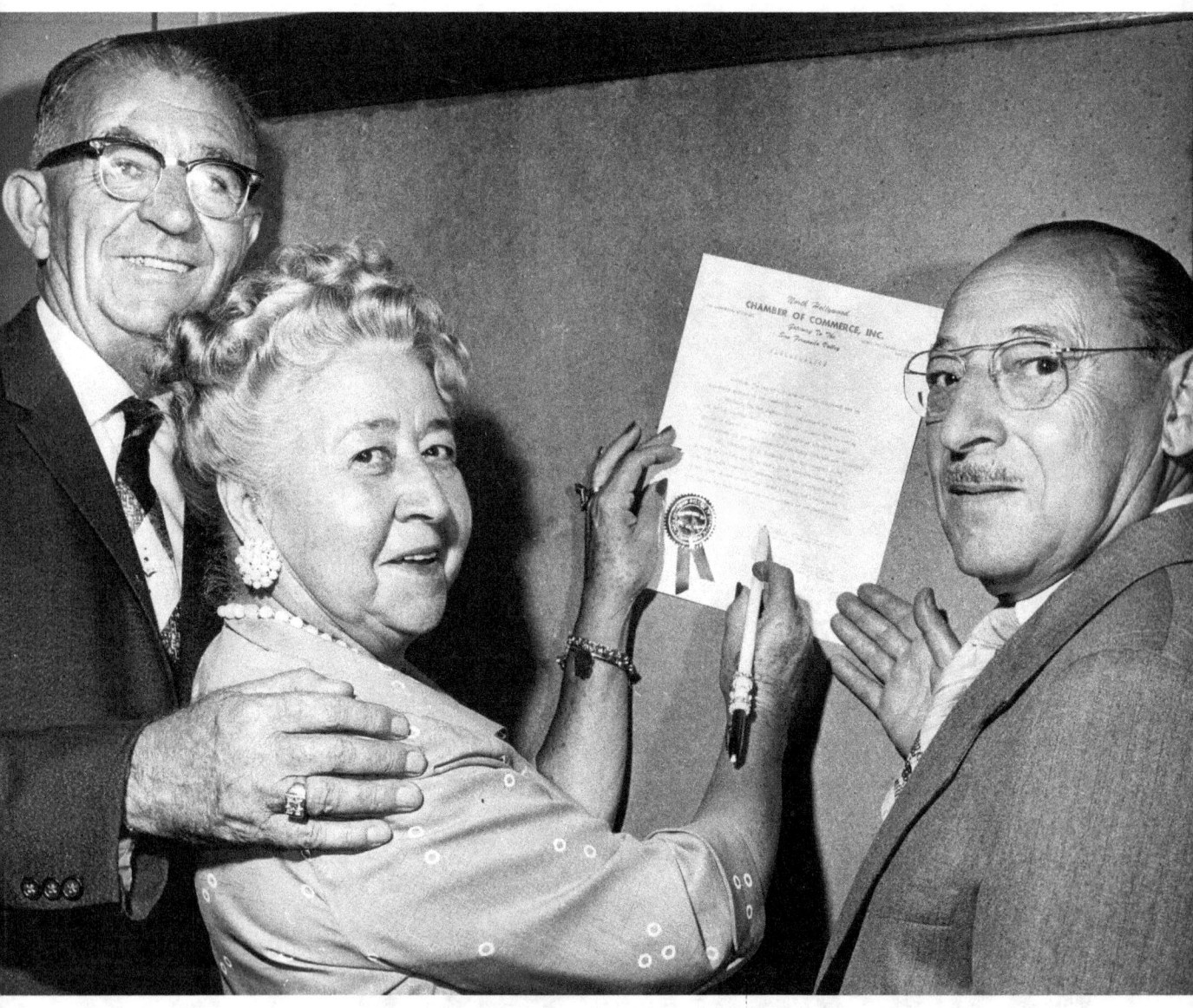

"Verna Felton, honorary mayor of North Hollywood, affixes signature to proclamation designating May as Senior Citizens' Month in North Hollywood. Proclamation was signed also by B. S. Hand, left, of Chamber of Commerce, in presence of Max Deutsch, president of Senior Citizens Club of North Hollywood."
May 23, 1960. (Order #00086288)

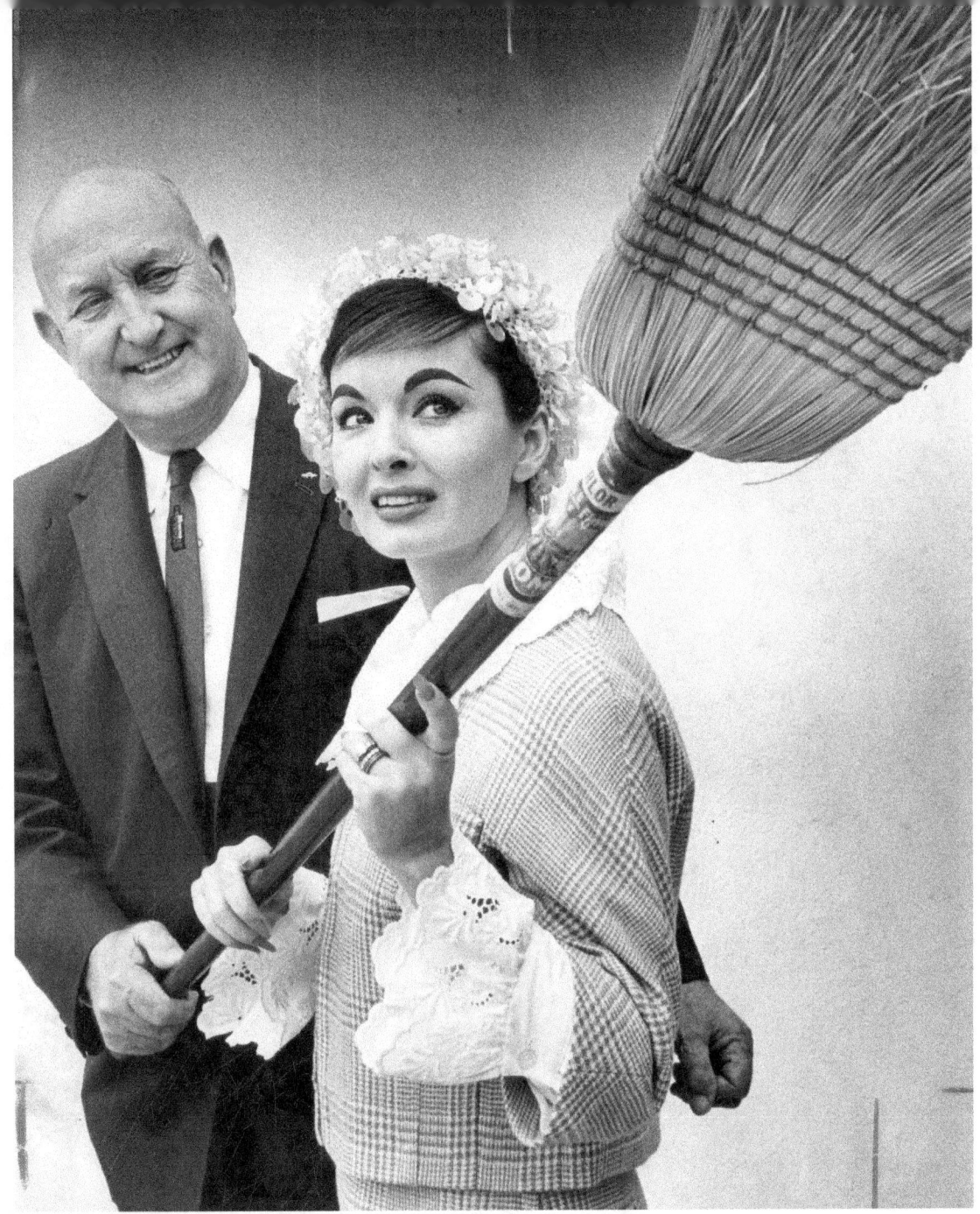

"Los Angeles City Councilman Everett Burkhalter stands behind actress Ann Blyth, Toluca Lake, to indicate his backing for Toluca Lake women who have formed a cleanup committee to make the community spotless. Burkhalter, 11005 Morrison St., North Hollywood, joined civic leaders as they met at Miss Blyth's home, 6 Toluca Lake Estates."
March 27, 1961. (George Brich)

(Order #00109661)

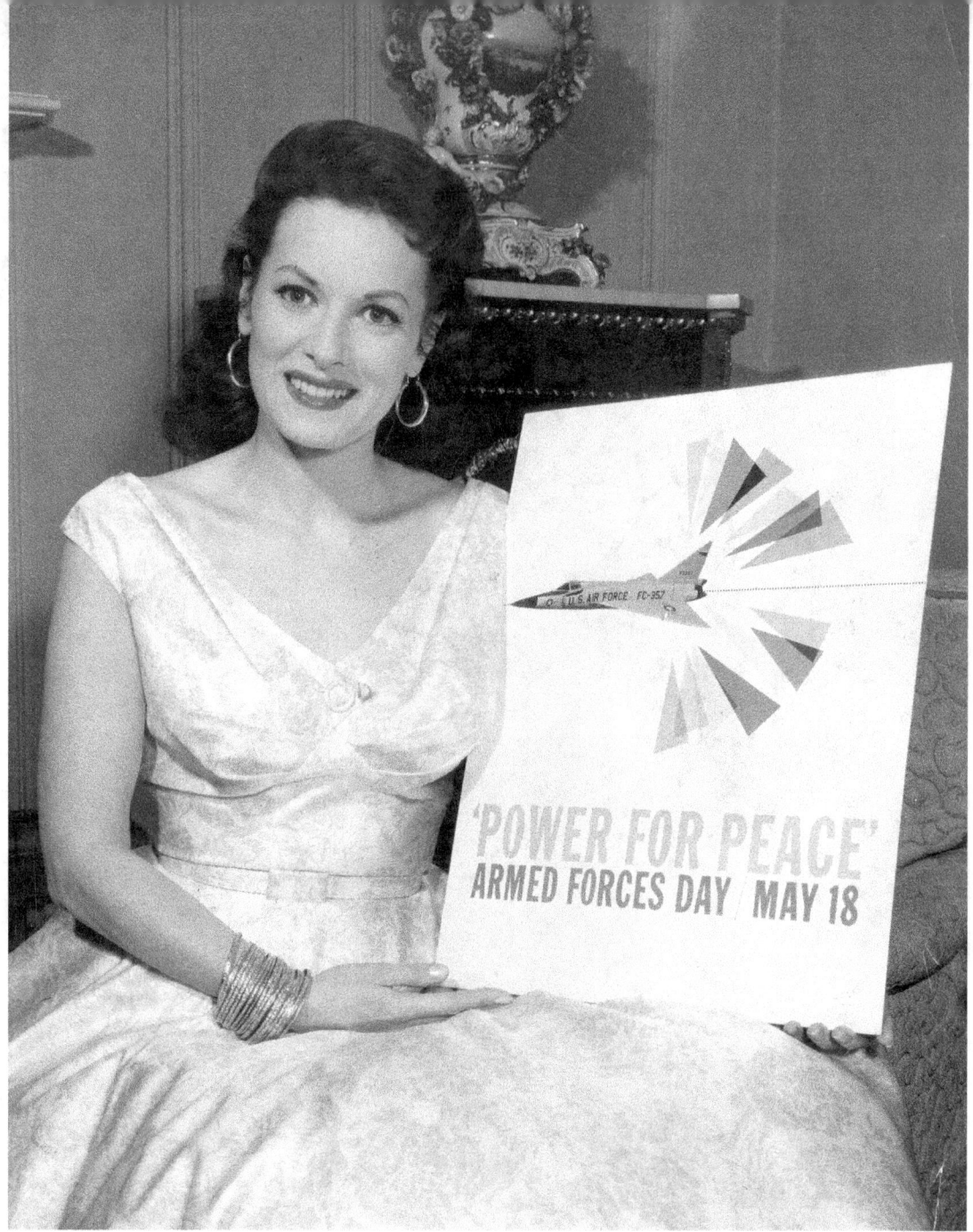

"Pretty actress Maureen O'Hara, born in Ireland, will join with millions of fellow Americans around world in observance of 10th annual Armed Forces Day May 18. Theme of this year's celebration is 'Power For Peace.' Air bases near Valley and Van Nuys Airports will hold open house to public to show latest air weapons. Navy and Army installations will also open their doors."

March 22, 1957. (Order #00109847)

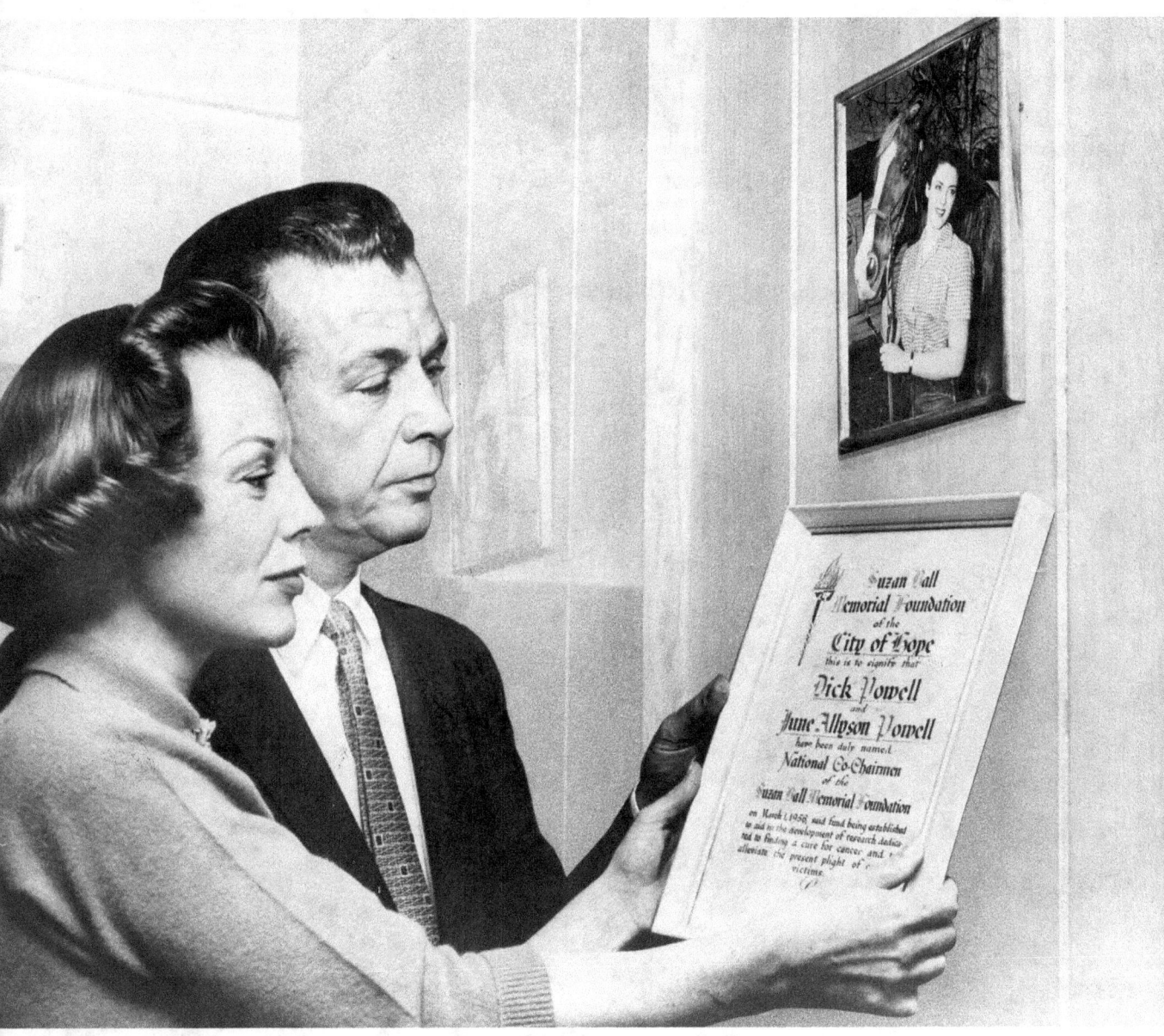

"Actress June Allyson and her actor-husband Dick Powell have been named as co-chairmen of the Suzan Ball Memorial Fund, a tribute to the late young Valley actress who fought courageous battle against cancer."
March 19, 1956. (Order #00111128)

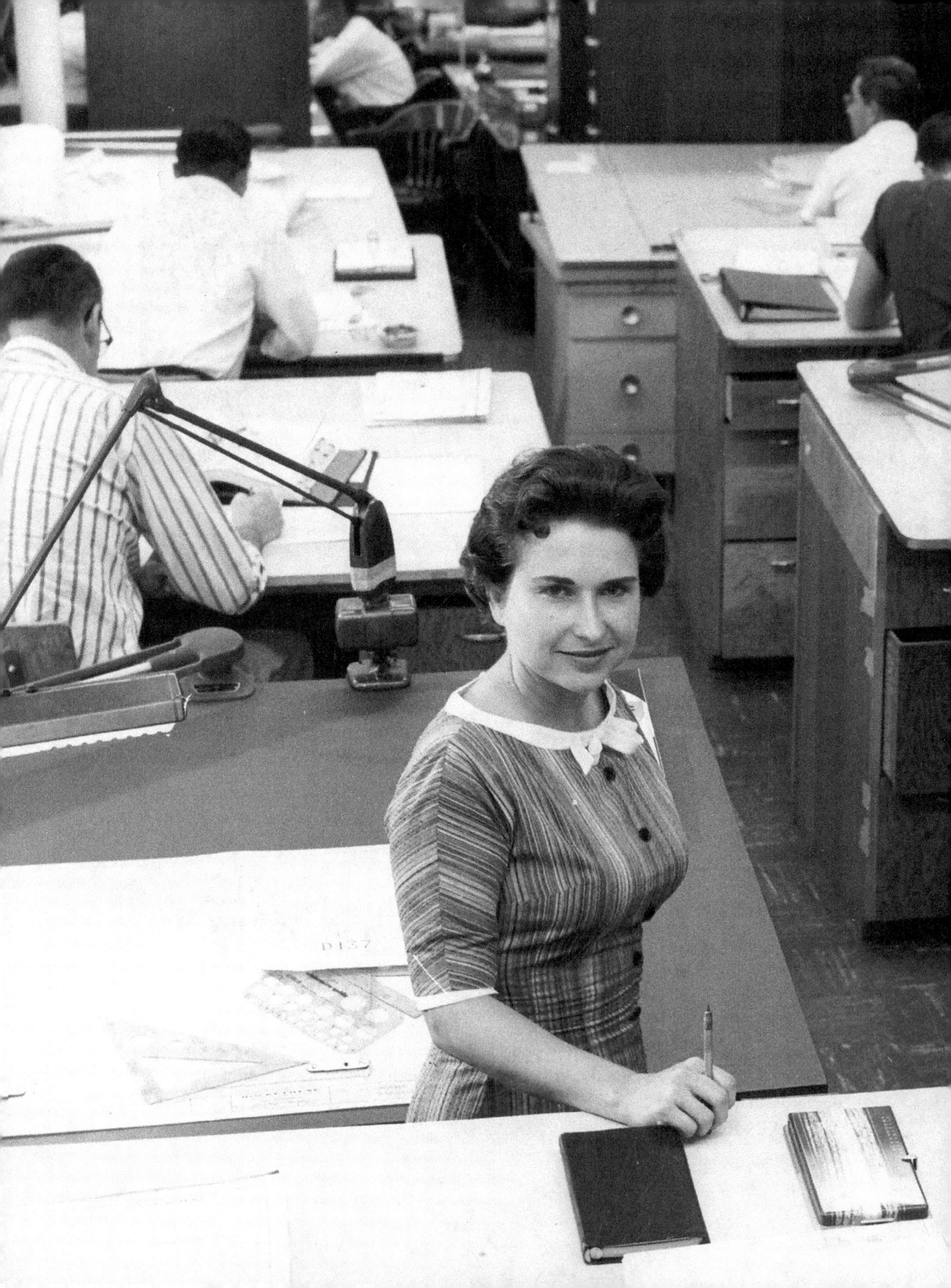

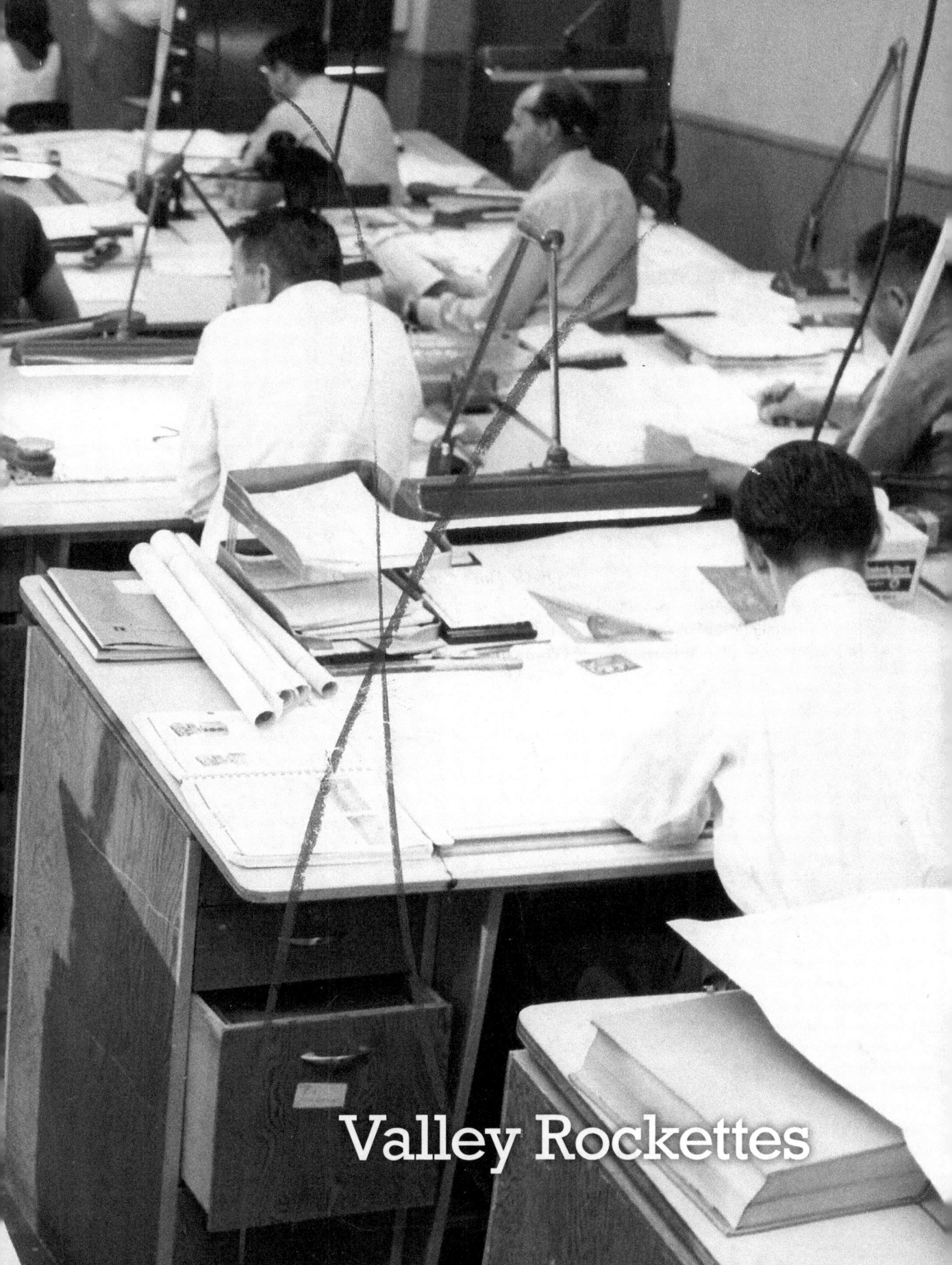

Valley Rockettes

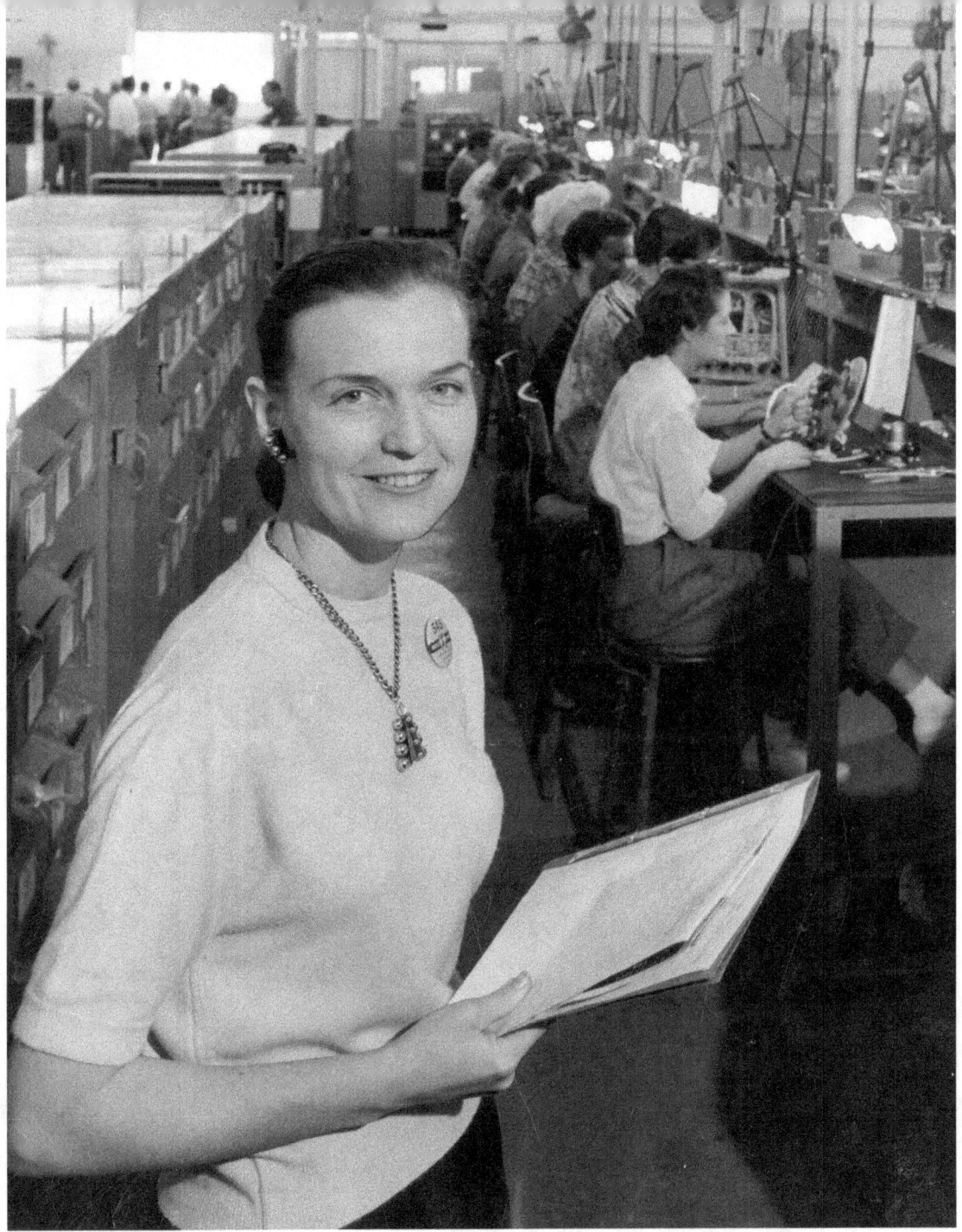

"Thelma Batchlor of Woodland Hills, 10-year veteran with North American Aviation, is lead woman in Rocketdyne electrical group supervising in wiring of junction boxes used in rocket engines that power nation's biggest ballistic missiles. There are 2,260 women at Valley plant who are backing space effort."
February 4, 1959. (Order #00086242)

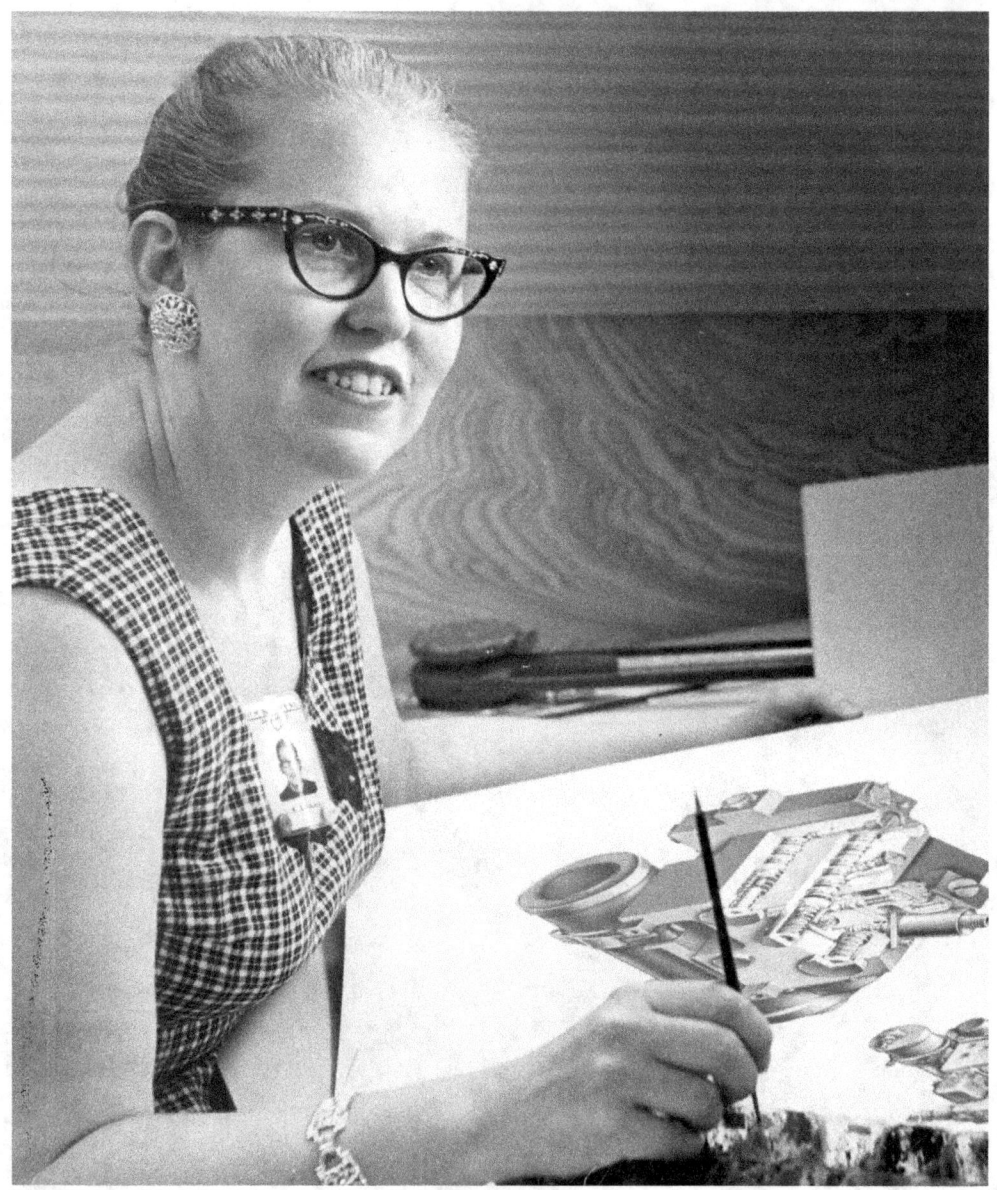

"Although fine art painting may seem far removed from illustration of rocketry hardware, Lauren Erickson is successful in both fields. A resident of Canoga Park, Mrs. Erickson is employed in the commercial, and air brush group of Rocketdyne's Canoga avenue installation."
August 8, 1960. (Jon Woods)
(Order #00108961)

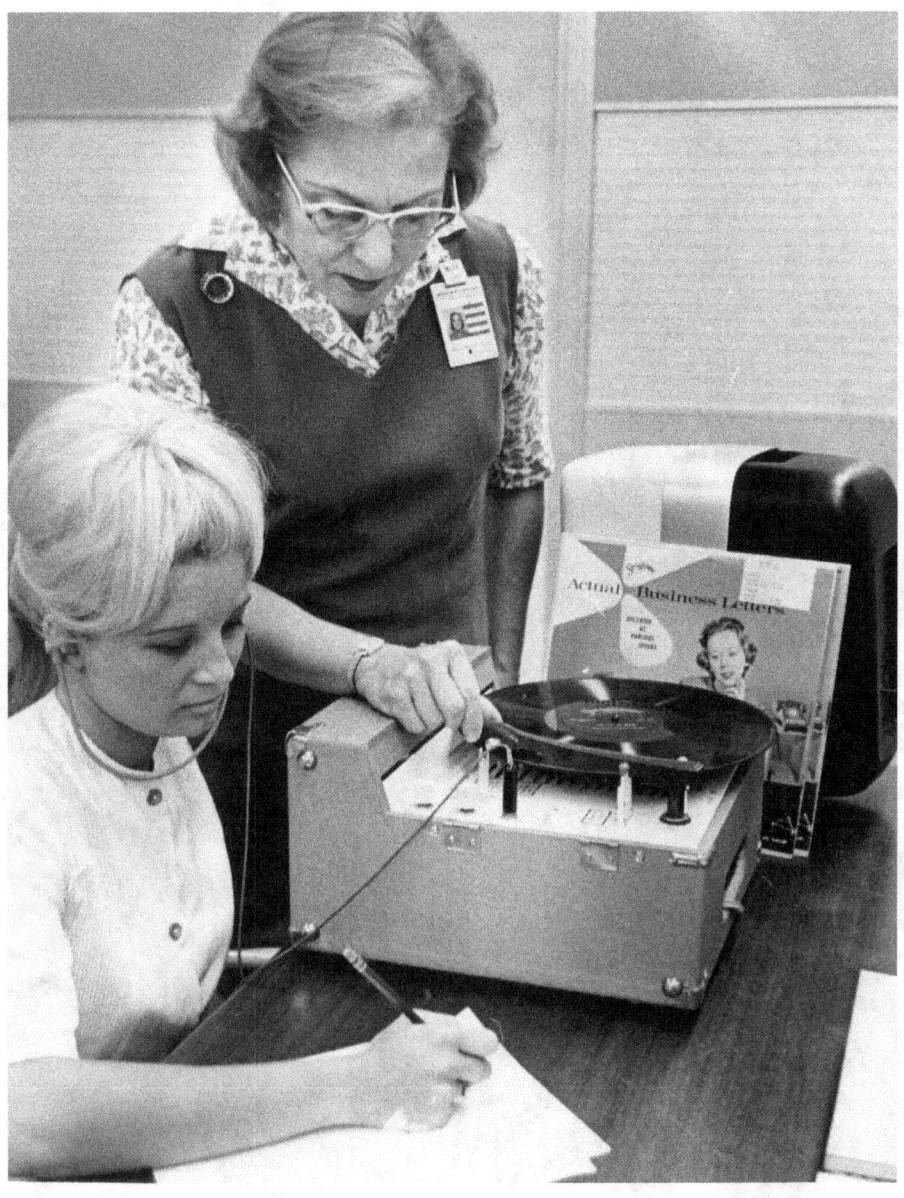

"Participating in Rocketdyne's internal secretarial training program, Mrs. Sharon Jones, left, of Chatsworth, takes a lesson on business letter writing from Mrs. Lani de Ganges, instructor for the company-sponsored program." July 12, 1965. (Jeff Goldwater)

(Order #00108918)

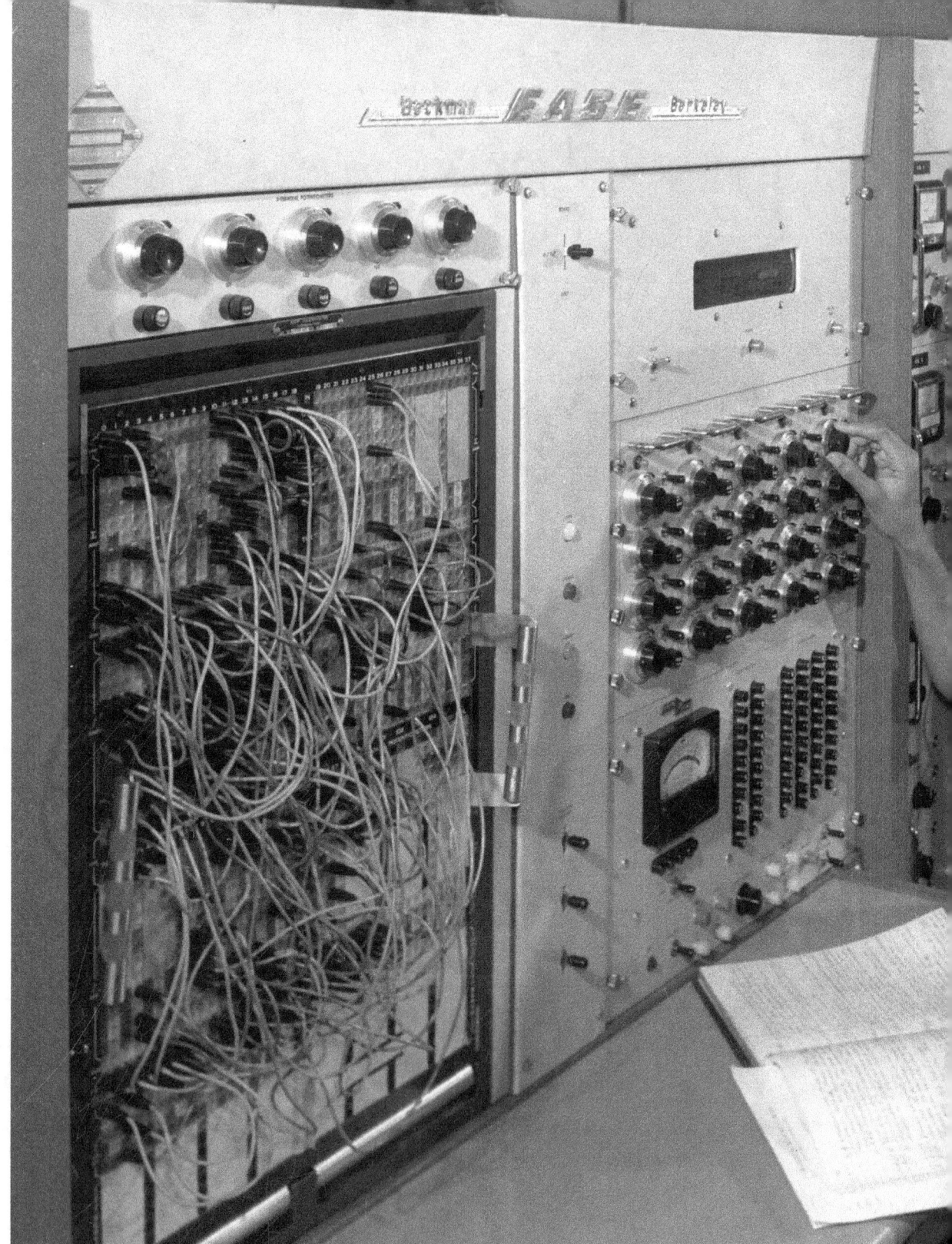

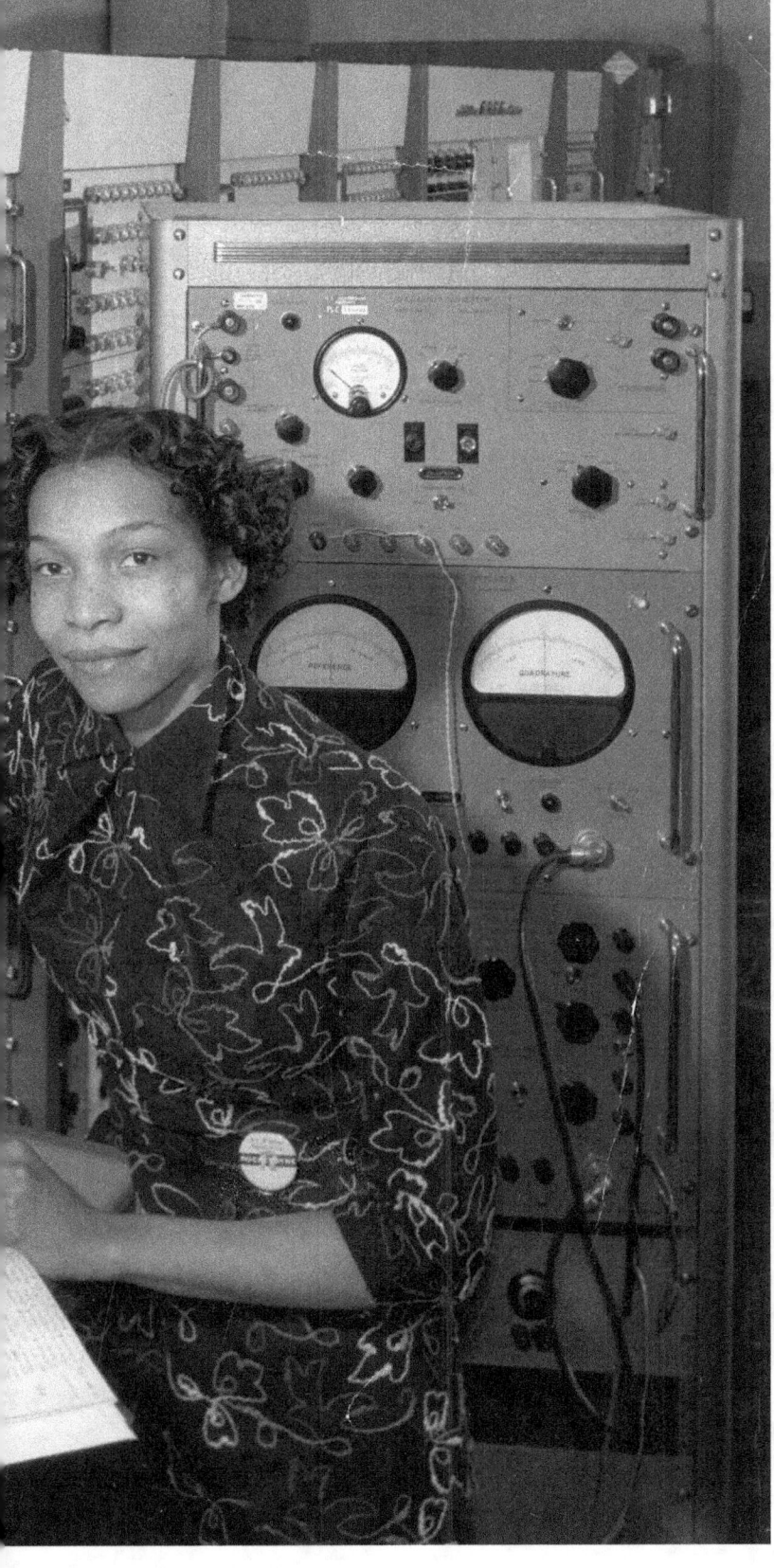

"Nasira Wilkins of Los Angeles is a graduate of Howard University with master's degree in physics. She spends her Rocketdyne hours studying new liquid propellant rocket engine concepts."
February 4, 1959.
(Order #00086244)

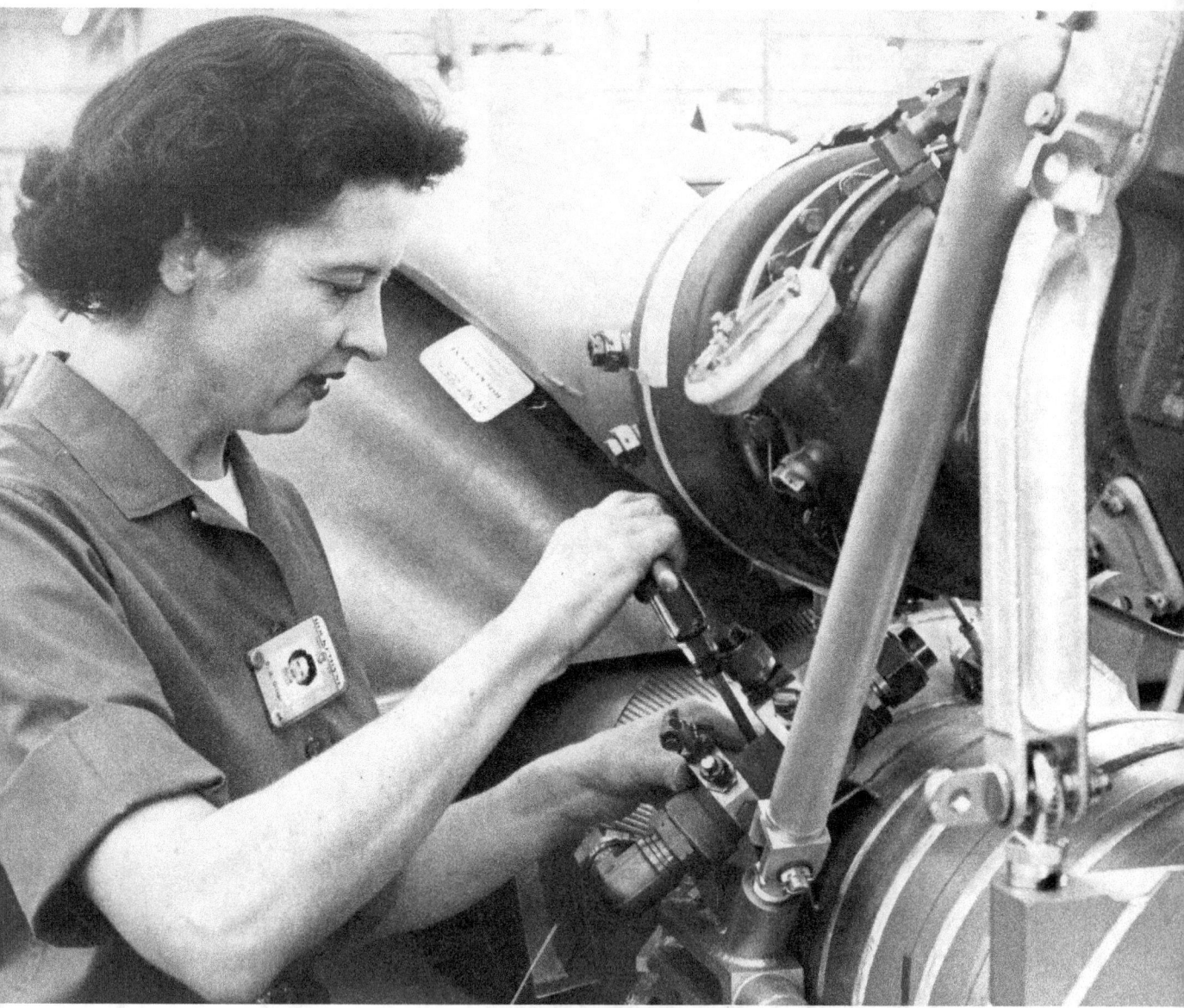

Donna Gilman who worked on one phase of astronaut John Glenn's historic orbit of Earth is back at work immediately following the launch.
February 20, 1962. (Alan Hyde)

(Order #00108913)

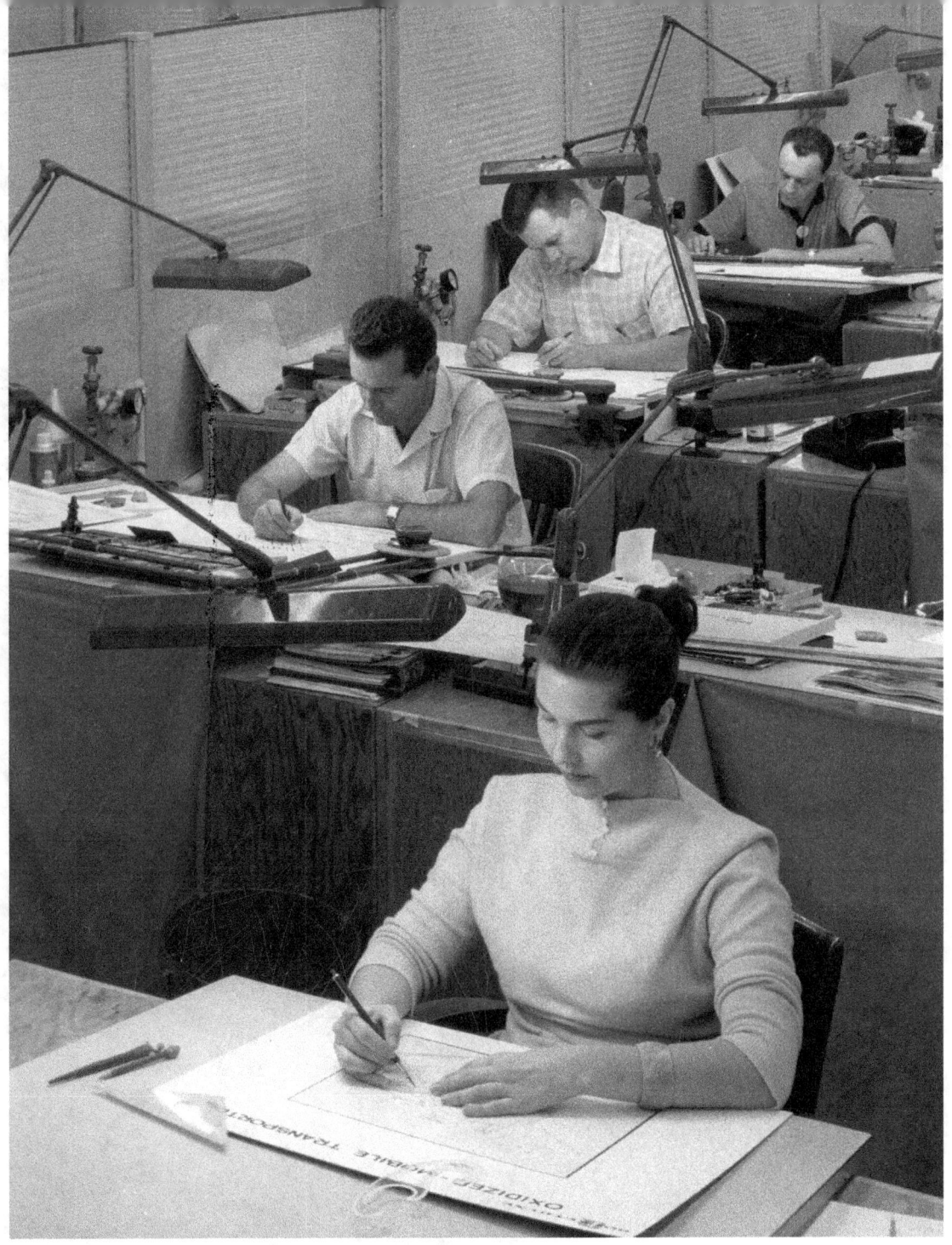

"Eva Major of Granada Hills makes drawings of structural detail of many Rocketdyne engines.
She is one of 132 artists and illustrators employed at West Valley installation."
February 4, 1959. (Order #00086246)

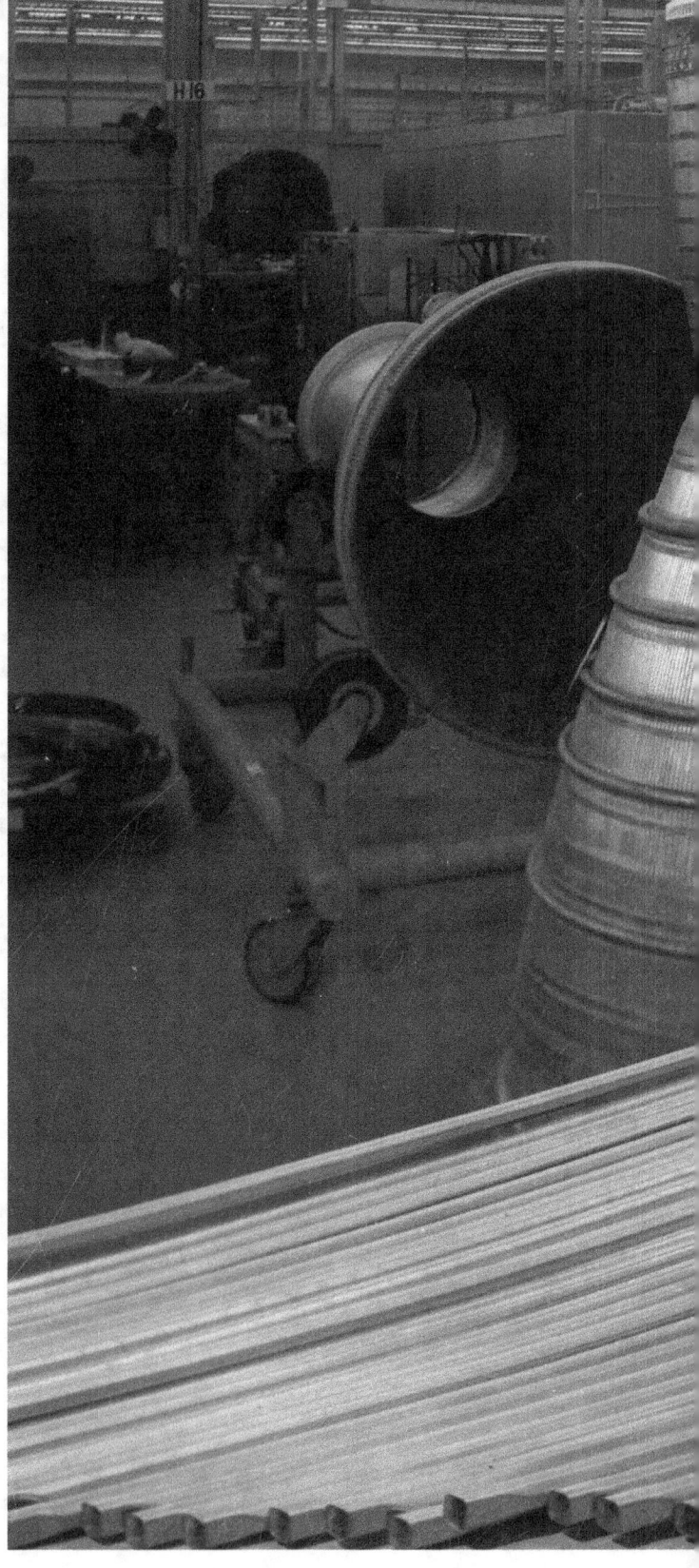

"Shirley Smith, of Woodland Hills, holds Master's degree in Mechanical engineering. She is specialist in heat transfer designing tubes that brave temperatures of 5,000 degrees." February 4, 1959. (Order #00086245)

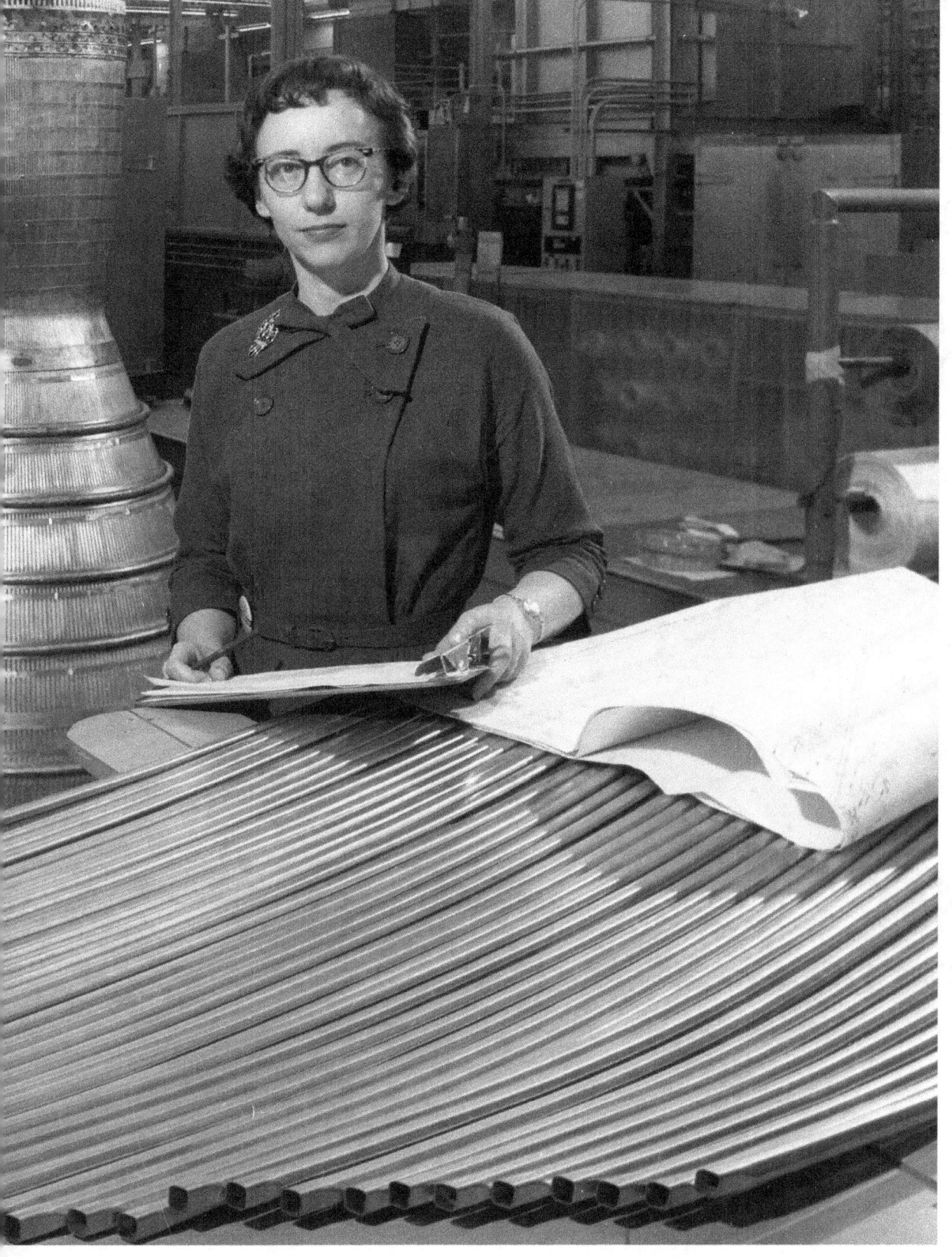

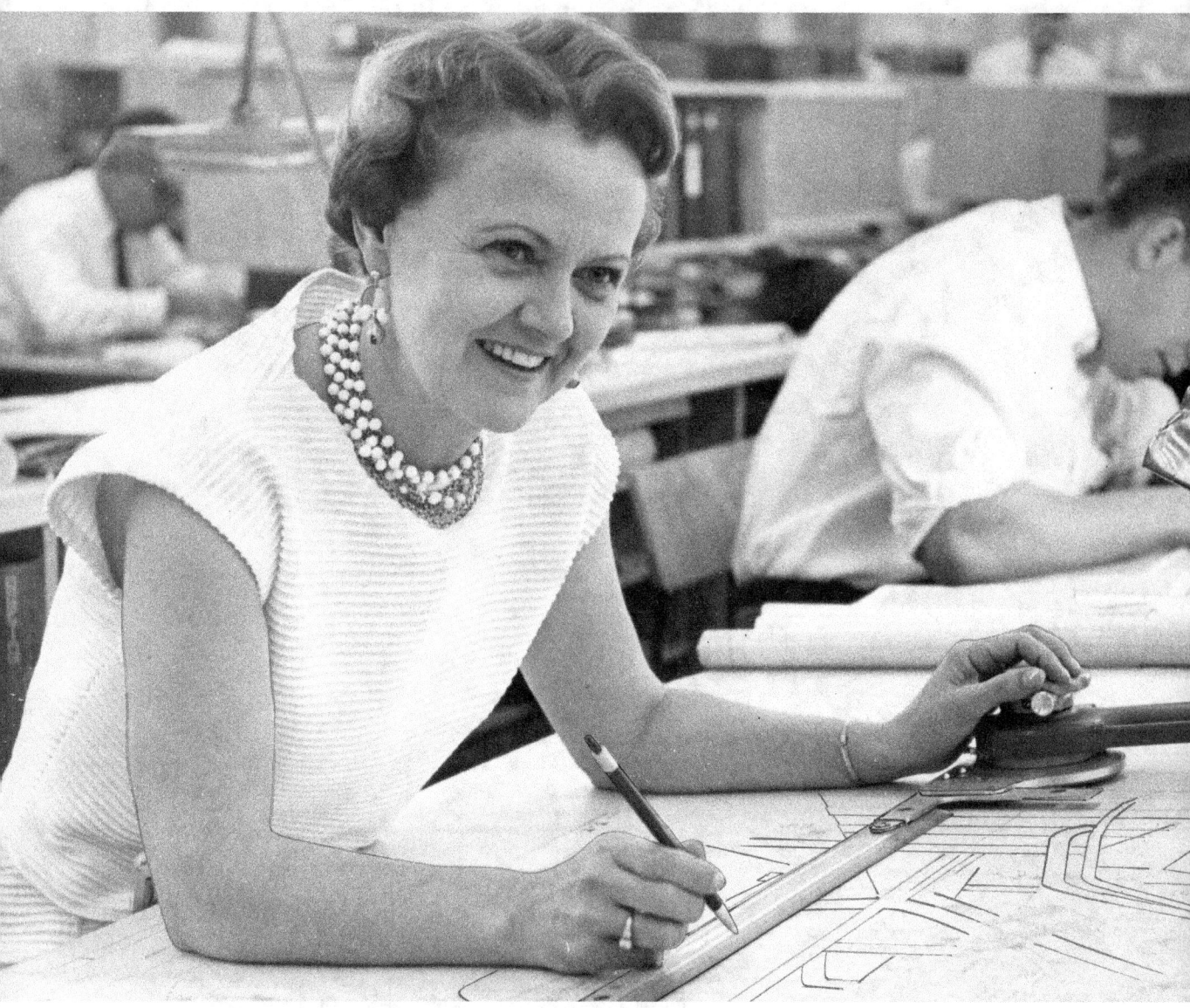

"Another test has taken place at Rocketdyne's Propulsion Field Laboratory, Canoga Park, where the Redstone, Thor, Jupiter and Atlas missiles have been given their first charge of life. But, back of these pace-setting missiles are the creative and technical contributions of thousands of people... among them, two Valley women, Faith McCollough and Ethlyn Ludolow, who spend eight hours a day in this world of tomorrow."
August 18, 1960. (Jon Woods)

(Order #00108999 & 00108998)

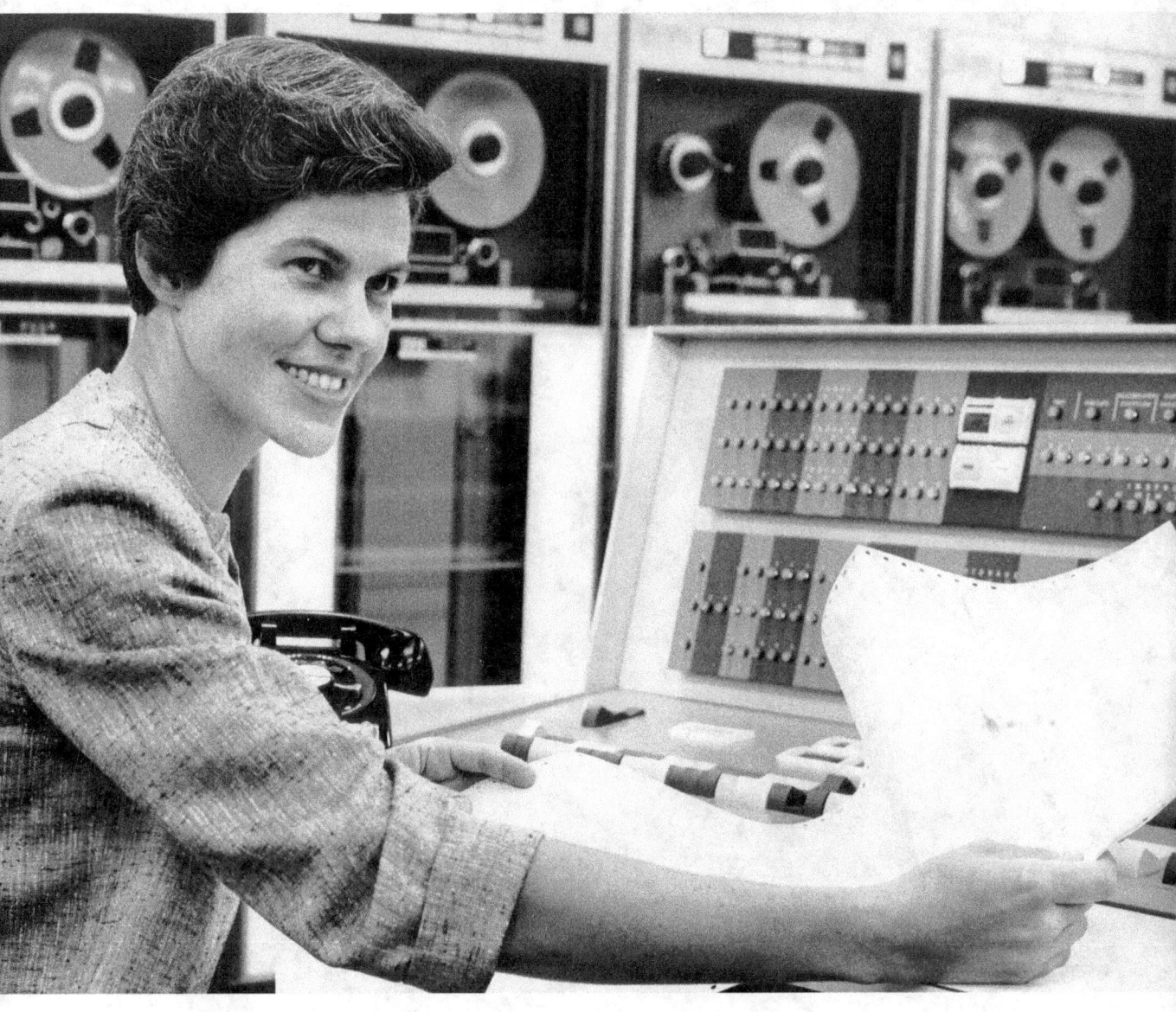

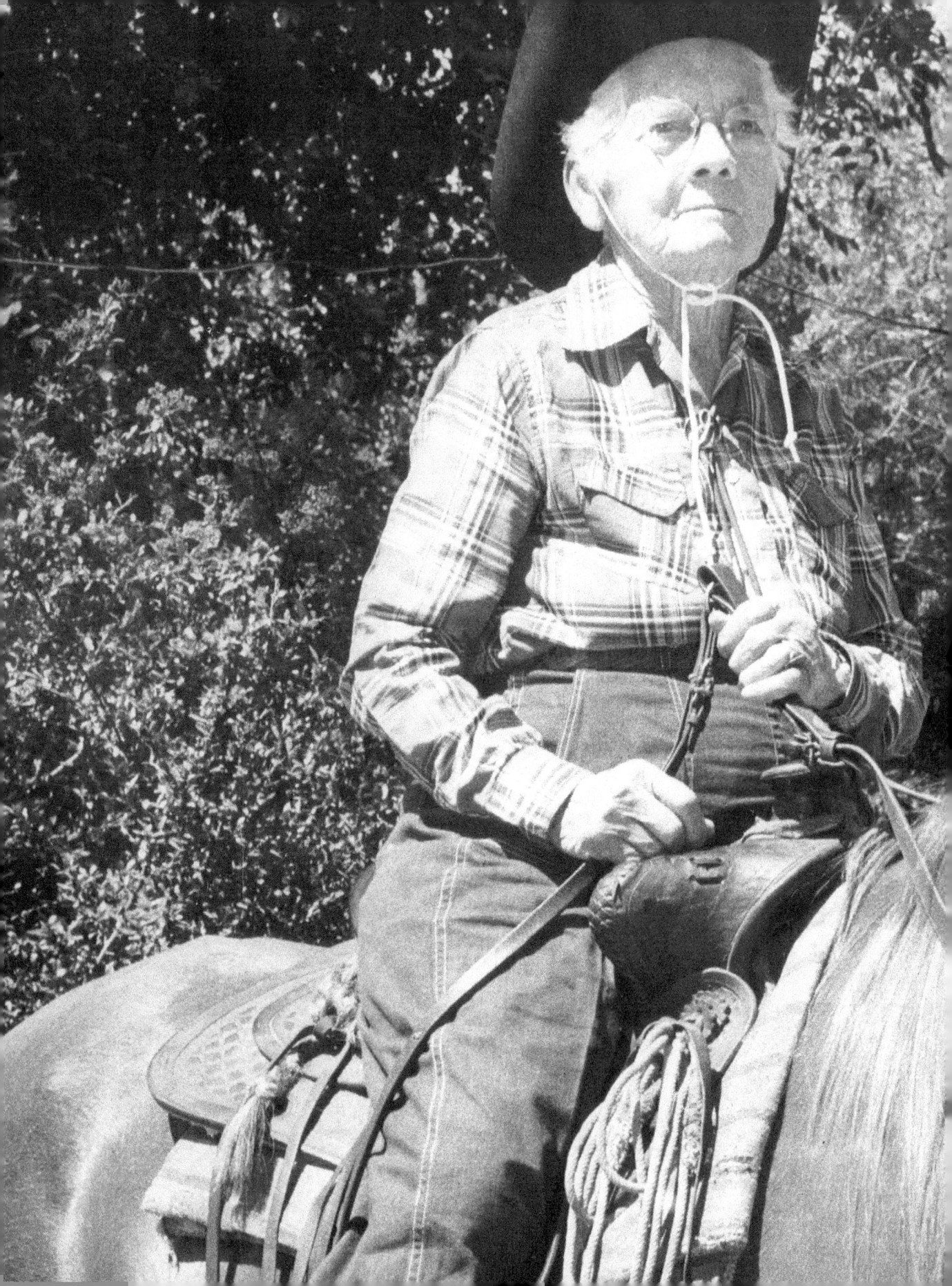

The Valley Pioneers

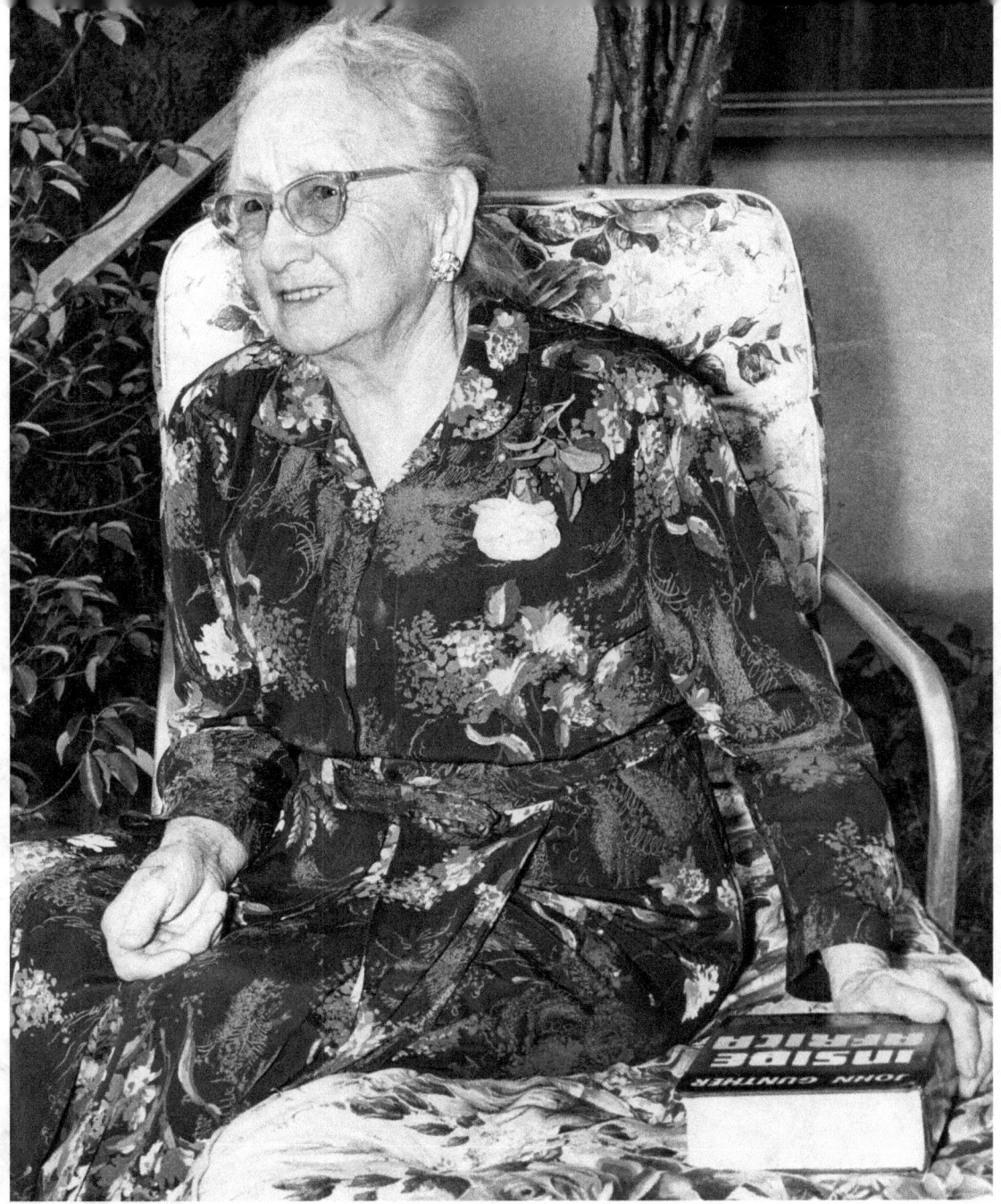

"Myra Milliken Sherwin, 90, interrupts her reading to look back over 50 years of Valley residence, during which she served as postmistress, nurse and mother." Myra Milliken Sherwin who moved to the Valley in 1909 and married Fred B. Sherwin, was appointed postmistress of the town of Lankershim (now North Hollywood) by Fred Weddington of the Weddington General Store on Lankershim Blvd. In 1929 she moved from Lankershim "because Lankershim was beginning to get crowded," to Pacoima where she passed away at age 93 in 1962. November 14, 1959. (Order #00085569)

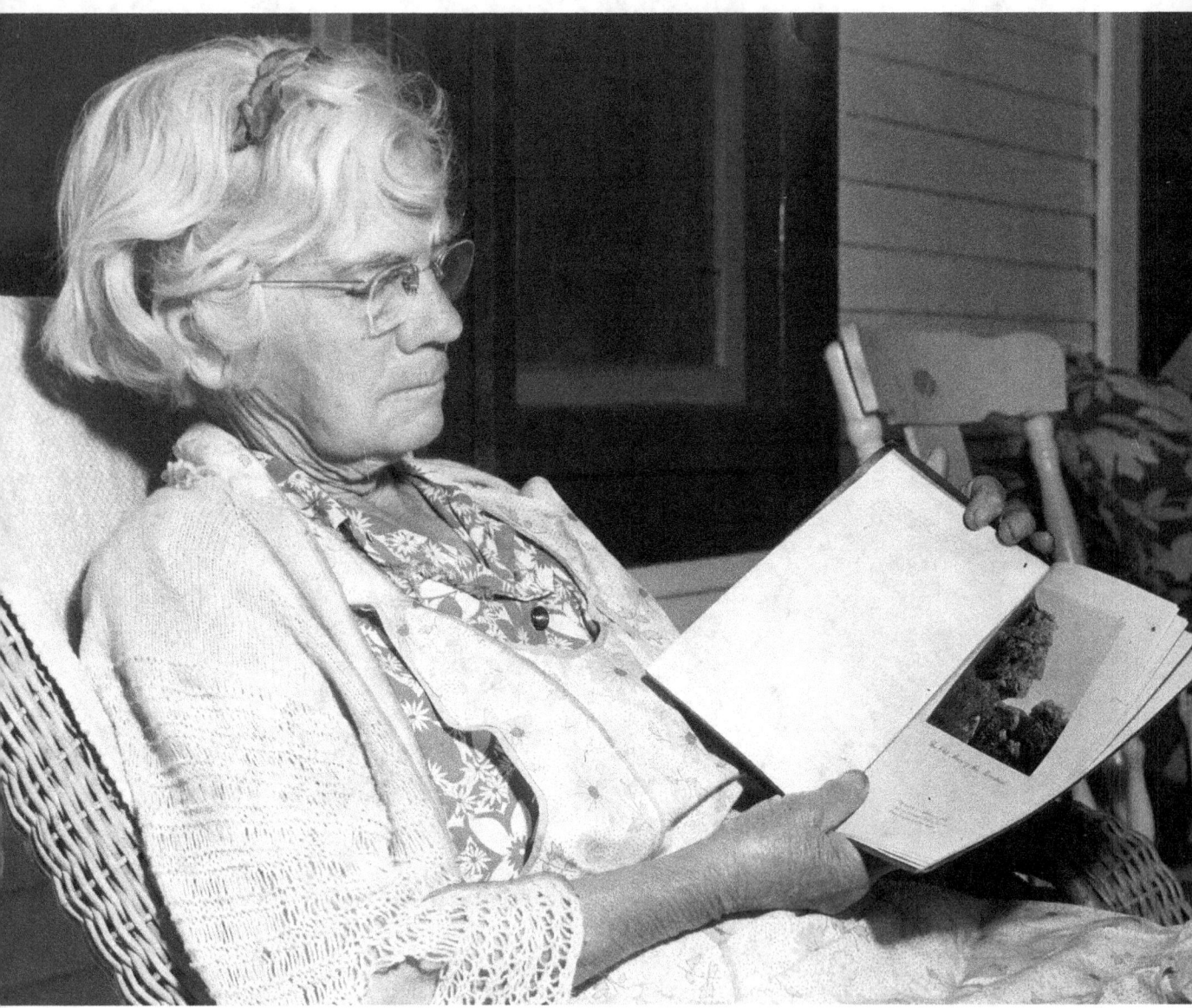

"Emma Graves views a photo of a stone monument she played around nearly three-fourths century ago."
May 26, 1948. (Order #00107969)

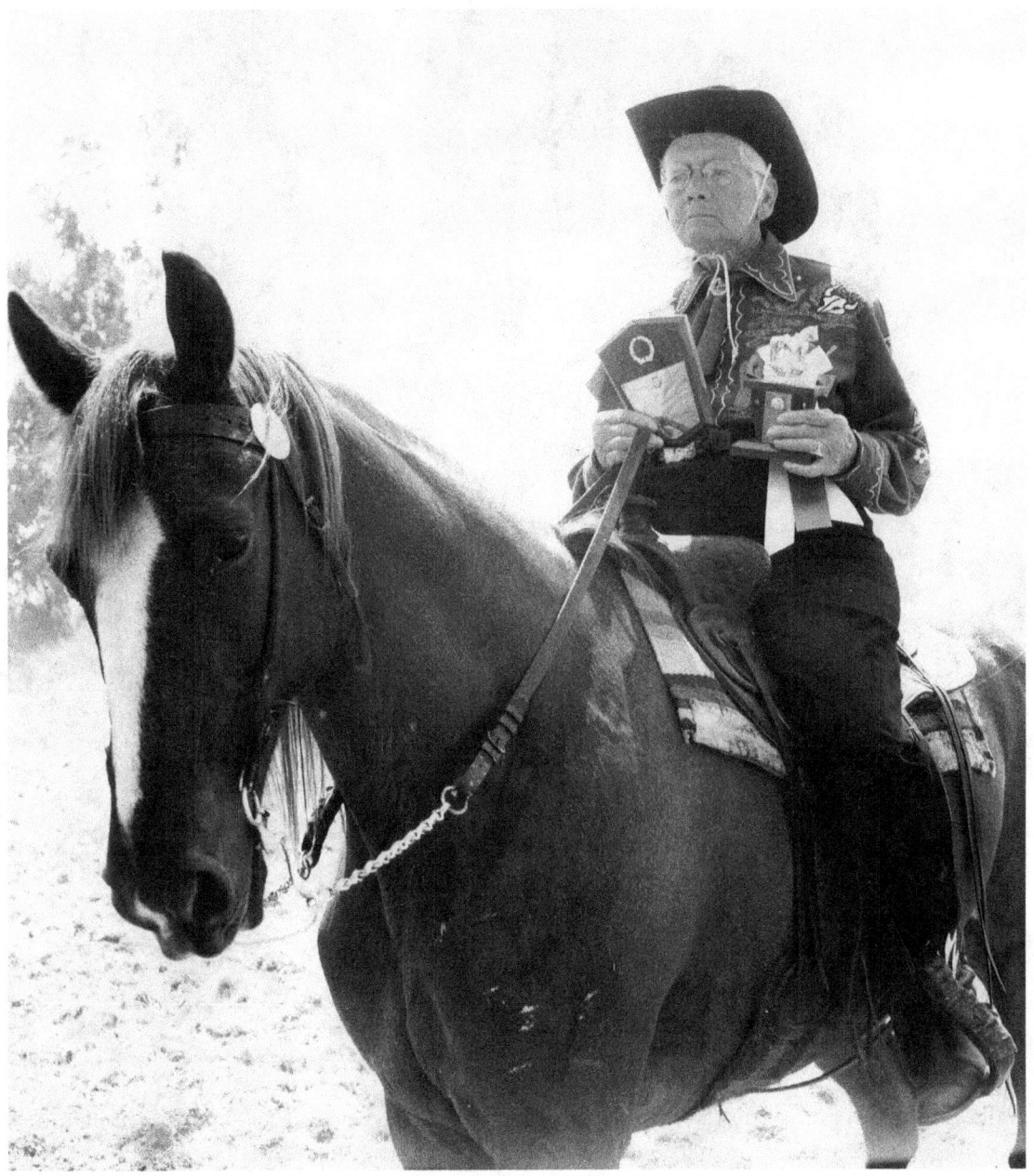

"Mrs. Emma Graves, 86, who was first white child born in Chatsworth area of Valley, rides her favorite mount, Hobby, as grand marshal of parade staged Saturday in observance of Chatsworth's 72nd anniversary."
June 15, 1959. (Order #00107978)

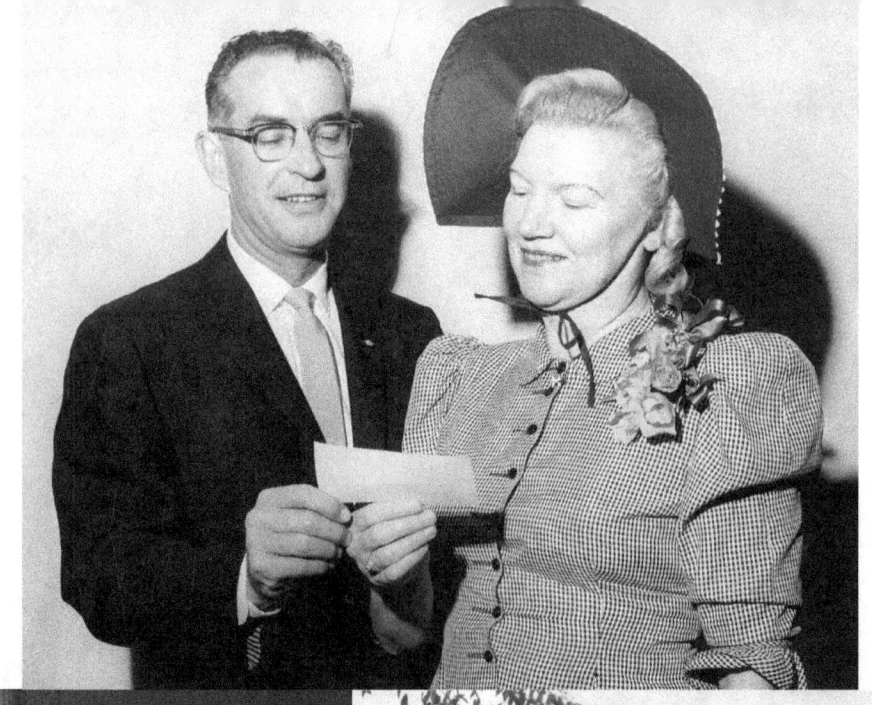

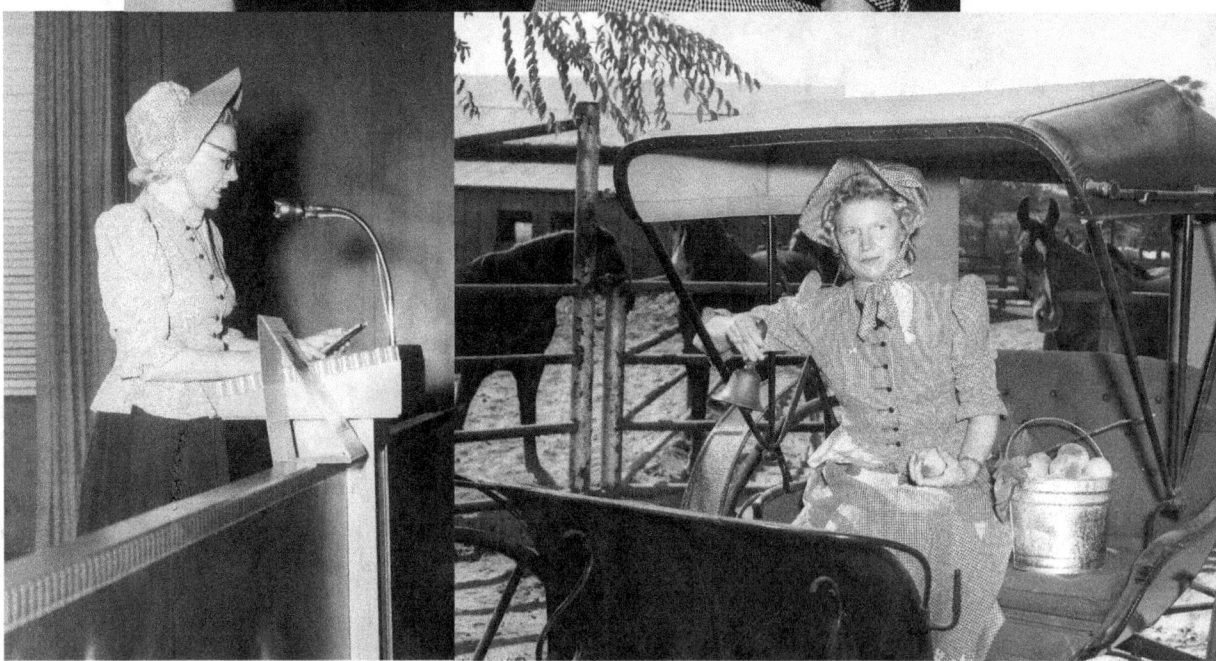

Valley historian Frances Muir Pomeroy moved to North Hollywood in 1907 from Farmington, Washington and grew up on a 50 acre fruit ranch where North Hollywood High School. A strong advocate of local history, Pomeroy, became known as the chief historian of the San Fernando Valley and served as president of the San Fernando Valley Historical Society. Frequently donning pioneer clothing, Pomeroy fought for the preservation of landmarks, installation of monuments, and general awareness of the Valley's history.

(Order #00109786, 00109785, 00109111, 00109784)

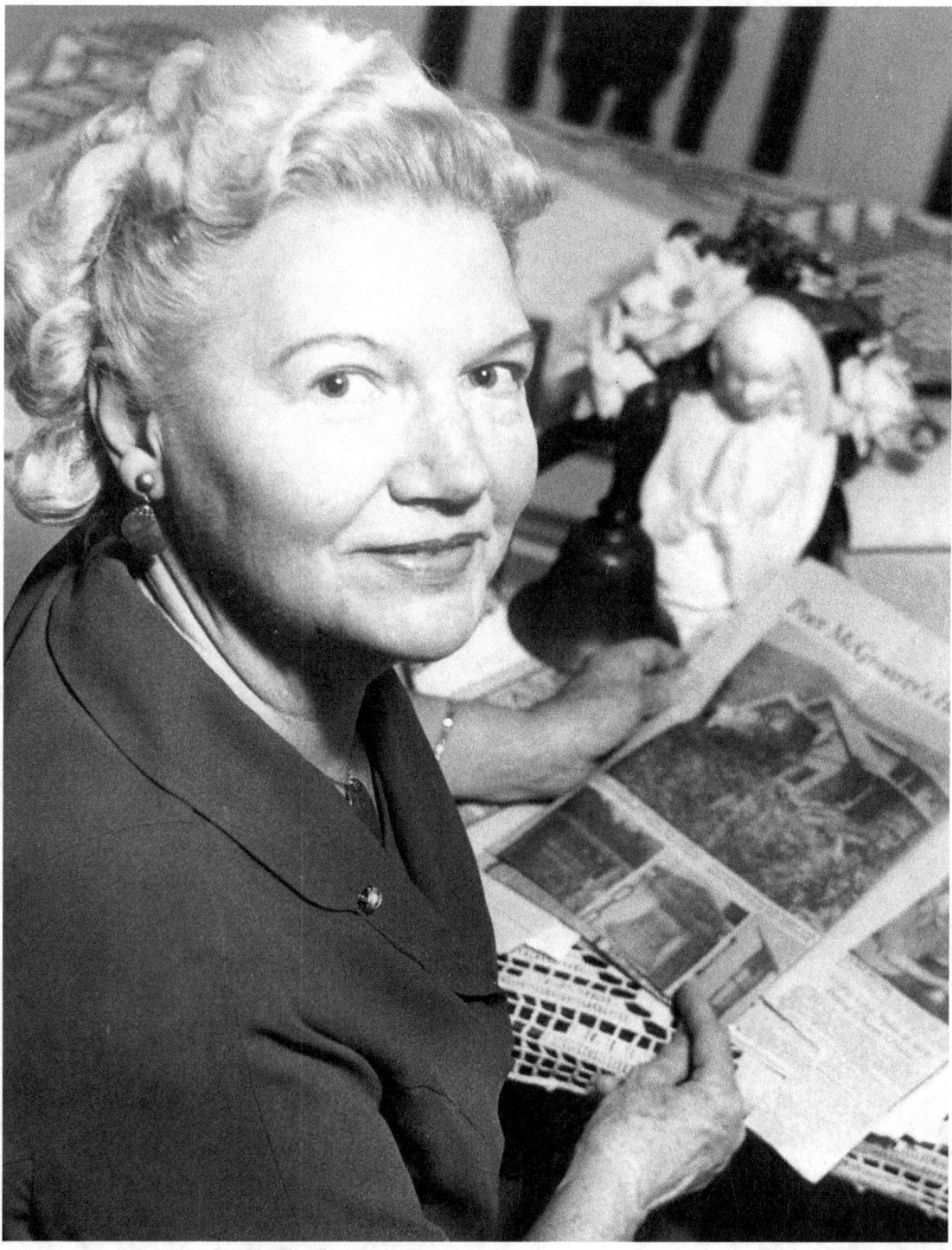

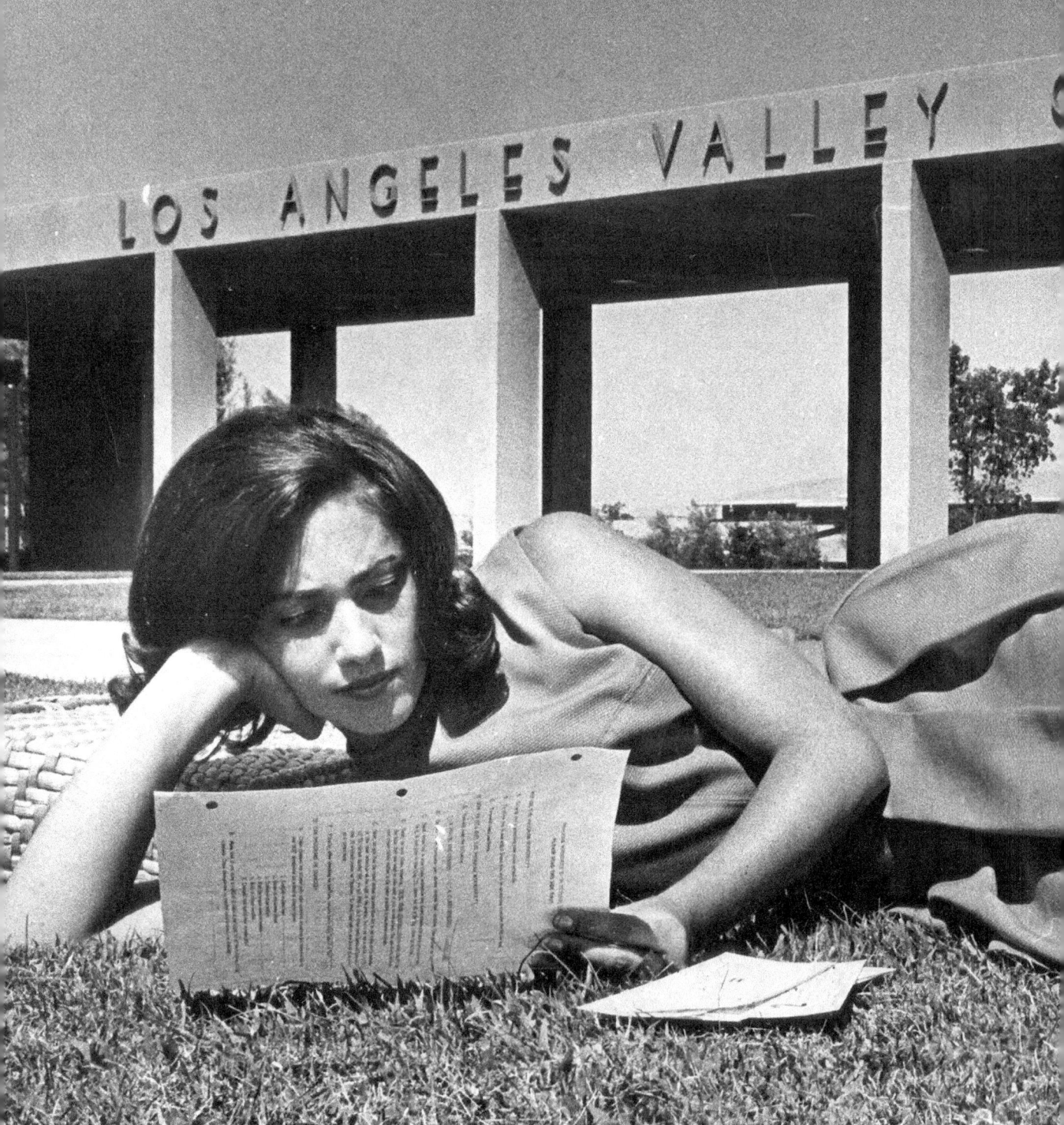

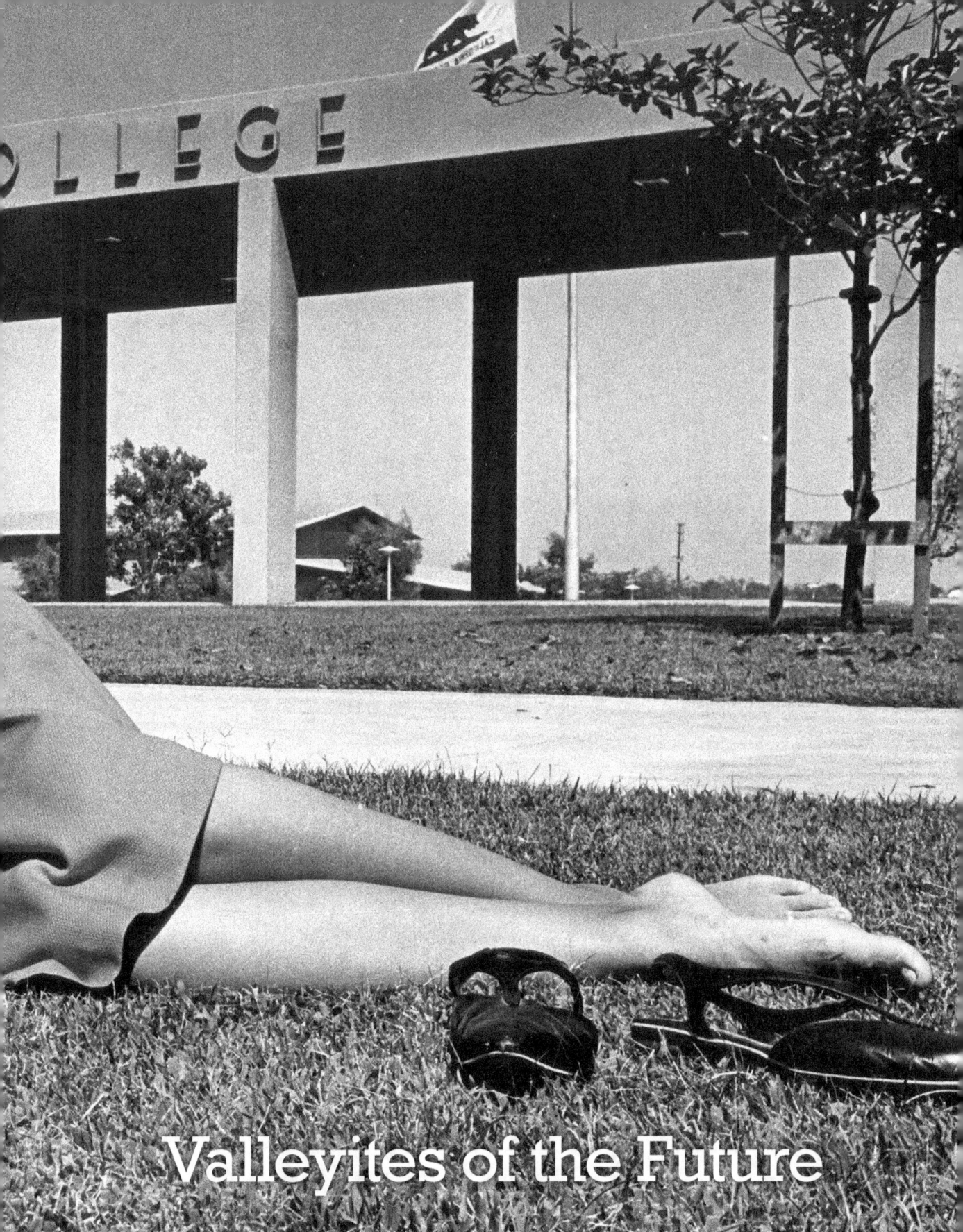

Valleyites of the Future

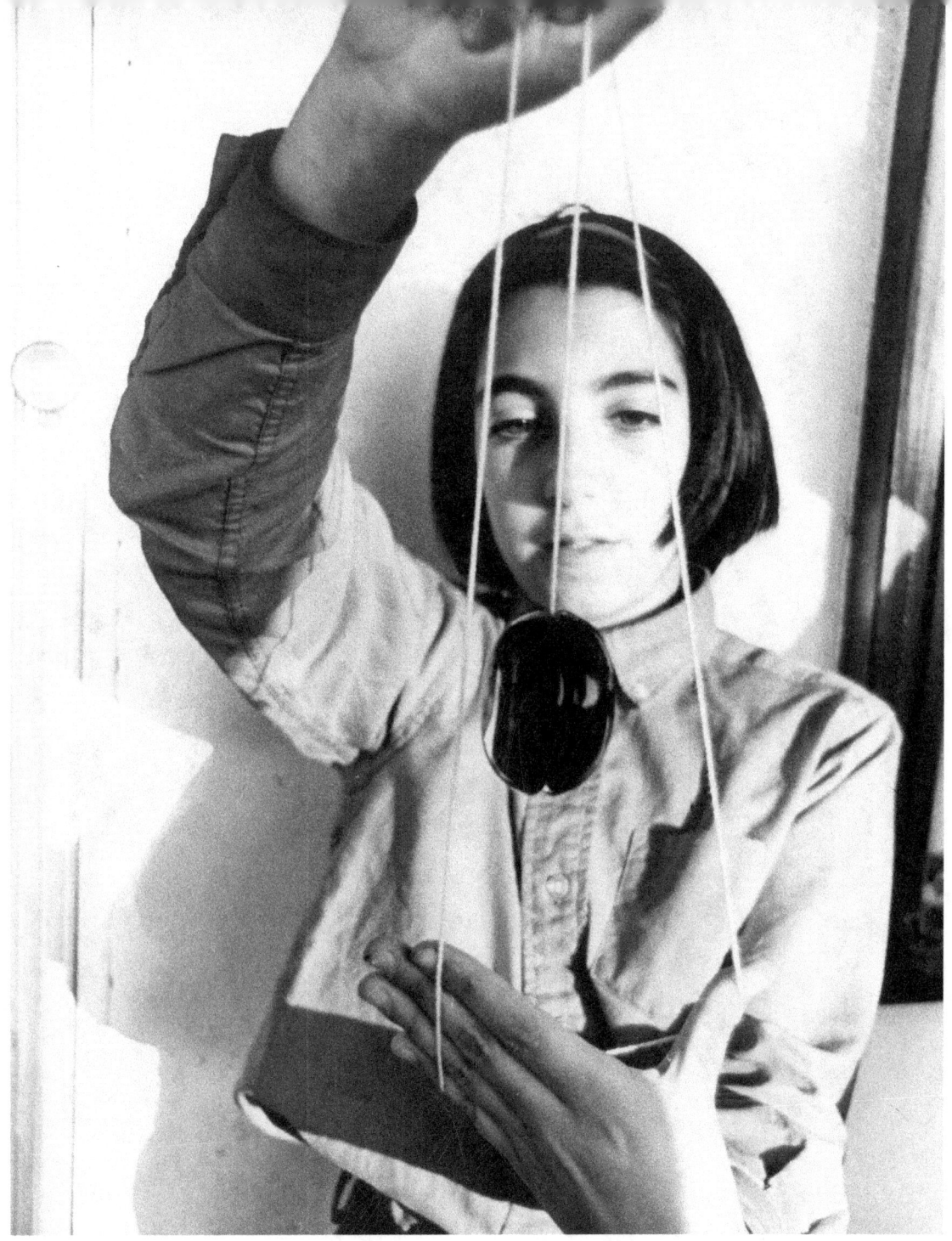

"Local yo-yo champion Susan Burke, 10, of Van Nuys, rocks the cradle as she practiced for city finals which were held in Los Angeles this afternoon."
February 13, 1965. (Bob Martin)
(Order #00109257)

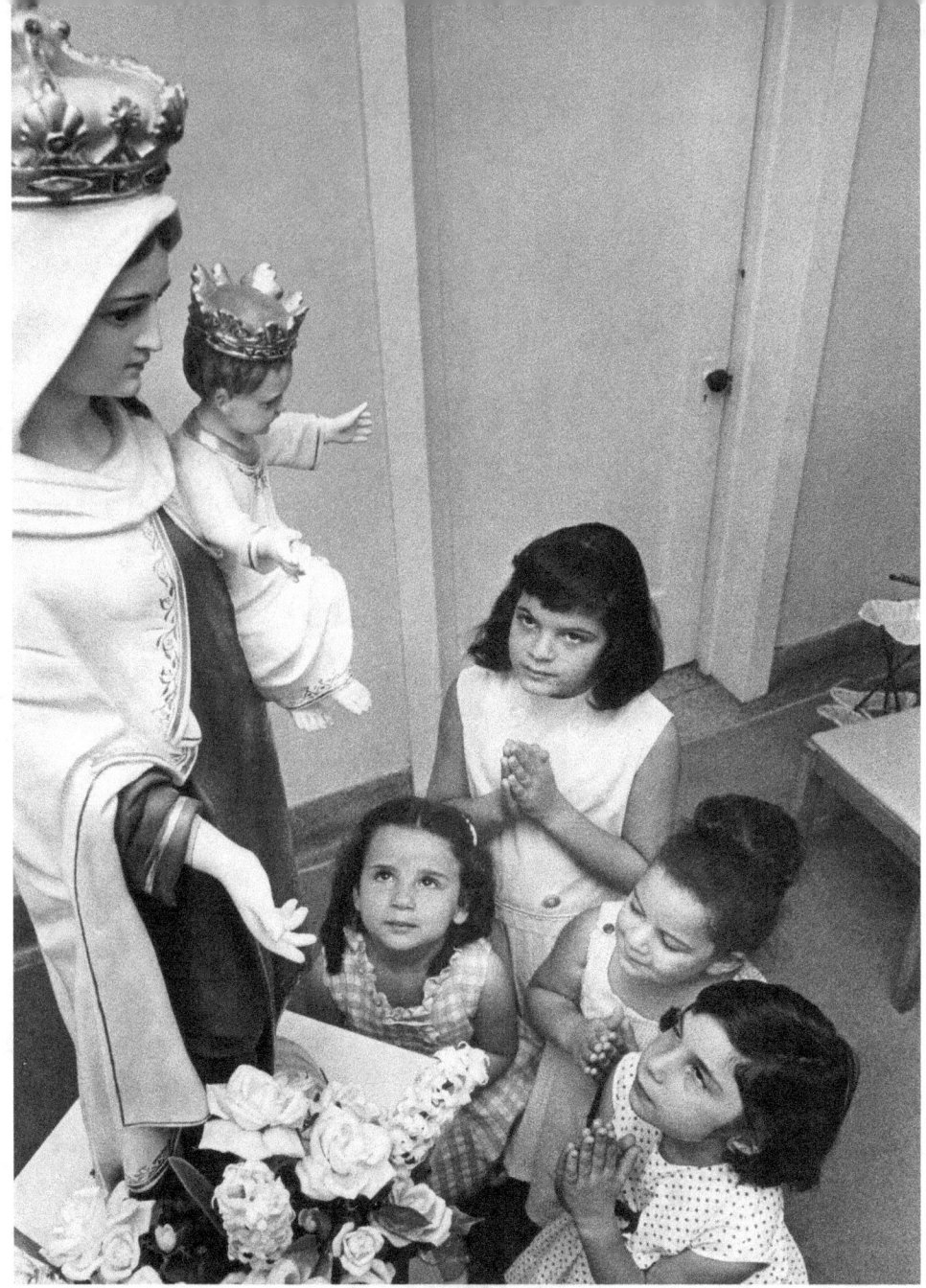

"Flower girls, front from left, Annette Bonde, 4, of Burbank; Cheryl Anne Garcia, 5; Dine Figliuzzi, 8, all of North Hollywood, offer prayers to Our Lady of Mount Carmel at Villa Cabrini Academy, 7500 Glenoaks Blvd., Burbank. They will lead a procession at the eighth annual feast of Our Lady of Mount Carmel at 11 a.m. tomorrow on the academy grounds."
July 10, 1965. (Jeff Goldwater)
(Order #00082774)

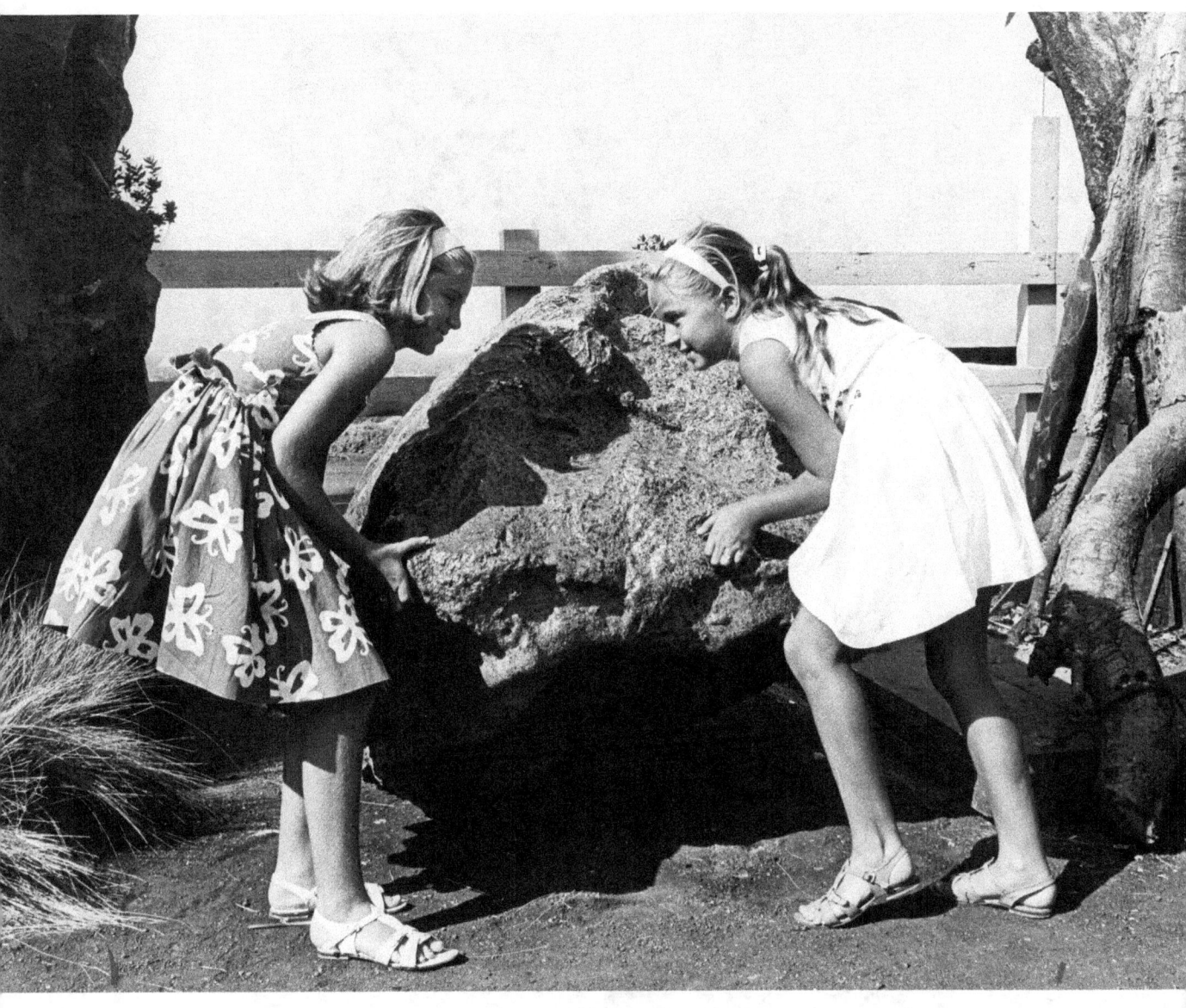

"To their surprise, Kathy Geelan, 11, left, and her sister Mary Beth, 9, find they can lift a 'boulder' larger than themselves at Universal City's Visitor's Center. The rubber rock was one of several movieland exhibits at the tour stop."
August 19, 1964. (Steve Young)
(Order #00109488)

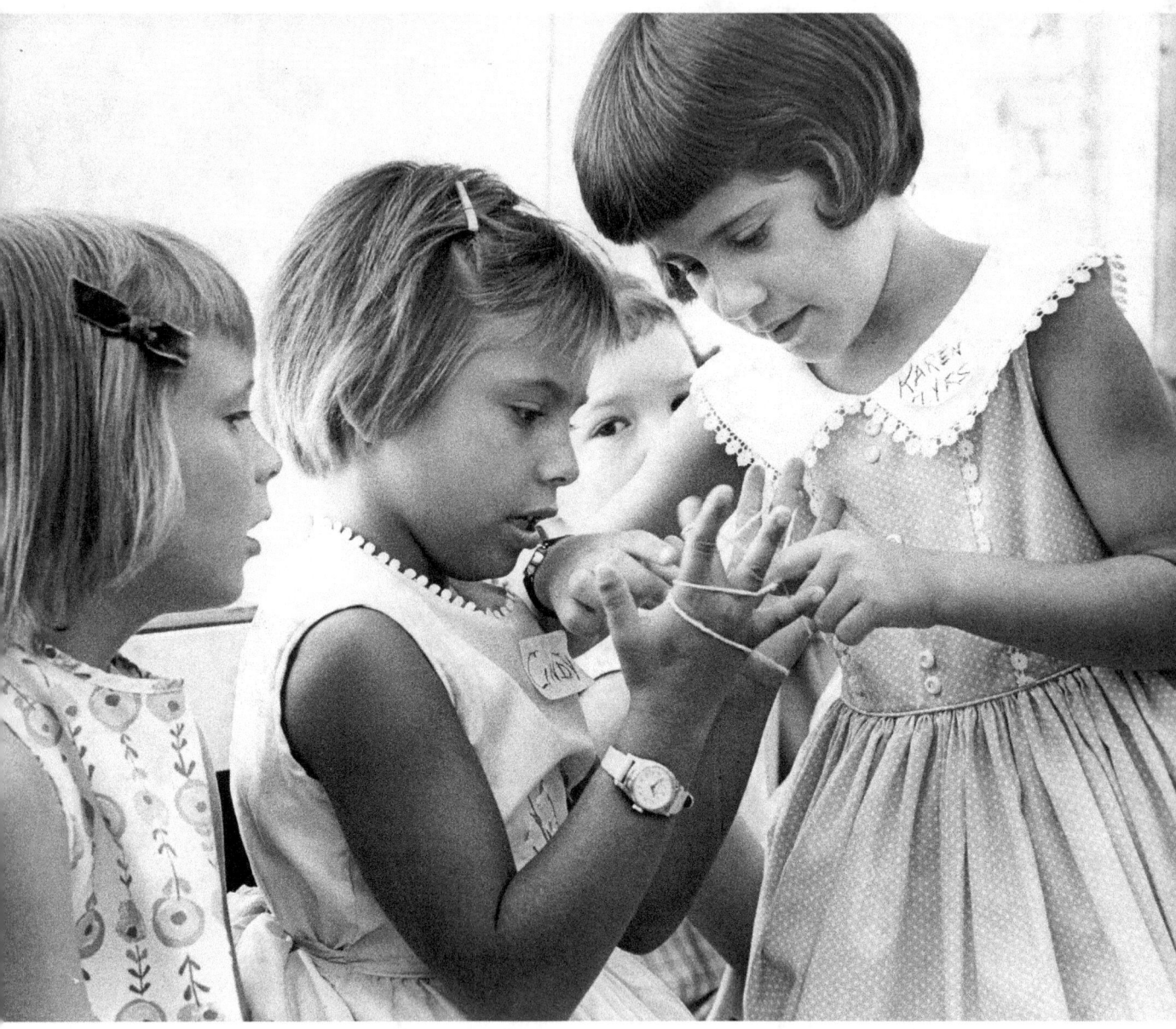

Karen Miller of Encino plays cat's cradle at a party held at Geniiland, a fantasy party place for young children.
August 5, 1964. (Bob Miller)
(Order #00082917)

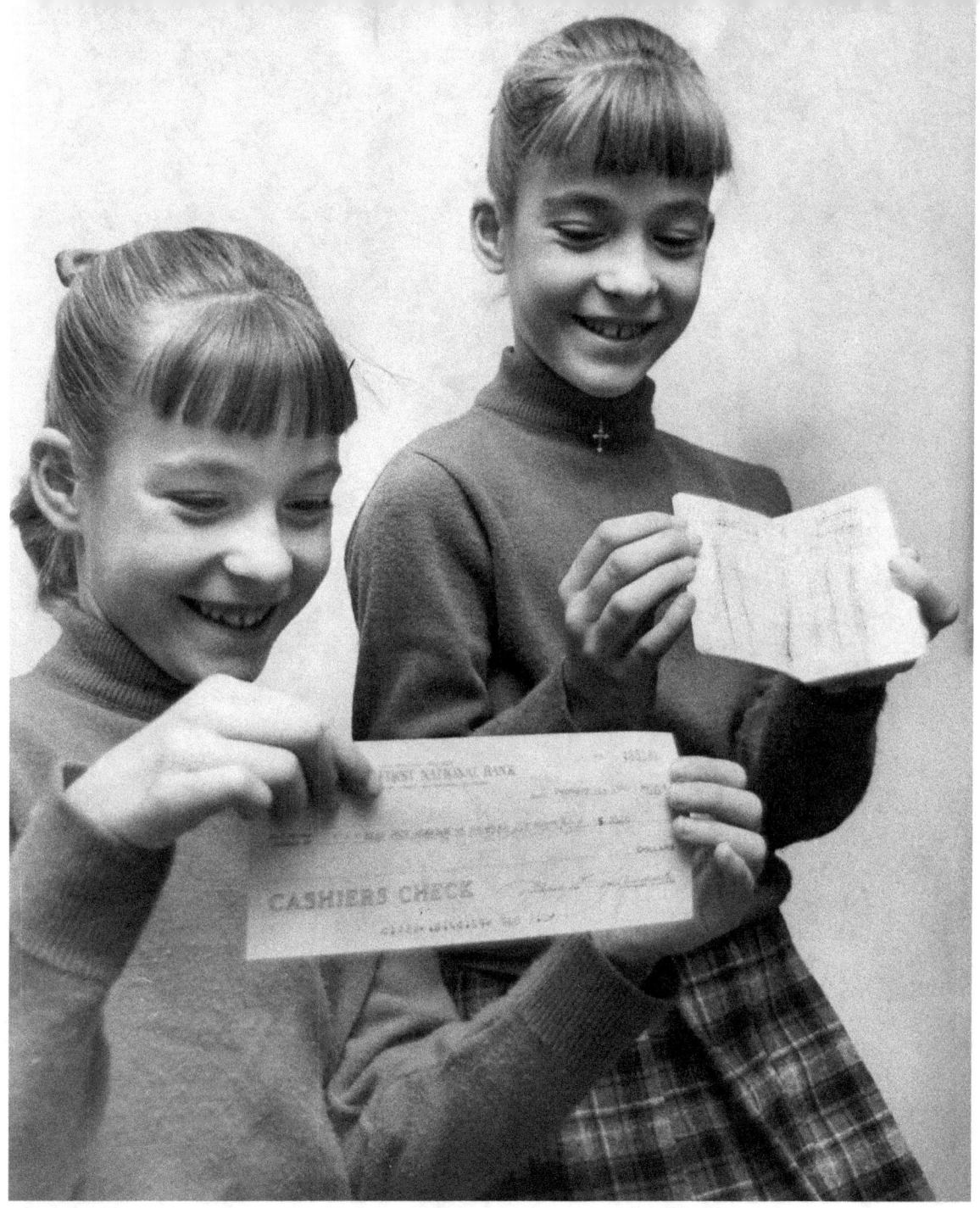

"Twins Judi and Jodi Simpson, 8, of Northridge, opened joint bank account with reward money they received when they returned $20, which they found, to the bank. The girls live at 8625 Calvin Ave."
April 6, 1965. (Bob Martin)
(Order #00112034)

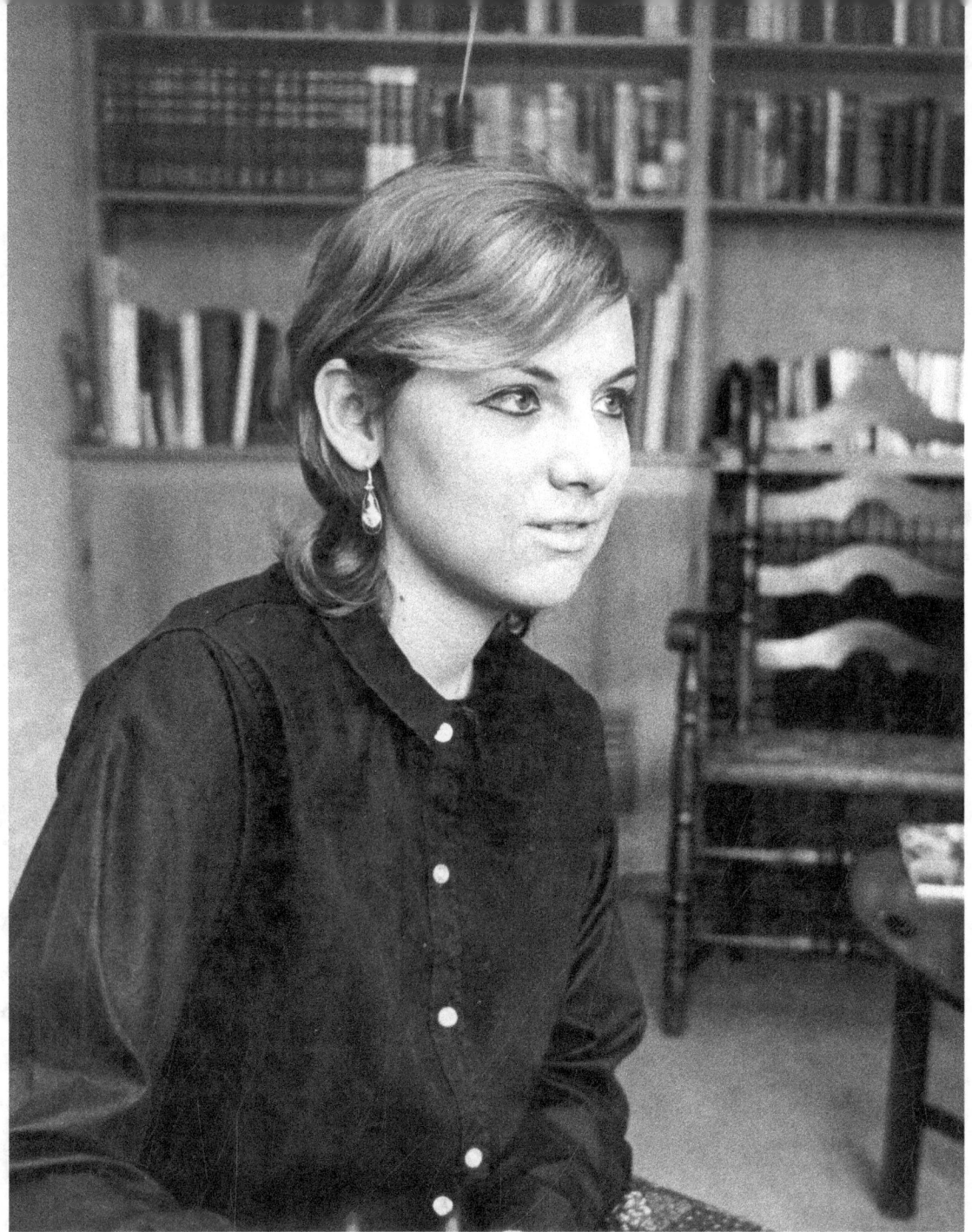

"Miss Susan Mintz, blue-eyed brunette graduate of Burbank High School is the proud winner of an essay contest on school dropout problem. Susan spent one-quarter of an hour on the essay which earned her $1, 725."
August 30, 1964. (Steve Young)

(Order #00109431)

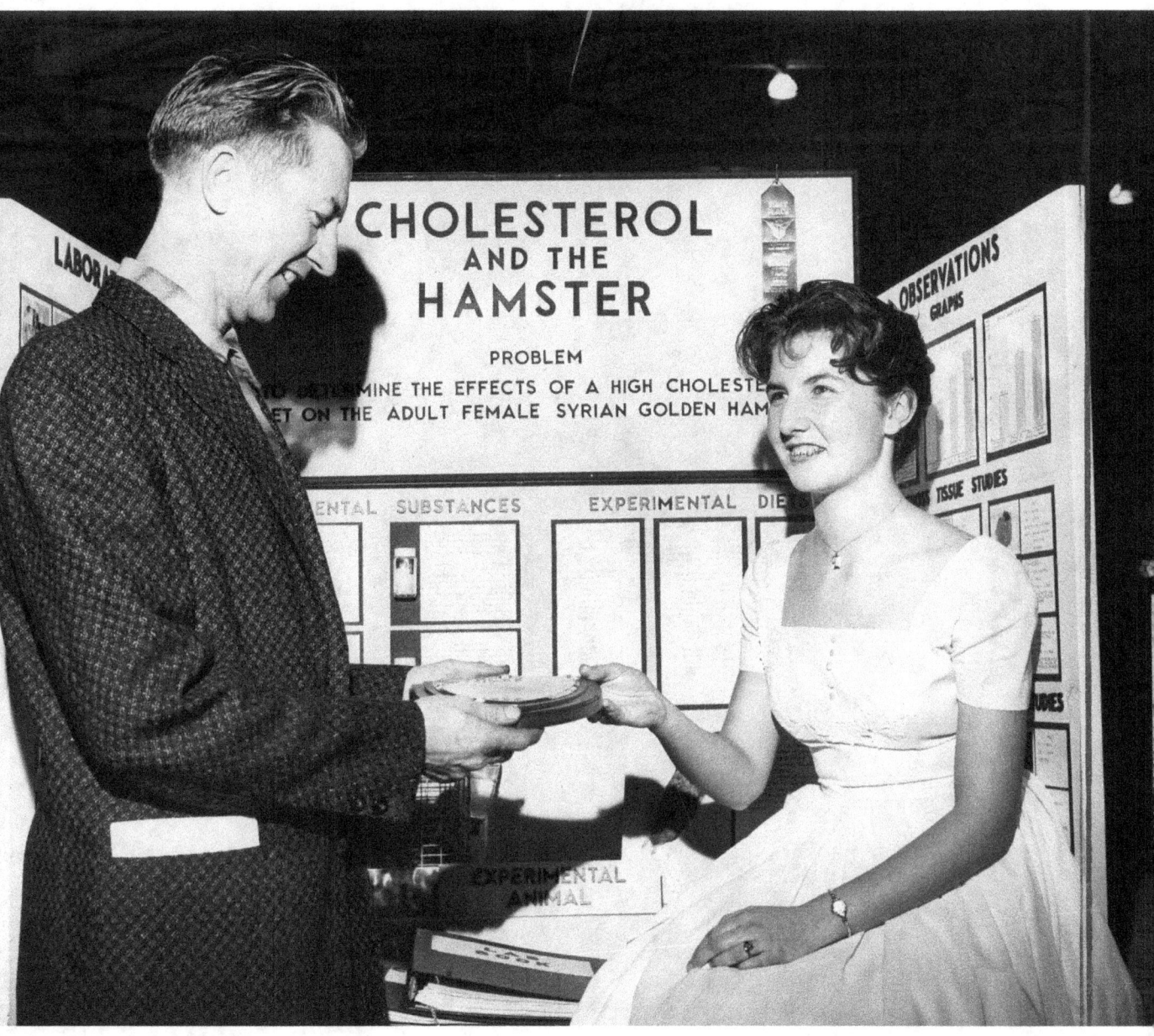

"Linda Ann Reynolds shows her father, Jay, exhibit on study of Hamsters which won her top award of Valley Science Fair. Reynolds expressed surprise at the completeness of the exhibit. 'I didn't realize she had done so much,' he said."
April 11, 1960. (Order #00086195)

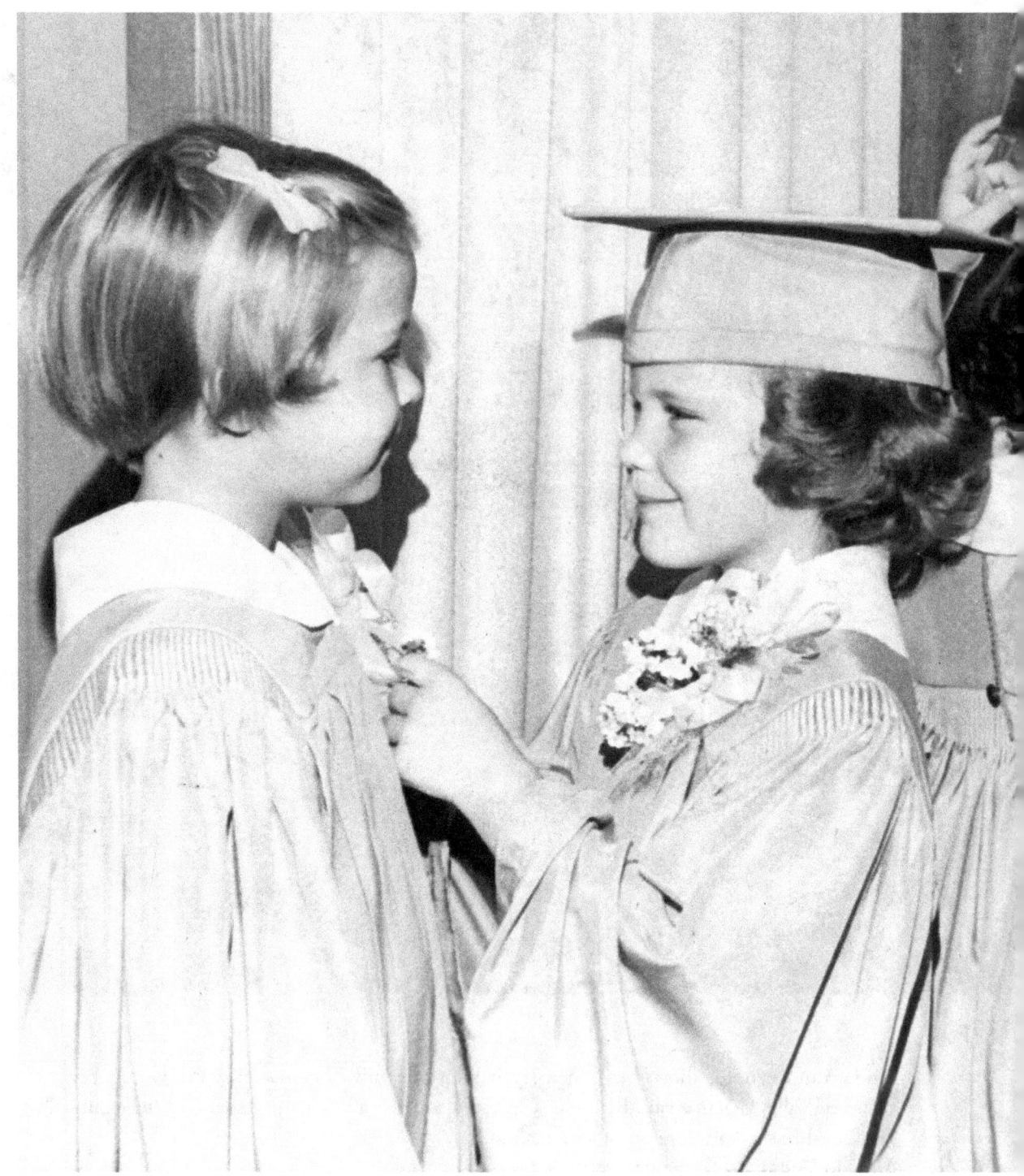

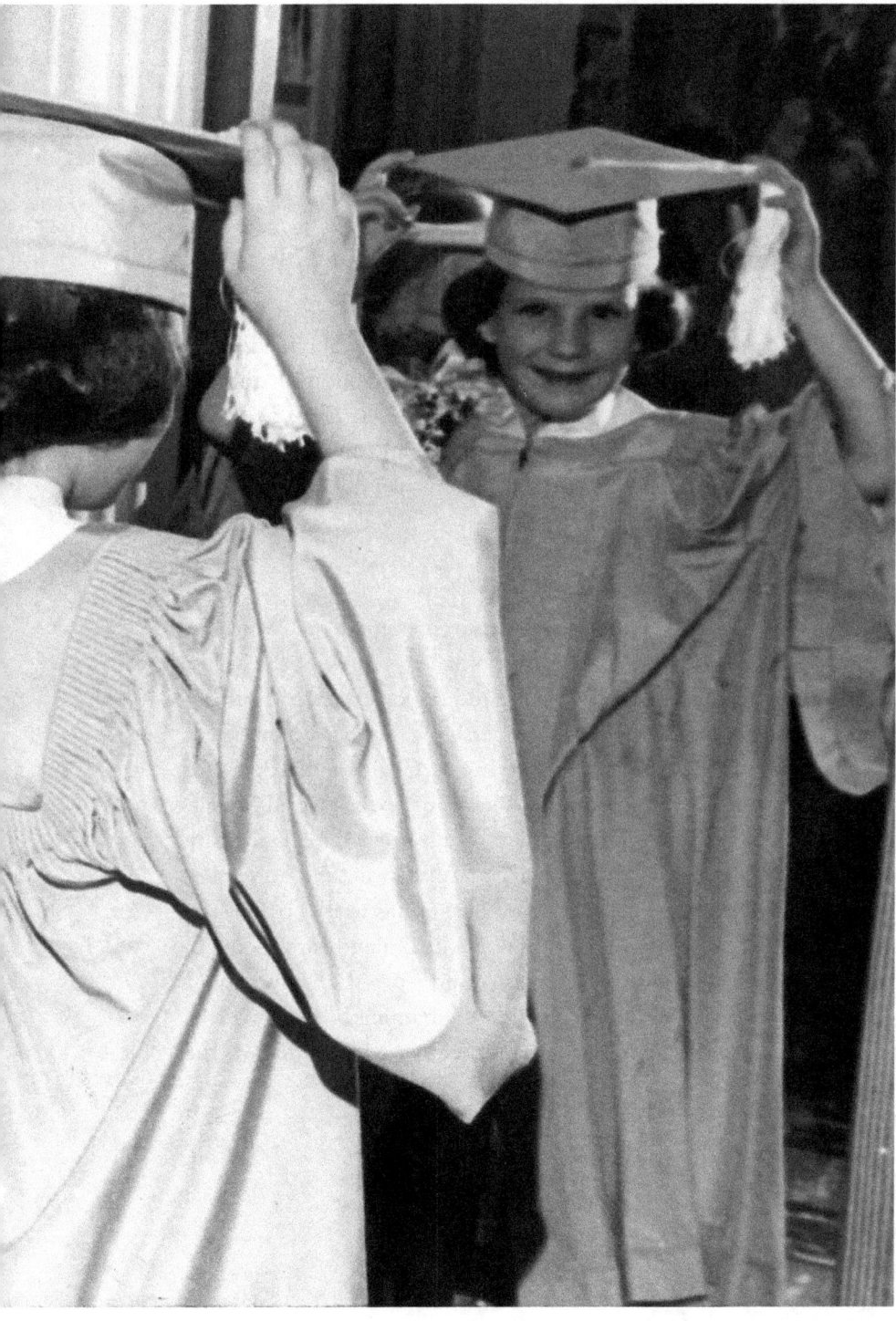

"Forty-five kindergarten students at Villa Cabrini Academy, 7500 Glenoaks Blvd., Burbank, will solemnly march down the aisle of the school auditorium at 2 p.m. Sunday to receive their diplomas. The proud graduates will be dressed in traditional blue gowns and mortar boards. Trying on caps and gowns for ceremony are (from left) Erica Koesler, 5; Laurie Kledvizik, 5, and Donna Reno, 5." May 20, 1963. (Gordon Dean) (Order #00108849)

About the Authors

Christina Rice is a librarian, archivist, author, wife and mother. She obtained an MLIS from San Jose State University and now oversees the photo collection at the Los Angeles Public Library. Her first book, *Ann Dvorak: Hollywood's Forgotten Rebel* was published in 2013 from University Press of Kentucky. She lives in Los Angeles with her husband, writer Joshua Hale Fialkov, their daughter, two dogs, and one disgruntled cat.

Former Los Angeles City Council Member **Joy Picus** represented the West San Fernando Valley from 1977-1993. She was the first woman to represent the Valley on the City Council. With a reputation as an effective and responsive elected official who got the job done, Picus continues her civic leadership as a board member of several nonprofit organizations. She is currently serving as Chair of the Board of Friends of the (Griffith) Observatory. She is on the Boards of Jewish World Watch, Community Partners, and the Foundation Board of California State University Northridge. She is a proud alumna of the University of Wisconsin, and a member of the Board of Visitors for the College of Letters and Science, as well as past Chair and current active member of the UW Foundation's Women's Philanthropy Council. She is proud of receiving the Distinguished Alumna Award from the University of Wisconsin in 2002. Other very special honors include the naming of the Joy Picus Child Development Center in LA's Civic Center, and being a Ms. Woman of the Year in 1985.

Support the Campaign to Preserve & Digitize the *Valley Times* Photo Collection

Photo Friends, a non-profit organization that supports the Los Angeles Public Library (LAPL) Photo Collection is seeking funds to aid the library's effort to make readily accessible to the public, researchers, and the educational community, through the LAPL website at lapl.org, approximately 45,000 photographs from the *Valley Times* newspaper collection.

All proceeds from the sale of this book will directly support the Los Angeles Public Library Photo Collection, and additional donations to the *Valley Times* project are always welcome! Photo Friends is a 501(c)(3) nonprofit organization; all contributions to the project are tax-deductible. The project is estimated to take 6½ years, with a total funding requirement of $475,000. Over $50,000 has been raised to date, and work on the project has begun, with several hundred images per month going online. Donations may be made in any amount, with checks made out to Photo Friends and sent to the address below, or by PayPal to photofriendsla@gmail.com.

c/o Future Studio • PO Box 292000 • Los Angeles CA 90029

Additional information about the *Valley Times* project can be found at
www.valleytimes.org.

Valley Times Advisory Council

Martin M. Cooper (chair)
President, Cooper Communications, Inc.; President, City of Los Angeles Quality & Productivity Commission

Steven Afriat
President, The Afriat Consulting Group, Inc.

Daniel Blake, Ph.D.
Emeritus Professor of Economics, California State University, Northridge

John Bunzel
Morgan Stanley

John Bwarie
Founder, Stratiscope

Robert Hertzberg
Partner, Mayer, Brown, Rowe & Maw, LLP; Chair Emeritus, California State Assembly

Coby King
President/CEO of High Point Strategies, LLC; Chairman of the Board, VICA

Mel Kohn
Partner, Kirsch, Kohn & Bridge, LLP

Cindy Mediavilla
Library Programs Consultant, California State Library

Joy Picus
Los Angeles City Council Member, Retired

Robert Rawitch
Executive Vice President, Winner & Associates; Former Executive Editor, Valley Edition, Los Angeles Times

Kevin Roderick
Editor and Publisher, LA Observed

Jan Sobel
President and CEO, Boys & Girls Club of the West Valley

Kathleen Sterling
Publisher, Valley News Group

Scott Sterling
President, Museum of the San Fernando Valley; Owner, Sterling Construction

Kevin Tamaki
Director, External Affairs, AT&T

Diana Williams
CEO, West Valley/Warner Center Chamber of Commerce

Valley Times Project Donors

John Randolph Haynes and Dora Haynes Foundation
Photo Friends
Steve and Christy McAvoy
Ralph M. Parsons Foundation
Tom La Bonge, Los Angeles City Council District 4
Bert Bachman, Galpin Motors
Friends of the Chatsworth Library

About the Photo Collection

The Los Angeles Public Library (LAPL) began collecting photographs sometime before World War II and had a collection of about 13,000 images by the late 1950s. In 1981, when Los Angeles celebrated its 200th birthday, Security Pacific National Bank gave its noted collection of historical photographs to the people of Los Angeles to be archived at the Central Library. Since then, LAPL has been fortunate to receive other major collections, making the Library a resource worldwide for visual images.

Notable collections include the "photo morgues" of the *Los Angeles Herald Examiner* and *Valley Times* newspapers, the Kelly-Holiday mid-Century collection of aerial photographs, the Works Progress Administration/Federal Writers Project collection, the Luther Ingersoll Portrait Collection, along with the landmark *Shades of L.A.*, which is an archive of images representing the contemporary and historic diversity of families in Los Angeles. Images were chosen from family albums and copied in a project sponsored by Photo Friends.

The Los Angeles Public Library Photo Collection also includes the works of individual photographers, including Ansel Adams, Herman Schultheis, William Reagh, Ralph Morris, Lucille Stewart, Gary Leonard, Stone Ishimaru, Carol Westwood, and Rolland Curtis.

Over 100,000 images from these collections have been digitized and are available to view through the LAPL website at **http://photos.lapl.org.**

About Photo Friends

Formed in 1990, Photo Friends is a nonprofit organization that supports the Los Angeles Public Library's Photograph Collection and History & Genealogy Department. Our goal is to improve access to the collections and promote them through programs, projects, exhibits, and books such as this one.

We are an enthusiastic group of photographers, writers, historians, business people, politicians, academics, and many others, all bonded by our passion for photography, history, and Los Angeles.

Since 1994, Photo Friends has presented a series called *The Photographer's Eye,* which spotlights local photographers and their work. These talks are presented bi-monthly. In 2011, Photo Friends inaugurated *L.A. in Focus,* a lecture series that features images drawn primarily from the Photo Collection. We have presented programs on L.A. crime, the San Fernando Valley, Kelly-Holiday aerial photographs, and L.A.'s themed environments, among others.

With initial funding from the Ralph M. Parsons Foundation, Photo Friends sponsored *L.A. Neighborhoods Project* by commissioning photographers to create a visual record of the neighborhoods of Los Angeles during the early part of the 21st century (all now part of the collection). To ensure the Library's Collection will continue to reflect such an important part of Los Angeles's history, a generous grant enabled Photo Friends to hire five contemporary photographers to document present-day industrial L.A. These images have become part of LAPL's permanent collection and are available through the Library's Photo Database. Photo Friends also curates photography exhibits on display in the History Department.

Photo Friends is a membership organization. Please consider becoming a member and helping us in our work to preserve and promote L.A.'s rich photographic resource. All proceeds from the sale of this book go to support Photo Friends' programs.

photofriends.org

This catalog was published in conjunction with a photo exhibit at
Los Angeles Central Library's History & Genealogy Department—
Defining Their Identity
The Changing Roles of Women in the Post-War Era
as Documented by the Valley Times *Newspaper*
July 7, 2014–January 4, 2015

Thank You!

George Brich, Kim Creighton, Maria Novoa, Lisa Ondoy, Anne Olivier, Matthew
Mattson, Evelyn Mercado, Michelle Olivier, Andrea Haw, and Zoey Smith.

Defining Their Identity:
The Changing Roles of Women in the Post-War Era as Documented by the Valley Times *Newspaper*
Edited by Christina Rice
Copyright © 2014 Photo Friends of the Los Angeles Public Library
Images © Los Angeles Public Library Photo Collection

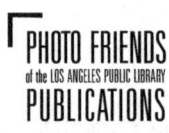

Published by:
Photo Friends of the Los Angeles Public Library
c/o Future Studio
P.O. Box 292000
Los Angeles, CA 90029
www.photofriends.org

Designed by Amy Inouye, Future Studio Los Angeles

Special quantity discounts available when purchased in bulk by corporations, organizations, or groups.
Please contact Photo Friends at: **photofriendsla@gmail.com**

ISBN-13: 978-0692702901

Printed in the United States